REFLECTING ON SOCIAL WORK –
DISCIPLINE AND PROFESSION

Contemporary Social Work Studies

Series Editor:
Robin Lovelock, University of Southampton, UK

Series Advisory Board:
Lena Dominelli, University of Southampton, UK
Peter Ford, University of Southampton, UK
Lorraine Gutiérrez, University of Michigan, USA
Walter Lorenz, Free University of Bozen/Bolzano, Italy
Karen Lyons, University of East London, UK
Joan Orme, University of Glasgow, UK
Jackie Powell, University of Southampton, UK
Chris Warren-Adamson, University of Southampton, UK

Contemporary Social Work Studies (CSWS) is a series disseminating high quality new research and scholarship in the discipline and profession of social work. The series promotes critical engagement with contemporary issues relevant across the social work community and captures the diversity of interests currently evident at national, international and local levels.

CSWS is located in the School of Social Sciences at the University of Southampton, and is a development from the successful series of books published by Ashgate in association with CEDR (the Centre for Evaluative and Developmental Research) from 1991.

Titles include:

Broadening Horizons: *International Exchanges in Social Work*
Edited by Lena Dominelli and Wanda Thomas Bernard

Beyond Racial Divides: *Ethnicities in Social Work Practice*
Edited by Lena Dominelli, Walter Lorenz and Haluk Soydan

Valuing the Field: Child Welfare in an International Context
Edited by Marilyn Callahan, Sven Hessle and Susan Strega

Social Work in Higher Education: *Demise or Development?*
Karen Lyons

Community Approaches to Child Welfare: *International Perspectives*
Edited by Lena Dominelli

Child Sexual Abuse and Adult Offenders: New Theory and Research
Edited by Christopher Bagley and Kanka Mallick

Reflecting on Social Work – Discipline and Profession

Edited by

ROBIN LOVELOCK
University of Southampton, UK

KAREN LYONS
University of East London, UK

JACKIE POWELL
University of Southampton, UK

ASHGATE

Published by
Ashgate Publishing Limited
Gower House
Croft Road
Aldershot
Hants GU11 3HR
England

Ashgate Publishing Company
Suite 420
101 Cherry Street
Burlington, VT 05401-4405
USA

Ashgate website: http://www.ashgate.com

British Library Cataloguing in Publication Data
Reflecting on social work - discipline and profession. -
   (Contemporary social work studies)
   1. Social service - Great Britain 2. Social service -
   Research - Great Britain
   I. Lovelock, Robin II. Lyons, K. H. (Karen Hamilton), 1944-
   III. Powell, Jackie
   361.3'2'0941

Library of Congress Cataloging-in-Publication Data
Reflecting on social work - discipline and profession / edited by Robin Lovelock, Karen
   Lyons, and Jackie Powell.
      p. cm. -- (Contemporary social work studies)
   Includes bibliographical references and index.
   ISBN 0-7546-1905-2
      1. Social service--Great Britain. I. Lovelock, Robin, 1946- II. Lyons, K. H. (Karen
   Hamilton), 1944- III. Powell, Jackie, 1946- IV. Series.

   HV245.R33 2004
   361.3'0941--dc22

                                                                    2003056932

ISBN 0 7546 1905 2

Printed and bound in Great Britain by MPG Books Ltd, Bodmin, Cornwall

10/18/04

Contents

Notes on Contributors

THE EDITORS

Robin Lovelock is a Visiting Senior Research Fellow in the School of Social Sciences (Social Work Studies Division), University of Southampton, having been Director of the Centre for Evaluative and Developmental Research (CEDR) in the then Department of Social Work Studies prior to taking early retirement in 1991. After gaining a BSc (Soc Sci) in Politics and Sociology, he studied for but did not complete a doctorate in political theory. He has a long-standing interest in research methodology, especially qualitative evaluative research, and in the role of research in relation to policy and practice. From 1974–2001 he researched mainly in the field of social and health care services, first at Portsmouth Polytechnic (now University) and from 1988 at the University of Southampton. Services at the social and health care interface were a particular focus, especially innovative community-based provision; later publications include *Disability: Britain in Europe* (Avebury, 1994, with Jackie Powell), *Visual Impairment; Social Support* (Avebury, 1995), and *Shared Territory: Assessing the Social Support Needs of Visually Impaired People* (Joseph Rowntree Foundation, 1995, with Jackie Powell and Sarah Craggs). His main scholarly interests in more recent years have been in the relationships between social work and political and social theory; he took an MSc (Soc Sci) in Political Theory during 1995–98 (part time). With Alan P. Brier he co-edited *Communication and Community: Anglo-German Perspectives* (Avebury, 1996), which includes 'Communication or incommensurability? Some contested issues in social work theory and practice' (with Jackie Powell).

Karen Lyons is Professor of International Social Work at the University of East London, where she has worked for many years following experience in social work practice and management, also mainly in east London. Having recently retired she continues to work part time at UEL as course tutor for an MA in International Social Work. Prior to professional qualification her disciplinary background was in geography, then social administration. In her more recent PhD studies she analysed social work education in the context of policy change and with reference to different theoretical perspectives on professions and disciplines. Her other main fields of research include: the effects of globalisation on welfare arrangements and social work education and practice; and the organisation of social work in the UK (particularly as reflected in the employment destinations of newly qualified social workers). Among her recent publications are *Social Work in Higher Education:*

Demise or Development? and *International Social Work: Themes and Perspectives* (both Ashgate, 1999).

Jackie Powell is a Reader in the School of Social Sciences (Social Work Studies Division) at the University of Southampton and was formerly Associate Director of the Centre for Evaluative and Developmental Research (CEDR). Qualifying as a social worker after taking a first degree in natural sciences, she worked in a number of mental health settings prior to becoming a 'jobbing researcher' for several years. Her main research and teaching interests include evaluative research methodologies and the impact of changing policy and organisational structures on patterns of service provision and professional practice. She is currently involved in several research projects exploring inter-agency and inter-professional working at the health and social care interface. Among her many publications are *Changing Patterns of Mental Health Care* (Avebury, 1992, with Robin Lovelock), *Understanding Social Research: Perspectives on Methodology and Practice* (Falmer, 1997, ed., with George McKenzie and Robin Usher), and more recently a series of articles on research practice, including 'The changing conditions of social work research' (*BJSW*, 2002).

OTHER CONTRIBUTORS

Ian Butler is Professor of Social Work at Keele University, before which he was Director of Social Work Studies at the University of Cardiff. He is a qualified social worker with considerable practice and managerial experience in residential and field settings, in the statutory, voluntary and independent sectors. His main research interests include children's accounts of their social worlds, the health care of looked-after children, and the practice of substitute family care. He is also interested in the development of social policy as it affects children and young people, especially young offenders. His most recent publications include *Social Policy, Social Welfare and Scandal: How British Public Policy is Made* (Palgrave Macmillan, 2002, with M. Drakeford), *Divorcing Children: Children and Family Breakdown* (Jessica Kingsley, forthcoming, with L. Scanlan and others), 'A code of ethics for social work and social care research' (*BJSW*, 2002), and 'Which Blair project? Communitarianism, social authoritarianism and social work' (*Journal of Social Work*, 2001, with M. Drakeford).

Nick Gould is Professor of Social Work at the University of Bath. He holds a BA and an MA in Politics, an MSc in Social Work, and gained his PhD for work using personal construct psychology to analyse experiential learning. He has been a social work practitioner in local authority and forensic settings, and maintains an involvement in mental health practice. He has published widely in the social work field, including: *Reflective Learning for Social Work* (Arena, 1996, ed., with Imogen Taylor), and *Qualitative Research in Social Work: Context and Method* (Sage, 2001, with Ian Shaw). His current research interests include professional learning, new technology and social inclusion, and the development of qualitative methodologies.

Beth Humphries is Reader in Social Work at Lancaster University. She has practised and researched in social work for many years, in Northern Ireland, Scotland and England. Her research interests include social work and inequality, and social work responses to people subject to immigration controls. She has published on these topics and her most recent book is *From Immigration Controls to Welfare Controls* (Routledge, 2002, ed., with Steve Cohen and Ed Mynott). She has also published widely on research methods, including *Research in Social Care and Social Welfare: Issues and Debates for Practice* (Jessica Kingsley, 2000, ed.).

Adrian James has been Professor of Applied Social Studies at the University of Bradford since April 1998, having taught at the University of Hull from 1978–98. After graduating in sociology and geography he qualified as a social worker in 1970, then worked in the probation service for eight years, during which time he had special responsibility for training and also took a part-time MA in Criminology. A stream of studies and publications reflect his particular and long-standing research interest in the work of family court welfare officers, including: a major ESRC-funded project (1989–92) which led to *Court Welfare in Action: Practice and Theory* (Harvester Wheatsheaf, 1993, with W. Hay); work forming part of a joint project funded by the Legal Services Commission to evaluate publicly-funded mediation as introduced by the Family Law Act, 1996; and, more recently, further ESRC-funded research comparing the work of family court welfare officers and guardians *ad litem* in the context of the new Children and Family Courts Advisory and Support Service. Other major publications include *Couples, Conflict and Change: Social Work with Marital Relationships* (Tavistock, 1986, with K. Wilson), and *Privatizing Prisons: Rhetoric and Reality* (Sage, 1997, with K. Bottomley, E. Clare and A. Liebling).

Bill Jordan is Professor in Social Policy at both the University of Exeter and the University of Huddersfield. Having qualified as a social worker in the 1960s he worked in the probation service and in the mental health field until the mid 1980s. He is the author of many books and articles in the fields of social policy, social work and political theory, most recently *Social Work and the Third Way: Tough Love as Social Policy* (Sage, 2000, with Charlie Jordan), and *Irregular Migration: Dilemmas of Transnational Mobility* (Edward Elgar, 2002, with Franck Düvell).

Jeremy Kearney is a qualified social worker and therapist, and currently Director of the Centre for Social Research and Practice at the University of Sunderland, where he was also Head of Applied Social Studies for eight years. The Centre provides a focus for developing systemic/social constructionist research within the School of Health, Natural and Social Sciences at the University, and is involved in a range of projects covering such areas as child protection, mental health, fatherhood and masculinity, and community-based work. With two Swedish colleagues he recently published a series of articles based on the findings of major comparative research on the ideals and realities of fatherhood and masculinity in England and Sweden. He has also published articles on the theory/practice relationship in social work, and on the assertive outreach model of mental health, and has written on the application of systemic ideas in social care and social work in *Working in Social Care: A Systemic Approach* (Arena, 1996, with Dave Evans). He is programme leader for an international Masters in Systemic Organisation and Management, which brings together managers and practitioners from multi-disciplinary settings and runs in four different countries. After undergraduate studies in English and philosophy he worked for many years as a community worker, social work practitioner and manager, and family therapist.

Walter Lorenz, a trained social worker with a background in philosophy and theology, is a Professor at the Free University of Bolzano, Italy. He formerly held a Jean Monnet Chair (Social Europe) at the National University of Ireland, University College Cork. He teaches a wide spectrum of social work and sociology modules, mainly from an inter-cultural and European perspective, while his research activities extend from issues arising from the history of different traditions of social work and social policy in Europe, to anti-racist and inter-cultural practice models. He has lectured in many parts of Europe and has published on his research topics in English, German and Italian. He co-founded the *European Journal of Social Work* and is a member of the editorial group of the e-journal *Social Work and Society*.

Nigel Parton is Professor in Child Care and Director of the Centre for Applied Childhood Studies at the University of Huddersfield. Formerly a social worker, he has been in higher education, involved in research and writing, for over 20 years. He is the author of numerous books and articles, among his most recent being: 'Some thoughts on the relationship between theory and practice in and for social work' (*BJSW*, 2000), *Constructive Social Work: Towards a New Practice* (Macmillan, 2000, with Patrick O'Byrne), and 'Rethinking *professional* practice: the contributions of social constructionism and the feminist "ethics of care"' (*BJSW*, 2003).

Richard Pugh is Senior Lecturer in Social Work at Keele University and has experience as both a residential and a field worker in Britain and the USA. He has published widely on language issues, social work theory, and child protection. He is also extensively involved with academics and practitioners throughout Europe, and from Australia and North America, in developing good practice from an anti-discriminatory perspective. His latest book is *Rural Social Work* (Russell House, 2000).

Imogen Taylor joined the University of Sussex as Professor of Social Work and Social Care in 2001, having previously been Senior Lecturer in the School for Policy Studies at the University of Bristol, where she also completed her doctorate. She is Co-Director of the multi-location UK Learning and Teaching Support Network Subject Centre for Social Policy and Social Work (SWAPltsn), funded by the four UK Higher Education Funding Councils. She qualified and practised as a social worker in Toronto, and was also a practice teacher there, before taking up an academic post in the University's School of Social Work. Her research and publishing interests are in the area of learning for professional and inter-professional practice. She has long-standing interests in gender issues in learning and practice, non-traditional learners, and critically reflective learning, culminating in her book *Developing Learning in Professional Education: Partnerships for Practice* (Society for Research into Higher Education/Open University Press, 1997). She is a member of the Editorial Board of *Social Work Education.*

Steve Trevillion took up the post of Head of Social Work Education at the General Social Care Council on 1 October 2003, having previously been Professor of Social Work at South Bank University and prior to that Head of the Social Work Department and Dean of Faculty at Brunel University, where he also held a personal chair. He studied anthropology at the Universities of London and Oxford and subsequently obtained qualifications in social policy and social work from the Universities of York and Exeter. He holds a PhD from Brunel for work on social networks. He spent most of the 1980s working as a social worker in busy area teams, both in Plymouth and in London. His long-standing interests in partnership and collaboration date back to his days as a community social worker and he has undertaken research on these subjects in London and Stockholm. He also began writing about cross-boundary issues when still practising and has been preoccupied with them ever since. The author of *Networking and Community Partnership* (Arena, 1999), he has, in recent years, played an active role in revitalising the debate about social work theory. Best known for his development of the 'networking' concept of cross-boundary practice, he believes that the future of social work research lies mainly in the contribution it can make to the evolution of a new kind of partnership practice.

Introduction

Jackie Powell, Robin Lovelock and Karen Lyons

Social work has always been a contested activity, characterised by a history of uncertainty and of continually shifting identities (Lorenz, 1994). Its search for meaning and coherence has taken place in the context of a series of crises in relation to its status as an academic discipline and a professional practice (Camilleri, 1999). Subject to competing challenges both from within and without, there is currently renewed interest in the theoretical and research dimensions of social work, at a time when recent and ongoing major changes in the broad social, political and economic context in which practice takes place require a further re-evaluation of social work's role and a re-examination of its identity. A continuing flow of texts is contributing to such a reappraisal, notable among them recent books by Fawcett *et al.* (2000), Ife (1997), Jordan (2000), Leonard (1997), Lyons (1999), Parton (1996a), Parton and O'Byrne (2000), and Pease and Fook (1999); Davies and Leonard's forthcoming collection (in the same series as this present one) will add to this list. Our own aim here is similarly to stimulate and contribute to further debate on the fundamental nature and role of social work, and about its future, in light of the dominant constraints and opportunities facing the discipline and the profession at the beginning of the twenty-first century. We envisage this collection as an exploratory conversation on these matters amongst the contributors and, by extension, with readers. We hope thence to promote wider discussion in a similar spirit.

The editors specifically invited a group of leading social work academics, mainly from the UK, to reflect critically on the nature of social work as both a professional activity and an academic, university-based discipline, and the contribution of the latter component to social work 'as a whole'. The relationships between research, theory and practice were indicated as a more specific area for contributors' consideration, and they were encouraged to reflect and to draw upon their own research, scholarship and experience in the broadest sense. The diversity of the emerging contributions reflects the complexity and creativity of contemporary social work research and scholarship. The majority of the following chapters have a predominantly UK focus, but the wider perspectives and experiences of the contributors and the way in which issues and developments are increasingly shared – and linked – throughout our globalising world gives the collection more general relevance.

From its early origins social work has had to grapple with and manage a number of tensions arising from its essentially ambiguous and uncertain nature, concerned for both individual and collective goods. These tensions can be seen in several related contexts: the role of social work in relation to the state on the one hand and to private individuals and families on the other; the organisation of social work services; the status of social work as a formally acknowledged activity or occupation; and its knowledge claims as an (autonomous) academic discipline and as the basis for professional education and practice. Such themes have been addressed in different ways over time, reflecting various changes in the social, economic and political contexts in which social work takes place. At the same time, the more narrowly focused concerns of an emerging profession of practitioners, social work managers, educators, researchers, and to a lesser extent the users of their services, have been influential.

The project which this collection represents had two related starting points. One was the nexus of questions concerning the contributions of empirical research and of theorising to the discipline and the profession – a variation on the long-standing theme of 'the relationship between theory and practice in social work'. In the immediate context of the origins and development of this book the issues involved were closely bound up with the series of six seminars which took place around the UK during 1999–2000 sponsored by the Economic and Social Research Council (ESRC) and the subsequent free-standing conference, collectively entitled *Theorising Social Work Research (TSWR)*.[1] The editors and most of the contributors to this collection participated in some or all of these events, and while each of the chapters now appearing here was written specifically for the book, much of the material included builds on the stimulating discussions which took place in the *TSWR* context, with several of the contributions incorporating substantially revised and developed versions of papers presented therein. The second starting point for this book was a theme which emerged from Karen Lyons's *Social Work in Higher Education: Demise or Development?* (1999), namely that social work academics tend on balance to look *either* to 'the discipline' *or* to 'the profession' as their primary reference point. These differences in self-identity reflect the biographies of many social work educators and their often strong and continuing commitment to social work practice, alongside the sometimes competing demands of the academy in relation to disciplinary development and knowledge creation *per se*. Such tensions were evident in many of the debates surfacing throughout the *TSWR* seminar series,

---

[1]   One innovative aspect of the *TSWR* seminars was that papers were made available in advance via a dedicated website hosted by the National Institute for Social Work (NISW). This not only helped maximise available discussion-time at the seminars themselves, but also facilitated on-line exchanges amongst a wider body of participants. NISW has now closed; some of its former functions have in effect 'moved' to the Social Care Institute for Excellence (SCIE), from whose website – more specifically the 'Electronic Library for Social Care' (eLSC) – many of the *TSWR* papers are now accessible, together with additional information about the seminar series and its aims and outputs. The main address for this material is <http://www.elsc.org.uk/socialcareresource/tswr/tswrindex.htm>. A number of the seminar papers are referred to in the various contributions to this book; where appropriate, electronic addresses are included in the listed references.

variously presented as the relevance of 'theory', the kind of research given priority by various stakeholders, the role envisaged for research in relation to practice and policy, and so on. An additional factor in all of this is the variety of disciplinary backgrounds among social work academics (and for that matter among practitioners). Because of our interest in this factor we invited authors to include some details of their own intellectual biographies in the information supplied for our use in Notes on Contributors, which precedes this introduction.

The dominant approach to the relationship between knowledge and practice within UK social work probably may still be characterised as 'applied social science plus social work values and skills', although this has been contested within academic social work and challenged by both practitioners and service users. Much of the argument has focused on the role and relevance of research in relation to day-to-day professional practice and the use and appropriateness of different research methodologies and techniques. Until relatively recently, rather less attention has been given to the pervasive deeper assumption that research and/or theory are, could, or should be somehow foundational, to be 'applied' to, or in, practice – as evident, for example, in some prominent conceptions of 'evidence-based practice'. This conventional view has been characterised via the notion of 'a captive triangle' (Usher and Bryant, 1989). However, as Usher and Bryant argue, acknowledging an inescapable three-way interaction between research, theory and practice does not necessitate picturing the links in terms of a triangle with theory and research situated at its base corners and practice at its apex. Rather, re-conceptualisation in terms of 'an open triangle' (*ibid.*) allows alternative ways of thinking about these elements of social work without any implication of privileging research and/or theory as the *basis* for practice. Moreover, it provides a means of exploring all three in a more creative and interactive fashion (Powell, 1997). Many of the contributions in the present book may be seen as challenging what remains a powerful orthodoxy in just this way, implicitly or explicitly pointing towards more dynamic links between and amongst theory, practice and research.

The chapters which follow variously emphasise and address these three inter-related elements, which may be said together to constitute social work, and in doing so explore and confirm social work's claim to be both an academic discipline appropriately established in higher education and at the same time a profession directly affecting the lives of individuals and families. The contributors draw upon their own biographies implicitly, rather than self-consciously reflecting upon them, but they are evident to varying degrees through the various voices heard and the different commitments expressed. The content of each chapter flows from and reflects the wider research and writing of its author(s). Inevitably there is a degree of overlap, even some repetition, but there are also interesting and significant differences of perspective and judgement. While as editors we have sought to highlight significant points of intersection between chapters via notes in the text, we have not attempted to eliminate restatement.

Before offering a summary of each chapter in turn by way of further and more detailed introduction, it may be helpful to take a more general overview of the structure of the book as a whole. The first three chapters present related and similarly critical perspectives on recent developments in the conception and role of social work, focusing on the UK; together, they indicate – among other things – the importance of context for any critical understanding. Chapter 4 examines the impact of gender across both the profession and the discipline, addressing key aspects of professional education and the tensions emanating from its competing interests and concerns in an academic context. The next three contributions share a more direct and primary focus on empirical research than is to be found in the other seven chapters, while at the same time each posing rather different questions about the nature and purpose of research in social work and its contribution to social work knowledge, practice and policy. The final three chapters adopt a self-consciously theoretical perspective, albeit that just what is meant by 'theoretical' in relation to social work, and how such 'theory' might inform research and/or practice, are very much part of what is under consideration. They draw variously on major traditions and key ideas in philosophy and the social sciences. In different ways each demonstrates the relevance of critical reflection, not least concerning the role of language itself, in the representation and understanding – indeed the constitution – of contemporary social work and its knowledge claims. We might suggest in a preliminary way that each seeks to reflect on social work by 'standing back from' but not 'above' it, thus hoping to provide an additional element of perspective and self-understanding to inform both practice and research.

Over the period during which these chapters were written and the collection as a whole edited for publication, perhaps the two major preoccupations in UK social work – certainly for academics – have been the continuing debate around 'evidence-based practice' and the development of the curriculum for the new degree-level qualifying award. The second of these in particular has associated with it all the issues around partnership arrangements with service users as well as employers (now including 'occupational standards' and 'codes of practice'), 'benchmarked' academic standards and the quality of learning and teaching, and – increasingly significant – inter-professional learning. Both broad areas – the evidence base and the qualifying curriculum – are of course in part associated with and linked by the New Labour Government's 'modernisation' agenda as it bears on social work and social care (see British Journal of Social Work, 2001). The huge impact and significance of all this notwithstanding – and we certainly do not mean to underestimate the importance of any or all of it – the central focus of this book as a whole is consciously elsewhere.

Not very long ago Nigel Parton observed that 'conceptual and theoretical debate about social work and for social work has been severely lacking in recent years at a time when such debate is needed more than ever' (1996b, p. 5). As already intimated, we see this book's primary contribution as being to the discipline's ongoing efforts to make good this deficit, and in that context to developing a broad and reflective conception of 'theory' in and for social work. In an important way this implicitly encompasses, or perhaps better subtends, is implicit in, the many and various 'more practical' issues around research and teaching. Most of the following chapters make mention of evidence-based practice, with contributors broadly sharing a perspective which is critical of the understanding of this which presently seems to prevail officially (i.e. is endorsed by the Government) in the UK, seeing a role for a variety of forms of research-based and other contributions to the development of policy and practice in social work and social care. In considerable measure this consensus is associated with a shared view, made explicit by several authors, that social work is best seen as primarily a moral and political, rather than a technical activity. In Chapters 2, 3 and 6 the 'what works' approach is directly discussed, without being *per se* the primary focus of concern, whilst in several other contributions the fundamental questions around what forms of research are appropriate to social work are considered in a variety of ways, with several chapters illuminating the issues surrounding methodological choices in undertaking social work research. A strong sense that social work is located amongst the social science disciplines is variously evident in each contribution, and this is one way in which although there is relatively little direct attention to matters of curriculum and teaching in this book – except to some extent in Chapter 4 – these are in a sense implicit throughout. Similarly, whilst little explicit attention is given to issues around service users' involvement in research and theorising, and/or in informing/influencing policy and practice, there is in each contribution an underlying recognition of this group's importance as key stakeholders. A need for dialogue, across the academy/ profession and other 'divides', is emphasised in several chapters and is directly taken up in the final section of Chapter 10.

In the opening chapter, Bill Jordan and Nigel Parton provide a broad and theoretically rich context for the book as a whole, drawing upon and bringing together ideas which each has presented separately in recent books (Jordan, 2000; Parton and O'Byrne, 2000). Drawing on their backgrounds in political and social theory respectively, they analyse changes over the past 25 years in the UK public sector, in social work itself, and in civil society. They emphasise the deliberate efforts of Conservative governments from 1979 to 1997 to redraw the public/ private boundary, and the way in which these 'reforms' have been taken forward by subsequent New Labour administrations whilst also acknowledging the incompleteness of the market-oriented approach of their predecessors. Jordan and Parton explore the various theories of economists and political scientists which have more or less explicitly underpinned successive changes: public choice theory, which lay behind the Conservative programme, and the communitarian ideas and the theories of social capital favoured by New Labour. The authors draw attention to the paradox that despite the pervasive sense of uncertainty as to the appropriateness and feasibility of large-scale planning and provision, and the consequent fragmentation and 'residualisation' of services, the last 25 years have seen the construction of increasingly complex systems of audit and accountability; meanwhile, the discrepancy between the respective resources and opportunities available to the 'haves' and 'have nots' persists – indeed has grown. The 'current hegemony of the idea of evidence-based practice' – for which they see a *limited* role in relation to social work practice – is viewed as part of an agenda which threatens to destroy professional, especially public-sector, social work. Yet, paradoxically, there has been a rejuvenation of the historic skills and values of the profession in voluntary-sector and community groups. Jordan and Parton sketch an alternative future in terms of 'constructive social work', with ambiguity and uncertainty consciously acknowledged as being at its heart and whose practitioners understand themselves as engaged in what is primarily a practical–moral rather than a technical–rational activity.

Each of the next two chapters, which overlap and complement each other, concentrates on a particular aspect of the contemporary context of social work in the UK and adopts a similar critical perspective to that of the opening contribution.

Adrian James subtly and provocatively uses Ritzer's[2] concept of the 'McDonaldization' of (American) society to characterise what has happened to social work in the UK in recent decades. He reviews the transition from the predominance of psychosocial casework, via the organisational changes following the 1968 Seebohm Report and the creation of the Central Council for Education and Training in Social Work (CCETSW), to the managerialism and evidence-based practice of the current era. He gives particular attention to changes in the probation service, showing how these provide a particularly clear – and early – example of the wider process of McDonaldization which, he argues, has affected social work in Britain. He suggests that we now have 'a highly rational approach to delivering a particular kind of service', and have in effect 'substitut[ed] fast food for … individually prepared and served meals'. Echoing Jordan and Parton, James argues both that successive governments have actively sought to undermine social work's professional status, and that some aspects of the whole, largely but not exclusively to be found in the voluntary and not-for-profit sectors, have 'escaped' McDonaldization, though at the cost of being marginalised and defined out of social work by the regulatory body for education and training[3] and the major employers – i.e. local authorities. In addition, he suggests that, under threat, some academics and professionals have embraced governments' narrowed definitions of practice and research, with a consequent loss of scope for innovation in the former and for critical analysis in the latter.

Ian Butler and Richard Pugh's focus is the depoliticisation of social work research and of social work as such. They suggest that the constrained and scientistic view of what constitutes knowledge which is embodied in the dominant conception of evidence-based practice goes hand-in-hand with and reinforces narrow ideas of welfare and of the role of social work therein. They express considerable unease over the 'apparent cosy coincidence of interests between policy makers, social work practitioners and researchers', noting in a similarly critical way to Adrian James – and Beth Humphries in Chapter 6 – that some applaud and seek to sustain and extend these closer symbiotic relationships. Butler and Pugh offer an overview of the origins and main tenets of the dominant

[2]   It is sometimes necessary in this introduction to indicate sources drawn upon by contributors; readers are directed to the chapters concerned for full bibliographic details, which are not generally included in the list of references appended here.
[3]   The functions of CCETSW (see above) in these respects were incorporated in the role of the newly-created General Social Care Council (GSCC) from 2001.

conception of evidence-based practice, and endorse the major critiques made of its epistemological assumptions and its political and professional consequences. They also acknowledge that this is neither the only possible or actual version of evidence-based practice, nor for that matter 'the only game [currently] in town' in terms of styles of social work research. They themselves argue for an eclectic approach to knowledge and research in the discipline and profession. Characterising their position as one of 'weak relativism', they embrace 'contingency and ultimate uncertainty' concerning the social world and on this basis reject the view of social work researchers as technicians. Emphasising the role of judgement, not least in interpreting and appraising evidence, they conclude that researchers should both seek to shape policy and practice and embrace the role of 'problematiser and critic'.

All three chapters in this first part of the book argue that social work academics have a key role to play in critically challenging current orthodoxies, especially the narrow, instrumental and reductionist view of research, the (associated) rather mechanical view of practice, and the (parallel) notion of competency-based training, all espoused not least by recent and current UK governments. They also each argue, with differences in detailed meaning and emphasis, that this involves embracing – in some senses *re*-embracing – a broader conception of social work, which acknowledges the moral values which lie at its heart and the unavoidably political dimensions which result from operating at the interface between individuals and families and the wider society as represented by the state.

Karen Lyons and Imogen Taylor foreground gender issues, as well as giving more direct and detailed attention than other contributors to the tensions between social work as a profession and as a discipline, especially as experienced by university-based social work academics who are both professional educators and researchers/theorists. They show that social work has been and in many respects still is regarded as a 'women's profession', and that with some justification. However, the numerical predominance of women in social work both in practice and in the academy is more than reversed amongst those in positions of power in either context. Drawing on feminist theory and empirical research informed by feminist perspectives, Lyons and Taylor explore some of the possible reasons for these gendered patterns, and how they have affected and continue to affect social work's development as a discipline and as a profession, both from within and from without. They highlight issues of gender and of status in relation to the creation and transmission of knowledge. At the end of their chapter they explore the gender dimensions and possible implications of some significant recent and current changes: managerialism in the public sector, the growth in the use of information and communication technologies, and the changing expectations of social work, specifically *vis-à-vis* qualifying training, its curriculum and methods.

The next three chapters focus – although not narrowly so – on different aspects of the complex agenda currently faced by social work research. All three of the authors concerned acknowledge and variously engage with the broader and multi-dimensional context explored in the contributions preceding them, while distancing themselves to differing degrees from the current broad direction being taken by social work in the UK, both academically and, especially, in terms of policy and practice.

Partnership between the academy and the profession – practitioners, managers, and policy makers – is a significant if largely implicit theme of this book and, as we have seen, a more direct concern of the chapter by Karen Lyons and Imogen Taylor. Steve Trevillion draws attention to the wider prominence of partnership in current UK policy discourses, and in doing so offers a rather different perspective on some of the broad changes highlighted by Jordan and Parton. He notes that the idea of partnership is by no means new, neither is its current popularity attended by widespread agreement on what precisely the concept means and/or to what it refers. He demonstrates that there is a particularly strong tradition not only of practice but of research concerning partnership in social work, characterised especially by a valuable focus on the complexities attending issues of 'difference' and crossing boundaries. He suggests that the area of social work research – including his own work – which through the 1990s began to explore partnership in new ways, drawing upon network analysis, is not only especially relevant to contemporary policy concerns but also presents social work research with a major opportunity to play a central role, based upon its long-standing concerns with process issues and with cultural as much as structural change. Some of the ideas Trevillion explores towards the end of his chapter point towards the discussions of social pedagogy and of democratic participation in the contributions of Walter Lorenz and of Robin Lovelock and Jackie Powell.

Beth Humphries takes up issues raised by earlier contributions, most directly by that of Ian Butler and Richard Pugh. She revisits Howard Becker's 1960s claim that social research in general cannot avoid 'taking sides' and that therefore researchers should do this consciously and explicitly, declaring their partiality; moreover, that they should take the side of 'the underdog'. In social work discourses it is arguably as common for an answer to the major questions involved here to be taken for granted, so to speak, often via implicit or explicit reference to 'social work values', as it is for discussion of the issue to be denied legitimacy by assumptions of a positivistic kind. Humphries broadly endorses the observations on Becker's views made at the time by Alvin Gouldner; namely that while partisanship is not incompatible with objectivity as he (Gouldner) understands it, the researcher's allegiance should be to particular values not to factions. With this in view, and focusing upon policy and practice in the field of immigration and asylum controls, Humphries challenges the claims of social work researchers – and social work more generally – to be on the side of 'the oppressed' in current UK contexts. In the process she seriously questions how far successive governments' policies on immigration and asylum have been based on evidence – which is often inconclusive anyway – rather than on ideological commitment and popular/ populist myth, sometimes in fact ignoring or flying in the face of substantial evidence. Drawing on studies – including her own recent research – which adopt a broader view than simply accepting the government of the day's policy goals and examining 'what works' in relation to them, she offers research messages of a rather different kind. She claims that 'taking sides against oppression' in the sense which she advocates implies no absence of rigour, no methodological sloppiness, and that in the current context social work research which fails to reflect critically on the bases of policy thereby aligns with 'forces that contradict social work's expressed values'.

Nick Gould suggests that recent debates in the UK concerning evidence-based practice in social care have seen a good deal of 'gladiatorial position-taking', not least in academic social work circles. He sees this as not only unhelpful but also as somewhat *passé*, notably in relation to contemporary discussions of evidence-based practice in the health field. He also echoes Beth Humphries's observations – and those of Ian Butler and Richard Pugh – that the Government's expressed commitment to evidence-based policy and practice is somewhat disingenuous, being honoured mainly in the breach. Seeking to move things forward, Gould surveys the contributions of qualitative research in social work, deliberately taking what he terms a 'non-hierarchical approach' to alternative methodologies, and he 'cuts the cake' in two different and complementary ways. First he applies to research in social work Denzin and Lincoln's analysis of the history of qualitative social research in general in terms of five periods or 'moments'. Then, drawing on Popay and Williams's thematic review of qualitative health research, he develops an equivalent picture of the enduring substantive preoccupations of qualitative social work researchers. Gould's chapter includes two further significant aspects. He attends briefly to the question of whether qualitative research has any particular affinity with – and therefore potentially some special contribution to make to – social work practice. This leads him to seek to identify a range of appropriate criteria by which the adequacy of qualitative research as evidence or knowledge might be judged. This is obviously a matter of no little concern if qualitative findings are to inform social work practice, along with quantitative research and practice-based or experiential knowledge, a trinity of resources whose combination Gould advocates.

As already indicated, Chapters 8, 9 and 10 explore ways in which different conceptions and forms of 'theory' might, among other possible roles, offer perspective and orientation to social work practice and research.

Walter Lorenz draws attention to the links between persisting questions about general approaches to social work practice, that is to say social work's core identity, and questions about the appropriate methodological orientation for social work research, bringing out the links between the two concerns and also drawing attention to parallels in Anglo-American and German debates and to the recurrence of the main themes at different periods. Among other things, this evidently offers a helpful critical perspective on typical contemporary discussions of evidence-based practice, while being broadly consistent with the views expressed in several earlier chapters. The aim of Lorenz's historical and conceptual analysis is to encourage the social work community to locate what are often seen as and seem to be polarised alternatives as, rather, a diversity reflecting the origins and fundamental 'location' of social work, with different perspectives dominating at different times and in different places, in turn reflecting the variety of forces in play. He sees as being at the centre of all this the tensions attendant on social work's dual concerns with individual well-being and with social order and solidarity, most familiar to English readers through the work of Nigel Parton, Bill Jordan and others and touched on near the beginning of this introduction. Lorenz presents this via Jürgen Habermas's philosophical/sociological/historical account of the development of modern societies, in particular his idea of a growing split between 'system' and 'lifeworld', with social work ambivalently located in a mediating position. Lorenz's key point is that controversies over research methodology are intimately bound up with the question of social work's overall identity, and that while epistemological as well as merely technical issues are involved, those epistemological issues must in turn be related – as Habermas does relate them – to a wider social theory. Only in that way, Lorenz argues, can the question of social work's professional and academic identity and status, its *fundamentally mediating* position, be 'resolved'. Recognition of this, he argues – drawing further on Habermas, in particular his sharp distinction between instrumental and communicative reason and action – releases the 'communicative potential constitutive of social work'.

Jeremy Kearney explores the complex relationships between research, theory and practice in a rather different way. He draws on the later work of the philosopher Ludwig Wittgenstein, and on the more recent and related ideas of John Shotter and other social constructionist thinkers, to present a view of language and meaning in which social worlds are made by 'persons-in-conversation'. From this perspective Kearney suggests ways of understanding and undertaking practice, research and theory in social work which involve consciously conceiving them as historically situated and as constructed and reconstructed in ongoing mutual inter-relationships. Among the key ideas he draws from Wittgenstein are those of 'language-games' and 'knowing how to go on' (in them), and he demonstrates the usefulness of these ways of looking at social work by applying them to a variety of contexts where there is some kind of 'block' to 'going on'. He argues that we should focus on specific situated moments of interaction and attend to what emerges or might emerge from them, suggesting that this may well be more productive, offering recognisably better ways of 'knowing how to go on', than many of our current ways of acting in social work practice, research and theory.

In Chapter 10, Robin Lovelock and Jackie Powell in effect seek to engage many of the questions arising during the course of the book as a whole by reference to major themes in contemporary political and social theory. They thus have a similar aim to Walter Lorenz, but confront some of the difficulties attending the tradition of 'Frankfurt School' critical theory on which he draws significantly. They present a necessarily brief overview of the extensive writings of two of the major intellectual figures of the second half of the twentieth century, Jürgen Habermas and Michel Foucault, in order to identify what is fundamentally at stake between them, namely that they offer two very different conceptions and practices of critical reflection. Lovelock and Powell then explore this further with reference to different understandings of state/society relations and the history and current form of the welfare state – as the context of social work practice, research and theorising. In some ways they argue ultimately for a rather similar self-consciousness of our being inescapably historically, socially and culturally situated as does Jeremy Kearney, thereby reflecting the resonances between in each case the later work of Wittgenstein and Foucault (see Tully, 1995, especially pp. 34–

43). Embracing Foucault's emphasis on the *historicity* of reason 'as against' Habermas's insistent search to sustain his regulative *theory* of reason (Hoy, 1998, p. 23), they nevertheless also argue for drawing upon Habermas's 'rules of discourse', but understood as involving ethical commitment to a practical historical project; a project to which they suggest social work, especially in the pedagogical tradition, could make a major contribution, both in terms of theory and of practice. This final chapter is not a 'conclusion' in the conventional sense, in that it neither attempts to bring the preceding contributions together into a coherent whole nor to chart in any detail a substantive way forward. What it might be seen as doing, through reaching for an over-arching understanding of 'theory' as critical reflection, is seeking to encourage greater (self-)awareness concerning how we think about thinking about social work and thus how we deploy and develop some of the arguments and perspectives offered in other chapters of the book – and indeed elsewhere. With this in mind, the chapter concludes by arguing for more broadly-based and more genuine dialogue on the nature and role of social work, as discipline and profession, both in the academy and amongst a wider community of interest and public. In so-doing it briefly addresses the often unacknowledged difficulties attending both the idea of dialogue and its pursuit in practice.

Thus a general claim that social work and political theory share much in common and have much to contribute to each other, including and not least around the vexed matter of 'the relation between theory and practice', is in effect advanced and explored in Chapter 10 by means of a close examination of a particularly significant 'confrontation' and some of its far-reaching ramifications. Support for the more general proposition is also evident in several of the other chapters in this book, notably those by Bill Jordan and Nigel Parton and by Walter Lorenz. Moreover, most if not all contributors to this collection, and doubtless many of its readers, share the view that social work is at root a political activity. However, when this point is made – as it often is – in social work discussions, it is not always entirely clear just what the implications are, in particular for social work as an academic pursuit; nor is it always evident what precisely is meant or understood by 'political' in this context. The meaning of 'the political' has in fact become a significant theme of much recent work in academic political theory, as the latter comes to terms with the overlapping challenges of postmodernist, feminist and multiculturalist ideas (see O'Sullivan, 1997, for a useful 'map'). A key question here, around which the final chapter in many ways turns and which is in effect implicit in the rest of the book, concerns the problem of how, in the current intellectual and cultural context, to reflect upon and discuss normative ideas.

With this in mind, a number of observations will be offered here, albeit summarily, relevant to thinking about social work as a discipline and profession in a way which acknowledges both its political nature and its important but under-developed links with political theory. We must preface these comments by noting that 'political theory' in the sense meant here – '[critical] reflection on "political and social relationships at the widest possible level of generality"' (White, 2002, p. 472, quoting Laslett, 1956, p. vii) – has been a largely academic pursuit for close to a century at least (see also below). In addition, like 'social work', political theory is far from being homogeneous – in either its academic or its wider frame of reference and meaning.

First, politics and systematic and critical thinking about politics in the sense just indicated – variously 'political theory' or 'political philosophy', sometimes 'political thought'[4] – are taken to involve moral issues. Second, such matters of political theory/philosophy, and political morality, as

> … Are there human rights and if so what are they? What is the role of the state? Do individuals have definable needs and if so who has an obligation to satisfy them? … Can we give an adequate account of the moral basis of social and political institutions? … (Plant, 1991, pp. 1–2)

are held to be, if neither susceptible of certainty nor of universal agreement, nevertheless '[not] just a matter of individual preferences and commitment' (*ibid.*, p. 2). Third, the contemporary conception of (academic) political theory in the English-speaking world which embodies the two foregoing understandings reflects the 're-emergence' of the discipline after a period in the middle of the twentieth century when its cognitive status was challenged – indeed there were many who (albeit only relatively briefly) believed it 'dead' (see Berlin, 1962; Laslett, 1956) – under the dominance of logical positivism in philosophy. On this latter view, substantive, and thus normative, political ideas, along with moral and aesthetic judgements, were regarded as merely the expression of subjective preferences; only the empirical study of political behaviour and the logical/linguistic analysis of political concepts were to be seen as proper academic concerns in this area.

In an effort to guard against a number of potential misunderstandings of what is being suggested here and in Chapter 10 with respect to 'theory' in social work and its actual and potential relationship with (academic) political theory/philosophy, two further and inter-related points must be noted, again of necessity all too briefly. The first concerns the multiple meanings of 'theory' in both contexts; the second the relationships between the respective academic disciplines and their 'real world' reference points.

The period has essentially passed when 'the death of political theory' and 'the behavioural revolution in political science' were being proclaimed; both 'normative' and putatively 'explanatory' theory are now generally acknowledged as having a place in the academic study of politics – with the former being what is usually meant by 'political theory'. The concerns of this book with the relationship between research and theory in social work in some ways parallel contemporary

---

[4]   The different nuances of meaning of 'political theory' and 'political philosophy' probably need not detain us for very long here. Although not strictly interchangeable they are often employed in that manner; they are anyway closely interlinked terms, with, when a distinction is made, the latter usually suggesting the more abstract and general conceptual and meta-theoretical end of the spectrum of reflection and discussion. In a number of places we use the formulation 'political theory/philosophy' to indicate reference to the whole, for which, in some contexts, here and elsewhere, 'political thought' sometimes similarly stands.

discussions of the relationships between political theory and political science (see, for example, Political Theory, 2002) in what let us for ease here call (generically) 'political studies'. That said, as Stephen White has recently argued:

> [A] perennial challenge to the activity of political theory has come from social science in general and political science in particular. ... [S]ome of our colleagues in political science departments still harbor disciplinary ideals that, at best, denigrate political philosophy or, at worst, leave no room whatsoever for it. (White, 2002, p. 479)

Hence, White continues, it remains

> ... a perennial task for political theorists ... to delineate the differences between theory and science, as well as show why the systematic study of politics requires both types of insight. (*ibid.*)

There are clearly parallels to be drawn as regards the social work academy, where the matter of the meaning(s) of 'theory' is arguably more complicated and certainly trickier to characterise. Developing and updating Barbour's (1984) discussion, which was based on an analysis of a survey of student understandings of 'theory and practice', now requires the addition of feminist and postmodernist ideas to her first category, sense or type of theory, which she exemplified by reference to Marx and Freud and referred to as 'comprehensive conceptual frameworks'. In addition, greater contemporary awareness of the philosophical difficulties attending what Barbour also called 'grand theory' must now be acknowledged, so that – as with political theory/philosophy (see above and, in a little more detail, below) a whole range of meta-theoretical discussion is part of what, broadly speaking, we ourselves mainly mean here by 'theory'. There is also a significant place in social work for theory in Barbour's second sense, namely would-be explanatory frameworks for specific areas or phenomena, such as bereavement, child development, child abuse; also for (possibly associated) theories or models of intervention, such as task-centred casework, groupwork – although these latter are perhaps more helpfully labelled 'social work methods' (or 'methodologies'). Finally, it is common for 'theory' to be used across the social work community to refer to what is presented and discussed in the university- or college-based components of social work education and training rather than what is encountered in placement situations – and of course there is a similar more general usage juxtaposing academic and practice contexts.

This third aspect of the meaning and use of 'theory' in social work links with the significant differences between the ways in which the respective academic disciplines of social work and political theory/philosophy relate to the world outside the academy. Whilst it is certainly the case that some academics based in departments of politics or similar have frequent and/or possibly influential contact with powerful figures in national and international public life – as for that matter do some social work academics – there is in what let us again call 'political studies' hardly the close and unavoidable ongoing inter-relationship between the academic discipline and the field of professional and public activity which characterises social work.

The publication of John Rawls's *A Theory of Justice* (1971) is widely seen as having been central to the 'resurrection' of normative, substantive 'Anglo-American' political theory referred to on the previous page – things were always rather different on the European mainland (West, 1996).[5] The ensuing 'liberal–communitarian debate', largely generated around Rawls's book (see Avineri and de-Shalit, 1992; Mulhall and Swift, 1996), and the more recently dominant major themes of 'democracy and difference' (see Benhabib, 1996; O'Sullivan, 1997) and 'recognition' (see Kymlicka, 1995; Tully, 1995), which like the preceding central or dominant focus revolve around issues of 'foundationalism' and 'contextualism', all merge into broader postmodernist, feminist and multiculturalist critiques of the Western philosophical tradition (see Good and Velody, 1998; Plant, 1998). Rawls's *Political Liberalism* (1993), substantially but not entirely a collection of papers published through the 1970s and 1980s clarifying and developing aspects of his theory and which he saw as a re-presentation rather than a revision or reformulation of his account of justice as fairness, is also particularly important in this context.

Lest the previous paragraph suggests an overly academic or intellectualist perspective, it should be noted – though without any implied determinism – that the wider social and political situation and climate of the 1960s, the decade of 'protest', was arguably the more fundamental 'cause' of the re-emergence of normative political theory, just as contemporary academic concerns with postmodernity and multiculturalism both reflect and inform wider social and political currents.

What remains crucially at stake involves how to 'do' political theory, including – but not only – substantive, normative political theory. What kind of activity is it, and what claims can legitimately be made for its content? And thence, similarly *and* relatedly so both this introduction and Chapter 10 seek to suggest, how, in a certain sense, should we frame 'doing' academic social work? How to think, write, speak coherently and critically about the kinds of questions indicated a little earlier (p. 12), given that pluralism is a scarcely controvertible fact of life, not only between but within cultures, and that 'foundationalism' has been under severe philosophical attack for some time. As Raymond Plant has put it:

> Is the project of political theory to provide some universal values as a foundation for practical reasoning in politics, or is it to bring to a fuller consciousness the values which are implicit in the communities of which we are a part? (Plant, 1991, p. 327)

Foundationalism in political thought has traditionally taken the form of invoking some account of human nature or human flourishing, which is in turn regarded as epistemologically grounded, as the basis for how social and political affairs should

---

[5]   The developments being alluded to in this paragraph have both reflected and contributed to the fact that Anglo-American and continental European philosophy are now more closely (re-)connected than was the case during much of the twentieth century.

be organised.[6] However, as Plant states, 'the fact/value distinction makes such arguments deeply problematic ... [even] with the collapse of the overall positivist programme' (*ibid.*, p. 323). This is because the logical principle that the conclusion of a valid argument can contain nothing not already contained in its premises means that

> ... if the theory of human nature is factual, it is difficult to see how it will support a conclusion about political principle and morality, in so far as it is evaluative it may support the moral conclusion, but will itself need to be grounded in something other than a subjective preference for one set of views about human nature rather than another. (*ibid.*, p. 71)

Many political theorists have, nevertheless, continued to look for some form of foundational support, albeit that in the work of liberals such as Rawls this has taken the form of notably 'thin' conceptions of human nature and of 'the good':

> [P]art of the liberal project in political theory ... has been to try to determine whether there are any rationally compelling rules which could underpin practical political reasoning in a world in which first order moral agreement has become fragmented. (Plant, 1991, p. 323)

Rawls's well-known principles of justice (1971, pp. 302–3) are a key example of what Plant has in mind here. Moreover, in *Political Liberalism* (1993) Rawls seeks to show that they remain compelling, and how this is to be understood, in a world where deep cultural differences cannot be ignored.

The idea that many reflections on social work could benefit from greater attention to the literature of moral and political philosophy is hardly an original thought (see, for example, Plant, 1970; Plant *et al.*, 1980; Timms and Watson, 1978), but it bears repeating. The relevance for social work of the themes and ideas sketched in the last few paragraphs – and the fact that there is some acknowledgement of this within the discipline – may be further and more concretely demonstrated by reference to the centrality of ideas about human needs in welfare discourses (e.g. Doyal and Gough, 1984; 1986; 1991; Leonard, 1997; Plant, 1991, especially pp. 54–71 and chapter 5; Plant *et al.*, 1980), by what for many is social work's defining commitment to social justice (e.g. British Journal of Social Work, 2002; Jordan, 1990; 1998b; 2000), and by the continuing search for a universal code of ethics for social work (e.g. Briskman and Noble, 1999; Butler, 2002). We might note in addition that the underpinnings of the dominant or officially (i.e. Governmentally) endorsed conception of evidence-based practice in the UK are strongly redolent of logical positivism (see Webb, 2001) – more usually expressed in terms of 'empirical practice' underpinned by 'logical empiricism' in

---

[6]   It is significant – and no accident – that the major figures in the Western philosophical tradition, such as Plato, Aristotle, Hobbes, Locke, Kant, Hegel, Mill, all addressed both epistemological issues and matters of political theory, and in inter-related ways. Thence the substantial and continuing overlap between the philosophy and methodology of the social sciences and specifically political philosophy.

the US – and that the persisting 'debates' around this are reminiscent of those of the period referred to above in which political theory was pronounced 'dead' but from which alleged demise it has re-emerged to flourish in recent decades.

Furthermore, we might pause to reflect, as social work writers such as Jim Ife (1997) have done, before too readily dismissing all forms of 'foundationalism'. Any conception of universal human rights seen as a way of limiting what might be done to persons, any idea of community or solidarity suggesting that we have obligations to meet the needs of others, and any conception of social justice appealed to as a basis for correcting market solutions, all seem to require some rationally compelling basis capable of transcending personal preferences and/or cultural, national or religious boundaries (Plant, 1992, pp. 139–40). Plant's interim 'conclusion' on these matters – and, relatedly, on the future of political theory – is that

> ... This argument still has a long way to go but I would imagine that we may move towards what might be called a left Hegelian position, in which we see a role for theorising about universal features of human life and reasons for action based upon them while allowing ... that what fills in these universal features is going to depend a great deal upon context and social meanings. (Plant, 1998, p. 103)

Much of what has been presented here in necessarily brief support of the proposal that increased contact and academic dialogue between social work and contemporary social and political theory would be mutually beneficial may well appear to be advocating one-way traffic. In urging fellow social work academics to deeper reflection on matters which continue to preoccupy political theorists, it has been and must be acknowledged that in its institutionalised academic form political theory/philosophy is often overly abstract, self-absorbed, and remote from 'the real world' (see Isaac, 1995, and the responses published together with Isaac's paper as a symposium, for recent discussion of this specifically in the US context). Indeed it is precisely in this that the importance – and potential – of a *two-way* exchange with social work lies. The Cambridge political philosopher John Dunn has argued for the central importance of a contemporary reassertion and democratisation of the classical virtue of prudence – 'the key virtue of human practical reason' (Dunn, 1990, p. 3). For Dunn (see especially his introduction and chapter 12) 'the major task of political theory [now is] showing human beings how they have good reason to act in the historical situation in which they find themselves', and he is correspondingly critical of contemporary academic political theory as preoccupied with 'interpreting itself, rather than the real political world'.[7] In this respect political theory could surely benefit from closer attention to social work, given the pressure on the latter to think in terms of context and action, often relatively immediate action, including – and in some sense perhaps primarily – action at an individual, or better an inter-personal, level.

The varied contributions which follow here may serve, *inter alia*, to further indicate how pursuing joint concerns in both theory and practice would be assisted

---

[7]   The two summary quotations in this sentence are from the jacket of Dunn's book.

by cross-fertilisation between social work and academic political thought. Yet in an important respect none of what has been said here on this theme has been adequately framed; for what is really needed is not so much dialogue *across* disciplinary boundaries as a *less discipline-bound* approach. To take just one – but a major – example, the challenge which postmodernist themes raise for the nature and role of political theory, of social work, and of a host of academic and other – including professional – practices as presently constituted, suggests that some of the most interesting and important contemporary discussions are of common concern. Bill Jordan's inter-related contributions to social policy (e.g. 1987; 1996; 1998b), political theory (e.g. 1989; 1997; 1998a) and social work (e.g. 1984; 1990; 2000) continue to demonstrate and exemplify the value of drawing upon, bringing together, and contributing to a number of disciplinary perspectives and literatures. This book attempts something similar through the diverse yet inter-connecting reference points of its contributors.

References

Avineri, S. and de-Shalit, A. (eds) (1992), *Communitarianism and Individualism*, Oxford University Press, Oxford.

Barbour, R.S. (1984), 'Social work education: tackling the theory–practice dilemma', *British Journal of Social Work*, **14**(6), pp. 557–77.

Benhabib, S. (ed.) (1996), *Democracy and Difference: Contesting the Boundaries of the Political*, Princeton University Press, Princeton, NJ.

Berlin, I. (1962), 'Does political theory still exist?', in Laslett, P. and Runciman, W.G. (eds), *Philosophy, Politics and Society*, 2nd Series, Blackwell, Oxford, pp. 1–33.

Briskman, L. and Noble, C. (1999), 'Social work ethics: embracing diversity?', in Pease and Fook, *op. cit.*, pp. 57–69.

British Journal of Social Work (2001), **31**(4), Special Issue: 'Social Work and New Labour: End of the First Term', eds I. Butler and M. Drakeford.

British Journal of Social Work (2002), **32**(6), Special Issue: 'Social Work and Social Justice', ed. M. Colton.

Butler, I. (2002), 'Critical Commentary: A code of ethics for social work and social care research', *British Journal of Social Work*, **32**(2), pp. 239–48. (An earlier version, presented in the *Theorising Social Work Research* seminar series, no. 6, 11 July 2000, University of Luton, is now available at
<http://www.elsc.org.uk/socialcareresource/tswr/seminar6/butler.htm>.
The Code itself is also available on the web page of the Joint Universities Council Social Work Education Committee (JUC/SWEC), which is in turn accessible via
<http://www.york.ac.uk/depts/poli/juc/jucwelc.htm>.)

Camilleri, P. (1999), 'Social work and its search for meaning: theories, narratives and practices', in Pease and Fook, *op. cit.*, pp. 25–39.

Davies, L. and Leonard, P. (eds) (forthcoming), *Social Work in a Corporate Era: Scepticism and Emancipation*, Ashgate, Aldershot.

Doyal, L. and Gough, I. (1984), 'A theory of human needs', *Critical Social Policy*, issue **10**, pp. 6–38.

Doyal, L. and Gough, I. (1986), 'Human needs and socialist welfare', *Praxis International*, **6**(1), pp. 43–69.

Doyal, L. and Gough, I. (1991), *A Theory of Human Need*, Macmillan, Basingstoke.

Dunn, J. (1990), *Interpreting Political Responsibility*, Princeton University Press, Princeton, NJ.

Fawcett, B., Featherstone, B., Fook, J. and Rossiter, A. (eds) (2000), *Practice and Research in Social Work: Postmodern Feminist Perspectives*, Routledge, London.

Good, J. and Velody, I. (eds) (1998), *The Politics of Postmodernity*, Cambridge University Press, Cambridge.

Hoy, D.C. (1998), 'Foucault and critical theory', in Moss, J. (ed.), *The Later Foucault: Politics and Philosophy*, Sage, London, pp. 18–32.

Ife, J. (1997), *Rethinking Social Work: Towards Critical Practice*, Longman, Melbourne.

Isaac, J.C. (1995), 'The strange silence of political theory', *Political Theory*, **23**(4), pp. 636–52 (with several responses and a rejoinder, pp. 653–88).

Jordan, B. (1984), *Invitation to Social Work*, Martin Robertson, Oxford.

Jordan, B. (1987), *Rethinking Welfare*, Blackwell, Oxford.

Jordan, B. (1989), *The Common Good: Citizenship, Morality and Self-Interest*, Blackwell, Oxford.

Jordan, B. (1990), *Social Work in an Unjust Society*, Harvester Wheatsheaf, Hemel Hempstead.

Jordan, B. (1996), *A Theory of Poverty and Social Exclusion*, Polity, Cambridge.

Jordan, B. (1997), 'Democratic community and public choice', in Eriksen, E.O. and Loftager, J. (eds), *The Rationality of the Welfare State*, Scandinavian University Press, Oslo, pp. 76–97.

Jordan, B. (1998a), 'Justice and reciprocity', *Critical Review of International Social and Political Philosophy*, **1**(1), pp. 63–85.

Jordan, B. (1998b), *The New Politics of Welfare: Social Justice in a Global Context*, Sage, London.

Jordan, B., with Jordan, C. (2000), *Social Work and the Third Way: Tough Love as Social Policy*, Sage, London.

Kymlicka, W. (1995), *Multicultural Citizenship: A Liberal Theory of Minority Rights*, Oxford University Press, Oxford.

Laslett, P. (1956), 'Introduction', in Laslett, P. (ed.), *Philosophy, Politics and Society*, 1st Series, Blackwell, Oxford, pp. vii–xiv.

Leonard, P. (1997), *Postmodern Welfare: Reconstructing an Emancipatory Project*, Sage, London.

Lorenz, W. (1994), *Social Work in a Changing Europe*, Routledge, London.

Lyons, K. (1999), *Social Work in Higher Education: Demise or Development?*, Ashgate, Aldershot.

Mulhall, S. and Swift, A. (1996), *Liberals and Communitarians* (2nd edn), Blackwell, Oxford.

O'Sullivan, N. (1997), 'Difference and the concept of the political in contemporary political philosophy', *Political Studies*, **45**(4), pp. 739–54.

Parton, N. (ed.) (1996a), *Social Theory, Social Change and Social Work*, Routledge, London.

Parton, N. (1996b), 'Social theory, social change and social work: an introduction', in Parton, 1996a, pp. 4–18.

Parton, N. and O'Byrne, P. (2000), *Constructive Social Work: Towards a New Practice*, Macmillan, Basingstoke.

Pease, B. and Fook, J. (eds) (1999), *Transforming Social Work Practice: Postmodern Critical Perspectives*, Routledge, London.

Plant, R. (1970), *Social and Moral Theory in Casework*, Routledge and Kegan Paul, London.

Plant, R. (1991), *Modern Political Thought*, Blackwell, Oxford.

Plant, R. (1992), 'Political theory without foundations', *History of the Human Sciences*, **5**(3), pp. 137–44.

Plant, R. (1998), 'Antinomies of modernist political thought: reasoning, context and community', in Good and Velody, *op. cit.*, pp. 76–106.

Plant, R., Lesser, H. and Taylor-Gooby, P. (1980), *Political Philosophy and Social Welfare: Essays on the Normative Basis of Welfare Provision*, Routledge and Kegan Paul, London.

Political Theory (2002), **30**(4), Special Issue: 'What Is Political Theory?', ed. S.K. White.

Powell, J. (1997), 'Researching social work and social care practices', in McKenzie, G., Powell, J. and Usher, R. (eds), *Understanding Social Research: Perspectives on Methodology and Practice*, Falmer, London, pp. 139–54.

Rawls, J. (1971), *A Theory of Justice*, Harvard University Press, Cambridge, MA.

Rawls, J. (1993), *Political Liberalism*, Columbia University Press, New York.

Timms, N. and Watson, D. (1978), *Philosophy in Social Work*, Routledge and Kegan Paul, London.

Tully, J. (1995), *Strange Multiplicity: Constitutionalism in an Age of Diversity*, Cambridge University Press, Cambridge.

Usher, R. and Bryant, I. (1989), *Adult Education as Theory, Practice and Research: The Captive Triangle*, Routledge, London.

Webb, S.A. (2001), 'Some considerations on the validity of evidence-based practice in social work', *British Journal of Social Work*, **31**(1), pp. 57–79.

West, D. (1996), *An Introduction to Continental Philosophy*, Polity, Cambridge.

White, S.K. (2002), 'Introduction – Pluralism, platitudes, and paradoxes: fifty years of Western political thought', in Political Theory, *op. cit.*, pp. 472–81.

Chapter 1

Social Work, the Public Sphere and Civil Society

Bill Jordan and Nigel Parton

The central aim of this chapter is to focus on what we see as an increasingly paradoxical feature of social work in the UK. Essentially the paradox recognises that the core skills associated with social work – creative, interpersonal, interactive, and concerned with negotiating and mediating over issues of interdependence, power and obligation – have somehow come to be at a discount in practice in public-sector social work agencies, yet in demand in other agencies and organisations, even including other branches of the public services. It is as if public-sector social workers are becoming little more than organisational functionaries in 'their own' agencies, being subject to (often seemingly alien) assessment, audit and inspection, along with increasing managerial oversight; yet in other kinds of public-sector organisations, and in the voluntary sector, their capacities, principles, ethics and approaches are at a premium, and adopted or borrowed by other occupational groups (Jordan, 2000; Parton and O'Byrne, 2000).

To understand what is happening, and perhaps to act to influence it in certain directions, we need to analyse a number of different processes that have been occurring more or less simultaneously. The first is the transformation of the whole public sector in the UK. This has occurred more quickly and more thoroughly than in other European countries, and even than in some other English-speaking countries, such as Australia (Harris and McDonald, 2000). The second is the transformation in social work itself, as a professional activity, in its organisation and methods, and in its education and training programmes. Because of UK social work's primary location in the public sector since the Second World War it has been more influenced by the first process than have its counterparts in most other countries, so that the changes to the discipline and profession itself have also been more rapid and more profound than elsewhere. Finally, there are changes in 'civil society', and in the relationship between non-government organisations (NGOs), associations and community groups, and the public sector.

These changes have not taken place spontaneously, or through the action of impersonal forces beyond human control. Like others ('globalisation', for example, or 'climate change') they have been partly the result of programmes pursued by governments and transnational organisations (including commercial firms), and partly the consequences of strategies pursued by groups and individuals (Jordan, 1996, chapter 2). Individuals, in turn, are not simply 'givens' in these processes; they are moulded by institutions, and governments often seek to 'reconstruct' them, as citizens, claimants, members of communities, economic actors, or whatever. They also respond to new opportunities and constraints in their environments and in these processes reconstruct themselves.

In this chapter, we relate the paradoxical situation of social work to the changed role of the public sector in the political, social and economic life of the United Kingdom. In the post-Second-World-War welfare state, the public services were seen as crucial elements in the maintenance of a cohesive society, sustaining the balance between freedom and security, restraining wasteful competition, dampening dangerous conflicts and ensuring adequate equality. In this sense, the public sector shaped the 'public sphere' – the polity, the economy and society – by providing the institutional and moral context for citizens' interactions with each other. Here we argue that the reforms of the public services, instituted by the Conservative governments led by Margaret Thatcher and John Major, and consolidated by New Labour under Tony Blair, have fundamentally changed these relationships.

Before 1979 the most important distinction widely made in discussing the broad structure of Britain was between the 'private sphere' of the family and household, and the 'public sphere' of political and economic activity, organised and served by public-sector services. After 1979 the most relevant distinction lay between the state and society, with the latter split between a market economy, and a 'civil society' made up of non-government bodies (voluntary organisations, associations and informal groups). Margaret Thatcher and her advisers were determined to reduce the role of the public sector, and to confine the state as far as possible to a regulatory role. Hence the aim was to transfer as many as possible of the functions of the public services either to the commercial sector, through market mechanisms, or to the voluntary organisations of civil society.

Social work provides an illustration of the problems and pitfalls of these ambitious aims. In the first place, as we will show in the next section, although social work had come to be located predominantly in the public sector, it had always resided in a space between the private sphere of the household and family, and the public sphere of economy, polity and society. In this sense, social work illustrates that the lines between 'private' and 'public' are moveable, permeable to some extent, and constantly being redrawn, both in the realm of ideas and in practice (Pateman, 1989).

Second, when it came to the reform of local authority social services departments (the Children Act, 1989, and the NHS and Community Care Act, 1990), the regulatory responsibility of the public services could not be separated from two other functions – the detailed assessment of needs and risks by trained professionals, and the allocation of public funds on the basis of such assessments ('purchasing' – now crucially contrasted with and split from 'providing' services directly, a role which local authorities were progressively to shed). Hence the continuing requirement for public-sector social services practitioners to be involved in the everyday relationships of family and communal life, albeit in a mainly assessing and rationing role. Indeed, the skills required for this work have been recognised as needed by a range of other public-service staff in new or reformed state agencies under New Labour.

Third, the restructuring of the public services created new opportunities for strategic action by citizens, in search of competitive advantage (Jordan *et al.*, 1994). Changes aimed at improving cost-effectiveness and efficiency ('value for money') not only transformed the ethos of the public services themselves, by introducing quasi-market principles; they also altered the attitudes and behaviour of citizens. Social services users were encouraged to see themselves as consumers, as choice and quality were promoted, at the expense of participation and solidarity.

Fourth, the relationship between 'reformed' (Thatcher/Major) or 'modernised' (Blair) public services and civil society organisations is very complex. The term 'civil society' itself has changed its meaning over time (Ashenden, 1999), and refers to or 'contains' both agencies closely involved in maintaining the extant social order and ones concerned with transformation and resistance. In the contemporary UK and elsewhere, while some of these rely on state funding and work closely with the public services, others are fiercely autonomous and even hostile to the state.

Social work's historic role and function involve it in all these ambiguities and conflicts, which are being worked out at the present time. This chapter explores these developments, and the scope for social workers to influence them.

'The social' and the public sphere

The emergence of social work (and of social policy more generally) was associated with the political and economic transformations that took place from the mid nineteenth century onwards, in response to a number of inter-related anxieties about the family and community (Parton, 1994). It developed as a hybrid in the space, 'the social' (Donzelot, 1980; 1988), between the private sphere of the household, and the public sphere of the state and wider polity. It operated in an intermediary zone. It was produced and is reproduced in new relations between the law, social security, medicine, the school and the family. The emergence of 'the social' and the practices of social workers, who were to be among its key actors, was seen as a positive solution to a major problem for the liberal state (Hirst, 1981) – how the state could sustain the healthy development of family members who were vulnerable and dependent, while promoting the family as the 'natural' sphere for caring for those individuals, and without intervening in *all* families. Social work developed at a midway point between individual initiative and the all-encompassing state. It provided a compromise between the liberal vision of unhindered individual freedom and private philanthropy, and the socialist vision of a planned, collectivised society that would take responsibility for all citizens' needs.

Thus one of social work's enduring characteristics is its essentially contested and ambiguous nature (Martinez-Brawley and Zorita, 1998). Most crucially, this ambiguity arises from its commitments to individuals and families and their needs on the one hand, and its allegiances to and legitimation by the state, in the guise of the court, and its statutory responsibilities on the other. This ambiguity captures the central but often submerged nature of modern social work as it emerged from the late nineteenth century onwards. Social work occupied the space between the respectable and the dangerous classes, and between those with access to political and speaking rights and those excluded (Philp, 1979; Stenson, 1993). Social work fulfilled an essentially mediating role between those who were – are – actually or potentially excluded and the mainstream of society. Part of what social workers have traditionally sought to do is to strengthen the bonds of inclusive membership by trying to nurture reciprocity, sharing and small-scale redistribution between individuals, in households, groups, communities and so on. Social work has also in part been concerned with the compulsory enforcement of social obligations, rules, laws and regulations. The two dimensions are intertwined and invariably the latter provides the ultimate mandate for the former – it is in this context that social work involves both *care* and *control*. While it has always been concerned to liberate and emancipate those with whom it works, it is also concerned with working on behalf of the state and the wider society to maintain social order.

For state, or public-sector social work to operate quietly and in a relatively uncontested way, it required a supportive social mandate together with an internal professional confidence and coherence. In many respects this was the case in the UK during the period of social work's rapid development in the post-war period, up until the early 1970s and the establishment of local authority social services departments. The post-war welfare state was based on a particular model of the economy and the family. Not only did it assume full male employment, it also assumed a traditional role for the patriarchal nuclear family. The family was also assumed to be white. The notion of the 'family wage' was central, linking the labour market to the distribution of social roles and dependency by age and gender within the family.

Within the family, women were to trade housework, childbirth and child rearing, and physical and emotional caring as a 'labour of love', in return for economic support (Finch and Groves, 1983). In practice, therefore, much welfare work was expected to be undertaken within the family, either using the family wage to buy goods and services, or by women caring for children and other dependants. The system of state welfare was intended to support the patriarchal nuclear family, which was seen as central, positive and beneficent.

However, local authority social work was also able to partake of the ethic in which public services were seen as serving the 'public interest', and shaping the 'common good'. Like other staff in these services, social workers tended to define their work as a 'vocation', and to regard it as making a special contribution to the community and to a sense of solidarity among its members. Support for, as well as work in, the public services represented a kind of public morality, the residue of which is still present in the UK, as was evidenced in an extensive survey carried out by the *Guardian* in March 2001 and replicated the following year (*Guardian*, 21 March 2002). At its most ambitious, this morality might be seen as providing the cultural resources from which citizens could generate some coherence out of their shared lives, and get a sense of belonging together, and of what they owed to each other.

Thus in the post-war period, social work in the UK seemed to have marked out a clear position and to have established an increasingly unified identity in the public sector as part of the wider welfare state. Yet this apparent strength, as part of a system of collective, compulsory solidarity and of a strategy of equality, turned out to be a potential weakness. Once the consensus around redistribution and the importance of public services began to erode, this apparent security was one of the first casualties.

The compromise solution to liberalism's problems which was embodied in the welfare state, though virtually universal in the First World of developed capitalist states, was by no means uncontested and unchallenged, nor did it take the same form in all of these regimes. In most countries, the voluntary sector continued to provide the bulk of social work services, albeit with state funding and within a legislative framework laid down by the state (Badelt, 1990; Jones and May, 1992). It was only in the UK and the Scandinavian countries that the public-sector social work agencies became dominant, defining the nature of the profession, and its training agenda. Indeed, in the UK the local authority social services departments have, since the early 1970s, been the 'fifth social service' (Townsend *et al.*, 1970), operating as partners (albeit junior partners) to education, health, housing and social security, as part of the public infrastructure of British citizens' lives.

The public sector: critique and reconstruction

It is this public infrastructure that has been purposefully redesigned by UK governments since 1979, and that is still being adapted and fine-tuned by New Labour according to the same set of principles. We need to look behind the details of such changes to understand the assumptions behind the reforms, and the intended and unintended consequences that they have produced. The whole new institutional landscape is not simply designed for greater efficiency (according to market measures), it is intended to reconstruct all the actors within it – managers, bureaucrats, professionals and service users – to change their beliefs, behaviour and orientations towards each other.

The theorists who informed this whole shift were committed to a reconstruction of the public sector, which they approached along the lines of the micro-economic analysis of markets, as systems for co-ordinating decisions about the production and distribution of private goods and services. That said, these theorists recognised that, although some of the activities of the public sector could be handed over to commercial companies, and other parts entrusted to voluntary organisations, the role of the state would always go beyond regulation through law and enforcement. Hence they looked for a way in which public services might be allocated efficiently, in ways more consistent with the priority they gave to individual freedom and choice.

The theory of markets holds that production and distribution will find their optimum equilibrium spontaneously when individuals and firms are free to move around in search of the best returns on their resources (assets and skills). They behave as rational economic actors, i.e. bargain hunters looking for the best available deal, and are directed by Adam Smith's 'invisible hand' to bring about the most efficient possible allocations overall. The counterpart for the public sector is called public choice theory, and was pioneered by economists committed to holding down taxation and 'taming the Leviathan' of government spending and regulation (Oates, 1985).

In the post-war 'golden age of welfare states' (Esping-Andersen, 1996), it was taken for granted that citizens would look to their government for protection from the contingencies of the life cycle, the arbitrary outcomes of the labour market, and the bad luck of illness and disability. The bigger and stronger the state, the more it was able to require both capital and labour to submit to its redistributive plans, the more reliable was this protection, and the bigger the welfare dividend. Public choice theorists set out to challenge this whole order, aided by the fact of its destabilisation during the 1970s oil shocks, fiscal crises and economic downturns. It is impossible to understand the changes that have impacted on the contexts in which public-sector social work operates in the UK, and the nature of the tasks it is expected to address, without analysing the basis of this challenge to the understanding and role of the public sector itself.

As early as 1956, an economist called Charles Tiebout had sketched the fundamentals of the new programme. He argued that government could work best if it was based on providing 'local and particular' collective goods, and if jurisdictions were required to compete for members on the basis of the quality and cost of these goods. In a short, path-breaking paper, he postulated such authorities, each able to exclude the residents of other authorities from their collective provision, and mobile citizens, fully informed about the tax rates and quality of public goods in each of these authorities, and choosing between a potentially infinite number of them (Tiebout, 1956). Clearly what was at stake here was the whole public infrastructure (hospitals, clinics, schools, libraries, transport, policing, social care and social control facilities), and citizens' ability to 'vote with their feet' by moving to another jurisdiction. It provided the public choice equivalent of market preference and consumer sovereignty in the economy.

This model was enthusiastically taken up by a group of economists, led by the very influential James Buchanan, whose best work was done in the late 1960s and early 1970s (Buchanan, 1968; Buchanan and Goetz, 1972). As in markets, populations are assumed to have diverse incomes and tastes, and hence the most efficient solution to these issues of diversity is not to try to equalise incomes through taxation, and standardise preferences by universal and uniform public services, but to allow local authorities to provide a variety of collective goods, and let those with similar incomes and tastes move to those best suited to them. The theory, which is called 'fiscal federalism' (Oates, 1972; 1999), argues that, in principle, for every public good (such as education, hospital treatment or residential care) there is an optimum (generally rather small) size of authority, which can supply this most efficiently, and at considerably lower cost than a standardised central government service.

This approach self-consciously adapts the economics of private clubs to the provision of public (including social) services. Buchanan (1965) pointed out that swimming clubs, whose members pay for access to a pool, are able to exclude those who cannot afford their dues, or who would congest the facilities for existing members. Applying the same logic to the provision of services (Foldvary, 1994), public choice theorists cheerfully acknowledge that the advantages are likely to be lost if groups are not rather homogeneous, in terms of incomes and tastes. 'There may be a tendency for zoning on the part of high-income groups in order to exclude the poor' (Cullis and Jones, 1994, p. 300). 'The rich tend to want to be away from the poor, but the poor want to be in the same jurisdiction as the rich' (*ibid.*, p. 297). It can be argued that the application of these principles of 'fiscal federalism' to the public sector provides the main explanation of the social exclusion that New Labour claims to be combating, but which it consolidates through policies still based on this model (Jordan, 1996; 2000, chapter 2).

Obviously, the whole intention of this approach is to bear down on public expenditure of all kinds, by making all public-sector workers conscious of costs and quality, whether they are providing the service concerned themselves or buying it from contractors. The basic mechanism is to devolve responsibility to smaller and smaller units, and to make them compete, through managing their budgets. But an even more fundamental shift is to make service users aware of differences in the quality of public provision, as well as council tax levels, and to encourage them to 'vote with their feet' by publishing league tables and outcome statistics. Very soon, better-off, mobile individuals and households are able and willing to act on this information, and cluster around the best facilities, while those with low income, or with strong ties to a less-favoured neighbourhood (through loyalty or caring commitments), are left with the worst. At the same time, budget holders and managers in turn act strategically to attract high-yield, low-cost pupils, patients, trainees or residents under new funding arrangements, and exclude low-yield, high-cost ones, with multiple social problems (Jordan, 1996, chapters 5 and 6).

It is easy to see that, in so far as these approaches to governance of the public sector have been successful in keeping down tax rates (both locally and nationally), they have also had other unintended consequences. For instance, the clustering of high-income residents in desirable areas has driven up house prices, so that in some parts of the country public service staff cannot afford to live near their work-base; hence (especially in London) overseas professionals have had to be recruited, who are prepared to live in cheaper accommodation and travel further to work (Jordan, 2001). For lower-skilled tasks, welfare-to-work programmes have had to be adapted so as to pay the travel expenses of lone parents and unemployed claimants, who can then take jobs in social care in other districts which are more favoured (HM Treasury, 2000, para. 4.33). Above all, concentrations of the poorest and most vulnerable citizens, in the worst material environments, have produced extremely costly demands on all the public services, in those districts least able to afford to tackle them. This has required a whole range of expensive central government initiatives, from the Employment Zones and Action Teams, to the Social Exclusion Unit, New Deal for Communities, and Single Regeneration Budget (Jordan, 2000, chapters 7 and 8).

Clearly these transformations have radically changed the environment in which public-sector social workers operate, both by redesigning the structures of the institutions in which they are employed, and by reconstructing the basis on which service users perceive their own interests, and act in relation to them. It is not just that the whole task of purchasing and providing such services has come to be about 'best value' for taxpayers' money, with the assessment of those most at risk, or causing risk to others, paramount in deciding who should get what is available. It is also that those service users themselves are supposed to be a new breed of 'citizen-consumers', with higher expectations, but also required to be more independent, to save, and to contribute to the costs of services (Department of Health, 1998, para. 108; Department of Social Security, 1998, p. 16 and p. 33).

In this new environment, those citizen-consumers who have been able to do so – because they can afford to live in the areas where they are available – have indeed moved to obtain the most advantageous package of education, health and social care. But a residualised public social services regime has been forced to ration resources, and to focus on those least able to adopt such strategies, often through formal, legal interventions, especially child protection and youth justice measures. In many respects the approach adopted by New Labour can be seen to have taken further many of the policies introduced by the previous Conservative administrations.

Civil society

Yet the incoming New Labour Government was also aware that this agenda – pursued by its Conservative predecessors for the previous 18 years – was in itself incomplete and potentially damaging. It therefore sought at the same time to compensate for the effects on social relations and communities, and the polarisation of residential districts and public infrastructures, that this programme was having. Thus its other preoccupation – alongside the reconstruction ('modernisation') of the public sector – was encompassed in the ideas of 'community' and 'social capital'. We can understand this as an attempt to balance 'the new social', by linking up the private sphere of informal activities and family life with the public sphere of official agencies, through the resurrected notion of a 'civil society' of groups, associations, and non-government organisations. And here again, of course, the whole idea of 'the new social' is that professions like social work (or similar activities, using similar skills, perhaps under other names) should help accomplish these links, and achieve the aims of social harmony, the protection of the most vulnerable individuals, and the prevention of damaging abuse of power, strength or cunning.

The idea of community of course has a long history, but it resurfaced prominently in political theory in the 1980s. The so-called 'liberal–communitarian debate' (see Avineri and de-Shalit, 1992; Mulhall and Swift, 1996) developed around the related critiques of John Rawls's *A Theory of Justice* (1971) advanced by a number of other North American philosophers (MacIntyre, 1981; Taylor, 1979; Sandel, 1982; Walzer, 1983). As Charles Taylor reflected later (1989), the wide-ranging 'debate' involved – and often failed to distinguish between – ontological issues, about the concept of the self and sources of identity, and advocacy issues, concerning the lack of 'community' in contemporary Western societies; this in a context in which both liberal theory and liberal practice were under fire. Aspects of these largely academic analyses were popularised by Amitai Etzioni in the 1990s (Etzioni, 1993; 1997; 1999; 2000), and his writings directly influenced both Bill Clinton and Tony Blair (see Jordan, 1998). This 'popular' 'communitarianism' emphasised the importance of responsibilities, as the counterpart to liberal rights, and of self-help, to balance the expectation of collective provision; in this sense it was essentially conservative, with its stress on the family, churches, and the importance of self-discipline and social control (Driver and Martell, 1997). It also justified New Labour's new authoritarianism, and especially the compulsory measures in the various New Deals, because these rested on the idea of enforcing responsibilities, and making rights more conditional (Jordan, 1998). Although Etzioni avoided the topic of state coercion, it could be seen that this thinking lay behind the new spirit of 'tough love' that pervaded Third Way policies on crime, drugs, homelessness, immigration and the family (Jordan, 2000).

The companion concept to 'community' in New Labour's lexicon is 'social capital', strongly associated with the work of Robert Putnam (Putnam, 1993; 2000). This idea now enjoys the support of the World Bank, in its World Development Programme (World Bank, 2000), and in the UK has pervaded many Government policy units, and even the Central Statistical Office (Harper, 2001), as attempts are made to quantify its distribution among individuals and communities. Essentially, the idea of social capital is that if we want to explain differences in the distribution of social harmony, economic prosperity, and good governance between and amongst collectivities, we need to take account of variables that deal in collective action (from families to global coalitions). Physical capital (the stock of material resources that are used for production) and human capital (the stock of skills and aptitudes acquired by individuals) will not alone account for these differences; we need also to take into consideration the stock of *shared* understandings, norms, rules and the expectations of individuals. Not only must physical capital be linked to human capital to be productive; human capital must be linked up through social capital, in order to achieve efficiency and effectiveness. Norms of trust, reciprocity and co-operation are seen as the most important aspects of social capital, with voluntary associations being their clearest expression (Ostrom, 2001). Institutions are in effect rules for co-operation (North, 1990), and allow organisations to mobilise individuals for collective action. Public policies as such can either promote or destroy social capital; top-down interventions often actually destroy it, for example when they seek to solve collective action problems by regulation or control (Ostrom, 1991).

One of the central questions addressed by theorists of social capital is how the stock of shared norms and cultural practices contributes either to various forms of harmony, solidarity and co-operation, or to conflict, mistrust and violence. After all, while self-help, kinship support networks, volunteering and charitable giving are all examples of collective action, so are drug dealing, mafia rackets, the trafficking of migrants and global terrorism. Social capital theory attempts to explain these differences in terms of 'bonding' and 'bridging' capital. Bonding capital is created and used when people act with others like themselves, according to shared characteristics, often to mobilise in competition with others unlike themselves. Bridging capital is created and used when individuals create solidarities with others unlike themselves, and act to solve problems that might otherwise divide them (Putnam, 2000).

Yet this distinction does not, on its own, explain very much – for example, why some societies, such as Sweden, have levels of trust among fellow citizens which are almost ten times higher than those of others, such as Brazil or Turkey (Rothstein and Stolle, 2001). Putnam's intuition, on the basis of his studies of Italian regions (Putnam, 1993), was that this was to do with the number and structure of associations, including such diverse organisations as sports clubs and churches. However, this has not proved very robust under research investigation.

Ironically, although Putnam (following James Coleman) chose the term 'social capital' to encourage economists to join the debate (Putnam, 2001), neither he nor his followers have attempted to link their ideas with public choice theory to any significant extent. Yet public choice theorists purport to explain the distribution of bonding and bridging capital very elegantly. Where governments redistribute large sums of money to equalise incomes, and promote common interests between diverse groups, this creates an environment highly favourable to bridging capital (large-scale solidarity). This is precisely the situation in the Scandinavian countries, especially Sweden. Where societies are very diverse and unequal, and split into competing regional, ethnic and religious factions, and where government spends little on welfare and much on control and enforcement, trust is inevitably much lower. This explains low levels of trust in Brazil and Turkey. Just to strengthen the point, researchers associated with Putnam found that recipients of universal social benefits in Sweden had almost the same very high levels of trust as those citizens receiving no benefits; but Swedes who received targeted, means-tested social assistance had levels of trust only about half as high, and those on the receiving end of compulsory workfare measures had levels close to those of Brazil and Turkey (Rothstein and Stolle, 2001).

Of course, the idea of social capital is very relevant to many aspects of 'the social'. For instance, bonding capital in poor districts, especially in female networks, can be crucial to the outcome of child protection issues (Jack, 1997; 2000). Social workers have always been concerned with strengthening networks, and repairing tears in the fabric of such relationships. But increasingly social work *per se* is not involved in action which bridges between bonding groups. This is because public-sector social work, engaged in the organisational nexus discussed in the last section, deals with service users as 'customers', assessing their individual needs and risks, and their capacities to pay for what they will receive, or protecting the most vulnerable from those who threaten their safety. What becomes evident, however, is that NGOs, voluntary-sector associations, and community groups have proliferated and filled the vacuum left by withdrawal of the public services into this arm's length proceduralism, with its formal, technical rationality.

These organisations and groups have taken an amazing variety of forms, stimulated by government funding (albeit often exploitative, arbitrary and short-term), and by the creative energies of communities themselves. On the one hand, there has been a renaissance of the old voluntary sector, together with a further flourishing of some newer organisations (especially in the field of disability) created in the 1960s and 1970s. On the other hand, many new, grassroots agencies and community groups, and a whole range of projects, units and teams, survivor and support groups, and local associations have also developed. Overall, these organisations and groups have given rise to many innovatory and creative practices, but they have also been constrained by certain structural factors. They have drawn on and attempted to build up bonding social capital among the excluded groups and communities where there is common ground among their users and members, but – except in the form of charitable giving and volunteering – they can do little to overcome the barriers to bridging between the communities and classes that have been institutionalised in the new order. As income inequalities have widened, trust and links between the 'haves' and 'have nots' have declined.

Growing fragmentation and residualisation

Policy on markets and decentralisation has fed into increased doubts about the rationality and viability of planning to meet large-scale needs, and of providing help through the large-scale organisations which characterised the welfare state. The current condition is increasingly marked by doubts about both the intelligibility and the shapeability of the social world, since greater awareness of the plurality and diversity of social practices makes it difficult to hold on to any set of ideas as self-evident and/or universal, and to imagine the collective actor who can intervene in their name. Risk, uncertainty and reflexivity are increasingly seen as characterising contemporary times, such that more and more social conflicts are perceived as having no easy and unambiguous solution. They are, rather, distinguished by fundamental ambivalences, which might be grasped, but certainly not removed, by calculations of probability. It seems we are now living in a world of multiple authorities and diverse, even divergent, bodies of knowledge (Wagner, 1994). In many respects the history of state or public-sector social work over the last quarter-century can be seen as a fascinating case study of these major and more wide-ranging social changes. It is as if the modern, certain, positivistic, forms of knowledge and practice which seemed so embedded some 25 years or so ago, have now become subjected to deepening critique.

Some of the consequences of this break-up of the old certainties have been paradoxical and unexpected. Just as 'market choice' sometimes produces a range of almost identical products, distinguishable only by brand names and logos (as in multiple commercial TV channels, or refrigerated soft-drinks cabinets in shops), so the devolution of budgets and fragmentation of organisations has led to a remarkable standardisation of practice [eds: see James, this volume, on the 'McDonaldization' of social work]. Across the UK and in other countries experiencing similar large-scale changes, public-sector social work has reverted to Poor-Law-style rationing, assessment, and protective intervention, in an approach increasingly reminiscent of that prevalent before the welfare state. The predominant response to the changes and challenges experienced since the early 1970s has been to construct ever-more-sophisticated systems of accountability, and in particular to attempt to rationalise and scientise increasing areas of social work activity with the introduction of ever-more-complex procedures and systems of audit – whereby it is assumed that the world can be subjected to prediction and calculation. With resources so limited, and the clientele's plight so desperate, the consequence has been the residualisation of public provision.

As argued above, the New Labour reforms of recent years have increased rather than reversed the trends originally introduced under Conservative administrations. The White Paper *Modernising Social Services* (Department of Health, 1998) is primarily concerned with regulating local authority departments through a series of supervisory and monitoring bodies, with setting new standards and targets by which to measure performance, and creating agencies to enforce these, and with establishing a new system for training social care workers under the guidance of a new regulatory body. The steady growth of audit and managerialism noted in the previous paragraph has proceeded inexorably, for example and in particular in the guise of the *Quality Protects* programme.

All these developments have been facilitated by a movement within research and training for social work that favours 'evidence-based' approaches to social care. Its proponents claim that a more rigorous application of critical appraisal skills to existing research findings can yield clear guidelines about appropriate interventions for definable categories of cases. Correlatively, it is argued that practitioners should be guided by detailed and instrumental instructions on how to assess and deal with service users in line with these scientifically validated methodologies. Clearly such reviews and the research on which they build have important contributions to make, but it is our view that 'evidence-based' approaches should take on a support role, rather than be promoted to the front line in the development of practice knowledge, as seems to be the case currently.

We believe that the reasons for the current hegemony of the idea of 'evidence-based practice' in regard to social work education have more to do with the political agendas of New Labour than with the needs of practitioners. While pursuing a rhetoric of improving standards, the Government is in danger of effectively deskilling the public-sector branch of the profession. Meanwhile, as we have seen, quite different practices have flourished in a huge number of projects, teams and units, and in community and survivor groups and neighbourhood associations. But these have often not recognised themselves as doing social work, or wanted professional training, or identified with the profession. They have often been underfunded and isolated, and in consequence have lacked a wider vision or links with other similar endeavours (Jordan, 2000).

All this raises important issues about the role of public services generally, as well as about the future of social work practice. On the one hand, what is now widely recognised as a 'crisis of the public services' appears to involve something deeper than the funding and accountability problems that have preoccupied New Labour. Although Tony Blair and his Ministers are highly ambivalent about this topic, they seem, reluctantly, to accept that the ethos of service to the whole community is an important asset, which needs to be conserved and enhanced. Beyond this, what is not yet acknowledged is that something like this ethos can help citizens to make sense of their common experiences, and to participate in improving their shared lives together. The 'public sphere' may have greater need of a culture of solidarity and belonging in a pluralistic polity and a globalised market-driven economy than it did in the notionally planned and rational era of the post-war welfare state.

Furthermore, it is becoming clear that public policy must be about more than regulating standards and allocating revenues. Citizens need to feel recognised and valued, in all their diversity, as well as efficiently served. In principle, social work – the giving of personal attention to people's subjective interpretations of their identities and needs – should be well suited to these tasks. But its present organisation in the UK does not make the most of this potential. Public-sector social work communicates stigma, blame and meanness as much as it gives recognition and value. Voluntary organisations and community groups provide identity and purpose for their memberships, but on the basis of very narrow mutualities, and often among very disadvantaged groups. Hence social work could contribute something more to the revival of the public sector, and to the revitalisation of a more public-spirited public sphere, if it was allowed to do so.

Alternative futures: constructive social work

The problems identified in the previous section, though strongly influenced by economic and political trends, are not inevitable. To develop an alternative approach, notions of ambiguity, indeterminacy and uncertainty need to be consciously conceived as at the core of social work, and thus should be built upon and not defined out (Jordan, 2000; Parton, 2000; 2003; Parton and O'Byrne, 2000). In the process this would open up the potential for a greater creativity and novel ways of thinking and acting. It is important to recognise that social work is better seen and understood as primarily a *practical–moral* activity, rather than as a *technical–rational* one. We would argue that in the current climate, approaches which are affirmative and reflexive, and focus on the importance of dialogue, are key to developing practice. The importance of power, process and plurality, of both knowledge and voice, are central, for they recognise that users have strengths and resources within and around them and that it is the way these are narrated which is key to revealing new and positive possibilities for change.

However, the transformation of 'the social' that has occurred in the last 20 years means that the social work profession cannot expect to have the same milieu and organisational systems in which to operate. The institutional landscape of the public sector is now designed for rational economic actors, exclusive 'clubs' of members/users, and citizen-consumers, seeking advantages over each other. Of course real people do not respond exactly according to institutional (re)designs, but they have certainly been influenced by them. This applies to public-sector social workers also. The overall style of practice has certainly shifted in the direction of formal, arm's-length, office-bound methods, suited for tasks of risk assessment and risk management.   But many of the practices and traditions that have been squeezed out of mainstream public-sector work have survived and flourished in civil society organisations, albeit fragmented between many kinds of agencies and groups. The social work profession has lost its unified structure and identity, but its aspirations and values have survived, and examples of social work in continental Europe and Australasia show that these more fragmented structures can provide a basis for development and growing strength, as well as new theoretical insights (Fook, 1996).

Progress in these directions in the UK requires more strategic awareness of the overall terrain of 'the social', and of the direction of New Labour policy.   The reason why public-sector social work in Britain has been boxed into its narrow role is that the Government does not trust the old public-sector professions (medicine and teaching, any more than social work), and prefers to create new agencies with specific, instrumental training for tasks, like New Deal Personal Advisers and National Asylum Support Service staff (Jordan, 2000). However, the Government has little idea how to reconstruct 'the social' in such a way as to link the old public services, these new agencies, and the burgeoning neighbourhood support and survivor groups of civil society into a coherent whole, and thereby to connect up excluded, marginalised people to the mainstream.   Policy consists mainly of Ministerial rhetoric and moral exhortations, combined with tough enforcement measures.   Although the Government is clearly serious about trying to change cultures and attitudes, it seems to have very little idea about how to develop a policy programme to implement this, apart from its increased reliance on the managerialist dimensions of welfare provision, not least as directed both at and through the professionals and workers in the agencies themselves.   As all the signals following the 2001 General Election suggested, this has proved to be the focus of even more intensive efforts during the second New Labour administration.

Social work as an occupation and as a profession in the UK has up to now been strongly identified with the public sector and has therefore become the object of the increasing regulation, standard-setting and enforcement we have described.   However, this is a particularly narrow view of social work. Our argument is that it is important to develop a much broader conception, one that embraces notions of community development (including economic and social regeneration projects) and encompasses all the various projects and units that have sprung up in recent years, employing a variety of street-level, outreach support workers of various kinds.   Many of these have been put together as part of various partnerships in order to take advantage of new Government initiatives; Sure Start programmes, Health Action Zones, and a variety of other initiatives, exemplify this. Much of the direct, face-to-face work that is required, both to implement Government policy and to create the spaces in which needs, norms and rules are negotiated between the state and civil society, is increasingly being carried out by voluntary organisations and community groups through these various new projects.   It is these sorts of developments that seem to fill the spaces which were previously associated with the idea and the actuality of 'the social', but which have become much more complex and fragmented, and even more ambiguous.   Yet this is just the terrain where social work previously operated; that is, social workers were the primary practitioners of 'the social'. It is important that this relationship is not lost.

We would argue that the current crisis in the public services signals a deeper malaise in our society; social work is showing the symptoms of that malaise, as much as demonstrating frailties of its own. While it would be inappropriate, *per impossibile*, to try to restore the fabric of the post-war welfare state, some substitute will eventually have to be found for the bonds of membership and mutuality that linked citizens of that time. To succeed, new institutions will be required to run on communication of value, not coercive regulation, and it is here that social work (in its broadest sense) is likely to find new opportunities and openings. Fortunately, the knowledge and practice methods that are needed for such work have continued to be developed, often in unlikely corners of society, and are still available to be deployed for future, wider purposes.

In conclusion, therefore, what we are arguing is that it is important that we have a broad conception of social work, which makes serious attempts to reflect the way it was originally conceived in the late nineteenth century and the social spaces to which it gave expression, yet developed in ways that take account of the important changes of more recent years. While a number of recent developments can be seen to compromise social work and to marginalise it from many other activities, it is important that we are not just concerned with changes which have a direct impact only on social work seen as a public-sector activity. Many of these new developments require a range of research, theorisation and skills in order to make them practicable and to articulate their central features and implications. A narrowly defined and instrumental view of social work is very unhelpful in this regard. Social work research and theory can play a critical role in a dynamic relationship with practice, rather than simply supply technocratic 'evidence' to guide narrowly instrumental interventions, based on 'what works'. These are difficult times but they are very interesting times, throwing up major issues from which we should not be deflected by the organisational and regulatory demands which will be made on us over the next few years.

References

Ashenden, S. (1999), 'Questions of criticism: Habermas and Foucault on civil society and resistance', in Ashenden, S. and Owen, D. (eds), *Foucault Contra Habermas: Recasting the Dialogue Between Genealogy and Critical Theory*, Sage, London, pp. 143–65.

Avineri, S. and de-Shalit, A. (eds) (1992), *Communitarianism and Individualism*, Oxford University Press, Oxford.

Badelt, C. (1990), 'Institutional choice and the nonprofit sector', in Anheier, H.K. and Seibel, W. (eds), *The Third Sector: Comparative Studies of Nonprofit Organizations*, de Gruyter, Berlin, pp. 53–63.

Buchanan, J.M. (1965), 'An economic theory of clubs', *Economica*, **32**(1), pp. 1–14.

Buchanan, J.M. (1968), *The Demand and Supply of Public Goods*, Rand McNally, New York.

Buchanan, J.M. and Goetz, C.J. (1972), 'Efficiency limits of fiscal mobility: an assessment of the Tiebout model', *Journal of Public Economics*, **1**(1), pp. 25–58.

Cullis, J. and Jones, P. (1994), *Public Finance and Public Choice: Analytical Perspectives*, McGraw Hill, London.

Department of Health (1998), *Modernising Social Services: Promoting Independence, Improving Protection, Raising Standards*, Cm 4169, Stationery Office, London.

Department of Social Security (1998), *A New Contract for Welfare*, Cm 3805, Stationery Office, London.

Donzelot, J. (1980), *The Policing of Families: Welfare Versus the State*, Hutchinson, London.

Donzelot, J. (1988), 'The promotion of the social', *Economy and Society*, **17**(3), pp. 395–427.

Driver, S. and Martell, L. (1997), 'New Labour's communitarianisms', *Critical Social Policy*, **17**(3) (issue 52), pp. 27–46.

Esping-Andersen, G. (1996), *Welfare States in Transition: National Adaptations in Global Economies*, Sage, London.

Etzioni, A. (1993), *The Spirit of Community: The Reinvention of American Society*, Touchstone, New York.

Etzioni, A. (1997), *The New Golden Rule: Community and Morality in a Democratic Society*, Profile Books, London.

Etzioni, A. (1999), *The Limits of Privacy*, Basic Books, New York.

Etzioni, A. (2000), *The Third Way to a Good Society*, Demos, London.

Finch, J. and Groves, D. (eds) (1983), *A Labour of Love: Women, Work and Caring*, Routledge and Kegan Paul, London.

Foldvary, F. (1994), *Public Goods and Private Communities: The Market Provision of Social Services*, Edward Elgar, Aldershot.

Fook, J. (ed.) (1996), *The Reflective Researcher: Social Workers' Theories of Practice Research*, Allen and Unwin, Melbourne.

Harper, R. (2001), 'Statistics on social capital', paper presented at a conference on *Social Capital: Interdisciplinary Perspectives*, University of Exeter, 15–20 September.

Harris, J. and McDonald, C. (2000), 'Post-Fordism and the welfare state: a comparison of Australia and Britain', *British Journal of Social Work*, **30**(1), pp. 51–70.

HM Treasury (2000), *Pre-Budget Report*, Stationery Office, London.

Hirst, P. (1981), 'The genesis of the social', *Politics and Power*, **3**, pp. 67–82.

Jack, G. (1997), 'An ecological approach to social work with children and families', *Child and Family Social Work*, **2**(1), pp. 109–20.

Jack, G. (2000), 'Ecological influences on parenting and child development', *British Journal of Social Work*, **30**(6), pp. 703–20.

Jones, A., and May, J. (1992), *Working in Human Service Organisations: A Critical Introduction*, Longman Cheshire, Melbourne.

Jordan, B. (1996), *A Theory of Poverty and Social Exclusion*, Polity, Cambridge.

Jordan, B. (1998), *The New Politics of Welfare: Social Justice in a Global Context*, Sage, London.

Jordan, B. (2001), 'Tough love: social work, social exclusion and the third way', *British Journal of Social Work*, **31**(4), pp. 527–46.

Jordan, B., with Jordan, C. (2000), *Social Work and the Third Way: Tough Love as Social Policy*, Sage, London.

Jordan, B., Redley, M. and James, S. (1994), *Putting the Family First: Identities, Decisions, Citizenship*, UCL Press, London.

MacIntyre, A. (1981), *After Virtue: A Study in Moral Theory*, Duckworth, London.

Martinez-Brawley, E. and Zorita, P. (1998), 'At the edge of the frame: beyond science and art in social work', *British Journal of Social Work*, **28**(2), pp. 197–212.

Mulhall, S. and Swift, A. (1996), *Liberals and Communitarians* (2nd edn), Blackwell, Oxford.

North, D.C. (1990), *Institutions, Institutional Change and Economic Performance*, Cambridge University Press, Cambridge.

Oates, W.E. (1972), *Fiscal Federalism*, Harcourt Brace Jovanovich, New York.

Oates, W.E. (1985), 'Searching for Leviathan: an empirical study', *American Economic Review*, **75**(4), pp. 748–57.

Oates, W.E. (1999), 'An essay on fiscal federalism', *Journal of Economic Literature*, **37**(3), pp. 1120–49.

Ostrom, E. (1991), *Governing the Commons: The Evolution of Institutions for Collective Action*, Cambridge University Press, Cambridge.

Ostrom, E. (2001), 'Social capital and collective action', paper presented at a conference on *Social Capital: Interdisciplinary Perspectives*, University of Exeter, 15–20 September.

Parton, N. (1994), '"Problematics of government", (post)modernity and social work', *British Journal of Social Work*, **24**(1), pp. 9–32.

Parton, N. (2000), 'Some thoughts on the relationship between theory and practice in and for social work', *British Journal of Social Work*, **30**(4), pp. 449–63. (An earlier version, presented in the *Theorising Social Work Research* seminar series, no. 1, 26 May 1999, Brunel University, is now available at
<http://www.elsc.org.uk/socialcareresource/tswr/seminar1/parton.htm>.)

Parton, N. (2003), 'Rethinking *professional* practice: the contributions of social constructionism and the feminist "ethics of care"', *British Journal of Social Work*, **33**(1) pp. 1–16.

Parton, N. and O'Byrne, P. (2000), *Constructive Social Work: Towards a New Practice*, Macmillan, Basingstoke.

Pateman, C. (1989), *The Disorder of Women: Democracy, Feminism and Political Theory*, Polity, Cambridge.

Philp, M. (1979), 'Notes on the form of knowledge in social work', *Sociological Review*, **27**(1), pp. 83–111.

Putnam, R.D. (1993), *Making Democracy Work: Civic Traditions in Modern Italy*, Princeton University Press, Princeton, NJ.

Putnam, R.D. (2000), *Bowling Alone: The Collapse and Revival of American Community*, Simon and Schuster, New York.

Putnam, R.D. (2001), 'Social capital: issues for research', paper presented at a conference on *Social Capital: Interdisciplinary Perspectives*, University of Exeter, 15–20 September.

Rothstein, B. and Stolle, D. (2001), 'Social capital and street-level bureaucracy: an institutional theory of generalized trust', paper presented at a conference on *Social Capital: Interdisciplinary Perspectives*, University of Exeter, 15–20 September.

Sandel, M. (1982), *Liberalism and the Limits of Justice*, Cambridge University Press, Cambridge.

Stenson, K. (1993), 'Social work discourse and the social work interview', *Economy and Society*, **22**(1), pp. 42–76.

Taylor, C. (1979), 'Atomism', in Kontos, A. (ed.), *Powers, Possessions and Freedom*, University of Toronto Press, Toronto, pp. 39–61.

Taylor, C. (1989), 'Cross-purposes: the liberal–communitarian debate', in Rosenblum, N. (ed.), *Liberalism and the Moral Life*, Harvard University Press, Cambridge, MA, pp. 159–82.

Tiebout, C. (1956), 'A pure theory of local expenditures', *Journal of Political Economy*, **64**(4), pp. 416–24.

Townsend, P., Sinfield, A., Kahan, B., Mittler, P., Rose, H., Meacher, M., Agate, J., Lynes, T. and Bull, D. (1970), *The Fifth Social Service: A Critical Analysis of the Seebohm Proposals*, Fabian Society, London.

Wagner, P. (1994), *A Sociology of Modernity: Liberty and Discipline*, Routledge, London.

Walzer, M. (1983), *Spheres of Justice: A Defence of Pluralism and Equality*, Martin Robertson, Oxford.

World Bank (2000), *World Development Report*, World Bank, Washington DC.

Chapter 2

The McDonaldization of Social Work – or 'Come Back Florence Hollis, All Is (or Should Be) Forgiven'

Adrian L. James

Somewhat unusually, the title of this chapter was the first thing to be written. Some readers may find it obscure or even pretentious. However, the juxtaposition of McDonald's and Florence Hollis somehow seemed to provide an evocative motif for the particular issues about which I wanted to write when I was asked to contribute to a book that was intended to explore the nature of social work as an academic discipline and its contribution to the profession of social work. In particular, what the image encapsulated was the notion that we have lost our way – that we are in danger of losing our critical edge in terms of understanding the meaning of quality in social work and have substituted fast food for *haute cuisine*, or at least for individually prepared and served meals.[1, 2]

---

[1] An alternative title for this chapter, given its nature and starting point, might have been that of Paul Simon's song 'A Simple Desultory Philippic', released by CBS on the 1965 album *The Paul Simon Songbook*; to this might have been added a personalised version of the sub-title – 'or "How I Was (Nearly) 'CCETSW'd' Into Submission"'. However, this allusion would probably have been lost on all but keen Paul Simon fans of a certain generation!

[2] Having decided upon the title, an alarm bell sounded, associated with a vague recollection that somebody, somewhere, had already written something along these lines. Being wary of the possibility of inadvertent plagiarism, I searched to try to bring this vague memory closer to the surface and, after considerable excavations, I found it – an article in the *Probation Journal* (Oldfield, 1994) about the increasing use of market-based concepts and approaches by probation service managers. And so, lest my subconscious has played tricks with my thought processes, let me acknowledge any possible debt to Mark Oldfield. I should also like to acknowledge, with many thanks, my debt to my friends and colleagues Allison James and Kate Wilson for their helpful comments on an earlier draft of this chapter. Responsibility for the final product is, however, mine alone.

The McDonaldization thesis

It is some years now – 1983 in fact – since George Ritzer first published his ideas about and analysis of the 'McDonaldization' of society. The fact that these have not only survived but have flourished into the new millennium gives some indication of the value of his insight, the durability of the main elements of his thesis, and the importance of the issues it raises. In brief, in Ritzer's terms, McDonaldization is 'the process by which the principles of the fast-food restaurant are coming to dominate more and more sectors of American society as well as the rest of the world' (Ritzer, 2000, p. 1). A very similar approach has been formulated recently by Bryman (1999), in the context of the spread of Disney theme parks, but for the purpose of this chapter I propose to stay with the more familiar and perhaps more self-evident process analysed by Ritzer.

The process of McDonaldization is based on applying the principles of efficiency, calculability, predictability and control to the processing and serving of a limited range of products. For Ritzer, efficiency means choosing the optimum means to a given end. Thus, 'McDonaldized systems function efficiently by following the steps in a pre-designed process ... Organizational rules and regulations also help to ensure highly efficient work' (2000, p. 12). By breaking down the process into a series of discrete and clearly specified tasks, a standardised, regulated, and therefore efficient process of production is designed. This ensures calculability, so that McDonald's can identify precisely the resources needed to produce their products, with the consequence that 'In McDonaldized systems, quantity has become equivalent to quality ... Workers in McDonaldized systems also tend to emphasize the quantitative rather than the qualitative aspects of their work' (*ibid.*, pp. 12–13). Calculating, counting and quantifying are therefore key features of McDonaldization. The importance of predictability for the consumer lies in 'the assurance that products and services will be the same over time and in all locales ... The workers in McDonaldized systems ... follow corporate rules as well as the dictates of their managers' (*ibid.*, p. 13).

In order to secure the operation of the above principles, control is an important part of McDonaldization, particularly control through the replacement of human with non-human technology. Importantly, however, 'technologies include not only the obvious, such as robots and computers, but also the less obvious, such as the assembly line, bureaucratic rules, and manuals prescribing accepted procedures and techniques' (*ibid.*, p. 104). In a McDonaldized system, workers are also 'trained to do a limited number of things in precisely the way they are told to do them' (*ibid.*, p. 14), and it is the use of such technologies 'that increases control over workers [and] helps McDonaldized systems assure customers that their products and service will be consistent' (*ibid.*, p. 15).

It is also important to note, however, that control 'is exerted over the people who enter the world of McDonald's' (*ibid.*, p. 14), from the management of the movement of customers though the restaurant or past the drive-through window, to the process of clearing up after they have eaten. Customers cease to be individuals under such a system, in spite of attempts to conceal this fact. As Finkelstein observes:

The training of restaurant personnel, as set out in the 600 page McDonald's staffing manual, includes suggestions for specific conversational exchanges. Greeting the customer is important: 'be pleasant, not mechanical' which means employ a convincing smile. Other suggested comments include 'Hi, I'm here to serve you,' 'Come and visit us again,' 'Have a nice day' ... These formulaic exchanges prevent any recognition of the other as unique. Each diner is treated indiscriminately ... the uniformity of the moral order of the fast-food restaurant is crucial to its commercial success. (Finkelstein, 1989, p. 11)

The above offers a very brief descriptive summary of the main elements of McDonaldization that between them produce what many might regard as a highly rational approach to delivering a particular kind of service. There are of course many advantages to this rationality, especially from the point of view of the producer of the service or product. It also has a number of disadvantages, however, not least to the extent that 'rational systems serve to deny human reason [and they] are often unreasonable' (Ritzer, 2000, p. 16), whilst 'assembly lines have been shown to be inhuman settings in which to work' (*ibid.*, p. 17). Importantly, the starting point for a McDonaldized service is the end product – it is driven by the need to produce, as quickly, as efficiently, and as cheaply as possible, a product of uniform size, quality and acceptability, rather than by the need to produce the *best* product or, more significantly, to produce something that caters for a range of individual customers, in different settings and with different needs.

The purpose of this brief consideration of McDonaldization is not, however, to make a detailed analysis of the latter's strengths and weaknesses as a means of production, nor to make a judgement about its social or other possible merits. Neither is there any claim from Ritzer or elsewhere that, in spite of the undoubted impact of McDonaldization throughout the world, the process has affected every organisation in the same way or to the same extent. Indeed, Ritzer argues that 'There are degrees of McDonaldization. Fast-food restaurants have been heavily McDonaldized, universities moderately McDonaldized, and mom-and-pop grocers only slightly McDonaldized' (2000, p. 19). Rather, my purpose is solely to identify the main features of the process in order to allow us to consider the extent to which changes in social work over the last three decades provide evidence of McDonaldization in that area too. Such changes include: increasing emphasis on the exercise of managerial control over professional discretion; the concern with efficiency and effectiveness; the emphasis on standardisation that is evident in the development of national standards (for example National Standards for Adoption, monitored by the National Care Standards Commission), codes of practice, and frameworks for assessment; the deconstruction of a wide range of professional tasks into bite-sized competencies, alongside the development of occupational standards; and the new hegemony of evidence-based practice. It is arguable that each and all of these might be said to reflect the process identified and described by Ritzer.

The McDonaldization of social work

When Florence Hollis wrote her book on psychosocial casework (Hollis, 1964), which influenced the practice of so many social workers in the 1960s and 1970s, the ethos of social work was rooted firmly in a highly individualised model of practice, in the sense that its primary perspective was that of the individual professional social worker, working and interacting with the individual client in his or her own particular family and social context. Entirely consistent with such an approach, there was little reference to the significance of the organisational or legal frameworks within which social workers practised; what was seen as important was the provision of a theoretical framework within which to understand and interpret the client's problems and underpinned by a set of values with which to guide practice.

Hollis's book was not the only text of its kind to explore 'the casework relationship' that lay at the heart of social work practice at that time (see also, for example, Biestek, 1957); neither was it the only theoretical perspective to have a widespread currency across the profession (see Roberts and Nee, 1970). However, I highlight it here because it *is* representative of the dominant social work ethos in post-war Britain, both in terms of the values it embodied and espoused and the theoretical perspectives that informed the work of many practising social workers of the period, not least because of the links it made, both implicitly and explicitly, between the individual and his or her social environment. As Simon argued at the time:

> In a society of paradoxes of poverty and affluence, of over-population and brilliant technology, of deeply disturbing contradictions that arise from accelerated complexity that produces dehumanization, social casework makes its contribution by its commitment to the individual in society. The commitment to understand, to differentiate, to act for and with the individual gives social casework crucial importance in alleviating the human suffering related to society's problems. (Simon, 1970, p. 355)

This is not the place to undertake a detailed review of the many changes that have taken place in social work since those words were written. There are, however, certain key dimensions that are worth identifying. One of the most fundamental of these, which acted as a catalyst for much that was to follow, was the modernisation of social work as a result of the Seebohm Report (Seebohm Committee, 1968). This brought together the main, previously separate, departments offering social work services to different client groups that had emerged in post-war Britain, into single, supposedly generic, social services departments that would rationalise access to and the delivery of social work services. It also heralded the arrival of a substantially unified and higher-profile profession of social work – albeit that that status (i.e. 'profession') has remained uncertain and contested – and, it was promised, would offer a more efficient way of organising and delivering services that would provide greater control over and more rational use of resources.

This single development therefore opened the door to some of the key elements of McDonaldization, since it led inexorably to the greater bureaucratisation of social work as an expression of the process of rationalisation. Paradoxically, however, this same process began progressively to undermine the new-found professional[3] status of social work. It also created fertile ground for the adoption and subsequent growth of the kind of public-sector managerialism that was so much a hallmark of the economic and political ideology of conservatism under Margaret Thatcher. This was typified by the search for the most 'rational' means of ensuring efficiency, economy, effectiveness and value for money, by securing greater degrees of predictability, calculability and control in the delivery of public-sector services.

Not unrelated to such developments was a growing emphasis during the 1970s and 1980s on short-term, task-centred, contract-based and behavioural methods of social work intervention. Buttressed by a growing understanding of the perspectives and feelings of service users and the wish to take account of these, such developments were not only intrinsic to the emergent social work profession, they also challenged the validity of the theoretical and practice foundations of the psychosocial approach advocated by Hollis. This was not only on the basis that there was little empirical evidence to demonstrate the latter's efficacy, so that those who used it seemed to do so more as a matter of faith, but also because it tended to involve long-term work at a time when increasing emphasis was being placed on the development of more economical short-term approaches. These, evidence suggested, were just as effective – if not more so. Moreover, apart from being more economical in terms of the use of resources, because they were time-limited rather than open-ended, such methods had the added advantage of requiring a much clearer specification of intended outcomes and timescales. This, in turn, made their empirical validation easier and encouraged the development of a more standardised (i.e. McDonaldized) approach to practice.

Another key development that occurred at the same time was the creation of the Central Council for Education and Training in Social Work (CCETSW). As Lyons observes,

> [T]he government strengthened the regulation of social work education through the establishment of the Central Council for Education and Training in Social Work (CCETSW) ... [which was] charged with promoting the growth, rationalisation and standardisation of social work education ... The legislation was amended in 1971 to give the new council extended powers, and again in 1983 when the size of the council was significantly reduced and became less representative of the profession and more subject to government influence, a trend continued into the 1990s. (Lyons, 1999, p. 10)

In describing the history of CCETSW and its impact upon social work, Lyons (*ibid.*, pp. 10–23) notes that the Council was heavily influenced from the outset by

---

[3]   It would be tedious to put 'scare quotes' around 'profession' in what follows, but the uncertain and contested status of social work in this respect must be kept in mind throughout; this will be mentioned explicitly again later, albeit briefly. [Eds: see also Lorenz, this volume; Lyons and Taylor, this volume.]

the needs of social workers' employers, the new local authority social services departments. The increasing regulation of social work was given added impetus, however, by the growing awareness of and concerns about child protection in the 1980s, in the course of which the training of social workers became the focus of considerable criticism (see, for example, Brandon and Davies, 1979). As part of this, there was particular concern about their lack of knowledge of the law, which gave rise to a close scrutiny of law teaching on social work qualifying courses. This led to the publication of the CCETSW Law Report (Ball *et al.*, 1988), which emphasised such concerns and focused on the need to ensure the legal knowledge and competence of social workers. As a consequence, Lyons argues, these developments 'led to an increasing emphasis on law teaching on courses … [which was] a significant theme in the recasting of qualifying training for the 1990s' (1999, pp. 13–14). This, in turn, added considerable weight to an increasing preoccupation with the technical skills and knowledge of social workers and the development and articulation of competencies, aimed at ensuring the acquisition of uniform minimum levels of knowledge and skill in practice, which increasingly shaped social work education and training.

This is not to say that CCETSW was not concerned with social work values – it was. However, discussion came to revolve primarily around issues of anti-discriminatory practice and was largely divorced from issues of methods, resources, and the changing policy context of social work. It therefore became increasingly difficult to reconcile the traditional values of social work – e.g. those identified by Hollis and Biestek – with the demands and expectations that were beginning to emerge from social services departments and the Government, not only about the nature of social work services and the mode of their delivery, but also about making effective use of increasingly scarce resources. Thus, the developing impact of managerialist responses to such issues and the 'hierarchical and bureaucratic structures which some saw as being at variance with professional values' (Lyons, 1999, p. 26) contributed to the McDonaldization of social work and therefore to the decline of those values that were based on dealing with social work clients as individuals.

Similarly, in February 1993, a report on a review of CCETSW by the Department of Health's Social Services Inspectorate emphasised, *inter alia*, the need for ensuring value for money from social work education, and for quality assurance and control in relation both to CCETSW and to social work training courses. It also argued, however, that it was 'important that CCETSW programmes and priorities are congruent with those of Government' (Department of Health (Social Services Inspectorate), 1993, p. 57). The report concluded that 'CCETSW must ensure that its programmes of work are systematically and thoroughly informed by the perspectives of the range of interests which comprise customers of CCETSW's services, and of the users of services in which those holding CCETSW qualifications work' (*ibid*, p. 58). However, it failed to recognise or acknowledge two important issues: firstly, that there may well be some tension between the priorities of governments and the perspectives of those who use such services; secondly, that the users[4] of social work services are not a homogeneous group necessarily sharing the same 'range of interests', either as individuals or as potential or actual members of a wide range of pressure groups. This failure also reflected the growing McDonaldization of social work.

The progressive distancing and eventual separation of probation from social work was another key development, not least because it split work with offenders from the rest of the profession's contribution. The significance of this lies partly in the fact that it demonstrates clearly the increasing political influence over the definition and construction of 'social work' and the inability of the social work profession or academy to resist this. More importantly, however, it represents a clear political *putsch* intended to remove social work values and perspectives from work with a particular and politically problematic client (or user) group – work that was undertaken by a service with one of the longest statutory associations with the social work profession. Probation therefore became increasingly separated from its professional social work foundations and from values that reflected an individualised view of the needs and problems of offenders.

This progressive separation also made possible the extension of managerial approaches and technologies (in Ritzer's terms) that constituted the earliest and clearest example of the McDonaldization of social work. Indeed, as Oldfield (1994) argues, a concern with efficiency was very much in evidence in probation from the late 1980s onwards, with a clear and growing emphasis on the effective use of resources, cost cutting, and the progressive introduction of performance indicators. Predictability, for example, was introduced in the form of National Standards, promulgated from the late 1980s onwards and quickly covering every aspect of the work of probation officers. This reflected an 'increasing concern to reduce the complex activities of probation officers to a set of formalised moves within a series of prescriptive guidelines … aimed at developing a standard product that has nothing to do with engendering creativity or innovation' (Oldfield, 1994, p. 187).

As Oldfield further argues, there was also a significant increase in managerial control over the practice of probation officers, by a variety of means, which resulted in 'deskilling and devaluing … the workers at the bottom of the hierarchy and reducing their control over their work' (*ibid.*). These developments were matched by a redefinition of the quality of practice, with a move away from concerns about the quality of relationships with offenders and their welfare and rehabilitation towards 'results that can be measured and evaluated by the use of technology, standardised working practices and adherence to the rules' (*ibid.*, p. 189). This was at least in part a consequence of the questioning of the value of existing and predominantly psychosocial/therapeutic approaches to working with

---

[4]   It is interesting to note, in passing, the increasing reluctance at the time to refer to those with whom social workers had contact as 'clients' and the emerging preference for terms such as 'service users', which subtly but significantly recast the nature of the relationship between social workers and social work agencies on the one hand, and those who had recourse to them on the other, by increasing the emotional distance between the two in a way that is strongly reminiscent of the view McDonald's takes of its customers.

offenders that resulted from negative research findings about their efficacy and, in particular, the impact of the political spin put on Martinson's (1974) overview of research, which was apparent in the deliberately overstated claim that 'nothing works'. This effectively undermined and destroyed not only the 'traditional' (i.e. historical) value base and ethical framework that had informed work with offenders, but also the methods that had been the mainstay of such work.

The vacuum that this created, as the probation service searched for a new sense of direction and purpose, allowed political rather than social work agendas to become paramount in shaping practice. Such developments were buttressed by the emergence of 'the new penology' (Feeley and Simon, 1992), less concerned with the individual offender than with groupings of offenders, classified and managed in terms of their dangerousness. The focus of the new penology was stated to be on 'the criminal justice *system*, and ... pursu[ing] systematic rationality and efficiency. It seeks to sort and classify, to separate the less from the more dangerous, and to deploy control strategies rationally' (*ibid.*, p. 452, emphasis in original). Its goal was not to eliminate crime but to make it tolerable through systematic co-ordination and it therefore reflected a dramatic shift from the values and practices of welfare and rehabilitation towards those of crime control.

As a consequence, the probation service increasingly adopted 'the bureaucratising and rationalising approaches that have been typical of the modern organisation's search for efficiency, predictability, calculability and control' (Oldfield, 1994, p. 189). In such a context, the interaction between probation officers and offenders became merely a means of achieving organisational and therefore political objectives, since it was a perspective that excluded 'the human skills, qualities and talents that make innovative and creative probation work possible and desirable' (*ibid.*, p. 192). Such an approach was and is impossible to reconcile with the individualised values and perspectives that are at the very heart of the work of Florence Hollis.

The Heineken factor

It is interesting to note that in spite of such widespread and large-scale shifts of emphasis, which amounted to nothing short of a redefinition of social work, there were some parts that the McDonaldization process did not reach. In the midst of this veritable sea-change in the nature of social work as an activity and as a profession (albeit that as noted earlier the claim to such status was and is far from uncontested), there remained a substantial penumbra of social work activity, largely in the voluntary or not-for-profit sector, which was resistant to such changes. This was mainly because the driving forces behind the McDonaldization of social work were in large part a product of the scale, complexity, and increasing politicisation of certain areas of practice. Thus a whole range of activities – for example, marriage/relationship guidance, counselling, conciliation/mediation, and community work – that, by virtue of their value base, theory, and methods either were or could have been included under the umbrella of traditional social work, remained largely untouched by McDonaldization. As a consequence, however, they were marginalised and effectively defined out of social work by the formulations and requirements of CCETSW and the major statutory employers of social workers.

A significant exception to this pattern was the area of family court welfare work, which continued for many years to be part of the probation service, albeit one that was increasingly seen as anomalous in the context of the service's primary work with offenders. Although latterly family court welfare became subject to National Standards, these were substantially less prescriptive than those for working with offenders. In addition, because it had been subject to a process of 'benign neglect' as a result of political imperatives that increasingly emphasised the work of probation officers with offenders (James and Hay, 1993), this area of work had also never been drawn into the 'what works' debate that had effectively redefined social work practice, both in the probation service and in other statutory agencies. As a result, it was progressively marginalised until it was eventually sloughed off in 2001, with the formation of the Children and Family Courts Advisory and Support Service, leaving the probation service free to concentrate on its responsibilities for crime control.

By contrast with the statutory sector, social work activities such as marriage guidance and relationship counselling more generally, the primary focus of which was on relationships rather than various kinds of social control or the delivery of various practical services, continued largely unaffected by the McDonaldization of the rest of social work. It is, for example, instructive to consider the development of family mediation in the voluntary sector as part of this brief review. 'Conciliation', later to become re-branded as 'mediation', emerged in Britain in the late 1970s as a means of working with families whose relationships had been affected by separation and divorce (see James, 1990). It drew heavily on a range of social work theory and methods (see James and Wilson, 1986), and was also firmly rooted in social work values. Indeed, given the ubiquity of conflict as an element of so many problems dealt with by social workers, it was a potentially valuable weapon in the armoury of methods of intervention available to them (James, 1987) and yet, for much of the 1980s and 1990s, mediation developed outwith the mainstream of social work and was therefore unaffected by the process of McDonaldization.

The continuing financial precariousness of many voluntary-sector mediation schemes, and an active and effective lobbying campaign, meant, however, that mediation began to move increasingly centre stage in the context of the debate surrounding the rising divorce rate and criticisms of the law relating to divorce. As a result, it figured prominently in the changes proposed by the ill-fated Family Law Act, 1996. However, having moved to the centre of the political stage and having become a key plank in the piloting by the Legal Aid Board (now the Legal Services Commission) of some of the money-saving provisions of the 1996 Act, mediation became an unwitting but collusive victim of the McDonaldization process, as it was compelled to respond to the rigours and ravages of the franchising process (which demanded standardisation, quality, and cost controls as part of contract compliance) through which the Legal Aid Board sought to ensure the widespread availability of mediation throughout Britain (Davis *et al.*, 2000).

The relationship between research, theory and practice

But why is the McDonaldization of social work important in terms of the relationship between research, theory and practice?

As noted, part of the reason for the shift away from psychosocial approaches and the entire body of theory and practice knowledge on which they were based was the progressive impact of the idea that 'nothing works'. Although located particularly in the context of therapeutic interventions with offenders, this notion also permeated more general discourse about social work, to the extent that increasing weight was given, both in terms of research and practice, to short-term and particularly behavioural methods, which provided clearer, more tightly structured approaches to intervention with clients (as they used to be called before they became simply offenders or service users), which were in turn more amenable to outcome research and therefore to empirical validation. It is surely at this time that the seeds of evidence-based practice were sown, not least because of the, at first implicit but latterly increasingly explicit, links made between theory, methods and outcomes, and therefore between methods, outcomes and resources.

The managerial discourse that increasingly permeated social work as part of this realignment of practice was, however, part of a much broader strategy of undermining the claims for and privileges associated with professional status, evident in many aspects of government policy during the 1980s. This is not the place to explore the finer conceptual arguments about, for example, what distinguishes a profession from a 'semi-profession' [eds: see Lyons and Taylor, this volume, for further discussion]. It is important to recognise, however, that the process of change under discussion increasingly eroded the epistemological, organisational, and therefore the ontological security of social workers, thereby creating fertile soil in which the seeds of the McDonaldization of social work were sown. Faced with this challenge, and in their continuing search for acceptance as a profession, social workers (both academic and practice-based) have increasingly embraced successive governments' agendas in terms of both research and practice. In order to understand the significance in this regard of the several inter-related changes which have been outlined, a short excursus is necessary, to consider these matters in a little more detail.

Epistemologically, it is still arguable that social work is not a discipline because it has no body of theory, values or skills that are unique to it. Although, for example, it may be configured in such a way that the particular constellation of attributes that are presented to the world as 'social work' are unique, they can equally be found contributing in different combinations to the construction of other disciplines, professions or vocations. A further part of this difficulty is that, increasingly, social work has come to exist only as part of particular organisational structures. This is not to say that social work does not exist outwith the context of increasingly monolithic local authority bureaucracies (see above), but rather to argue that it has increasingly been defined on the basis of particular functions, in particular organisational contexts, as these have come to dominate the delivery of social work services and therefore the practice of social work.

For social workers as professionals this has generated a growing sense of uncertainty – being located in an organisational context in which their practice has increasingly been defined and regulated not by the values, theories and methods of their profession but by the requirements, concerns and accountabilities of their employers and the political concerns of both the central and the local state. This, combined with the sometimes overt criticism of and hostility towards social work and social workers that was generated particularly in the context of the widespread moral panic about child protection that surfaced in the mid 1970s, has weakened the identity of the profession progressively. In turn, and in conjunction with the other influences outlined above, this has created a sense of ontological insecurity amongst social workers that has rendered them both individually and as a profession highly vulnerable to the process of McDonaldization.

Before returning to my main theme, it may be helpful to pose one further question: 'To what extent are social work academics part of the social work profession?'[5] Just as overcoming the putative split between theory and practice has long dominated the concerns of social work educators – not to mention their students or CCETSW – it can also be argued that that there is an equivalent split between social work academics and practitioners. This is partly a matter of fact, to the extent that the social work enterprise has never successfully bridged this gap by enabling easy movement between settings in the way that professions such as medicine and the law have, although this is itself also a matter of organisational context.

More importantly, however, and this goes to the heart of the issue, as I have already argued there is no corpus of knowledge, values, skills or methods, whether these be to do with either research or practice, that are intrinsic to social work and that therefore serve effectively to differentiate it from other academic disciplines. With few exceptions, social work in UK universities is so closely related to, for example, psychology, sociology and social policy, that it has no clear and separate academic identity. As Lyons argues, 'The lack of clarity about the theoretical core, the competing disciplinary paradigms and the disputed nature of the professional territory, are reflected in the wide range of departments within which the subject is located' (1999, p. 90). This same problem of identity is reflected in the fact that both the panel that recently drafted the benchmarking statement for academic social work programmes produced by the Quality Assurance Agency for Higher Education, and the panel for the 2001 Research Assessment Exercise conducted by the four Higher Education Funding Councils in the UK, were joint panels bringing together social policy and social work.

It can be argued – and the matters just referred to offer some evidence – that the concerns of social work academics are increasingly becoming primarily

---

[5]   UK universities are also increasingly undergoing the process of McDonaldization; witness the nature and impact of quality assurance language and technologies. This, however, is not an issue for this chapter. [Eds: see Lyons and Taylor, this volume, for discussion of the 'double dose' of managerialism suffered by social work academics in recent years, reflecting, but also in addition to, the 'normal' tensions inherent in the academy/practice 'divide'.]

academic, in the highly instrumental sense of chasing research funding, including government funding for evaluation studies [eds: see also Humphries, this volume], whilst those of social work practitioners and managers now lie primarily with the realities and constraints of practice and service delivery, and their effective management.

This long-standing gap, which is arguably becoming a schism as a consequence of the recent developments highlighted, is seldom acknowledged, let alone articulated, since to do so is to strike at the very heart of the philosophy of partnership that has, with increasing difficulty in recent years, held academics and practitioners together in a semblance of unity [eds: see Lyons and Taylor, this volume, *passim*].   In its current form it is, however, a product of the de-professionalisation and McDonaldization of social work, and the fact that neither academics nor practitioners are able to resist these processes because both groups – and social work as a whole – are dependent upon external and largely political influences, structural and situational.   Hence neither group has effective control over the construction and definition of social work, in the way in which, for example, the medical and legal professions control the way in which medicine and the law are constructed, defined, maintained and developed – *viz.* in a reflexive relationship between theory and practice, academics and practitioners, universities and hospitals/legal institutions.

It is the epistemological vacuum indicated a little earlier that evidence-based practice has filled, restoring some credibility and some sense of professional identity to both social work academics and practitioners. The former can validate their role as academics by generating research income (especially from central and local government departments), employing research skills and methods to evaluate polices and practices, and publishing their results in learned journals, thereby further legitimating their academic status through the achievement of research credibility.   In parallel, practitioners can adopt evidence-based practices that, because they have been 'proven' empirically 'to work', can be and are endorsed as 'valid' forms of social work practice and service delivery and thence seen as legitimate by employers and government alike.   The nature of social work has thereby been transformed in recent years.

Implications of the McDonaldization of social work

It is clear that there is a price to be paid by social workers, whether based in practice or in academia, for going down this road. For social work in general, that price is the loss of scope for innovation and creativity, because McDonaldized services are, by definition, standardised. For academics, it also means a narrowing of the research agenda, with the attendant risk of a real loss of academic freedom in terms of the ability to research into and comment critically upon important social issues. This may have profound implications for clients and practitioners alike. As Lorenz has argued:

It is not the choice of a particular research method that determines social work's position socially and politically. Rather it is the ability to engage critically in the political agenda of defining the terms on which knowledge and truth can be established which should form the basis for the search of [*sic*] appropriate research approaches in social work. (Lorenz, 2000, p. 10)

Achieving such a critical engagement becomes ever more problematic, given the increasing level of political control over academic research inherent in the Government's enthusiasm for funding 'what works' research with which to underpin its drive to promote evidence-based policy and practice. Thus, social work research, which is inherently political, has recently become more specifically politicised; it is certainly arguable that any independent academic research agenda has been hijacked and swamped by the current emphasis on evaluation studies aimed at the promulgation of evidence-based practice.

As Mair has argued, the distinction between research and evaluation, whilst not acknowledged by all, is an important one.

Evaluation is ... different from research in its pure form – although it may be difficult to see any differences in practice between the two. There is no doubt that research can be evaluative, and that an evaluation study will include some (if not wholly consist of) research. But evaluation implies some form of assessment of success or failure, some kind of measure of how well or how badly a programme or initiative is meeting its objectives; in other words, evaluation has to do with effectiveness. Evaluation is also connected with the policy process and with 'politics' in a much more intimate fashion than research. (Mair, 1997, p. xix)

Similarly, Kazi has argued that 'The pressures on social work practice to demonstrate its effectiveness have continued to grow in the last two decades and there has been a growth in evaluation publications, particularly in the 1990s' (2000, p. 755).

This heavy emphasis on evaluation studies has seen a consequent marginalisation of social work research; theoretical, organisational, 'blue skies', and socio-legal research all run the risk of being sacrificed on the altar of instrumentality and effectiveness, driving home once again the wedge between theory and practice that has for so long been problematic for social work. Increasingly, social work research reflects the dominance of the Government's agenda. This is evident, for example, in the impact of Department of Health funding on child care research and, to some extent, that of the charitable funding of community care research. Increasingly too, the focus of such research (or, more accurately, evaluation) is on policy implementation and user-relevance, rather than on the direction and values that underpin such policies and the broader social and structural context in which they are being promulgated [eds: see also Humphries, this volume].

The investment of £1.5 million in 1996 by the Department of Health in the development of evidence-based practice for social services departments, which involved the establishment of the Centre for Evidence-Based Social Services at the University of Exeter, provides additional evidence of this trend (Webb, 2001, p.

58). It is further underlined by the commitment of the Training Organisation for the Personal Social Services (TOPSS), the new social care training agency that has taken over from CCETSW those functions not assumed by the General Social Care Council (GSCC), to the centrality of evidence-based practice (Webb, 2001, p. 59). Such constraints have been necessarily, if not willingly, accepted by academics in order that they can meet the demands of increasingly McDonaldized higher education institutions. It is salutary to note, however, that as long ago as 1984, Raynor felt it necessary to warn about the dangers of 'evaluation with one eye closed', observing that without an awareness of the

> normative and interpretative dimensions of the social worker's task and the conceptual equipment to consider them rationally (if not scientifically), the empiricist approach to technical effectiveness is an insufficient guide. If we rely too heavily on it we run the risk of a naïve reductionism which may in the long run reduce the effectiveness and accountability of social workers, as well as lending itself to unwitting ideological bias through its failure to consider political and moral issues. (Raynor, 1984, p. 9)

In the light of the above analysis, Raynor's argument seems remarkably prescient, for it certainly appears to be the case that social work has adopted just such a Nelsonian stance towards these risks during the latter part of the twentieth century and the beginning of the twenty-first, turning a blind eye to these and related developments that have facilitated its McDonaldization. For social work practitioners, this has resulted in precisely the 'naïve reductionism' and the consequent reduction in 'the effectiveness and accountability of social workers' against which Raynor warned. It has also seen the degradation of theory, knowledge, skill and creativity – the *art* of social work as England (1986) wrote – into role, function, task and uniformity. As Webb has recently argued, 'Evidence-based practice entraps professional practice within an instrumental framework which regiments, systematizes and manages social work within a technocratic framework of routinized operations' (Webb, 2001, p. 71). This is, of course, the very essence and, more importantly, the *purpose* of the process of McDonaldization.

Raynor's earlier highlighting of the moral issues raised by such a shift also foreshadows recent renewed concerns about the erosion and impoverishment of social work values, which are now so clearly subservient to agency and Government policies that the claims of social work to the professional status it had in the 1950s and 1960s are hard to sustain. As Preston-Shoot and colleagues have recently argued, '[the] social work values of respect for person, partnership, and empowerment are being undermined by the reality of resource-driven and service-led provision' (Preston-Shoot *et al.*, 2001, p. 2). Although these authors go on to suggest that 'the increasingly extensive use of policy and practice guidance may reflect an increasing preoccupation with values' (*ibid.*, p. 4), it is clear that the values contained in such guidance may be political or instrumental values, rather than the more substantive moral values of social work(ers). Their use may also reflect a desire for greater control over social work rather than a concern to re-imbue social work practice with a social work value base.

This possibility is also identified by Webb, who argues that

> by attempting to root out value laden, professional judgement or 'opinion-based ideas' evidence-based practice entails an implicit value base of its own. It embodies a formal (means–end) rationality and centres its interest on efficiency, economy and outcome-based predictions ... [I]ts ideological function is the legitimation of a particular type of formal rationality in social work. (Webb, 2001, pp. 72–3)

Webb goes further, however, and suggests that

> social work should abandon mechanistic approaches, such as evidential practice and those characteristic of experimental and behavioural research ... Unless this is done, the emerging panacea of evidence-based work can have the effect of neutralizing social work's role in moral and political discourse and undermining its professional autonomy. (*ibid.*, p. 76)

With the announcement in 2001 of the Government's intention to establish a Social Care Institute for Excellence (SCIE), and the subsequent emergence of the latter with a key role in promulgating evidence-based practice, it is doubtful whether social work is in a position to abandon such approaches, or whether social work practitioners in particular are in a position to resist such developments.

Social work academics, however, *are* in a position – if they so choose – to retain sufficient freedom to enable them to offer a critique of such developments and to act as the conscience of the profession. As England put it so well:

> Good social work rests upon the process of criticism, a process of experience and understanding, of analysis and comparison. A widespread and critical dialogue is the only means whereby the canons of professional judgement and evaluation can be established in social work. (England, 1986, p. 125)

It is clear therefore, as Lyons has recently proposed, that social work values 'must remain central to the conduct of social work as a professional activity' (1999, p. 179), just as they must also figure prominently in the concerns of social work researchers. They must also, indeed, remain central to the teaching of social work, since the reductionist tendencies of evidence-based practice are both mirrored and buttressed by the continuing emphasis on competency-based practice in training. As Lyons observes,

> Henkel (1994) described competencies at NVQ level as 'reductionist and atomistic' and suggested that the challenge to professional education is to devise competencies which reflect the holistic and reflective conceptions of professional practice. (Lyons, 1999, p. 66)

In this sense, as in so many others, teaching and research in social work must go hand-in-hand and must be sufficiently reflexive to be properly critical of recent developments in the organisation and practice of social work.

Conclusion

None of the above is to argue that the baby was ever completely thrown out with the bath water. It is of course true that highly individualised approaches, based on traditional social work values, have continued in some areas of practice, such as adoption and foster care, or working with survivors of child abuse. Nonetheless, there is widespread evidence of the McDonaldization of social work and, in conjunction with the growing emphasis on evidence-based practice, this undoubtedly represents a very different 'epistemic view of human agency and thereby the nature of social work' (Webb, 2001, p. 61) from the holistic, humanistic and individualised approach that was the very essence of the understandings typified by the writings of Florence Hollis and her contemporaries.

Yet voices are beginning to be raised about the growing hegemony of McDonaldization and related managerial mechanisms, including the drive towards evidence-based practice, not only in social work but also in other spheres of service delivery in the public sector. This is occurring not least because of the instrumental, atomistic and reductionist impact that they are having, which is so much at odds with what social work used, and still *ought*, to represent, given the values on which the profession was founded, on which it grew, and which were central to the view of social work practice espoused by Hollis. As Webb argues:

> [S]ocial work requires a model which is much more nuanced and sensitive to local and contextual factors. That is, a model which recognizes, in line with research in connectionist and network analysis, that social actors operate with a limited rationality due to the indeterminacy, uncertainty and spontaneous effects of networked systems which change over time ... (Webb, 2001, p. 76)[6]

The language may be different, but such ideas would not sound unfamiliar to Florence Hollis if translated into terms of understanding the relationship between the psychological aspects of human behaviour (agency) and the social context in which this takes place – or, in her terms, 'the person–situation configuration'. What sounds less familiar in terms of social work today is her view that casework is

> both art and science. Intuitive insights and spontaneity are combined with continuous efforts to develop and systematize knowledge and understanding ... It is assumed that man [*sic*] is not only acted upon but is capable of spontaneous activity ... that adults can still change and develop towards fuller self-realization. (Hollis, 1970, p. 38)

This is a truly heretical perspective in terms of the McDonaldized approach to the help currently delivered to social work service users at the beginning of the twenty-first century. For Hollis, the nature of social work is characterised

---

6   [Eds: for discussion of the potential of social work research adopting a network perspective, see Trevillion, this volume.]

by its direct concern for the well-being of the individual. It is not primarily an organ of social control, designed to bring the individual into conformity with society ... [it is] a response to the needs of human beings for protection against social and natural deprivations and catastrophes ... [and] [f]rom its inception it has stressed the value of the individual. (1964, p. 12)

Might now perhaps be the time for us to acknowledge the impact of McDonaldization on social work, and for social workers, be they academics or practitioners, to revisit some of the values and perspectives of Florence Hollis and her contemporaries and to seek to re-establish the position of social work, both socially and politically, by responding to Lorenz's exhortation (2000, p. 9) 'to engage critically in the political agenda of defining the terms on which knowledge and truth can be established'?

In the course of writing this chapter, certain issues have been elided, others have not been addressed, and yet others have been insufficiently substantiated or perhaps glossed over. It is perhaps also inevitable that some readers will find it too critical of recent developments, or too polemical. Yet others will simply disagree with the arguments put forward and will be quick to formulate counter-arguments and identify contra-indications in order to rebut the McDonaldization thesis as I have sought to apply it to the case of social work. Having at least opened up this proposition for debate, however, I would ask the critical reader one question: does it have what Matza (1964) called the 'ring of truth'? If the answer to this question is either wholly or even partially in the affirmative, I hope this will give pause for further reflection about the current and future direction of social work.

References

Ball, C., Harris, R., Roberts, G. and Vernon, S. (1988), *The Law Report: Teaching and Assessment of Law in Social Work Education* (Paper 4.1), Central Council for Education and Training in Social Work (CCETSW), London.

Biestek, F. (1957), *The Casework Relationship*, Unwin University Books, London.

Brandon, J. and Davies, M. (1979), 'The limits of competence in social work: the assessment of marginal students in social work education', *British Journal of Social Work*, 9(3), pp. 295–347.

Bryman, A. (1999), 'The Disneyization of society', *Sociological Review*, 47(1), pp. 25–47.

Davis, G., Bevan, G., Clisby, S., Cumming, Z., Dingwall, R., Fenn, P., Finch, S., Fitzgerald, R., Goldie, S., Greatbatch, D., James, A. and Pearce, J. (2000), *Monitoring Publicly Funded Family Mediation: Report to the Legal Services Commission*, Legal Services Commission, London.

Department of Health (Social Services Inspectorate) (1993), *Report of a Policy and Financial Management Review of the Central Council for Education and Training in Social Work*, DoH, London.

England, H. (1986), *Social Work as Art: Making Sense for Good Practice*, Allen and Unwin, London.

Feeley, M. and Simon, J. (1992), 'The new penology: notes on the emerging strategy of corrections and its implications', *Criminology*, 30(4), pp. 449–74.

Finkelstein, J. (1989), *Dining Out: A Sociology of Modern Manners*, Polity, Cambridge.

Henkel, M. (1994), 'Social work: an incorrigibly marginal profession?', in Becher, T. (ed.), *Governments and Professional Education*, Society for Research into Higher Education/ Open University Press, Buckingham, pp. 86–103, cited in Lyons, *op. cit.*

Hollis, F. (1964), *Casework: A Psychosocial Therapy*, Random House, New York.

Hollis, F. (1970), 'The psychosocial approach to casework', in Roberts and Nee, *op. cit.*, pp. 33–75.

James, A.L. (1987), 'Conflicts, conciliation and social work', *British Journal of Social Work*, **17**(4), pp. 347–64.

James, A.L. (1990), 'Conciliation and social change', in Fisher, T. (ed.), *Family Conciliation within the UK: Policy and Practice*, National Family Conciliation Council/*Family Law*, Bristol, pp. 19–27.

James, A.L. and Hay, W. (1993), *Court Welfare in Action: Practice and Theory*, Harvester Wheatsheaf, Hemel Hempstead.

James, A.L. and Wilson, K. (1986), *Couples, Conflict and Change: Social Work with Marital Relationships*, Tavistock, London.

Kazi, M.A.F. (2000), 'Contemporary perspectives in the evaluation of practice', *British Journal of Social Work*, **30**(6), pp. 755–68.

Lorenz, W. (2000), 'Contentious identities – social work research and the search for professional and personal identities', paper presented in the *Theorising Social Work Research* seminar series, no. 4, 6 March, University of Edinburgh, and now available at <http://www.elsc.org.uk/socialcareresource/tswr/seminar4/lorenz.htm>.

Lyons, K. (1999), *Social Work in Higher Education: Demise or Development?*, Ashgate, Aldershot.

Mair, G. (ed.) (1997), *Evaluating the Effectiveness of Community Penalties*, Avebury, Aldershot.

Martinson, R. (1974), 'What works? – questions and answers about prison reform', *The Public Interest*, **35** (Spring), pp. 22–54.

Matza, D. (1964), *Delinquency and Drift*, Wiley, New York.

Oldfield, M. (1994), 'Talking quality, meaning control: McDonalds, the market and the probation service', *Probation Journal*, **41**(4), pp. 186–92.

Preston-Shoot, M., Roberts, G. and Vernon, S. (2001), 'Values in social work law: strained relations or sustaining relationships?', *Journal of Social Welfare and Family Law*, **23**(1), pp. 1–22.

Raynor, P. (1984), 'Evaluation with one eye closed: the empiricist agenda in social work research', *British Journal of Social Work*, **14**(1), pp. 1–10.

Ritzer, G. (2000), *The McDonaldization of Society* (New Century edn), Pine Forge, Thousand Oaks, CA.

Roberts, R.W. and Nee, R.H. (eds) (1970), *Theories of Social Casework*, University of Chicago Press, London.

Seebohm Committee (1968), *Report of the Committee on Local Authority and Allied Personal Social Services*, Cmnd 3703, HMSO, London.

Simon, B. (1970), 'Social casework theory: an overview', in Roberts and Nee, *op. cit.*, pp. 353–94.

Webb, S.A. (2001), 'Some considerations on the validity of evidence-based practice in social work', *British Journal of Social Work*, **31**(1), pp. 57–79.

Chapter 3

The Politics of Social Work Research

Ian Butler and Richard Pugh

Introduction

Not for many years has interest in social work research been as widespread and as earnest as it is currently in the UK. Amongst social work practitioners, there is a growing appetite for the means of bringing research into the workplace. From the 'Research Briefings' prepared as part of the Government's *Quality Protects* programme, to the more formal collaborative arrangements developed by many service providers with key producers of social work research (such as *Making Research Count* and *Research in Practice*), researchers and practitioners appear to be encountering each other with new-found enthusiasm. Within the academy itself, social work research is beginning to emerge from the shadows of cognate disciplines. For example, this book has its origins in the ESRC-sponsored seminar series *Theorising Social Work Research*, which was an explicit, well-organised and effective device to secure more formal recognition of social work by its most prestigious potential funder as a distinctive (if not discrete) academic discipline amongst the social sciences. In government too, new organisations and structures are beginning to take shape that seek to engage directly with social work research. These include the advent of the Social Care Institute for Excellence (SCIE) and the Department of Health's Research Governance Framework (Department of Health, 2001).

It might be tempting – to echo the poet Wordsworth's sentiments (1805) concerning a revolution of another sort – to settle for 'the bliss' of being alive 'in such a dawn'. This chapter will suggest, however, that in the apparent cosy coincidence of interests between policy makers, social work practitioners, and researchers – typical of the rather self-congratulatory and uncritical relationships that accompany much of the politics of 'the third way' – there lies the potential for social work research to be transformed into a much-reduced, colourless, and almost entirely depoliticised form of practice. Our starting point is that social work is a political activity and as such intrinsically un-amenable to consensus. We suggest that the production of social work knowledge, through research, is equally a contested, sectional and partisan practice – or at least it should be if it is to be of service to social work, as we understand it. We will end by suggesting that the social work researcher, who may not wish to take sides, at least has to recognise that there are sides to be taken [eds: see also Humphries, this volume], and that there is an important role for us as problematisers and critics as well as technically efficient and 'on-message' contributors to any developing 'new' epistemological, methodological or practice orthodoxy.

The politics of social work

To appreciate the complexity of the relationship between politics and social work research, it is important first to recover the several senses in which social work – 'a disputed and even a dangerous activity' (Butler and Drakeford, 2000) – may be seen as a form of political practice. At one level, it has long been understood that social work has a particular part to play in managing 'the social' (Donzelot, 1980; 1988), the disciplinary interface between the individual and the state. Social work would appear to have an established place in the mechanisms of 'tutelage', a subtle balance of moralisation, normalisation and occasionally compulsion which, it has been suggested, is essentially a compromise reached by the modern, liberal state. The possibility that this might involve a reciprocal process, whereby the agents of social work are 'subverted' to perform acts of resistance in association with those relatively powerless groups with which they work, has an equally long though less frequently remembered history.

Even in the nineteenth century, the Charity Organisation Society feared that its workers might become politicised through contact with the lives of their clients (Jones, 1983). Much later, Kenneth Pray reached positively for a conception of social work as a two-way process, contending that it was about

> ... helping individuals meet the problems of their constantly shifting relations with one another and with the whole society, and helping the whole society, at the same time, adjust its demands upon its members and its services to them in accordance with the real needs of the individuals that compose and determine its life ... (Pray, 1949, pp. 33–4)

Indeed – 'going further', as it were – it has often been argued that social work is 'heir to a radical, emancipatory and transformative ... ideal' (Butler and Drakeford, 2001b, p. 16). Yet, despite a (modest) tradition of radical practice (see, for example, Bailey and Brake, 1975; Jordan, 1990), as recently as 1997 Ife was able to note that 'There is still a tendency ... to treat social work as ideologically neutral, rather than to define it as an essentially ideological activity ... essentially as political practice' (p. 199). While, in the UK anyway, the practice of social work continues to be an object of political interest, not least through its close association with the public sector, nevertheless Ife's point holds. It is easy to see how and why one might confuse neutered social work with neutral social work.

The recent history of social work in the UK has seen a steady disengagement from its more overtly political forms: community development, for example. In part this is attributable to having had to contend with the ideological forces at play during the long years of Tory government, which led to the weakened and weakening 'bargaining position' of social work and produced a series of uneasy compromises, made in order to ensure personal and professional survival. This involved acquiescence in the commodification (Drakeford, 2000) and marketisation of welfare, and an earnest enthusiasm for the managerialism that the 'politics of enforcement' (Parton, 1999, p. 17) requires (see Butler and Drakeford, 1997; 2001a). Nor did this process of accommodation to the political imperatives of the day end with the election of a Labour Government in 1997, as the opportunities for collaboration – or collusion (depending on your point of view) – with a less than emancipatory social project have continued undiminished. Specific instances are detailed by, for example, Blyth (2001), Bywaters and McLeod (2001), Jones (2001), Jordan (2001). Thus an argument can be advanced that the alliances or 'accommodations' (Butler and Drakeford, 2001b, p. 7) which social work has made with New Labour, as much as with previous administrations, may be operating to the detriment not only of service users but also to that of social work as a form of welfare practice (see also Shaw and Shaw, 1997).

During this period, social work has maintained a form of dialogue with politics, both in the general sense and in terms of the agenda of the particular government of the day. This has most frequently been expressed through a language of anti-oppressive practice, social work's most recent form of 'values-speak'. Clark (2000, p. 45) describes social work's 'perennial appeal to values' as evidence that it sees itself charged with 'moral purpose'. On examination, it is clear that many of the various declarations of social work's moral purpose borrow explicitly from a political vocabulary of equality, human rights and social justice – see, for example, the 'mission statement' of the International Association of Schools of Social Work (2002), or the statement of ethical 'principles and standards' of the International Federation of Social Workers (2002, paras 2.2.1–5). Whether this represents more than a rhetorical association is beyond the scope of this chapter, although it is difficult to resist Simpkin's contention of more than 20 years ago that 'such values are either so universal as to be empty of significance or else part of a particular liberal ideology whose particular conceit is a denial of its own existence as an ideology' (1979, p. 150). 'Values-speak' may be seen, however, as at the very least an oblique acknowledgement of social work as a political practice.

We proceed in this chapter from the premise that social work in its dominant form in the UK is intrinsically and necessarily a political practice. It cannot be otherwise if one accepts that it routinely engages with those who are confronted with asymmetrical and unjust social relations (including those based on class, sexuality, gender, race and age) and those whose relationships with social institutions (including the state and the family) are tense or divergent from the norm. This is not necessarily to romanticise radical forms of practice. In any case, as Jones has pointed out:

> For all its trappings of liberalism and concern, there has been no sustained or substantial tradition of radicalism within British social work ... [H]ad social work

acquired such a perspective, it would not have enjoyed state sponsorship since 1945. (Jones, 1998, p. 38)

Ferguson (2001) has even suggested that contemporary social work would do well to disengage from its spectral struggle with Beck's 'zombie institutions' – social structures and disciplinary forms (such as class, religion and the family) 'which have been clinically dead for a long time, but are unable to die' (Beck, 1994, p. 40). Instead, in the brave, new, 'post-traditional order', the emphasis is and should – in his view – be

> ... not simply on safety, equality and the securing of rights (emancipation), but on self-actualization (life politics) as evidenced by how social work and other counselling and self-help initiatives are used as resources to deepen self-understanding, construct a new narrative of the self, and find healing. (Ferguson, 2001, p. 53)

How widely this perspective would be shared in most social services departments is open to debate. It is our view that many of the realities of poverty, racism and structured inequality have survived from modernity into the postmodern lives of social workers' clients, largely unaltered either in their origins or effects. In one sense, however, it doesn't matter for our purposes whether injustice is encountered in terms of structure or of identity. Social work is still left operating at the interface between the state and its citizens and is still engaged in the arbitration and negotiation of power and control. It remains, therefore, a political practice, however widespread the failure to acknowledge it as such.

The politics of social research

We have suggested that social work has often denied its nature as a political practice, both implicitly and explicitly, both passively and actively. The question of how far and in what ways social work can claim to be or to have been a research-driven enterprise is perhaps at first sight more straightforward, although as soon as we begin to look for – and at – the evidence, difficulties arise. Certainly in its Fabian past and earlier the collection of social data was important in establishing a rationale for a wide range of welfare practices, from the sanitation crusaders of the early nineteenth century to the redistributive socialism of the Webbs themselves. However, according to Beresford and Evans (1999) the current place of social research in the UK needs to be expressed in more modest terms:

> ... social research now mainly plays a subsidiary role in the construction and development of social policies, including social work. Its role has increasingly been one of evaluating, monitoring and legitimating policy developments, rather than initiating them. (p. 672)

The relationship between social research and the production of public policy can never be a straightforward one of course; as Glass has noted (2001), the political and the 'scientific' processes conform to different rationalities. Be that as it may, the development described by Beresford and Evans was clearly well in train by the end of the 1970s when, in admiring the 'fruitfulness' of public 'controversy over the policy conclusions to be drawn from research' in 1960s America, Martin Bulmer (1978) had to work hard to cheer up his British contemporaries who had little to enthuse them back at home. Bulmer's account of the research community and the type of social research demanded by policy makers in the UK at that time is cautious, yet sufficiently optimistic for him to encourage continuing involvement in what would appear to have been a strained relationship between policy makers and researchers. For Bulmer (*ibid.*, p. 19), the production of social research was consequent on the interaction between the radically-Left-inclined, suspicious-of-the-state, campaigning social researcher, and the pragmatic, equally suspicious and increasingly cynical, central or local government administrator.

In Bulmer's account one can sense, even at this interval, an echo of frustrated optimism, as the research universe created by the social policy 'big bang' of the Wilson years collapsed in the face of the IMF-induced chill of the Callaghan Administration. Bulmer captured the mood of those times exactly when he noted – in the UK at least – 'a powerful current of radical pessimism, among sociologists in particular, about the contribution of social research to policy making' (*ibid.*, p. 25). The pessimism of policy makers drew on what they saw as the continuing failure of social scientists to deliver quantified, accurate and reliable predictions of use to politicians, comparable to those deriving from the natural sciences and of a sort that had already begun to be produced and to find an audience in the US when Bulmer was writing home (see Bell, 1982). On both sides of the Atlantic, the social sciences had been struggling since at least the late 1950s to make a case for their utility on similar terms to those made by the natural sciences (Lewis, 2002), and in this way to secure a meaningful place in the political processes that shape public policy.

Hammersley (2000), reflecting on the distinctive forms of social inquiry that have emerged over the last 20 years, distinguishes between the 'practical' and the 'scientific' in research, and characterises 'practical inquiry' as

> ... geared directly to providing information that is needed to deal with some practical problem, so that here the immediate audience for research reports is people with a practical interest in the issue; notably, but not exclusively, policy makers and occupational practitioners of the relevant kind. (p. 224)

Williams (2000, p. 162) sees alongside this the advent of the social researcher as 'technologist', 'engineering solutions to problems', equipped with little more than a 'set of tools for investigation' and little by way of 'ontological foundations'.

This is perhaps an overstatement (see Everitt and Hardiker, 1996), but it is difficult to avoid Lewis's conclusion that, over several decades, the social sciences have striven in their pursuit of demonstrating their utility, their practicality, and their reliability in providing 'real' solutions to 'real' problems, to become '... more "scientific"; more methodologically rigorous and above all more quantitative, in short, more hard' (2002, p. 3).

This would be, we would argue, an accurate description of the ambitions for contemporary social work research held by many social work practitioners and social work researchers, and by government(s). Currently, such ambitions are commonly couched in the language of 'evidence-based practice'.

Evidence-based practice

The immediate origins of evidence-based practice are usually traced (see Gibbs and Gambrill, 2002) to the 'research/practice gap' in medicine. More specifically, there was a perception in the United States that front-line medical practitioners did not have ready access to research findings, with the consequence that their formal knowledge base was commonly out-of-date; moreover, this situation could not easily be remedied by programmes of continuing professional education. This could lead in turn to the continuing use of interventions/treatments that, at best, had little or no demonstrated efficacy or, at worst, were positively harmful. Possibly the most widely quoted definition of evidence-based practice was developed in this context:

> Evidence-based practice is the conscientious, explicit and judicious use of current best evidence in making decisions about the care of individual patients, based on skills which allow the doctor to evaluate both personal experience and external evidence in a systematic and objective manner. (Sackett *et al.*, 1997, p. 2)

In the UK, advocacy for and the development of evidence-based practice in the context of social work draws additionally on several traditions, most notably on behavioural social work (see, for example, Macdonald, 1994; 1998; Macdonald and Sheldon, 1992) and the empirical practice movement (Bloom, 1994; Corcoran and Fischer, 1987; McGuire, 1995; Reid, 1994). During the last few years the approach has been most prominently pursued and extended by the Centre for Evidence-Based Social Services at Exeter University, with the main emphasis being upon seeking the practical goal – much-loved by the present Government – of discovering and applying 'what works'. The core assumption, at once 'scientific' and political, as Webb (2001) notes in a powerful critique, is 'the idea that a formal rationality of practice based on scientific methods can produce a more effective and economically accountable means of [delivering] social service[s]' (p. 60).

As already indicated, evidence-based practice has 'making decisions' as its central concern (Webb, *ibid.*, p. 61). Critiques of evidence-based practice typically question the epistemological assumptions which lie behind its understanding of how decisions should, are, and could be made in practice, *and* the professional/

political consequences of pursuing the 'evidence-based' approach. Thus Webb argues:

> Evidence-based practice proposes a particular version of rational inference on the part of decision makers. It assumes that there exist reliable criteria of inferential evidence based on objectively veridical or optimal modes of information processing. In other words it creates a picture of social workers engaged in an *epistemic process* of sorting and prioritizing information and using this to optimize practice to its best effect. (*ibid.*, p. 63; emphasis in original)

The epistemological criticisms levelled at evidence-based practice broadly restate long-standing and familiar philosophical critiques of positivism and empiricism, which will not be rehearsed in detail here. Suffice it to say that there are fundamental problems surrounding the assumptions made by proponents of evidence-based practice regarding the 'objectivity' – not to mention the certainty or reliability – of observation itself, of assessing different bodies or sorts of evidence, and of the processes of inference which lead from evidence to explanation. Despite efforts to construct notions of justification which are 'objective', 'value-free', or 'neutral' in terms of standpoint, all judgements of what constitutes evidence, what is 'good enough' in this regard, or what is 'evident' from data, are in our view perspectival, both informed by normative presumptions about values and interests, as well as by conceptual and theoretical frames of reference, and inevitably bound by context (including the political context). As Owen (1995, p. 33) neatly puts it, there is no 'view from nowhere'. We return to the centrality of judgement and justification later.

There are, of course – the foregoing paragraphs notwithstanding – several versions of evidence-based practice, and differences in the extent to which its exponents accept or adopt a positivistic understanding of possible knowledge concerning social life. However, in our view much of what social workers have, for good or ill, come to call 'evidence-based practice' reflects the nomothetic, utilitarian and pragmatic tendencies still operating across the social sciences more generally (see Trinder, 1996). Thus, whilst few contemporary British writers in the subject area would accept Thyer's assertion that 'there is no substitute for controlled experimental research, guided by the philosophy of science known as logical positivism and the tenets of the hypothetico-deductive process' (1989, p. 320), many do, nevertheless, conceive of a hierarchy of methodologies, with the randomised controlled trial and the single case experimental design being at the top and 'softer' subjective approaches such as narrative accounts of personal experience at the bottom.

Furthermore, there are differences in the degree to which exponents of evidence-based practice acknowledge and engage with epistemological concerns. For example, in his summary response to Webb (2001), Sheldon (2001, pp. 802–3) acknowledges that humans are prone to see what they wish (or expect) to see and frequently make unwarranted leaps from observations to explanations, mislead-ingly interpreting Webb's whole case in these terms and suggesting that he (Webb) regards this as 'intractable' (Sheldon, 2001, p. 802). However, Sheldon himself provides no account of how we might respond to the uncertainty inherent in our perceptions and knowledge, other than a brief reference to the possible potential in (essentially social) processes of conjecture and refutation (Popper, 1963). Most tellingly, there is no recognition of the idealistic positivism – and/or positivistic idealism – that Sheldon embraces. In this regard, he is typical of those exponents of evidence-based practice who may be characterised as 'careless epistemologists'. They either take epistemology as being quite unproblematic, or they concede uncertainty but offer little reflection upon its implications as they carry on with their work.

Peile and McCouat note that there are

> ... many positivists [who] have taken seriously the epistemological criticisms of the approach and now accept the limitations of objectivity ... They have recognized the benefits of qualitative approaches in strengthening and triangulating quantitative results ... [and] the value of appropriating alternative approaches ... (1997, p. 348)

However, these 'postpositivists' (Fraser *et al.*, 1991) '[retain] the positivist object-ives as ideals' (Peile and McCouat, 1997, p. 348).

This remains a narrow view of both the epistemology and the epistemic processes of social work, but it has come to dominate and define what constitutes legitimate or preferred forms of social work research (see Cheetham and Deakin, 1997). The predominance of such a view has, arguably, been reinforced by a range of regulatory mechanisms, such as the Research Assessment Exercise(s), the Research Governance Framework, and the Social Care Institute for Excellence (Butler, 2003).

In reflecting on the most influential – or 'official' – conception of evidence-based practice in Britain with regard to its political context and consequences and its implications for the actual production of social work research, we agree with Webb (2001) that it inclines to the imposition of an orthodoxy in terms of desirable and acceptable knowledge. We would go further and suggest that the scientism implicit in the dominant conception of evidence-based practice that has infiltrated social work suggests that it is both possible and desirable for us to don a metaphorical white coat in approaching the social. That is, to isolate actions, events and processes antiseptically from the broader contexts within which they are situated. Such scientism tends to the depoliticisation of social work research, mirroring a similar depoliticisation of social work itself.

This narrowly conceived understanding of what constitutes evidence (and hence legitimate forms of research) pays allegiance to the 'flag of truth, while saying nothing about the country for which it stands' (Gouldner, 1973, p. 65). Putting the emphasis on exploring the 'effectiveness, efficiency and economy of policy ... [as] reflected in its increasing preoccupation with managerially and professionally defined outcomes and outcome measurement' (Beresford and Evans, 1999, p. 672), evidence-based practice thus conceived leaves – or rather seeks to leave – unexplored the more fundamental causes of the 'social problems' to which it attends. It also seeks to bracket the essentially political questions concerning our society's collective aims and purposes [eds: see also Humphries, this volume]. One can immediately see the attraction of these implicit claims to objectivity and technical efficiency for the politicians of the 'third way'; their appeal to calm rationality seems beyond the choice between Left and Right. For Webb, the 'legitimation of a particular type of formal rationality in social work' (2001 p. 73) constitutes the main ideological function of evidence-based practice.

It is not necessary to take a simplistic 'conspiratorial' view either of the causes or the consequences of the emergence of certain forms of evidence-based practice, in the UK and elsewhere. Social workers and social work researchers may voluntarily succumb to the inducements of orthodoxy. As Hopkins has noted (1996, p. 33):

> The gravest danger to the status of the [*sic*] professional intellectuals lies not from ministers ... but from the possibility of corruption of the professional ideal by those amongst their ranks who distort their judgement in return for personal advantage.

Our point is that social work research in its currently privileged form has become subject to the 'politics of enforcement' and the drive to 'modernise, rationalise, managerialise and order' (Parton, 2000, p. 461), much as social work itself has, and for many of the same reasons. Not only are we being led to a narrowly constructed notion of welfare, but also to a similarly constrained notion of what constitutes knowledge. A kind of cross-contamination has occurred whereby the scientism of the one reinforces the depoliticisation of the other.

Knowledge and power

Evidence-based practice has not been the only game in town, however. Beresford and Evans (1999) have described the emergence of participatory and emancipatory forms of research, contributory elements in a 'progressive response' (as opposed to the 'reactionary' one) to the changing contours of the welfare state. These are approaches which

> [i]nstead of endorsing the traditional 'scientific' research values of neutrality, objectivity and distance, which 'evidence based' inquiry has re-emphasised ... [question] both their desirability and feasibility ... [and value] people's first-hand direct experience as a basis for knowledge. (Beresford and Evans, 1999, pp. 672–3)

Emancipatory approaches to social work research, with their roots in feminist, disability, and black people's movements, have been seen to offer a possible means of resisting managerialist and narrowly instrumental research agendas (Beresford and Evans, 1999; Dullea and Mullender, 1999). But beyond this, such approaches imply, according to the 'Toronto Group' (see Beresford and Evans, 1999) 'changing the role and relations of research with research participants ...

from extending professional knowledge, power and control to the liberation and emancipation of research participants' (Beresford and Evans, 1999, p. 673). By contrast with the statements of even the most radical postpositivists this reads like a manifesto. It is, at the very least, an unequivocal assertion of the political potential of social work research.

This is not an unreasonable argument to make if one accepts, following Foucault (1980; 1988), the intimate inter-relationship of knowledge and power, and acknowledges 'the link between the empowerment of oppressed people and the development and distribution of knowledge' (Pease, 2002, p. 141). Pease's argument (after Ranson, 1993) is that 'political struggle can ... be conceptualised as the struggle between different knowledges'. That is to say that the production of social work knowledge, in this instance through research, by its very nature also operates politically. This point is mirrored in Peile and McCouat's assertion that

> ... we need to get on with the collective job of exploring a creative way forward which allows and preserves social work's capacity, on the one hand, to understand a variety of voices and to critique dominating voices ... and, on the other hand, to be able to respond in a clear, enthusiastic, imaginative way to unlock the potential of the people with whom social workers work, particularly those who have been the most constrained and limited. (Peile and McCouat, 1997, p. 357)

This observation implicitly draws together ideas about 'emancipatory' social work research and the parallel development of 'empowerment practice' in social work. The discourse of empowerment has come to be regarded in many circles as the hallmark of progressive social work theory, research and practice (see Adams, 1996; Baistow, 1994; Cruickshank, 1993). The common thread linking these three contexts is the idea that service users' knowledge has an epistemically privileged status (Narayan, 1989) yet is ignored or underutilised in both research and practice. Taylor (1997) notes the re-emergence of interest in 'grass roots' knowledge in both social work practice and in social work research, and this is seen by Powell (2002, p. 20) as 'no accident', given the context of 'deepening inequality, poverty and social exclusion'. Some attempts have been made to locate empowering forms of practice in an explicit recognition of social work's more radical potential. For example, Wise has suggested that empowerment practice '... involves the commitment to encourage oppressed people to understand how structural oppression in its various forms impacts upon them as individuals and to enable them thereby to take back some control in their lives' (1995, p. 108).

Nonetheless, we should be wary of unsophisticated approaches to emancipatory research. As Powell (2002) has noted, these can sometimes lead to the neglect of structural considerations in favour of 'local' solutions; to an uncritical consumerism; to a naïve privileging of particular 'voices'; to a paralysing relativism; and, possibly, to the neglect of theory building.

To overcome these limitations, Powell advocates the development of a 'form of dialogic communication within the research process ...' (*ibid.*, p. 30). She also highlights 'the centrality of negotiating skills and reflexivity, alongside a more creative use of conventional research skills ...' (*ibid.*). Such a conception of research recognises that

> Social work research, like social work practice, involves multiple accountabilities. For the researcher, this demands attention to theoretical and methodological issues underpinning the research, alongside the pursuit of an approach congruent with social work's commitment to participation and empowering forms of practice. (*ibid.*, pp. 22–3)

Examples of what this might look like on the ground remain fairly few and far between, although there are some (see Hayes and Humphries, 1999; Higham, 2001).

Back to basics: epistemology, judgement and justification

It is a great irony that while the central contention of evidence-based practice is the appeal to the 'facts', to the empirical evidence, there is, as Gibbs and Gambrill (2002) have noted, little evidence to support the contention that *it* (i.e. evidence-based practice) 'works'. Yet, it is this question of justification, how to justify choosing between different accounts, goals, methods, explanations, that lies at the heart of the practice of social work, the doing of social work research, and the development and critique of theories of knowledge. As regards the research contribution to social work, our view is that we should not seek to privilege one methodological approach over others. Unlike those who are dogmatic proponents of evidence-based practice, and those who cannot embrace contingency other than in statements of statistical error and probability, we would wish to continue to acknowledge the tentative and contingent nature of both their ideas and 'knowledge' and those of others – including ourselves – who occupy different positions. We remain epistemological agnostics, unconvinced, but, philosophically at least, open to a variety of possibilities.

In adopting this stance – one that might be termed a 'weak' relativist position – we nonetheless think that some empirical statements remain more accurate than others, and that some theoretical propositions are more adequately developed than others, both conceptually and logically. We accept the need to develop some system of/for checking our efforts at gaining more valid and more reliable knowledge, as well as for also employing the analytical tools of logic and the social processes of argumentation in challenging what might seem to be 'natural', intuitive, or uncontentious suppositions about social phenomena. Indeed, in contrast to the epistemological certainty espoused within the evidence-based practice movement, this is precisely where those who are antagonistic to such positivistic simplicities are directing their efforts. Within recent social work writing there are a number of different examples of this. In his exposition of qualitative research approaches, Gould (2000) suggests seven standards that might be applied to the question of the adequacy of the evidence thereby gathered [eds:

see also Gould, this volume]. These include the adequacy of the description of the events, the claims for typicality, and theoretical and conceptual adequacy. Sheppard and his colleagues (2000) take a different direction, proposing a 'reflexive process model' for the generation, refinement and analysis of hypotheses.

Significant though these efforts are, not least in so far as they are taking place within social work, our main point is not simply to argue for the merits of qualitative approaches in contradistinction to the 'knowledge' produced by other research methods, or for relevance or validity as arising from some form of reflexive procedure. While epistemology is often presented and understood as a meta-narrative, that is, an account or analysis that seeks to place itself conceptually 'above' other more substantive debates, such as those in the social sciences, or in social and political life, it is, nonetheless, itself a human creation. Thus, while it offers useful and challenging perspectives on other discussions, it should not, ultimately, be privileged. As Smith observes, 'man [*sic*] is the measure of all the measures that man has' (1997, p. 86). Ultimately, epistemology too can be seen to be a normative enterprise. That is, one which seeks to make claims of preference, in this case discriminating between differing accounts, explanations or positions. Thus while like others we may seek the chimerical goal of 'truth', and sift and select propositions according to whichever epistemological principles and procedures we espouse, we are only too well aware that these latter should not be reified or given the status of 'rules for the direction of mind', such as Descartes hoped to establish. For, as Morton (1997) notes:

> The history of epistemology and the history of knowledge itself, has shown that this assumption is at best extremely dubious … In this way epistemology is like our other beliefs: we begin with assumptions, use them to evaluate evidence and form new beliefs, and then eventually abandon the assumptions with which we began. (p. 219)

Resistance to intellectual imperialism, whether the impetus to orthodoxy arises from the best intentions of some exponents of evidence-based practice or from more deliberate efforts to marginalise or exclude critical voices, must in part be based upon a critical and reflexive understanding of the possibilities of knowledge. Here we find ourselves in a difficult – if not entirely unfamiliar – situation. Like others, we would seek the comfort of a coherent and all-embracing epistemological and ontological position. But this is not available to us. In the final analysis, we must live with uncertainty and contingency in our assumptions and statements about our social worlds. There are many ways of knowing and many types of knowledge (Hartman, 1994). In this, we detect a strong echo of what constitutes social work practice itself. Much of what is done at an individual, interpersonal level in social work involves some attempt to appreciate another person's perceptions and emotions. These interactions involve subjective elements, which are communicated and received subjectively, and cannot have precisely the same meanings for others, whether party to the discussion or not. The recognition of this phenomenological dimension to human experience does not, however, mean that effective communication or intervention is impossible, rather than often 'merely' difficult; rather, it reinforces our recognition of the particularity and subjectivity of human experience.

Conclusion

'Objectivists' might see our 'weak relativism' as epistemological weakness, but we see it as a mark of our engagement with the world as it is. That is, with a social world of contingency and ultimate uncertainty, but, nonetheless, a world in which it is neither unreasonable nor irrational to expect some predictability and reliability in daily life, even if our capacity for generalisation is limited by the cognitive, epistemological and social considerations that both mediate and shape the acts of 'knowing'. Implicit within contemporary debates about social work knowledge there is often an assumption that a more authoritative and less contested position can be achieved. We contend that it is unlikely that such a point can be reached, for both epistemological and social/historical reasons.

If we accept that social work is an interstitial profession, located between the wider society and particular groups and individuals, it is inevitable that we will occupy contested territory. That is where we belong. We see no contradiction in accepting different ways of knowing and different forms of knowledge in response to these contingencies. While we wish to reassert the importance of meaning and subjectivity, we also wish to lay claim to the tools of reason and logic, for these are not irrevocably wedded to an objectivist epistemology (O'Neill, 1995; Smith, 1997). When we acknowledge the fact of multiple perspectives we do not wish to romanticise narratives of oppression, or necessarily to privilege them. While we accept the important sense in which people do have privileged knowledge of their own particular situations, that is, that no one else knows better than the person directly concerned what her/his life is like, we agree with Narayan (1989) that they do not necessarily know best why it is that way or how best to change it. Thus we would, for example, wish to seek 'evidence' about the poor life chances and social marginalisation in which claims of oppression consist. Obviously, one cannot proceed in any endeavour that is laden with meaning and subjectivity without some consideration of how different realities are to be engaged with and new ones shaped. Consequently, our goal in this context is to find ways of engaging, recording, reconciling, or even selecting among multiple accounts, without resorting to any hubristic presumptions of infallibility.

More broadly, we insist that many of the questions to which we might seek answers in the field of social work and social welfare are not amenable to the procedures of technical–rational enquiry advocated by proponents of evidence-based practice who claim simply to seek and apply an appraisal of the 'facts'. Nor can they be resolved through epistemological reflection. They are questions whose answers lie in a different domain of human social life, the political–moral. That being so, social work researchers should not only seek to shape practice and influence policy, but also to embrace the intellectual role of problematiser and critic and enjoy being disputatious, controversial, sectional and partisan. Just like the best social workers.

References

Adams, R. (1996), *Social Work and Empowerment*, Macmillan, Basingstoke.

Bailey, R. and Brake, M. (eds) (1975), *Radical Social Work*, Edward Arnold, London.

Baistow, K. (1994), 'Liberation and regulation: some paradoxes of empowerment', *Critical Social Policy*, **14**(3) (issue 42), pp. 34–46.

Beck, U. (1994), 'The reinvention of politics: towards a theory of reflexive modernization', in Beck, U., Giddens, A. and Lash, S., *Reflexive Modernization: Politics, Tradition and Aesthetics in the Modern Social Order*, Polity, Cambridge, pp. 1–55.

Bell, D. (1982), *The Social Sciences Since the Second World War*, Transaction Books, New Brunswick, NJ.

Beresford, P. and Evans, C. (1999), 'Research Note: Research and empowerment', *British Journal of Social Work*, **29**(5), pp. 671–7.

Bloom, M. (ed.) (1994), *Single-System Designs in the Social Services: Issues and Options for the 1990s*, Haworth, New York.

Blyth, E. (2001), 'The impact of the first term of the New Labour Government on social work in Britain: the interface between education policy and social work', *British Journal of Social Work*, **31**(4), pp. 563–77.

Bulmer, M. (ed.) (1978), *Social Policy Research*, Macmillan, London.

Butler, I. (2003), 'Doing good research and doing it well: ethical awareness and the production of social work research', *Social Work Education*, **22**(1), pp. 19–30.

Butler, I. and Drakeford, M. (1997), 'Tough guise? The politics of youth justice', *Probation Journal*, **44**(4), pp. 216–19.

Butler, I and Drakeford, M. (2000), 'Editorial', *British Journal of Social Work*, **30**(1), pp. 1–2.

Butler, I. and Drakeford, M. (2001a), 'Tough justice? Youth justice under New Labour', *Probation Journal*, **48**(2), pp. 119–24.

Butler, I. and Drakeford, M. (2001b), 'Which Blair project? Communitarianism, social authoritarianism and social work', *Journal of Social Work*, **1**(1), pp. 7–19.

Bywaters, P. and McLeod, E. (2001), 'The impact of New Labour health policy on social services: a new deal for service users' health?', *British Journal of Social Work*, **31**(4), pp. 579–94.

Cheetham, J. and Deakin, N. (1997), 'Research Note: Assessing the assessment – some reflections on the 1996 Higher Education Funding Council's Research Assessment Exercise', *British Journal of Social Work*, **27**(3), pp. 435–42.

Clark, C.L. (2000), *Social Work Ethics: Politics, Principles and Practice*, Macmillan, Basingstoke.

Corcoran, K. and Fischer, J. (1987), *Measures for Clinical Practice*, Free Press, New York.

Cruickshank, B. (1993), 'Revolutions within: self government and self esteem', *Economy and Society*, **22**(3), pp. 327–44.

Department of Health (2001), *Research Governance Framework for Health and Social Care*, <http://www.doh.gov.uk/research/rd3/nhsrandd/researchgovernance.htm>.

Donzelot, J. (1980), *The Policing of Families: Welfare Versus the State*, Hutchinson, London.

Donzelot, J. (1988), 'The promotion of the social', *Economy and Society*, **17**(3), pp. 395–427.

Drakeford, M. (2000), *Privatisation and Social Policy*, Longman, Harlow.

Dullea, K. and Mullender, A. (1999), 'Evaluation and empowerment', in Shaw, I. and Lishman, J. (eds), *Evaluation and Social Work Practice*, Sage, London, pp. 81–100.

Everitt, A. and Hardiker, P. (1996), *Evaluating for Good Practice*, Macmillan, Basingstoke.

Ferguson, H. (2001), 'Social work, individualization and life politics', *British Journal of Social Work*, **31**(1), pp. 41–55.

Foucault, M. (1980), *Power/Knowledge: Selected Interviews and Other Writings 1972–1977*, ed. C. Gordon, Harvester, Brighton.

Foucault, M. (1988), 'Technologies of the self', in Martin, L.H., Gutman, H. and Hutton, P.H. (eds), *Technologies of the Self: A Seminar with Michel Foucault*, University of Massachusetts Press, Amherst, MA., pp. 16–49.

Fraser, M., Taylor, M.J., Jackson, R. and O'Jack, J. (1991), 'Social work and science: many ways of knowing?', *Social Work Research and Abstracts*, **27**(4), pp. 5–15.

Gibbs, L. and Gambrill, E. (2002), 'Evidence-based practice: counterarguments to objections', *Research on Social Work Practice*, **12**(3), pp. 452–76.

Glass, N. (2001), 'What works for children – the political issues', *Children and Society*, **15**(1), pp. 14–20.

Gould, N. (2000), 'Qualitative research and the development of best attainable knowledge in social work', paper presented in the *Theorising Social Work Research* seminar series, no. 5, 27 April, University of Wales, Cardiff, and now available at <http:www.elsc.org.uk/socialcareresource/tswr/seminar5/gould.htm>.

Gouldner, A.W. (1973), *For Sociology: Renewal and Critique in Sociology Today*, Allen Lane, London.

Hammersley, M. (2000), 'Varieties of social research: a typology', *International Journal of Social Research Methodology*, **3**(3), pp. 221–9.

Hartman, A. (1994), 'Setting the theme: many ways of knowing', in Sherman, E. and Reid, W.J. (eds), *Qualitative Research in Social Work*, Columbia University Press, New York, pp. 459–63.

Hayes, D. and Humphries, B. (1999), 'Negotiating contentious research topics', in Broad, B. (ed.), *The Politics of Social Work Research and Evaluation*, Birmingham, Venture Press, pp. 19–30.

Higham, P.E. (2001), 'Developing an interactive approach in social work research: the example of a research study on head injury', *British Journal of Social Work*, **31**(2), pp. 197–212.

Hopkins, J. (1996), 'Social work through the looking glass', in Parton, N. (ed.), *Social Theory, Social Change and Social Work*, Routledge, London, pp. 19–35.

Ife, J. (1997), *Rethinking Social Work: Towards Critical Practice*, Longman, Melbourne.

International Association of Schools of Social Work (2002), *Mission Statement*, <http://www.iassw.soton.ac.uk/Generic/mission.asp?lang=en>.

International Federation of Social Workers (2002), *The Ethics of Social Work – Principles and Standards*, <http://www.ifsw.org/Publications/4.4pub.html>.

Jones, C. (1983), *State Social Work and the Working Class*, Macmillan, London.

Jones, C. (1998), 'Social work and society', in Adams, R., Dominelli, L. and Payne, M. (eds), *Social Work: Themes, Issues and Critical Debates*, Macmillan, Basingstoke, pp. 34–43.

Jones, C. (2001), 'Voices from the front line: state social workers and New Labour', *British Journal of Social Work*, **31**(4), pp. 547–62.

Jordan, B. (1990), *Social Work in an Unjust Society*, Harvester Wheatsheaf, Hemel Hempstead.

Jordan, B. (2001), 'Tough love: social work, social exclusion and the third way', *British Journal of Social Work*, **31**(4), pp. 527–46.

Lewis, J. (2002), *Fluctuating Fortunes of the Social Sciences Since 1945*. A Working Paper for the Commission on the Future of the Social Sciences, Academy of Learned Societies for the Social Sciences, <http://www.the-academy.org.uk/docs/LewisFluctuatingFortunes.doc>.

Macdonald, G. (1994), 'Developing empirically-based practice in probation', *British Journal of Social Work*, **24**(4), pp. 405–27.

Macdonald, G. (1998), 'Promoting evidence-based practice in child protection', *Clinical Child Psychology and Psychiatry*, **3**(1), pp. 71–85.

Macdonald, G. and Sheldon, B., with Gillespie, J. (1992), 'Contemporary studies of the effectiveness of social work', *British Journal of Social Work*, **22**(6), pp. 615–43.

McGuire, J. (ed.) (1995), *What Works: Reducing Reoffending – Guidelines from Research and Practice*, Wiley, Chichester.

Morton, A. (1997), *A Guide Through the Theory of Knowledge*, Blackwell, Oxford.

Narayan, U. (1989), 'Working together across differences', in Compton, B. and Galaway, B. (eds), *Social Work Processes*, Brooks-Cole, Pacific Grove, CA., pp. 317–28.

O'Neill, J. (1995), *The Poverty of Postmodernism*, Routledge, London.

Owen, D. (1995), *Nietzsche, Politics and Modernity: A Critique of Liberal Reason*, Sage, London.

Parton, N. (1999), 'Ideology, politics and policy', in Stevenson, O. (ed.), *Child Welfare in the UK: 1948–1998*, Blackwell Science, Oxford, pp. 3–21.

Parton, N. (2000), 'Some thoughts on the relationship between theory and practice in and for social work', *British Journal of Social Work*, **30**(4), pp. 449–63. (An earlier version, presented in the *Theorising Social Work Research* seminar series, no. 1, 26 May 1999, Brunel University, is now available at <http://www.elsc.org.uk/socialcareresource/tswr/seminar1/parton.htm>.)

Pease, B. (2002), 'Rethinking empowerment: a postmodern reappraisal for emancipatory practice', *British Journal of Social Work*, **32**(2), pp. 135–47.

Peile, C. and McCouat, M. (1997), 'The rise of relativism: the future of theory and knowledge development in social work', *British Journal of Social Work*, **27**(3), pp. 343–60.

Popper, K.R. (1963), *Conjectures and Refutations: The Growth of Scientific Knowledge*, Routledge and Kegan Paul, London.

Powell, J. (2002), 'The changing conditions of social work research', *British Journal of Social Work*, **32**(1), pp. 17–33.

Pray, K. (1949), *Social Work in a Revolutionary Age*, University of Pennsylvania Press, Philadelphia, PA.

Ranson, J. (1993), 'Feminism, difference and discourse: the limits of discursive analysis for feminism', in Ramazanoglu, C. (ed.), *Up Against Foucault: Explorations of Some Tensions Between Foucault and Feminism*, Routledge, London, pp. 123–46.

Reid, W.J. (1994), 'Reframing the epistemological debate', in Sherman, E., and Reid, W.J. (eds), *Qualitative Research in Social Work*, Columbia University Press, New York, pp. 464–81.

Sackett, D.L., Richardson, W.S., Rosenberg, W. and Haynes, R.B. (1997), *Evidence-Based Medicine: How to Practice and Teach EBP*, Churchill Livingstone, New York.

Shaw, I. and Shaw, A. (1997), 'Keeping social work honest; evaluating as profession and practice', *British Journal of Social Work*, **27**(6), pp. 847–69.

Sheldon, B. (2001), 'The validity of evidence-based practice in social work: a reply to Stephen Webb', *British Journal of Social Work*, **31**(5), pp. 801–9.

Sheppard, M., Newstead, S., Di Caccavo, A. and Ryan, K. (2000), 'Reflexivity and the development of process knowledge in social work: a classification and empirical study', *British Journal of Social Work*, **30**(4), pp. 465–88. (Some of the material discussed in this article was presented (by Sheppard), in the *Theorising Social Work Research* seminar series, no. 1, 26 May 1999, Brunel University, under the title 'Reflection, reflexivity and knowledge for social work practice'.)

Simpkin, M. (1979), *Trapped Within Welfare*, Macmillan, London.

Smith, B.H. (1997), *Belief and Resistance: Dynamics of Contemporary Intellectual Controversy*, Harvard University Press, Cambridge, MA.

Taylor, G. (1997), 'Ethical issues in practice: participatory social research and groups', *Groupwork*, **9**(2), pp. 110–27.

Thyer, B. (1989), 'First principles of practice research', *British Journal of Social Work*, **19**(4), pp. 309–23.

Trinder, L. (1996), 'Social work research: the state of the art (or science)', *Child and Family Social Work*, **1**(4), pp. 233–42.

Webb, S.A. (2001), 'Some considerations on the validity of evidence-based practice in social work', *British Journal of Social Work*, **31**(1), pp. 57–79.

Williams, M. (2000), 'Social research – the emergence of a discipline?', *International Journal of Social Research Methodology*, **3**(2), pp. 157–66.

Wise, S. (1995), 'Feminist ethics in practice', in Hugman, R. and Smith, D. (eds), *Ethical Issues in Social Work*, Routledge, London, pp. 104–19.

Chapter 4

Gender and Knowledge in Social Work

Karen Lyons and Imogen Taylor

Introduction

Social work has been and continues generally to be viewed as a 'women's profession', both in Britain, ever since its inception there over 100 years ago (Walton, 1975), and in most of its current manifestations in other countries around the world (Lyons, 1999). This chapter reviews the gender (im)balance in social work, its influence on recent developments, and its implications for the future of UK social work in the field and in the academy. In so-doing we (re-)examine some ideas about the status of social work as a profession and as a discipline, and about knowledge. More specifically, we draw on recent research and scholarship to explore the relationship between gender and the drive towards professionalisation, the development of social work as an academic discipline, and the creation and transmission of knowledge in social work. We argue that the gender dimension has been one factor (among several) that has influenced the development of social work in its struggle to assert professional and academic credibility; and we suggest ways in which some recent changes in external environments might exacerbate or mitigate past and present patterns.

It has been suggested that, because most of its practitioners, service users and students are women, there is widespread commitment to feminism in social work (Payne, 2001). While the breadth and depth of such commitment might be questioned, we concur with the view that feminist perspectives have had considerable relevance and influence in informing the development of social work knowledge and practice, and we draw on feminist ideas in our analysis in this chapter. Dominelli states that 'feminism has placed gender issues on the social work map and transformed its gender-blind nature ... [although] given that social work is a profession comprised primarily of women, its impact has not been as widespread as one would have expected' (2002, p. 99). She identifies possible reasons for this, including that it seems still to be the case, despite the predominance of women numerically, that men are disproportionately represented in positions of power, both in the field and in the academy, and are thus best-placed to influence the ways in which knowledge is constructed and used. Additionally, social work is significantly subject to external direction and control, in ways that may also have a gender dimension.

We should preface our discussion with an acknowledgement both of the differences between and amongst women, *and* of the ways in which other factors, such as class and race, interact with gender to shape the experiences of women as social work practitioners, managers, academics, students and service users. As Acker observes, 'In recent years feminists have furiously debated how differences among women can be accorded the respect and analytical importance they deserve without destroying the integrity of the concept of "women"' (Acker, 1994, p. 134, quoted in Brooks, 1997, p. 4). However, we are concerned here specifically with the gender dimension, and our analysis draws on studies that suggest that there are differences between (most) women and (most) men in terms of how they relate, learn and know. These differences are very relevant to social work; we shall argue that they operate both as 'internal gender factors' influencing the development of both the discipline and the profession, and as 'external gender factors' in terms of the effects of gendered norms and power systems in the 'external' environments in which social work is practised, studied and researched.

Social work as a 'women's profession'

Historically, despite there being grounds for viewing it as a 'women's profession', social work has consistently been managed by men and/or subject to the influence of men, including men based outside the profession, for instance in philanthropic or political roles (Howe, 1986; Walton, 1975). Annual studies in the UK in the 1990s indicated that about 80 per cent of all students completing qualifying social work training were women and that about 80 per cent of all newly qualified social workers entered employment in local authority social services or social work departments (Wallis-Jones and Lyons, 2000). However, a recent study of those employed in a range of roles within the statutory-sector social care workforce found that whereas 86 per cent of such staff in English local authority social services departments were female, only 65 per cent of the managers surveyed (one of the broad groups in the study) were women (Ginn and Fisher, 1999, p. 129). Furthermore, the more senior the management position, the less likely it is to be occupied by a woman. Ginn and Fisher cite various Department of Health/Social Services Inspectorate statistics to show how little this changed through the 1990s, with by 1997 only 20 per cent of the directors heading the 192 social services authorities across the UK as a whole being women (*ibid.*, p. 130). We speculate later about the implications of recent and current organisational and cultural changes in the public sector for women in – or aspiring to – managerial positions in social work. Meanwhile, what might be the implications of this gender imbalance for the status of social work as an occupation?

It has been suggested that the so-called 'women's professions' developed when women transferred the caring functions they had learned and practised at home to new contexts of paid employment, including nursing, teaching and social work, bringing with them 'an ethic of care' (Baines, 1991, p. 36). The origins and history of these developments specifically in relation to social work have been addressed elsewhere (Lorenz, 1994; Walton, 1975) and will be alluded to here only briefly. Baines suggests that the development of a strong core of career women in these several fields was limited during the first half of the twentieth century, when these professions were viewed mainly as a stepping-stone to marriage. (An alternative formulation might suggest that the career aspirations of some women were in fact denied on marriage.) There were some early signs of moves towards professionalisation through the establishment of training courses (see later). In the case of social work, Perry and Cree suggest that notwithstanding the predominance of women in the occupation, 'men were seen as critical to the professionalisation project since only then would social workers command a salary "better than that of a shorthand typist"' (Perry and Cree, 2003, p. 376, quoting a phrase from Younghusband, 1947).

Work on the sociology of professions led Etzioni (1969) to designate the 'women's professions' as 'semi-professions'. However, Witz has more recently linked the notion of professionalisation to patriarchy and power, suggesting that 'the generic notion of profession is also a gendered notion as it takes what are, in fact, the successful professional projects of class-privileged male actors at a particular point in history and in particular societies to be the paradigmatic case of professions' (Witz, 1991, p. 675). One defining characteristic of a profession has been its capacity to regulate entry (Friedson, 1986), and male dominance in the traditional professions (the church, the law, medicine and the military services) made it difficult for women to gain access to these fields until almost the middle of the twentieth century. A second, and related, key characteristic is control of a specialised knowledge base. The contested question of the knowledge base of social work will be discussed in more detail later, but each 'semi-profession' has certainly been concerned to increase its status, in the eyes both of other professions and the public, by raising its educational requirements and strengthening its regulatory institutions. This is further evidenced in social work in the UK by recent and ongoing changes in regulatory arrangements and the move to a degree-level qualifying award, although in the changed conditions of the twenty-first century this is arguably attributable as much to external forces as to internal manoeuvres.

In the terms of Witz's analysis, one might speculate that as each semi-profession has sought to formalise its training programmes and institute forms of self-regulation it has risked replicating the male paradigm of professionalisation. But there may be other significant differences between what have traditionally been regarded as male professions and those chosen by (or seen as suitable for) women. For instance, Baines (1991) has argued that while men have emphasised expertise, women have emphasised an ethic of service. Glazer and Slater, studying the first half of the twentieth century, noted (1987, p. 229) that '... successful professionals were objective, competitive, individualistic and predictable: they were also scornful of nurturant, expressive and familial styles of interaction' (quoted in Baines, 1991, p. 55). In the case of social work, both the nature of one aspect of the role ('caring') and professionalisation have reinforced gendered patterns, and Baines again draws on other work to suggest that when men demonstrate interpersonal skills in business they are highly valued, whereas when women apply them in caring they can be viewed as sentimental and unscientific. Baines's proposal in the light of this (Baines, 1991, p. 66, citing Daniels, 1987) is that 'The challenge is to identify the knowledge and skills derived from women's caring and value these in the same way as knowledge derived from more traditional modes of inquiry'. We shall return to this later in discussing knowledge; meanwhile, we next consider how gender might affect the development and status of social work in the academy.

Disciplinary development and the gender factor

Before exploring ideas about the development of social work as an academic discipline, and the relevance of gender to this process, it might be useful to consider the gender aspects of the overall higher education context within which social work education and some of social work's overall output of research takes place. Brooks (1997) describes higher education institutions (HEIs) as 'masculinist', with limited and rigid career patterns for women, thereby suggesting that there has been little change in what were earlier dubbed 'bastions of male power and privilege' (Hansard Society, 1990). Brooks's research concerned academic women in the UK and New Zealand, and she points to a contradiction between the image of an academic community as characterised by equality and the reality for academic women; many of those in her study identified sex discrimination as impacting on their careers. Ramazanoglu (1987, cited in Brooks, 1997, p. 5) takes this further, claiming that women in higher education are perceived as actual or potential threats to order and that mechanisms to subordinate women need to be understood as forms of violence.

Brooks's research identified academic women as being under-represented in positions of leadership. Among the obstacles to promotion to senior positions that she reported was lack of a perceived career structure, particularly for research staff and staff on temporary contracts. Additionally, she found that women academics were more likely to be involved in a range of additional responsibilities which did not enhance career prospects and were a drain on energies required for research and publishing. Women were also more likely to be on departmental or faculty, rather than university, committees. In turn, strategies to support women, such as mentorship and role modelling, were difficult to operationalise due to the limited number of women in senior positions. Women's disadvantaged situation tended to be compounded by limited provisions for child care and a lack of recognition of the impact of pregnancy and care roles on their careers. Lyons (1999) has identified a further factor that may be significant in professional education, namely the later stage at which those involved typically enter academic work, having chosen to engage in professional practice after initial qualification. This seems likely to have an additional impact on female academics in the women's professions, since more 'late starters' will be women than men.

Research relating gender factors to specific disciplines remains limited (Brooks, 1997). However, the factors identified in Brooks's analysis as constraining women's careers in higher education have also been suggested by Cree (1997), writing specifically about social work. Mirroring social work in the field, social work in the academy is traditionally an area where women outnumber men, both as staff and as students. However, with regard to staffing, there is evidence that men are more likely to hold professorial or managerial posts. For instance, in the UK, membership of the Association of Professors of Social Work suggests that less than one in three professors of social work are women (Dominelli, 2002, p. 102), whereas the female-to-male proportion of lecturers may be as high as 6:1 (Lyons, 1999, p. 130). The predominance of women overall differentiates social work from many other academic subject areas, including across the social sciences and in some other fields of professional education; this, we suggest, may have a bearing on perceptions of the discipline by other academics. This raises the question of whether the often covert or even unconscious views about women, and their unfair treatment in HEIs, both evidenced above, may extend to disciplines where women are in the majority.

We turn now to the development of social work as a discipline. Toulmin (1972) suggested that each discipline is characterised by 'its own body of concepts, methods and fundamental aims' (p. 139), and that disciplinary knowledge, expressed in a complex web of concepts, is created and changed by what may be called 'communities of knowers' (see Lyons, 1999, p. 62). Thus academics are concerned with stability (through transmission of knowledge) and change (through critical discussion and research). Social work's development to its current state in the UK from a form of professional training, albeit importantly university-based, drawing heavily on knowledge from other disciplines as well as learning from practice placements (Smith, 1965) has spanned a century, and has been a difficult process (Lyons, 1999). Social work has frequently been characterised as unable to generate its own knowledge base and as only minimally engaged in research and theorising. We would argue that these criticisms are now being more actively addressed, but also that there may be a gender dimension to both the reasons for and the perceptions of this situation (as discussed later).

At this stage in the discussion we can note in passing some ambivalence about ownership of the title 'academic' among social work educators (Lyons, 1999), and one might question whether this reflects the anti-intellectualism evident to some degree in the wider profession (Jones, 1996) and/or discomfort with the 'elitism' often associated with specialisation, of which social work in the academy can be seen as one form. Both possibilities might have a gender basis, in that they may reflect feminist ideals about the value to be attributed to personal experience and concerning egalitarian relationships, which the high proportion of (women) educators in this area may share (Belenky *et al.*, 1986). In addition, there may be suspicion of the term 'academic' as conveying an expert status and a particular mode of relationship and pedagogy that would not be thought appropriate in professional education. Perhaps the long association of the term 'academic' with male post-holders has imbued the role with assumptions about particular values and ways of behaving which could be questioned and modified, rather than rejected, since the issue of a secure professional identity is surely as important to social work educators in the academy as it is to practitioners in the field.

With regard to students, Toulmin (1972) suggests that they are 'enculturated' into disciplines through a form of apprenticeship, completion of which is marked by the student's ability not only to internalise the relevant concepts, aims and methods, but also to engage critically with current knowledge and to develop it through her/his own research. We would argue that students participating in forms of professional education are expected to develop a professional (rather more than a disciplinary) identity and that experience in the field (rather than in the academy) is crucial to this process. There has thus been relatively little attention given, for instance, to the development of doctoral studies – induction into the role of academic and researcher – until recently (Lyons, 2002), although arguably the emphasis placed on reflexivity in practice (Schön, 1983) and growing interest in practitioner research (Fuller and Petch, 1995) mirror the development of critical and research capacities generally seen as fundamental to the future development of subjects traditionally labelled 'disciplines'.

The foregoing points raise wider questions about the differences between professional education – a term which we use here to refer to a complex of activities located in higher education and thus including research and theorising in and about the professional field as well as the provision of qualifying and advanced training – and disciplines as conventionally understood; and whether there might be gender dimensions in the research and debate in this area. Taylor (1997) has suggested that exploration of the cultures and predominant epistemological assumptions of those disciplines which involve professional education has largely been neglected until relatively recently. A significant study of 12 disciplines by Becher included three which train people for particular forms of professional practice, namely engineering, law and pharmacy; all three could be regarded as traditionally 'male' in terms of their staff and student populations. He noted that 'women are significantly under-represented in the physical and social sciences but they appear in sizeable numbers in female orientated subject areas such as ... home economics and in relatively low status fields such as library science and education' (Becher, 1989, p. 125). The lack of attention hitherto to 'women's disciplines' has been partly addressed in more recent studies of nurse, teacher or social work education (e.g. Eraut, 1995; Lyons, 1999), and the revised edition of Becher's book includes a chapter on gender (Becher and Trowler, 2001).

Becher (1989) attributed the lack of research into professional education to the difficulty of distinguishing the subject from the surrounding domains of professional practice. This relates to another distinguishing feature, namely the significance of the relationship between the academic arm and the professional field, as reflected in Harman's (1989) study of six social work schools in Australia and in more recent, larger-scale research in England and Wales (Lyons, 1999). One explanation advanced for the continuing orientation to the professional field found among the academics surveyed in the latter study was that it was common for them to have been engaged previously in social work practice and/or management themselves. It seems likely that such experience has been (and in some cases still is) more highly rated in recruitment to social work lecturing posts than is the possession of higher academic qualifications, and while this may partly be related to the nature of the task, it is also possible that it reflects other findings about the value which women (in particular) place on knowledge derived from experience (Belenky *et al.*, 1986).

The consequence of this necessary orientation to the field is that a third dimension is added to the role of social work (and other professional) educators.

Most academics experience normative tensions between teaching and research; those involved in professional education have a three-way set of demands, between knowledge transmission, knowledge creation, and 'attention to the field/an external orientation'. In the case of social work, attention to the field has been identified as one possible factor detracting from the research capacity of the discipline (Lyons, 1999); arguably, it could account in part for the low ranking – in the terms of the UK Higher Education Funding Councils' periodic Research Assessment Exercises – of social work and other 'women's subjects', such as teaching and nursing. There are also indications of 'specialisation' within (academic) social work staff teams, with men more likely to be engaged in more academically prestigious areas of research and publishing and women more heavily involved in teaching and tutorial work, including placement visiting (Cree, 1997).

Finally, the degree of internal autonomy which might be suggested by the idea of a 'community of knowers', implicit in Toulmin's (1972) analysis, seems less applicable to various forms of professional education, where academics must negotiate with significant stakeholders outside the academy who are concerned to influence the definition of the subject matter and the 'relevance' of particular kinds of training and research. These include the most powerful of arbiters, the government of the day; and as the contributors to Becher's (1994) edited collection demonstrate, governments in many countries have taken a more active role since the 1980s *vis-à-vis* the regulation of most professions, with knock-on effects for professional education. Less directly, changes in generally held notions of professional roles and accountabilities raise difficult issues for the education of professionals in HEIs. Similar demands for change have also been made of higher education itself (i.e. *per se*), both as regards explicitly demonstrating 'quality' in research and teaching and in terms of the conception of the sector's role, accessibility, accountability, etc. Arguably, all this has been felt particularly acutely by social work and teaching because of their roles in maintaining and promoting the social order (Henkel, 1994; Taylor, 1994). One can also wonder whether these have been 'soft targets' relative to other professions where male networks and voices are more in evidence. 'On the academic side', as it were, perhaps gendered ideas of what constitutes a 'proper' discipline have been in play, along similar lines to Witz's (1991) analysis of professionalisation (see above), with a consequent disregard of large parts of professional education. Ironically, social work may be in sight of achieving disciplinary status – in the sense that its knowledge base and research activity are now more in evidence – at a point when greater accountability is required of all in higher education and when 'disciplinarity' itself may be going out of fashion.

Gender issues in relation to knowledge, its creation, and its transmission

In the previous section we noted Toulmin's (1972) account of disciplines as having their own concepts, methods and aims, and thence their own (changing) knowledge. While the aims and methods of social work (meaning here the academic subject area) might be recognised as distinctive – though not universally agreed in terms of their substantive content – there has been extensive dispute about the nature – and the very notion – of a body of social work knowledge and the extent to which this is distinctive and created by the discipline itself. It is apparent that social work has drawn, and continues to draw, on 'knowledge' from a wide variety of other disciplines and professional subject areas (Lyons, 1999), but this is also true of other fields involving professional education, such as medicine, where it does not seem to detract from the discipline's status. The distinctiveness of social work knowledge may lie in the way in which such knowledge – or understanding – is integrated and applied in professional practice (Payne, 2001). In this sense Payne's suggestion that we should think in terms of knowledge biases (rather than bases) has some merit, and social work might be seen as espousing a particular form of inter-disciplinarity. Barnett (1994) has suggested that the latter is more favoured in the abstract than in practice in higher education generally, and we may therefore presume that social work's apparent inter-disciplinarity does not work to its advantage (but see later). Nevertheless, it is possible that the wish to 'connect', which Belenky *et al.* (1986) describe as a characteristic of women, may render social work staff especially sympathetic to forms of knowledge that require synthesis.

A number of feminists (e.g. Harding, 1986; 1987; 1991; Rose, 1994; Stanley, 1990) have argued that knowledge is gendered; 'feminine knowledge' is conceptualised as holistic and contextual, whereas knowledge that privileges competence, its measurement, and evidence, might be conceptualised as 'masculine'. In some part these ideas connect with the fundamental critiques of conceptions of knowledge, including in particular conceptions of the kind of knowledge produced in the social sciences, which rest on assumptions from – or rather on outdated assumptions about – the natural sciences (e.g. Habermas, 1972; Taylor, 1971).

Ideas about knowledge that seem particularly relevant in thinking about social work include Polanyi's concepts of 'personal knowledge' (1958) and 'tacit knowledge' (1967). For Polanyi, all new learning takes place in the context of existing knowledge, which in turn is derived from the totality of individual experience, including that beyond the conscious recollection of the learner. Also of particular interest is Habermas's sustained critical analysis of how technical rationality and scientific knowledge have come to be valued in the contemporary world at the expense of comprehending and communicating with each other. Habermas first advanced these ideas in the mid/late 1960s; he (1966; 1972) posited three 'knowledge-guiding' interests – a 'technical' interest in the control of the world around us; a 'practical' interest in mutual understanding in the conduct of life; and an 'emancipatory' interest in freeing ourselves from seemingly 'natural' constraints. In his subsequent theory of communicative action and communicative reason (1984; 1987) – concepts which remain the core of his continuing contribution – he offers an account of the 'colonisation of the lifeworld' by system imperatives [eds: see also Lorenz, this volume; Lovelock and Powell, this volume].

In writing about professional knowledge in particular, Henkel (1995) draws on the hermeneutic dimension of Habermas's work to argue that knowledge has moral, intellectual and personal dimensions, and that its development requires dialogue between – as well as within – communities. This resonates with the requirement that professional educators work across boundaries, collaborate with a variety of stakeholders, and engage in negotiations with power systems, both inside and outside the university. Those most directly involved in professional education in a particular area bear a major responsibility in relation to entry to the profession concerned; however, decisions about the nature of the knowledge to be transmitted and the creation of new knowledge are appropriately shared with the wider profession and other stakeholders. In the particular case of social work – and perhaps this is the case with other 'women's professions' – many of the relevant stakeholder groups are more powerful (and more male-dominated) than social work educators as a group, and indeed than the social work community as a whole. This would be true of political interest groups, government departments, and the major employers, although user groups would be an exception. We return to a consideration of the nature of the knowledge required for social work later, in the context of curriculum change.

Turning to the task of 'knowledge transmission', issues about the learning styles of students should be considered. Early research on this topic tended to be based largely on male experience (e.g. Perry, 1970). A later study suggested that the female experience of learning may be different; Belenky *et al.* (1986), on the basis of research carried out in the USA, propose that women view the world from one or another of five perspectives. In the first of these, the women concerned feel alienated from received knowledge and the means of knowing, and find themselves voiceless or silent; in the second, women have adapted to the male order of the educational process and are able to receive and reproduce knowledge provided by the experts. In the third perspective, women place an over-reliance on intuitive or subjective knowledge to the exclusion of other forms, while in the fourth the emphasis is placed on learning procedures for obtaining and communicating knowledge rather than for generating it. Only from the fifth perspective is knowledge viewed as contextual, and based on the woman's own objective and subjective strategies for learning and research. Attainment of this last stage is clearly important if women (as academics and practitioners) are to engage in creating disciplinary knowledge through research and theorising (in the sense indicated by Toulmin (1972)).

In considering the development of professional knowledge, Fook and her fellow Australian colleagues (2000), writing from a feminist perspective and on the basis of a longitudinal study of social workers, conceptualise professional expertise as being holistic and contextual, rather than abstract, fixed and generalisable. They distinguish between substantive knowledge and procedural knowledge, describing the first as based on analysis of 'facts', concepts and relationships. This may be specialist knowledge, specific to a particular domain or context. Procedural knowledge is concerned with how to use substantive knowledge in situations that are conflictual and unpredictable. Procedural knowledge can be transferred across domains and assist in rapidly learning new substantive knowledge, crucial to practising effectively in conditions of change (Kemshall, 2000). The emphasis therefore shifts away from protecting elite domains of knowledge to its transferability.

In Fook *et al.*'s (2000) theory of learning, professional expertise involves the ability to create knowledge from experience in context and to transfer this knowledge to different situations. Expertise is seen as context-relevant but not context-specific. This has implications for curriculum design and pedagogy, and Fook *et al.* build on the Dreyfus and Dreyfus (1986) model of skill acquisition by adult learners, which identifies stages through which the learner advances, taking account within this framework of learning which has taken place both before students enter the formal educational setting and outside it (Polanyi, 1967; Taylor, 1997). We would suggest that personal knowledge (Eraut, 1995; Polanyi, 1958) is perhaps not sufficiently emphasised in this model, and that development of the capacity to reflect critically on the impact of one's self on both substantive and procedural knowledge is also crucial to the development of professional expertise and must be integrated into the curriculum and into teaching and learning strategies (Gould and Taylor, 1996; Taylor, 1997).

The commonly used pedagogical approaches recently in evidence in social work education (Lyons, 1999) – skills workshops, experiential activities, and tutorial work – are reflected in Fook *et al.*'s analysis. While perhaps acknowledged more widely as appropriate to the 'transmission' (or development) of professional knowledge, they might also be seen as labour-intensive and as over-concerned with 'care' (by women, for the professional development of other women), not least in the context of the resource-constrained environments which most universities have become (Cree, 1997). However, as touched on earlier, the role of higher education itself has come under increasing scrutiny in recent decades, resulting, for instance, in the expectations that all students will be equipped with skills for the workplace and that universities will 'relate' to their wider communities. Such requirements might suggest more general acceptance of methods that promote learning about interpersonal skills and/or ideas and approaches derived from outside the university. In that case, HEIs might now be a more comfortable place for social work and other forms of professional education, notwithstanding the challenge of knowledge creation – to which we now turn.

One of the rationales for the location of social work in higher education is the expectation that social work academics will contribute to new knowledge through research. We indicated earlier that the extent to which this goal has been realised has been limited and that both this and the reasons for it may have gender dimensions. There is little evidence of involvement on the part of social work or social workers in the growth in social science research during much of the twentieth century. In the UK in the 1950s and 1960s, for example, this tended to be largely within a positivist paradigm, drawing heavily on quantitative methods, and it can be noted in this regard that the often-presumed differences between men and women in respective attitudes to and aptitudes for engaging with mathematical and statistical material have apparently been confirmed – in the USA at least (Fitzgerald *et al.*, 1995). Additionally, some of the research of this kind carried out on social work in the USA in the 1960s appeared to call into question the efficacy of the casework that was then the practice norm (see Cheetham *et al.*, 1992, pp. 3–4; Sheldon, 1986). Overall, therefore, it seems likely that UK social workers themselves generally felt alienated from or suspicious of research, and that the latter was seen as an activity for experts and as unlikely to be helpful to practice. Of course there were exceptions to the positivistic orientation, such as the study by Mayer and Timms (1970); the latter was important not only in terms of its findings but as marking both an engagement with research on the part of British social work academics and a particular (qualitative) approach.

Another factor in the lack of integration of research into the activities of many members of the social work community, both inside and outside the academy, might have had its roots in the perceived need for more social workers and, somewhat ironically, in the expansion of social work training. The Younghusband Reports of the late 1940s and 1950s (1947; 1951; 1959) led to a change from social work occupying a very small place at postgraduate level in a few older universities, to its rapid expansion at sub-degree level during the 1960s and 1970s, mainly in the new polytechnics. The latter generally lacked established research traditions, and it was not until their incorporation into the university sector in 1992 that research began to take a higher priority in many institutions where social work was and is taught (Lyons, 1999). It could be argued, therefore, that the majority of social work educators were more concerned with the transmission of knowledge than with its creation; a position exacerbated by the previously mentioned preference for field experience with regard to staff appointments and by the intensive teaching styles associated with 'skills-based' training courses.

Research activities on the part of UK social work academics have nevertheless grown throughout the 1990s, as evidenced in the increased number of submissions to the periodic Research Assessment Exercises (Lyons and Orme, 1998). It also seems likely that an apparently new-found confidence in undertaking research partly reflects the influence of feminist perspectives on ideas about research design and process. In a recent text about social work evaluation, Humphries (1999) has suggested that 'feminist consciousness can inform both topics and methods', although the focus of research 'need not be exclusively on women's experiences ... nor need it be exclusively qualitative research' (p. 118). Nor, we should add, do feminist perspectives only inform research undertaken *by* women. Humphries (*ibid.*) charts the influence of feminist thinking on social research and, like previous writers (e.g. Dominelli and McLeod, 1989; Orme, 1997), identifies the significance of congruence between the values underlying social work and those reflected in the research approach. Orme (1997) sees both social work and feminism as being committed to social and personal change and concerned with relating private and public worlds. She also sees them both as stressing the iterative relationship between theory and practice, and as valuing self-knowledge and feelings as facts.

Both Orme and Humphries draw attention to Mies's writing (1993) as relevant to a consideration of knowledge creation in the professional field through research *praxis*. This requires a partnership between those who know (theorise and research) and those who do (practise), involving a reduction in the power gap between the researcher (previously seen as the expert) and those who become participants in the research process, rather than merely 'respondents' (or indeed 'objects'). This can be said to mirror a basic tenet of feminist thinking, and it has been argued that participative research designs and methodologies carry this tenet to a logical conclusion and achieve the goal of empowerment (Beresford and Evans, 1999; Everitt and Hardiker, 1996; Everitt *et al.*, 1992), a goal shared by both feminists and social workers.

Alongside the congruence in values already mentioned, Powell (1996) has suggested that some research approaches can build on skills already developed for social work practice, and that, while the differences between the respective roles and purposes of researchers and practitioners must be respected, the concept of practitioner/researcher is one that can be further developed in social work. Significant recent developments in qualitative research methodology more generally promise to facilitate this, for example, the 'narrative turn' in social research (Andrews *et al.*, 2000) [eds: see also Gould, this volume]. In addition, as Humphries (1999) demonstrates, feminist critiques of quantitative methods in social research do not mean that these methods should be excluded from the social work researcher's repertoire. Nor, as already mentioned, need adopting feminist perspectives in social (including social work) research narrow the focus (Humphries, *ibid.*); among other things they can support any approaches which 'give voice' to the subjective reality of marginalised and oppressed groups. Such a use of research accords both with the value of empowerment espoused in social work, and with concerns for 'connection' (for example in social relationships) and 'care', identified as particularly characteristic of women's roles and practices (Belenky *et al.*, 1986).

The gender dimension in some recent developments and current changes

In the foregoing sections we have discussed the 'reality' of the description of social work (whether in the field or the academy) as an occupational sphere in which women predominate (in numbers if not in positions of power), together with some of the possible explanations for and implications of this situation. We now turn to some recent developments and current changes, identify their continuing gender dimensions and possible consequences. Focusing mainly on the UK, we have selected three developments in particular: the prevalence of managerialism in public-sector services and institutions; growth in the use of information and communication technologies; and changing expectations of social work education, specifically in terms of the qualifying curriculum and associated issues about knowledge transmission and knowledge creation.

Before proceeding we should confirm an important aspect of our broad frame of reference. There is evidence to suggest that, despite some indications of a rise in the number of men in the occupation in the preceding period, the years since the mid 1990s have been marked by an apparent increase in the proportion of women in UK social work, alongside concerns about the overall numbers entering. With regard to the latter, figures from the Central Council for Education and Training in Social Work (CCETSW) indicated a 55 per cent drop in applications to Diploma in Social Work (DipSW) courses across the UK between 1994 and 1999; there was also a fall (from 4660 to 4071) in the numbers qualifying over the same period (Steel, 2001). Recent publicity and Government initiatives to address the issues of social worker recruitment and retention – including those which will coincide with changes to social work qualifying training (see below) which will have come into effect by the time this book is published – suggest that these are now recognised as problematic, alongside similar concerns about recruitment and retention in other public-sector (and women's) occupations such as teaching and nursing.

It is possible that the fall in recruitment to social work may be due in part to external factors such as changing notions of suitable work for women and increasing availability of opportunities. Vocational psychologists in the USA have identified how the range of jobs open to women has increased, including in non-traditional occupations (Fitzgerald *et al.*, 1995). Similar patterns are evident in the UK, where equal opportunities legislation has enabled recruitment to, for example, fire and police services. As the range of opportunities has increased, there has also been a growing expectation that women, including lone mothers, will work. For instance, there has been an expansion in the number of posts (usually part-time and low-paid) for women in a broadly-conceived 'child care sector', often in projects involving health or education services (Lyons, 2000). The creation of new or revised roles with a narrow remit, commonly in a social control context, has also been observed (Jordan, 2000), along with the fact that many such roles do not require people to have social work qualifications although they may require similar skills. For example, probation officers now have a separate service-specific qualification, and people with various – and limited – qualifications are recruited to 'Connexions', which offers a personal communication service to young people. We can also note in passing that women now exceed men in recruitment to the probation service, an area where men traditionally predominated (Perry and Cree, 2003, pp. 380–81).

Meanwhile, although women continue to predominate in numerical terms in the women's professions, opportunities for male employment in manufacturing have declined considerably with the overall decline in the UK's manufacturing base, while impressionistic evidence suggests that relatively more men than in the past now seek work in the service sector and the broad field of caring professions, such as psychiatric nursing or physiotherapy. This trend does not appear to have benefited social work specifically, where, as mentioned above, decreasing numbers of men have been entering at the training stage (Perry and Cree, 2003, pp. 376–7; Wallis-Jones and Lyons, 2000).

Age interacts with gender as a factor affecting recruitment to social work, where traditionally the majority of new entrants to qualifying training in the UK have been 'mature students' (i.e. over 25 years of age), most of them women, and often with family and domestic responsibilities. Such students usually need to study locally, and arguably they (including the men in these situations) have been harder hit by the withdrawal of local authority student grants than have their younger peers, who are typically still dependent on their family of origin and/or prepared to enter into debt in anticipation of good returns in a future career. That this factor is significant may be assumed on the basis of some reported improvement in recruitment to nursing and teaching, following the Government's investment in recruitment campaigns and in the introduction of bursaries for training in these fields. Thus similar current and forthcoming initiatives *vis-à-vis* social work are to be welcomed.

With regard to retention in social work, it seems likely that limited recognition for senior practitioners and increased managerialism (see below) may be two factors currently affecting the career plans of social workers employed in and committed to direct practice. Harlow (2000) has examined the consequences of managerialism for social workers, and also the relationship between gender and managerial aspirations and opportunities. She suggests that while the advent of 'the new public sector management' may mean that men experience enhanced opportunities, women may be less attracted to posts concerned mainly with setting budgets and achieving performance targets; also that, in general, women may feel alienated from the more competitive milieu. Furthermore, Harlow (*ibid.*) suggests that the recruitment of managers without social work qualifications will reduce career opportunities for practitioners – who, as detailed, are predominantly women. However, conversely, we can speculate that the apparent decline in the status of social work, coupled with the decrease in the number of men entering the profession, could mean increased opportunities for women as managers.

Finally, falling recruitment to social work courses, and the staffing difficulties faced by social services departments, may also both be partly attributable to the persistently negative media attention given to social workers. This, together with changes in the overall working environment associated with increasing managerialism and, more specifically, changes in working practices associated with implementation of the NHS and Community Care Act, 1990 (Orme, 2001), may have reduced the attractions of local authority social work, which might previously have been seen as a secure form of employment in a 'women-friendly' environment. In addition, the significant changes currently taking place in the framework of qualifications and regulatory arrangements may suggest that social work is a turbulent profession, subject to considerable change that is beyond its own control.

Gender, social work and managerialism

Since the 1980s, the UK public sector has been characterised by an increasingly managerial culture (Pollitt, 1990), in which professional practitioners have had decreasing control over their work and diminishing influence over policy or resource allocation. This culture change has been evident in higher education, as touched upon earlier, as well as in local authority and other personal social services, thus affecting the social work community across a range of settings.

Clarke and Newman's (1997) analysis of the 'managerial state' highlights the implications for men and women of the restructuring of the welfare state. They identify three different but now coexisting 'organisational orders'. In the 'traditional' order, the welfare state was organised around bureaucratic structures peopled by bureau-professionals. These structures were characterised by strong gender divisions, both vertically (with women predominating on the front line of practice and men in positions of control) and horizontally (with some professions identified as male and others, notably the 'semi-professions' (see above), as female). A second, 'competitive', organisational order emerged during the Thatcherite years (in the 1980s and into the early 1990s), when many public-sector organisations adopted competitive behaviour, including specific mechanisms such as compulsory competitive tendering and performance measurement. In this order, previously established equal opportunities provisions were weakened and women lost the paternalistic protectiveness of the traditional order, with all staff exposed to the full rigours of a 'macho' style of working. As Clarke and Newman suggest,

> It is as if the unshackling of bureaucratic constraints has allowed public sector managers to become 'real men', released at last from the second class status of public functionaries by their exposure to the 'real world' of the market place. (1997, p. 70)

Clarke and Newman also identify a third, 'transformational', order, which they describe as an 'excellence model'. This is characterised by responsiveness to staff, empowerment, commitment to service values, and a belief that all staff have a contribution to make to the organisation. In this order, differences in power – and thus gender divisions – may be less in evidence.

Clarke and Newman suggest that with these three organisational orders now coexisting we face contradictory images – and lived experiences. The traditional order places low priority on personal interactions and views work that primarily involves them as feminine and adjunct. The competitive order is characterised by 'leaner and fitter' organisations, and by plans, technologies, strong boundaries, rationality, calculation, and linear thought. The transformational order is more 'people-orientated', requiring the 'feminisation' of management, with more emphasis on communication skills, culture rebuilding, and network and partnership management (*ibid.*, p. 73). Significantly – for women and men – both competitive and transformational orders demand an intensification of 'emotional labour':

> If second wave feminism fought for greater access to male bastions of power in the market place, women in the 1990s are beginning to find this something of a poisoned chalice. Just as women have been allowed to become managers, management itself has been transformed into containment of the uncertainties, pressures, stresses, and discontents of public sector restructuring, organisational downsizing and cuts in services to users and communities. Whether in managing these tensions within organisations or in interactions with service users, there has been an intensification of 'emotional labour' involved in providing public services. (*ibid.*, p. 75)

At the time of writing, welfare services are being further restructured across the UK, with new constellations such as Health and Social Care Trusts (see the National Health Service Plan (Department of Health, 2000)) and some local authorities adopting a 'Cabinet' style of decision making. An increase rather than a decrease in managerialism seems to be the norm, along with the increased requirement for emotional labour suggested by Clarke and Newman. Additionally, Witz's point that 'the creation and control of occupational boundaries and inter-occupational relations may be crucially mediated by patriarchal power relations' (1991, p. 675) may have continuing resonance in relation to the establishment of new occupational groupings. It will be a challenge in this changing scenario not to replicate the previous gendered division of labour (see discussion of Witz's analysis of professionalisation earlier in this chapter).

Gender, social work and information and communication technologies

Another recent and significant change in the workplace, again with gendered implications, is the rapidly increasing use of information and communication technologies (ICTs). As Hafkin and Taggart (2001) suggest, the United Nations statement that access to IT is the third most important issue facing women globally, after poverty and violence against their persons, emphasises the high profile of this issue. In their discussion of gender and information technology in developing countries, these authors report that, although IT is a new field, a gendered division of labour is already emerging within it. Women tend to be concentrated in lower-skilled IT jobs related to word processing or data entry – the 'high-tech' equivalent of the secretarial roles that women have traditionally filled.

In her introduction to a new text about ICTs and social welfare, Harlow (2003) explores how women employed in welfare services in the UK are responding to the increasing application of ICTs. She alerts us to the fact that in the IT sector itself, 'men outnumber women by over five to one' (Haughton, 2002, p. 2, quoted in Harlow, 2003, p. 16). Harlow surveys both empirical and theoretical work on gender differences and the use of ICTs, finding a complex picture. On the one hand, she points us to the work of feminist theorists such as Wajcman, who suggests (1994, p. 224, cited in Harlow, 2003, p. 17) that technology is not gender neutral, but rather is associated with masculinity, and that technical expertise provides men with actual or potential power over women. On the other hand, Harlow notes (2003, p. 17), for example, that middle-class women in particular may be developing sophisticated ICT skills and are the most active users of internet health sites. However, Hafkin and Taggart (2001) warn that women internet users are part of a small, educated, urban elite, and that as GDP rises the overall dominance of men edges lower the percentage of such users who are female. In the UK the percentage of women employed in IT has actually dropped in the past two decades (Spence, 2000). Hafkin and Taggart argue strongly for an 'engendered' approach to providing women and girls with IT education and skills. They also argue that to benefit fully from the new technology, women must act as leaders in its development and as agents of change.

Knowledge management and e-learning are further important issues to be considered here. A study by Ulster academics (Larmour and Tener, 2000) suggests an increasing gender imbalance in computing education, in the context of what its authors call 'a systematic "masculinisation" of the computer industry' over the last 20 years. In 1975, women comprised 25 per cent of the applicants for university computer science courses and this figure was expected to grow. In the event the number has instead declined, and today only 18 per cent of such students are female (Spence, 2000). However, Larmour and Tener report an interesting exception to the general pattern and trend; in each year from 1993–94 through 1998–99 around 60 per cent of those enrolling on part-time/evening computing courses at Belfast Institute of Further and Higher Education were women, with, in addition, a rise over this same period of 88 per cent in the number of women enrolling as compared with a rise of 73 per cent in male enrolments. Nonetheless, considered together, the data from these several sources arouse concern that the transmission of e-knowledge may be largely in the control of and to the benefit of men, with implications for effective use of ICTs in professions and disciplines where women predominate.

Changing expectations of social work education

At the time of writing, we are at a crucial stage in the UK in defining the knowledge needed for obtaining an initial qualification in social work, through a period of consultation and debate about the curriculum for a new three-year degree (to be implemented from 2003–04). What parts will different stakeholders play in shaping the curriculum? Following the example of teacher education, will a national curriculum be prescribed by the Department of Health and the General Social Care Council (GSCC)? Or will the curriculum for the new award be designed by individual HEIs based on learning outcomes established by the GSCC, echoing the preceding relationship between DipSW programmes and CCETSW? On what basis will either a national curriculum or learning outcomes be defined? And how will they be informed by the occupational standards defined by the Training Organisation for the Personal Social Services (TOPSS) (2001) and the benchmark statement of academic standards for the new degree agreed by the Quality Assurance Agency for Higher Education (QAA) (2000)?

A key issue in this process is how 'knowledge' is understood. If the knowledge thought to be required by social workers is understood in 'positivistic' terms, then prescription would seem to be the obvious route, with little requirement for debate; i.e. it is simply a question of applying 'what works'. However, this suggestion is highly contentious, seemingly being rooted in the view that social life is predictable in a law-like way. Postmodern perspectives identify uncertainty and unpredictability as characteristic of the current times – and for that matter in some sense as 'always' having been the lot of social work (Parton, 1994a; b; 1996). Two decades ago, Schön (1983) described professional practice as characterised by 'complexity, uncertainty, instability, uniqueness and value conflict' (p. 18). With the positivistic flavour of many current policy responses to risk in mind, Parton similarly and more recently proposes that 'the vast majority of social work ... is much better characterized in terms of uncertainty than of risk, and ... the notion of ambiguity is central to its operation ...' (1998, pp. 22–3).

In considering the development of a curriculum for qualifying training, therefore, the arguments against prescription and in favour of viewing knowledge as contingent and contextual seem incontrovertible (Eraut, 1995; Fook *et al.*, 2000; Taylor, 1997). It has been suggested that what Eraut (1995) described as the 'functional relevance' of theoretical knowledge to professional practice

> ... is often determined by the ability and willingness of people to use it, rather than any presumed external validity. In turn, the ability and willingness to use particular

knowledge is affected by work context, the way knowledge is introduced, and the way it is linked to professional concerns. (Fook *et al.*, 2000, p. 192)

As discussed earlier, Fook and her colleagues, writing from a feminist perspective, have recently identified principles that can be used to guide social work educators in curriculum design, and which assist us in considering the pedagogical models appropriate to 'knowledge transmission'. Other writers have also stressed the need to move away from a hierarchical model of expertise (familiar in traditional disciplines) to one that emphasises partnership and mutual learning (Miley *et al.*, 1998; Rossiter, 1993; Schön, 1987), a position consistent with principles of both feminism and adult learning.

One further substantive point merits consideration in this discussion of ongoing changes in social work education; it relates to knowledge creation. There has been increasing emphasis on the part of UK policy makers and managers – and many researchers – in the field of social work and social care on the establishment of 'reliable evidence' about 'what works' as the basis for practice, and the recently established (Autumn 2001) Social Care Institute for Excellence (SCIE) has been given a key mediating role in taking this forward. Major research funders, such as the Department of Health and the Home Office, appropriately concerned about effective responses to social problems, tend to assume that reliable evidence comes predominantly from research carried out in the positivistic tradition – and are supported in this by some social work academics (e.g. Macdonald and Sheldon, 1992; Sheldon, 1986; 2001). This paradigm would seem to echo the previously mentioned 'masculine' conception of knowledge.

As will be clear from discussion earlier, we would argue the case for due regard to be paid to research carried out using interpretive and qualitative approaches, including those with designs directly informed by feminist and participatory perspectives, which might more directly reflect the views and experiences of women and other minority groups as service users and carers, as well as those of social work professionals in the field and the academy. In this connection we can also note in passing – and welcome – that increased attention is currently being given to the promotion of a range of different kinds of opportunities for doctoral study (Lyons, 2002). This should be taken into account as likely to increase both the research capacity of the discipline and the availability of research findings (from a variety of perspectives) with potential relevance to practice.

Concluding comments

In this discussion we have reviewed selected literature and recent research to illustrate that social work is still in many respects appropriately regarded as a 'women's profession', notwithstanding a similarly continuing tendency for men to predominate in positions of power both in the field and in the academy. We have suggested that via this prevalence of women in social work, gender has had a bearing on several aspects of its development, both as a profession and as a discipline. Some of these influences might be seen as 'internal', for example through the likelihood that members of the predominantly female workforce view the world and behave in particular ways. However, there are also significant and similarly gendered 'external' influences affecting social work, for instance the (masculine) culture of the larger organisations in which social work is located, or the extent of external direction.

We have drawn on feminist perspectives to suggest that some of the debates about the status of social work – as a profession and/or as a discipline – are commonly framed within a 'male discourse' which attributes lesser status to 'women's professions' and to forms of professional education where women have traditionally predominated. This is in part related to debates about the nature of knowledge and the status attributed to 'masculine' knowledge and research paradigms, relative to other ways of knowing. We would argue that, given the nature of the task, feminist perspectives and some of the skills and values generally seen as more typically attributes of women rather than of men, can play a significant role in promoting the development of social work, as a form of practice and as a discipline which facilitates both professional development and the creation of knowledge for action.

We have suggested that two recent trends in the UK, namely increasing managerialism in the public sector and growth in the use of information and communication technologies, have conceivably disadvantaged and/or alienated women, with adverse consequences for recruitment to social work and thus potentially for its management and delivery. We have also explored the tensions in ongoing changes in social work education in the UK, including how they reflect changing approaches to accountability, showing that these too may be seen to have a gender dimension. All of these changes together present significant challenges to social work educators, who in negotiation with other stakeholders must ensure that social work education achieves its related goals of training reflective practitioners and carrying out varied forms of research on the social conditions of user groups and on interventions and forms of service delivery, so that in turn social work can most appropriately address the concerns of users and of the wider society.

References

Acker, S. (1994), *Gendered Education: Sociological Reflections on Women, Teaching and Feminism*, Open University Press, Buckingham, quoted in Brooks, *op. cit.*

Andrews, M., Sclater, S.D., Squires, C. and Treacher, A. (eds) (2000), *Lines of Narrative: Psychosocial Perspectives*, Routledge, London.

Baines, C.T. (1991), 'The professions and an ethic of care', in Baines, C.T., Evans, P.M. and Neysmith, S.M. (eds), *Women's Caring: Feminist Perspectives on Social Welfare*, McClelland and Stewart, Toronto, pp. 36–72.

Barnett, R. (1994), *The Limits of Competence: Knowledge, Higher Education and Society*, Society for Research into Higher Education/Open University Press, Buckingham.

Becher, T. (1989), *Academic Tribes and Territories: Intellectual Enquiry and the Cultures of Disciplines*, Society for Research into Higher Education/Open University Press, Buckingham.

Becher, T. (ed.) (1994), *Governments and Professional Education*, Society for Research into Higher Education/Open University Press, Buckingham.

Becher, T. and Trowler, P. (2001), *Academic Tribes and Territories: Intellectual Enquiry and the Cultures of Disciplines* (2nd edn), Society for Research into Higher Education/ Open University Press, Buckingham.

Belenky, M.F., Clinchy, B.M., Goldberger, N.R. and Tarule, J.M. (1986), *Women's Ways of Knowing: The Development of Self, Voice and Mind*, Basic Books, New York.

Beresford, P. and Evans, C. (1999), 'Research Note: Research and empowerment', *British Journal of Social Work*, **29**(5), pp. 671–7.

Brooks, A. (1997), *Academic Women*, Society for Research into Higher Education/Open University Press, Buckingham.

Cheetham, J., Fuller, R., McIvor, G. and Petch, A. (1992), *Evaluating Social Work Effectiveness*, Open University Press, Buckingham.

Clarke, J. and Newman, J. (1997), *The Managerial State*, Sage, London.

Cree, V.E. (1997), 'Surviving on the inside: reflections on being a woman and a feminist in a male academic institution', *Social Work Education*, **16**(3), pp. 37–60.

Daniels, A.K. (1987), 'Invisible work', *Social Problems*, **34**(5), pp. 403–15, cited in Baines, *op. cit.*

Department of Health (2000), *The NHS Plan. A Plan for Investment; A Plan for Reform*, Cm 4818 – I, HMSO, London.
   (Available at <http://www.doh.gov.uk/nhsplan/index.htm>.)

Dominelli, L. (2002), 'Feminist theory', in Davies, M. (ed.), *The Blackwell Companion to Social Work* (2nd edn), Blackwell, Oxford, pp. 96–105.

Dominelli, L. and McLeod, E. (1989), *Feminist Social Work*, Macmillan, Basingstoke.

Dreyfus, H. and Dreyfus, S. (1986), *Mind Over Machine: The Power of Human Intuition and Expertise in the Era of the Computer*, Blackwell, Oxford.

Eraut, M. (1995), *Developing Professional Knowledge and Competence*, Falmer, London.

Etzioni, A. (ed.) (1969), *The Semi-Professions and Their Organization: Nurses, Teachers, Social Workers*, Free Press, New York.

Everitt, A. and Hardiker, P. (1996), *Evaluating for Good Practice*, Macmillan, Basingstoke.

Everitt, A., Hardiker, P., Littlewood, J. and Mullender, A. (1992), *Applied Research for Better Practice*, Macmillan, Basingstoke.

Fitzgerald, L., Fassinger, R. and Betz, N. (1995), 'Theoretical advances in the study of women's career development', in Walsh, W.B. and Osipow, S.H. (eds), *The Handbook of Vocational Psychology: Theory, Research, and Practice* (2nd edn), Erlbaum, Mahwah, NJ, pp. 67–109.

Fook, J., Ryan, M. and Hawkins, L. (2000), *Professional Expertise: Practice, Theory and Education for Working in Uncertainty*, Whiting and Birch, London.

Friedson, E. (1986), *Professional Powers: A Study of the Institutionalization of Formal Knowledge*, University of Chicago Press, Chicago.

Fuller, R. and Petch, A. (1995), *Practitioner Research: The Reflexive Social Worker*, Open University Press, Buckingham.

Ginn, J. and Fisher, M. (1999), 'Gender and career progression', in Balloch, S., McLean, J. and Fisher, M. (eds), with several others, *Social Services: Working Under Pressure*, Policy Press, Bristol, pp. 129–40.

Glazer, P. and Slater M. (1987), *Unequal Colleagues: The Entrance of Women into the Professions, 1890–1945*, Rutgers University Press, Piscataway, NJ, quoted in Baines, *op. cit.*

Gould, N. and Taylor, I. (eds) (1996), *Reflective Learning for Social Work*, Arena, Aldershot.

Habermas, J. (1966), 'Knowledge and interest', trans. G. Flöistad, *Inquiry*, **9**(4), pp. 285–300. [Eds: Habermas's Inaugural Lecture as Professor of Philosophy and Sociology at the University of Frankfurt, 28 June 1965. Also appears (in a different translation) as an appendix to Habermas, 1972, pp. 301–17.]

Habermas, J. (1972), *Knowledge and Human Interests*, trans. J.J. Shapiro, Heinemann, London.

Habermas, J. (1984), *The Theory of Communicative Action*, Vol. I: *Reason and the Rationalization of Society*, trans. T. McCarthy, Polity, Cambridge.

Habermas, J. (1987), *The Theory of Communicative Action*, Vol. II: *Lifeworld and System – A Critique of Functionalist Reason*, trans. T. McCarthy, Polity, Cambridge.

Hafkin, N. and Taggart, N. (2001), *Gender, Information Technology, and Developing Countries: An Analytic Study*, Academy for Educational Development (AED), for the US Agency for International Development (USAID)'s Office of Women in Development, Washington, DC. (Available at <http://www.usaid.gov/wid/pubs/it01.htm> and at <http://learnlink.aed.org/Publications/Gender_Book/Home.htm>.)

Hansard Society (1990), *Report of the Hansard Society Commission on Women at the Top*, Hansard Society for Parliamentary Government, London.

Harding, S. (1986), *The Science Question in Feminism*, Open University Press, Milton Keynes.

Harding, S. (ed.) (1987), *Feminism and Methodology: Social Science Issues*, Open University Press, Milton Keynes.

Harding, S. (1991), *Whose Science? Whose Knowledge? Thinking from Women's Lives*, Open University Press, Milton Keynes.

Harlow, E. (2000), 'New managerialism and social work: changing women's work', in Harlow, E. and Lawler, J. (eds), *Management, Social Work and Change*, Ashgate, Aldershot, pp. 73–91.

Harlow, E. (2003), 'Information and communication technologies in the welfare services: wired wonderland or hypertext hell?', in Harlow, E. and Webb, S.A. (eds), *Information and Communication Technologies in the Welfare Services*, Jessica Kingsley, London, pp. 7–26.

Harman, K.M. (1989), 'Professional versus academic values: cultural ambivalence in university professional school in Australia', *Higher Education*, **18**(5), pp. 491–509.

Haughton, E. (2002), 'Gender split', *Education Guardian*, 5 March, <http://education.guardian.co.uk/itforschools/story/0,5500,661709,00.html>, quoted in Harlow, 2003.

Henkel, M. (1994), 'Social work: an incorrigibly marginal profession?', in Becher, 1994, pp. 86–103.

Henkel, M. (1995), 'Conceptions of knowledge and social work education', in Yelloly, M. and Henkel, M. (eds), *Learning and Teaching in Social Work: Towards Reflective Practice*, Jessica Kingsley, London, pp. 67–82.

Howe, D. (1986), *Social Workers and Their Practice in Welfare Bureaucracies*, Gower, Aldershot.

Humphries, B. (1999), 'Feminist evaluation', in Shaw, I. and Lishman, J. (eds), *Evaluation and Social Work Practice*, Sage, London, pp. 118–32.

Jones, C. (1996), 'Anti-intellectualism and the peculiarities of British social work education', in Parton, N. (ed.), *Social Theory, Social Change and Social Work*, Routledge, London, pp. 190–210.

Jordan, B., with Jordan, C. (2000), *Social Work and the Third Way: Tough Love as Social Policy*, Sage, London.

Kemshall, H. (2000), 'Competence, risk assessment and transfer of learning', in Cree, V.E. and Macaulay, C. (eds), *Transfer of Learning in Professional and Vocational Education*, Routledge, London, pp. 53–76.

Larmour, R. and Tener, D. (2000), 'A study of the gender imbalance in computer science education', <http://www.ics.ltsn.ac.uk/pub/conf2000/Posters/larmour.htm>.

Lorenz, W. (1994), *Social Work in a Changing Europe*, Routledge, London.

Lyons, K. (1999), *Social Work in Higher Education: Demise or Development?*, Ashgate, Aldershot.

Lyons, K (2000), 'UK policy designed to combat child poverty', in Link, R. and Bibus, A., with Lyons, K., *When Children Pay: US Welfare Reform and its Implications for UK Policy*, Child Poverty Action Group, London, pp. 70–103.

Lyons, K. (2002), 'Researching social work: doctoral work in the UK', *Social Work Education*, 21(3), pp. 337–46.

Lyons, K. and Orme, J. (1998), 'The 1996 Research Assessment Exercise and the response of social work academics', *British Journal of Social Work*, 28(5), pp. 783–92.

Macdonald, G. and Sheldon, B., with Gillespie, J. (1992), 'Contemporary studies of the effectiveness of social work', *British Journal of Social Work*, 22(6), pp. 615–43.

Mayer, J.E. and Timms, N. (1970), *The Client Speaks: Working Class Impressions of Casework*, Routledge and Kegan Paul, London.

Mies, M. (1993), 'Feminist research: science, violence and responsibility', in Mies, M. and Shiva, V. (eds), *Ecofeminism*, Zed Books, London, pp. 36–54.

Miley, K.K., O'Melia, M. and DuBois, B. (1998), *Generalist Social Work Practice: An Empowering Approach* (2nd edn), Allyn and Bacon, Boston, MA.

Orme, J. (1997), 'The case for research into practice', in McKenzie, G., Powell, J. and Usher, R. (eds), *Understanding Social Research: Perspectives on Methodology and Practice*, Falmer, London, pp. 112–23.

Orme, J. (2001), *Gender and Community Care: Social Work and Social Care Perspectives*, Palgrave, Basingstoke.

Parton, N. (1994a), 'The nature of social work under conditions of (post)modernity', *Social Work and Social Sciences Review*, 5(2), pp. 93–112.

Parton, N. (1994b), '"Problematics of government", (post)modernity and social work', *British Journal of Social Work*, 24(1), pp. 9–32.

Parton, N. (1996), 'Social theory, social change and social work: an introduction', in Parton, N. (ed.), *Social Theory, Social Change and Social Work*, Routledge, London, pp. 4–18.

Parton, N. (1998), 'Risk, advanced liberalism and child welfare: the need to rediscover uncertainty and ambiguity', *British Journal of Social Work*, 28(1), pp. 5–27.

Payne, M. (2001), 'Knowledge bases and knowledge biases in social work', *Journal of Social Work*, 1(2), pp. 133–46.

Perry, R.W. and Cree, V.E. (2003), 'The changing gender profile of applicants to qualifying social work training in the UK', *Social Work Education*, 22(4), pp. 375–83.

Perry, W. (1970), *Forms of Intellectual and Ethical Development in College Years*, Holt, Rinehart and Winston, New York.

Polanyi, M. (1958), *Personal Knowledge: Towards a Post-Critical Philosophy*, Routledge and Kegan Paul, London.

Polanyi, M. (1967), *The Tacit Dimension*, Routledge and Kegan Paul, London.

Pollitt, C. (1990), *Managerialism and the Public Services* (2nd edn), Blackwell, Oxford.

Powell, J. (1996), 'The social work practitioner as researcher: learning about research', in Ford, P. and Hayes, P. (eds), *Educating for Social Work: Arguments for Optimism*, Avebury, Aldershot, pp. 160–75.

Powell, J. (2000), 'Accountability and social work research', in Paylor, I., Froggett, L. and Harris, J. (eds), *Reclaiming Social Work*, The Southport Papers, Vol. 2, Venture Press, Birmingham, pp. 47–60.

Quality Assurance Agency (2000), *Subject Benchmarking: Academic Standards Statements*, <http://www.qaa.ac.uk/crntwork/benchmark/index.htm>.

Ramazanoglu, C. (1987), 'Sex and violence in academic life or you can keep a good woman down', in Hanmer, J. and Maynard, M. (eds), *Women, Violence and Social Control*, Macmillan, Basingstoke, pp. 61–74, cited in Brooks, *op. cit.*

Rose, H. (1994), *Love, Power and Knowledge: Towards a Feminist Transformation of the Sciences*, Polity, Cambridge.

Rossiter, A. (1993), 'Teaching social work from a critical perspective', *Canadian Social Work Review*, **10**(1), pp. 76–90.

Schön, D.A. (1983), *The Reflective Practitioner: How Professionals Think in Action*, Basic Books, New York.

Schön, D.A. (1987), *Educating the Reflective Practitioner*, Jossey-Bass, San Francisco.

Sheldon, B. (1986), 'Social work effectiveness experiments: review and implications', *British Journal of Social Work*, **16**(3), pp. 223–42.

Sheldon, B. (2001), 'The validity of evidence-based practice in social work: a reply to Stephen Webb', *British Journal of Social Work*, **31**(5), pp. 801–9.

Smith, M. (1965), *Professional Education for Social Work in Poverty – An Historical Account*, National Institute for Social Work, London.

Spence, R. (2000), 'Logging on to the fact that a woman's place is in the IT department', *Guardian*, 29 April, <http://www.guardian.co.uk/guardian_jobs_and_money/story/0,3605,215366,00.html>.

Stanley, L. (ed.) (1990), *Feminist Praxis: Research, Theory and Epistemology in Feminist Sociology*, Routledge, London.

Steel, L. (2001), 'Golden handcuffs: what local authorities are doing to keep the best staff', *Care and Health Guide*, issue **9**, pp. 10–11.

Taylor, C. (1971), 'Interpretation and the sciences of man', *Review of Metaphysics*, **25**(1), pp. 3–51.

Taylor, I. (1997), *Developing Learning in Professional Education: Partnerships for Practice*, Society for Research into Higher Education/Open University Press, Buckingham.

Taylor, W. (1994), 'Teacher education: backstage to centre stage', in Becher, 1994, pp. 43–59.

Toulmin, S. (1972), *Human Understanding*, Vol. I: *General Introduction* and *Part I*, Clarendon Press, Oxford.

Training Organisation for the Personal Social Services (2001), *The National Occupational Standards for Social Work*, TOPSS England, Leeds, <http://www.topss.org.uk/uk_eng/framesets/engindex.htm>.

Wajcman, J. (1994), 'Technology as masculine culture', in *The Polity Reader in Gender Studies*, Polity, Cambridge, pp. 216–25, cited in Harlow, 2003.

Wallis-Jones, M. and Lyons, K. (2000), *1999 Employment Survey of Newly Qualified Social Workers*, CCETSW, London.

Walton, R. (1975), *Women in Social Work*, Routledge, London.

Witz, A. (1991), 'Patriarchy and the professions: the gendered politics of occupational closure', *Sociology*, **24**(4), pp. 675–90.

Younghusband, E. (1947), *Report on the Employment and Training of Social Workers*, Carnegie UK Trust, London.

Younghusband, E. (1951), *Social Work in Britain: A Supplementary Report on the Employment and Training of Social Workers*, Carnegie UK Trust, Dunfermline.

Younghusband, E. (1959), *Report of the Working Party on Social Workers in the Local Authority Health and Welfare Services*, London, HMSO.

Chapter 5

Social Work Research and the Partnership Agenda

Steve Trevillion

Introduction

In recent years, 'partnership' between organisations, across different sectors, or with service users, has become one of the most talked-about issues in UK policy making. Some of the most controversial features of cross-boundary working, especially those associated with public/private partnerships, regularly make the headlines of the national press, as in the following extract from the *Guardian*: 'Stephen Byers, the transport secretary, was plunged into a new political crisis last night after it emerged that the taxpayer is to throw a £30m life-line to the part-privatised national air traffic control system' (Treanor, Wintour and Harper, 2002).

This does not mean that partnership is a new idea. On the contrary, it has a long history within social policy; neither is it associated with any one political party. It was a previous Conservative Government which claimed that co-operation between different organisations and professions would lead to a 'seamless' delivery of community care services (Department of Health (Social Services Inspectorate) 1991, pp. 2–30). The current New Labour emphasis is on the way an 'integrated' and 'multi-skilled' approach will generate 'best value' (Department of Health, 2000). The language may have changed but the broad thrust of the argument has remained the same. What is different is that partnership has now become a matter of ideology rather than of pragmatism; partnership has come to be intimately associated with the core New Labour principle of 'modernisation' (Department of Health, 1998) and, as such, is now part of the philosophical underpinning of contemporary welfare reform.

The fact that it has cross-party support does not imply that there is widespread agreement about what partnership really is or, indeed, whether it always operates in the interests of service users (Mackintosh, 2000). While there may be some acceptance on all sides that the basic idea of 'partnership' or 'collaboration' refers to the processes involved in 'working closely with somebody else' (Rao, 1991, p. 14), as soon as this apparently unobjectionable principle is linked to policy objectives, disagreements begin to surface. The gap which has opened up between those who see partnership as part of the authoritarianism of New Labour (Parton, 2000, p. 460), based on a 'strictly top-down approach to institution building and cultural change' (Jordan, 2000, p. 64), and those who see partnership as a key element in a 'capacity building' and 'empowering' strategy designed to shift power away from producers and governments and towards consumers and citizens (Mayo and Taylor, 2001, pp. 40–44), appears to be unbridgeable.

At first sight, social work research on partnership appears to be divided similarly between partnership protagonists and partnership antagonists, and therefore to offer few ways of breaking out of what seems a theoretical and practical impasse. However, appearances can be deceptive. This chapter will suggest that, although there is no consensus view about the merits or demerits of particular versions of partnership, and certainly no uniformity of opinion about the current Government's policy making, there is a remarkably robust and enduring paradigm of partnership research within the social work tradition. It will also be suggested that a revitalised version of this paradigm might enable the whole field of partnership research to move into new and productive areas of work.

Although the focus throughout is on the UK, what follows may be of much wider interest. There is growing enthusiasm for partnership working in many parts of the European Union as well as in the USA[1] and the issues debated here may well have relevance for all those interested in rethinking the fundamentals of partnership research.

Partnership: redefining the research field

One of the great ironies of partnership research is that it has become so fragmented. There is more than one reason for this; there are clear ideological schisms, but the sheer diversity and complexity of partnership practices has also played a part. As Balloch and Taylor put it:

> Variously identified as interagency, interprofessional, collaborative or joined-up working, joined-up thinking or a whole systems or holistic approach, that which we have chosen to call 'partnership working' exists along a broad continuum of theory and practice. (Balloch and Taylor, 2001, p. 6)

Partnership initiatives now cover education, urban regeneration, social housing, transport, and criminal justice, as well as health and social care. Given the wide range of organisations, social issues, and types of 'commitment' involved (Pratt *et al.*, 1998) definitional problems are hardly surprising. This goes to the heart of the problem facing partnership researchers. If it is difficult to define 'partnership' in a satisfactory way, how can we ever define 'partnership research';

---

[1]   At a recent seminar held at the Hogeschool Zuyd in Maastricht as part of an MA course in Comparative European Studies, social workers from Germany, Denmark, Norway and the Netherlands agreed that social policy in their own countries was coming to be increasingly influenced by ideas associated with various forms of partnership and collaboration. In the USA, following initiatives by the former Clinton Administration, new inter-agency networks and alliances have come to the fore in the fields of health and social care.

and if we cannot define 'partnership research', how can we argue that the social work tradition has something to contribute to it? The answers involve thinking about partnership in a new way. We need to look primarily at the kinds of boundaries that are crossed or changed as a result of partnership initiatives.

Contemporary partnerships in the UK seek to make connections between the traditionally separate public, private and voluntary sectors, while also breaking down the perceived barriers between actual or potential users of services on the one hand, and planners, purchasers and providers of services on the other. As Jordan points out, this amounts to an attempt to 'recast the whole administrative system of the UK' (Jordan, 2000, p. 64). More than this, however, it is an attempt to re-engineer the space inhabited by all those involved in social welfare, whether as users, providers, purchasers, or members of communities [eds: see also Jordan and Parton, this volume]. So, the most obvious unifying characteristic of contemporary welfare partnerships is that, by bringing together that which was (and to some extent still is) separate, they also bring about the possibility of a corresponding shift in the assumptive worlds of those involved.

Partnership can be understood not only (in structural terms) as a wide range of inter-organisational or inter-sectoral linkages (Balloch and Taylor, 2001), but also (in epistemological and ontological terms) as a way of creating new spaces for thinking and being in the post-welfare-state world. The defining characteristic of these new cross-boundary partnership spaces is that they are charged with the hopes and dreams of those who see in them a new form of social solidarity and a new kind of social contract.

Throughout Europe and the USA, attempts are being made to fashion a new sense of community that goes beyond the individualism of the market place but does not depend on state services. This is sometimes referred to as 'the third way' (Giddens, 1998); at other times it is linked to an idea of rebuilding 'civil society', creating a 'stakeholder economy and society' (Hutton, 1997, p. 62), or, as in France, developing a new, de-sectorised, '*espace sociale*' (Cannan, 1995, p. 306). If the Thatcherites, with their emphasis on the individual and the family, presided over the run-down of public services, the rise of Blair and the new meritocratic social democrats of continental Europe has seen a renewed interest in social solidarity, with partnership emerging as the preferred route to this new type of society.

In this context, the discourse about partnership is nothing less than a coded agenda for social reconstruction – an attempt at healing social wounds and generating a sense of shared purpose and values. As such it is deeply ambiguous. The very existence of a need for partnership is an acknowledgement of the depth of fragmentation and alienation in contemporary society. At the same time, the partnership concept represents a solution to social problems and contains an optimistic vision of an integrated and just society. At this level the 'partnership' ideal functions in a very similar way to that of 'community', but whereas community ideals assume that differences will disappear, partnership ideals assume that differences will remain but that social boundaries will become flexible and permeable rather than remaining fixed and immutable. The partnership concept may well be expressed in a wide range of organisational forms, but whatever their superficial differences, an attempt to fashion a new market-friendly and user-friendly type of social solidarity, that manages rather than abolishes difference, is involved.

The pursuit of the partnership ideal has had consequences for the process of policy implementation. It has inevitably become focused on discovering ways of embracing diversity and forging cross-sectoral links, while simultaneously looking for new solidarities based on shared principles and values.

These considerations about policy and practice have important implications for partnership research. To begin with, they suggest that the focus should be on understanding the nature of the epistemological and ontological shifts now taking place (see above) and should not be limited to the search for a series of quick, short-term organisational fixes. They also suggest that partnership research should be research into communal as well as organisational issues. This is something that social work researchers have been among the first to recognise. In arguing for the importance of a new 'public health' framework in debates about partnership, Daphne Statham, the last Director of the National Institute for Social Work, has also emphasised that the partnership between health and social care will only be successfully developed if those involved grasp the over-arching aim of 'well-being' for the community as a whole (Statham, 2000).

Partnership with service users and communities

If partnership research is fundamental research, it also needs to be practical research, focusing on people's experiences. But in trying to find out what really makes a difference to people's lives we discover the limitations of the type of research that underpins orthodox managerial approaches to partnership based on reorganisation and structural realignment. A recent study of collaboration between health and social services has shown that joint arrangements do not necessarily lead to improved services. Their review of joint commissioning led Greig and Poxton to conclude that there is 'little evidence that strategic partnership working actually results in changes for people' (2001, p. 34). Partnership structures and processes, it seems, too often become ends in themselves. If 'community well-being' is to be more than just a slogan, it seems we require models of partnership that do more than generate new organisational structures.

Perhaps the problem is that too much faith has been placed in theories that fail to take account of the complex relationship between macro and micro. As Statham (2000, p. 88) puts it, 'At the micro level partnership has multiple meanings and levels that have to be negotiated'. We ignore this at our peril. Any model of policy implementation has to engage with the complexities of a micro-world where little can be taken for granted, and where an ability to handle issues of power and identity may be as significant as an ability to plan or deliver new kinds of services. Politicians and policy makers may see the problem of partnership in terms of a relatively small set of boundaries between large organisations, but close-to the picture looks much more complicated.

The distinctive community- and user-oriented tradition of partnership in social work research has much to contribute to the development of flexible models of policy implementation. In so far as social work research has been engaged in an extended exploration of how new patterns of joint or collective working can transform not only the immediate service environment but also the world views of those involved, it could be said to have specialised in developing models of partnership that link micro-level processes to a more ambitious agenda for social and personal change. The nature of these models will become clearer if we look briefly at the history of partnership practice and research in social work.

Social work may not have invented partnership; however, both nationally and internationally, the profession has long identified itself with partnership principles and values, and it has done so in a specific way. Long before partnership surfaced as a key theme in broader areas of UK social policy, the British Association of Social Workers (1980) declared that 'clients are fellow citizens', committing social workers to a continuing search for ways of working *with* rather than simply *for* the users of services. Shortly afterwards, in an effort to define social work as 'community social work', the Barclay Report described 'an attitude of mind in all social workers from the director of the department or agency to front-line workers which regards members of the public as partners in the provision of social care' (Barclay, 1982, p. 198).

These two ideas, treating individual service users as fellow citizens and working with the community, have sometimes been in conflict with one another, but together they have been responsible for most of what has been distinctive about the social work approach to partnership over the last 20 years. This characteristic flexibility and inclusiveness stems largely from the particular view about what working with and in the community might mean that has underpinned professional thinking in social work ever since the publication of the Barclay Report. It embraces not only individuals and their families, but also what are variously described as 'other professions', 'social and professional networks' and 'social care networks', in a variety of settings from neighbourhoods to hospitals (Barclay, 1982, pp. 207–8).

Social work research on partnership has largely mirrored social work practice in these respects. It too has focused on various forms of community partnership, rather than looking at inter-professional issues, inter-agency working, or neighbourhood development as if they were separate and distinct topics. Partnership with clients or service users has remained central, but interest in it has generally coexisted with attention to other forms of partnership as well. Community social work (as *circa* 1982) may no longer exist as an organised movement, but it has bequeathed to subsequent generations of social workers a rich inheritance of ideas about inclusive patterns of partnership, and an equally rich set of questions for social work researchers, many of which are still being answered.

The topic of partnership is so vast that many different disciplines can offer useful insights, but the strength of social work research in this context lies in its traditional focus on issues around citizenship and community, and in particular the complexities of boundary crossing in situations characterised by troubled relationships, power differentials, miscommunication, and divergent interests. It is precisely these issues that have now become central to the general debate about partnership: 'Partnership working has too often been dominated by the more powerful partners and has not "delivered", especially for the communities and service users who are now a required part of most partnerships' (Balloch and Taylor, 2001, pp. 7–9).

So, partnerships not only solve problems; they also generate new but fundamental tensions between what is and what could be, between unity and division, and between being oneself and being a good partner. With this in mind, the next section explores the contribution of social work research to our understanding of boundaries and boundary crossing.

Understanding boundary-crossing processes

Social work theory has always contained within it concepts of 'difference'. At an early stage, the importance of differences between workers and clients was noted (Jordan, 1970). Over the years this has evolved into a frank acknowledgement of the way difference can be related to disadvantage and how there is a potential for oppression and discrimination even in apparently caring or therapeutic relationships (Dominelli, 1988). One consistent thread has been the attempt to accept and sometimes to celebrate differences while asserting the possibility of communication across boundaries and between people. When social work researchers investigate partnership they bring with them a long tradition of thinking in terms of interactions or transactions in a context of difference. This is particularly helpful because partnership can be conceptualised in terms of a cross-boundary traffic of ideas or resources that mediates differences without finally dissolving them. Social work researchers are at home in this rather paradoxical universe in ways that others may not be.

Social workers and social work researchers are especially sensitive to the fact that partnership involves working *with* difference and *through* boundaries. Their day-to-day practice experience also reinforces the need to attend to important nuances in the nature and number of boundaries and the differences that cluster around them. To take one example: an 'intermediate care' partnership linking a user and his or her family with a social worker, a nurse and a physiotherapist can be classified as consisting of only two groups – professionals and non-professionals – and a single lay/professional boundary; but whatever the official rhetoric says about integrated services the partnership is likely to run into difficulty if the care manager fails to recognise the existence of other boundaries – for example between nurses and physiotherapists. This is not just a matter of attitude or perception. If social workers are especially sensitive to the complexities of partnership working it is because their partnerships are frequently very complex. The reasons for this become obvious as soon as we consider what 'complexity' actually consists of in relation to partnership working.

The complexity of partnership working may be seen as a product of the relationship between levels of difference and numbers of boundaries. It is both quantitative and qualitative. It is not just the number of people in a partnership that makes it challenging, but the level of difference between them. A major boundary marking a high level of difference is likely to be much more difficult to manage than one where differences are less obvious to those involved. It follows that a partnership with a large number of minor boundaries may be less complex than one involving a much smaller number of major boundaries. On this understanding, few professionals work with a more complex set of boundaries than do social workers. A child protection specialist linking with similarly specialist police, education, psychiatry, and community nursing colleagues, as well as children, parents, and wider family, is involved in a complex set of community relationships. A care manager working with a general practitioner, an occupational therapist, a volunteer, day centre staff, and a service user, together with neighbours and family members, is involved in an equally ambitious undertaking.

In a partnership, boundaries are much less solid and concrete than they might at first appear, and boundary-crossing processes can only be inferred from interaction data about people. It is also interaction data that tell us which boundaries are proving difficult to manage and which are not. In so far as partnership problems are boundary management problems, it is likely that over time they may move around the partnership system. It is only by becoming finely attuned to the experiences of participants that researchers are able to track these shifts when and where they occur. The tradition of practice-oriented and practitioner research within the social work research community is a particular strength in relation to dealing with some of these micro-level issues.

One of the aims of a successful health and social care partnership is to effect changes in precisely those areas that contribute to the high levels of differentiation in the partnership. So, a partnership is not only a way of managing a series of boundary-crossing processes, it is also a process that changes the nature of those boundaries and therefore the boundary structure of the partnership itself. Social workers have to address the shifting nature of boundaries on a daily basis, and they have become closely associated – for good or ill – with the interplay between identity politics, inter-professional and inter-organisational questions, and the management of change.

Drawing on its strengths in user- and community-oriented research, social work research has much to say about the dynamic cross-boundary processes involved in partnership working. The next section begins to examine this contribution in more detail by looking at a number of specific partnership models developed by social work researchers.

Some social work models of partnership

Local partnerships

Social services departments were originally conceived of in the context of a partnership between local authorities and local communities, including the voluntary sector (Seebohm Committee, 1968). This 'community orientation' has frequently been lost sight of, but it regularly resurfaces to energise debates about social work and social care. At an early stage, social work research in the UK began to focus on the potential of 'interweaving' and partnership building within this broad community orientation; for example, in 1973 the case was made for a partnership between local social services and the friends, families or neighbours of people with learning difficulties living in the community (Bayley, 1973).

There has always been a tendency for social work research on partnership to look beyond 'the welfare environment', if this is defined as 'the established pattern of formally organised services' (Abrams *et al.*, 1989, p. 140). This was very marked throughout the 1970s and 1980s, and while such ideas may not have seemed relevant in the harsh managerial climate of the 1990s, they now look remarkably in tune with the new focus on the connections between partnership, citizenship and community well-being, and the relationship between public health and general environmental issues.

In the early 1980s there was a groundswell of interest in 'holistic', 'community-oriented' methods and perspectives on both sides of the Atlantic. In the USA many academics and practitioners began to see localised network practices as means by which social workers and community workers might unlock new forms of individual, community, organisational, business and volunteer support for marginalised groups and individuals (Gottlieb, 1981). In the UK a number of similar ideas were put forward; given the current widespread interest in the relationship between health and social care, it is worth noting that one early focus for community social work was what would now be described as 'community well-being' but was then described simply as 'an experiment in health and welfare co-operation' (Bayley and Parker, 1980). The project concerned began in 1976, in Dinnington, with the aim of 'integrating all health and welfare services, statutory and voluntary and informal, at a neighbourhood level' (*ibid.*, p. 71). What is striking here is the dual emphasis on integrated services and the involvement of local people.

The study concluded that, in Dinnington at least, community services for older people had to be centred much more on supporting the wardens of sheltered housing and home helps because of 'the way they bestride the boundary between the statutory services and informal care' (*ibid.*, p. 73). The need for closer co-operation between health and social work professionals was certainly recognised, but it was argued that this could only come about by working with informal caring networks. This study illustrates the way that social work researchers exploring the UK situation have tended to see the primary boundary in terms of the gap between the professional and non-professional domains rather than that between the NHS and local authorities. It also shows how such a perspective can lead to radical ideas for delivering front-line services.

In the Dinnington study and much of the general 'patch' or 'neighbourhood' social work literature, there is little explicit attention given to boundaries and boundary crossing. However, in an attempt to remedy this, one influential book defined boundaries as barriers to chains of interaction, and the building of a community as the process of 'punctuating' unhelpful boundaries so as to promote social interaction (Smale *et al.*, 1988, pp. 65–6). The authors went on to examine social work as a 'meta-level' activity, promoting change, with the social worker seen as a 'broker' (*ibid.*, p. 122). This analysis of the Dinnington experiment emphasised the close links between community and partnership debates in social work. It also raised important questions about partnership and empowerment by identifying a shift towards joint definitions of problems as well as joint solutions to problems. However, in so-doing it also encouraged a rather uncritical and simplistic account of the process of partnership formation.

Power sharing between professionals and service users

Seeing boundaries only as problems or as barriers to co-operation has its dangers. One is the tendency to underestimate the importance of the differences they mark, especially differences in relation to power and control. Within the community social work research tradition there was a tendency to ignore the diversity of interests within partnerships, and to downplay the dangers of colonisation, while making the case for alliances at a local or neighbourhood level. By the end of the 1980s, however, it was no longer possible to ignore the relationship between partnership and power sharing. Controversies surrounding the power of social workers in relation to parents were partly responsible for the inclusion of partnership principles in The Children Act, 1989, and led to a large volume of associated research on partnership with parents, especially in relation to child protection (Department of Health, 1995).

The power-sharing debate began to go far beyond the idea of consultation when feminists, anti-racists and disability activists successfully challenged the assumption that social work agencies dominated by white, male, middle-class, and able-bodied individuals should be able to impose their ideas of partnership on others (Beresford and Trevillion, 1995, p. 11). Since then, models of partnership that focus on the professional/user relationship have continued to develop. Some of these have become increasingly radical, forming an integral part of a wide-ranging and diverse campaign for user-led services and a user-led welfare system. User-researchers have emerged at the forefront of this movement. While some have been reluctant to identify themselves with social work research, a strong argument has recently been put forward for including 'user knowledges' in a broader and more inclusive conception of social work 'theory-building' (Beresford, 2000, p. 489).

Applied social network analysis

In the 1990s the organisational and professional landscape of UK social work was transformed. This period witnessed the rise of specialisation and the disappearance of the post-Seebohm concept of 'genericism' that had underpinned many of the older community social work approaches to partnership. It also saw statutory local authority social work moving into a new assessment-focused, enabling and facilitating role as a result of new legislation (Department of Health, 1990). This made some of the older approaches seem irrelevant. In this context of change, some researchers began to develop a new way of thinking about partnership, heavily influenced by network analysis.

While much of the earlier literature had referred to networks, it had done so in a 'metaphorical' way (Mitchell, 1969, p. 1), as a means of talking generally about relationships and connections. A new 'relational perspective', associated with applied social network analysis (Wasserman and Faust, 1994), offered partnership researchers an opportunity to shift the focus from one of 'punctuating' boundaries to one that was more respectful of difference and sensitive to the need for organisational autonomy, while still pursuing the goal of working together. For some, the major focus continued to be on finding ways of working with families (Speck and Attneave, 1973) or 'natural' communities (Maguire, 1983), although the language used became more sophisticated. However, the American school of case management contained the seeds of a new approach to practice and research, one that opened up the possibility of seeing the process of integrating social care networks as a way of enabling distinct organisations to merge their interests – losing autonomy so as to gain more control of the environment in which they operated (Austin, 1983, p. 17).

The concept of 'conferencing', introduced in 1988, revolved around the idea of a network process capable of transforming a set of conflicted and fragmented relationships into a cohesive social care group (Trevillion, 1988, pp. 302–6). It was based on the idea that the process of building or strengthening social networks was a distinctive helping strategy (Garbarino, 1986), and paved the way for other attempts to model case-level micro-processes in network terms. The question was no longer how boundaries could be dissolved, but what kinds of boundaries were needed to develop and maintain a partnership. In the conferencing model, partnership was seen not as an automatic consequence of any close relationship, but as a product of a certain shift in the pattern of interdependency. A major focus was on the role of the social worker as a broker, enabler, or facilitator of partnership, and as a 'holder' of the boundaries around the partnership concerned. One characteristic feature of the approach was to see partnership in terms of working with and even consolidating boundaries, rather than as something that could only exist if boundaries were eradicated. This separates it from much of the earlier work on partnership within the community social work tradition.

Although network conferencing was widely adopted by care managers in the 1990s as a way of dealing with complex relationship issues, the idea that lay behind it – that a social network could be seen as a partnership system – was not. A more short-term and pragmatic view of social networks came to dominate the care management and community care literature, and issues around boundaries and boundary crossing were neglected. This was, perhaps, inevitable, given the way in which care management in the UK became linked to purchasing and the associated pressure to exercise direct control over service providers through contractual mechanisms. The result was that the diversity of the care management partnership was all too easily pictured as a weakness rather than as a source of strength.

Another reason for the relative neglect of partnership issues lay with the social network concept itself. From an instrumental perspective a social support network can be seen primarily as a resource system. If individual family members and other organisations are seen only as potential resources, the question of difference is reduced to one of differences between various kinds of resources. Instead of ushering in a new era of partnership studies, the adoption of the social network approach at first led to the neglect of partnership issues in favour of a narrow concern with service outcomes. Ironically, although there was an explicit focus on community care policy, social work researchers seemed to lose sight of the community dimension that had underpinned earlier work. There continued to be strong interest in exploring how best to meet the needs of service users, but relationships between service providers, family members and others were neglected or seen as irrelevant.

Of all the work done at this time, that of Peter Day and Philip Seed stands out in terms of originality. Peter Day was one of the first to suggest that applied network analysis could make a major contribution to decarceration initiatives designed to help individuals to establish 'normal' lifestyles and access appropriate kinds of social support. He emphasised that 'network building' could be seen as a distinct social care role (Day, 1988, p. 281). Seed and Kaye took this further with their concept of an 'opportunities approach' to care management and assessment, linked to the use of applied social network analysis (Seed and Kaye, 1994). Unfortunately, although these studies marked a major technical advance for social work research they stayed firmly within the dominant 'instrumental' paradigm, barely touching on the way in which a social support network could be seen as a partnership. They also did not fully integrate ideas about network opportunities and resources with concepts of power sharing and user control, even though these were already being developed by user-researchers (Barnes, 1991, pp. 129–30).

Community partnership and networking models

The 1990s saw the debate about social networks move gradually away from purely instrumental concerns about engineering social support, and towards new questions about the idea of an active community partnership. This shift took place in the context of different attempts to articulate the concept of 'networking'. If Seed saw 'networking' mainly in terms of building up information about key social networks (Seed, 1990), for Malcolm Payne the concept focused on 'making and maintaining links between community and voluntary organisations' (Payne, 1993, p. 1). While there is little explicit discussion of partnership issues and values in Payne's work, he sees relationships as central to the overall success or failure of initiatives. This idea of networking as a community development strategy has since been taken much further by Gilchrist, who sees 'networking' as a 'radical strategy for empowerment' and 'interpersonal relationships and informal networks as crucial elements of a community's capacity to involve people in decision-making and to take collective action' (Gilchrist, 1997, p. 100).

There is no need, however, to see networking only as a community development strategy. The process of theory building has increasingly served to integrate individual and community perspectives. Recent research on networking has generally been characterised by an interest in the management of complex cross-boundary 'sets' (Trevillion, 1999, p. 6). The questions it poses embrace both the meaning of 'partnership' for those involved and the nature of the 'communities' that come into existence as a result of partnership initiatives. Issues include somewhat 'technical' matters about the optimum kind of communication pattern or mobilisation strategy for a particular situation, as well as more political or value-laden questions such as how organisational cultures and systems can be made more open and flexible (*ibid.*, pp. 35–51).

Although networking research has developed out of a desire to build a specific body of practice knowledge for those working in the fields of social care, health and education, the issues it deals with are not exclusively micro-level ones. As well as assisting the development of particular partnership relations, it also explores the organisational preconditions for partnership as such.

One key insight associated with this body of work is that partnership is best described not as an outcome or even an end-state, but as a qualitative characteristic of cross-boundary linkages. Partnership is in this way 'integral to all the cross-boundary linkages with which networking is concerned' (*ibid.*, p. 6). By focusing on cross-boundary processes, partnership working can be described in terms of how new networks are generated alongside shifts in the nature and pattern of key boundaries. This approach can encompass work on motivation, cultural change, mobilisation, and many other specific topics. Overall, partnership is pictured as something that is constantly *in process*, or in the making. The message is that without constant attention to issues of engagement and communication, ideas about partnership have little meaning. In research terms this has led to an interest in such themes as the relationship between modes of interaction and perceptions of self and others.

The significance of these ideas for the broad debate about partnership lies in the light shed on the complexities of cross-boundary interaction. In particular, as a result of research on networks and networking we now know much more than before about the importance of human agency in the construction of partnership arrangements. The concept of a 'community broker', first introduced by the community social work movement, is now seen as central to all forms of partnership working which depend on complex networks of separate individuals, groups or organisations held together by highly active boundary mediators (*ibid.*, p. 72).

Some new problems

It could be argued with some force that there is nothing really new in partnership work. However, this is not true of partnership research. It is only now, in the context of a developing knowledge base, that it has become possible to think of some new, 'second generation' questions. Moreover, the changing nature of debates about partnership, and – perhaps especially – the changing nature of the aspirations associated with it, have made three of these new questions very pressing. One relates to the emotional life of partnerships, another to political context, while the third concerns cognition and learning.

Partnership emotions

For some time it has been recognised that social networks represent the 'personal order of society' (Mitchell, 1969, p. 10), in so far as they describe society from the point of view of particular individuals and their ways of interacting with others. However, in a situation where the language of partnership has become debased and where some partnerships endure while others disappear without trace, we need to ask again what a partnership network might mean to its participants, and in particular, perhaps, the part it might play in their emotional landscape. What do those involved feel about a particular partnership? How strong is the bond that it represents? How prepared are people to accept a possible loss of partnership relationships? How far will they go to continue with partnership relationships in a hostile environment? Trying to answer questions like these in terms solely of organisational interests and advantages may not be sufficient. And what is true of smaller and more personal partnerships is also likely to be true of large-scale international partnerships such as the United Nations or the European Union. Big or small, partnerships are not emotionally neutral; they matter to people and strong emotions may circulate within and around them. The impact of emotions on partnerships is likely to become increasingly obvious as we begin to obtain longitudinal data on partnership development. In fact, we may not be able to interpret these data adequately without ways of modelling the interplay between emotions, actions and events.

The politics of partnership

The hopes of a generation of political leaders now focus on partnership. For many people the partnership agenda has become identified with the ambitious project of creating a more participatory form of democracy in which citizenship rights will be enhanced. So the attempt to conceptualise partnership cannot be divorced from the wider debate about the relationship between the state and its citizens. If we are to understand a particular partnership fully we need to know how it relates to the wider social and political environment. In particular, we need to consider how we might evaluate its legitimacy in relation to concepts of representational and/or direct democracy [eds: see also Lovelock and Powell, this volume].

In this connection, the concept of a 'stakeholder network' is helpful, albeit in the end inadequate. The stakeholder model suggests that the actions of a partnership network will be seen as legitimate only to the extent to which they are supported by a linked stakeholder network. In the stakeholder model, political legitimacy is defined in both representational and structural terms. However, this is not a full answer because the division between an active partnership or 'action set' (Mitchell, 1969, p. 40) and a wider stakeholder network could be seen as simply reproducing the divisions between people and politicians, service providers and service users, state and community, which partnership working should be seeking to ameliorate. Introducing cross-boundary interaction and overlapping membership into the model may still not be enough; researching the issue of legitimacy may require a different approach. Perhaps we need to look again at the concept of a 'collaboration culture' (Beresford and Trevillion, 1995, pp. 16–18). This emphasises the active involvement of a wide range of different participants. In network terms this approach to partnership working effectively draws the stakeholder network into the 'action set'. In political terms it represents a strategy for introducing elements of direct democracy.

It has already been suggested that social work research on partnership has been characterised by a focus on users and communities. As a consequence, it has generally adopted a wider perspective than approaches in other fields in which only inter-professional or inter-organisational issues have been explored. Within social work, debates about partnership are regularly linked to ideas of anti-oppressive, anti-discriminatory, and empowerment practice. While this has led its critics to accuse social work research – as well as social work itself – of being in thrall to political correctness, it has also enabled it to develop a critical approach and to explore what partnership with users and carers might actually mean in practice. The challenge now is to apply these tools to the analysis of the ways in which particular partnerships enhance or diminish citizenship.

Partnership knowledge

The bulk of the research on partnership has focused on developing new ways of working together, but another consequence of thinking about partnership in network terms is that it becomes possible to ask new questions about partnership knowledge by framing them as questions about network knowledge. To date, most research on partnership knowledge has been constrained by inadequate conceptualisations of teamwork; in particular, there has been an uncritical acceptance of Senge's dictum that 'teams, not individuals are the fundamental learning unit in modern organisations' (Senge, 1990, p. 10). The problem facing researchers here has been that neither 'team' nor 'teamwork' has proved easy to define (Jones, 1992). In addition, there has been a tendency to assume that teamwork is essentially groupwork (Bond, 1997; Dechant *et al.*, 1993), and that new kinds of team knowledge are associated with the emergence of group norms (Bond, 1997, p. 92). The further common claim that all this is associated with experimentation, innovation and tolerance of diversity seems inherently dubious. In contrast, a focus on network knowledge asks questions about the kind of culture associated with a particular pattern of cross-boundary relationships, and by implication with a particular kind of cross-boundary community; this framework encompasses both diversity and unity. The key assumption is that partnership is a transformative phenomenon. It changes not only what we do, but also what we know.

The roots of these concerns lie in the peculiar conditions of the social work research enterprise, with its interest in process knowledge. How do new partnerships, new networks, new patterns of social interaction start to see the world together? What are the processes that lead partnerships to become cultures as well as systems? In particular, how do partnerships learn how to *be* partnerships?

It has become evident that successful partnership working requires what has been described as 'innovative knowledge-management schemes that cross current boundaries of care' (Foote and Pisek, 2001, p. 33). These schemes do not have to be – indeed in some sense cannot be – imposed. The contribution of social work research has been to identify the cultural conditions under which new learning might take place and to show that an open kind of inter-organisational and cross-boundary culture evolves its own way of seeing the world (Beresford and Trevillion, 1995).

We can now go further, however; and, ironically, this may mean returning to the original insight of community social work, that partnership involves a process of collective thinking. Of all the new lines of inquiry possible, this is the one whose implications are most radical. What it suggests is that cross-boundary networks are intelligent. In the absence of a holistic way of thinking about cross-boundary processes such an idea seems absurd. But if we think of partnerships as communities, albeit communities of difference, then the divisions between the different groups or organisations making up such a community can be reframed as the starting point for a process of 'dynamic learning' within that community. From this perspective, partnerships resemble 'forms of life'. As individuals learn, so too does the partnership as a whole. If we could chart this process we would be looking at a new form of social life learning how to be.

What this line of research suggests is that partnerships are much more than a set of different organisations connected to one another for a particular purpose. They are likely to develop their own views about the world and to act upon those views. Another way of posing the question is in terms of cultural change. Recent research confirms that it is culture rather than structure that holds the key to partnership working (Greig and Poxton, 2001), and so thinking about this process of cultural change in community and network terms may be very productive. As the partnership learns, so those within it begin to think differently and their 'contextual sense-making' alters (Pedison and Sorenson, 1989, p. 2). Cultural change is at once a product of the process of autonomous learning and a marker that it is taking place.

What is striking about most of what is written by management theorists and policy analysts is that it ignores these social/community education issues. In contrast, the traditions of social work research ensure that it is well-positioned to attend to them. Within the UK there is a tendency to ignore the substantial contribution played by social work theorists in developing concepts of social education, whereas this latter is the bedrock of European social pedagogy [eds: see Lorenz, this volume], with its emphasis on human potential and on social interaction as an opportunity for personal and cultural transformation (Higham, 2001). As soon as we start to conceptualise partnerships as vehicles for personal and cultural transformation the relevance of these ideas becomes obvious, even if the focus is a new one.

Conclusion

The partnership agenda has come to dominate contemporary social policy in the UK in the same way that competition and market ideology pervaded all aspects of policy making in the Thatcherite era. While discourses that were essentially mechanistic and rationalistic inevitably marginalised social work research, renewed interest in community and social solidarity under New Labour has created a far more favourable environment for it. Social work researchers have been discussing and debating partnership for over 20 years, and much of what they have been preoccupied with is now proving to be central to the further development of the partnership agenda.

In this way, and almost by accident, social work research has found a place at the centre of contemporary social and political debate. All of this is very timely. Social work research has in the past been uncertain about its nature and role, and it still frequently divides into warring camps; but in the analysis of collaboration and the interactive complexities of partnership practice it has found a natural home. One reason for this is that social work research is intimately connected with precisely those kinds of 'relational concepts or processes' (Wasserman and Faust, 1994, p. 4) that have been seen as characteristic of social networks and which underpin all partnership activity.

Social work research has already made a substantial contribution to the partnership research agenda. It has focused on patterns of cross-boundary working involving user groups and local communities as well as professionals. It has also generated some distinctive models of partnership construction and development based on networking theory. If cultural questions are going to replace structural ones at the centre of the partnership debate, then social work research is well positioned to respond. In particular, social work researchers could play a key role in helping us to understand the nature of the interplay between complex, cross-boundary communication, the creation of new cross-boundary communities, and the development of forms of partnership which genuinely make a difference to people's lives.

References

Abrams, P., Abrams, S., Humphrey, R. and Snaith, R. (1989), *Neighbourhood Care and Social Policy*, HMSO, London.

Austin, C.D. (1983), 'Case management in long-term care: options and opportunities', *Health and Social Work*, **8**(1), pp. 16–30.

Balloch, S. and Taylor, M. (2001), 'Introduction', in Balloch, S. and Taylor, M. (eds), *Partnership Working: Policy and Practice*, Policy Press, Bristol, pp. 1–14.

Barclay, P.M. (1982), *Social Workers: Their Role and Tasks*, National Institute for Social Work/Bedford Square Press, London.

Barnes, C. (1991), *Disabled People in Britain and Discrimination: A Case for Anti-Discrimination Legislation*, British Council of Disabled People/Hurst, London.

Bayley, M. (1973), *Mental Handicap and Community Care: A Study of Mentally Handicapped People in Sheffield*, Routledge and Kegan Paul, London.

Bayley, M. and Parker, P. (1980), 'Dinnington: an experiment in health and welfare co-operation', in Hadley, R. and McGrath, M. (eds), *Going Local: Neighbourhood Social Services*, National Council for Voluntary Organisations Occasional Paper One, Bedford Square Press, London, pp. 71–80.

Beresford, P. (2000), 'Service users' knowledges and social work theory: conflict or collaboration?', *British Journal of Social Work*, **30**(4), pp. 489–503. (An earlier version, presented in the *Theorising Social Work Research* seminar series, no. 1, 26 May 1999, Brunel University, is now available at <http://www.elsc.org.uk/socialcareresource/tswr/seminar1/beresford.htm>.)

Beresford, P. and Trevillion, S. (1995), *Developing Skills for Community Care: A Collaborative Approach*, Arena, Aldershot.

Bond, M. (1997), 'A learning team in the making', *Journal of Interprofessional Care*, **11**(1), pp. 89–98.

British Association of Social Workers (1980), *Clients Are Fellow Citizens: Report of the Working Party on Client Participation in Social Work*, BASW, Birmingham.

Cannan, C. (1995), 'New pedagogies of citizenship? Social workers and the enterprise culture in Britain and France', in Baldock, J. and May, M. (eds), *Social Policy Review* 7, Social Policy Association, Canterbury, pp. 299–316.

Day, P.R. (1988), 'Social networks and social work practice', *Practice*, **2**(3), pp. 269–84.

Dechant, K., Marsick,V.J. and Kasl, E. (1993), 'Towards a model of team learning', *Studies in Continuing Education*, **15**(1), pp. 1–14.

Department of Health (1990), *Community Care in the Next Decade and Beyond (Policy Guidance)*, HMSO, London.

Department of Health (Social Services Inspectorate) (1991), *Training for Community Care: A Joint Approach*, HMSO, London.

Department of Health (1995), *Messages from Research and Challenges of Partnership in Child Protection*, DoH, London.

Department of Health (1998), *Modernising Social Services: Promoting Independence, Improving Protection, Raising Standards*, Cm 4169, Stationery Office, London.

Department of Health (2000), *A Quality Strategy for Social Care*, DoH, London.

Dominelli, L. (1988), *Anti-Racist Social Work*, Macmillan, Basingstoke.

Foote, C. and Pisek, P. (2001), 'Thinking out of the box', *Health Service Journal*, **111** (no. 5750), pp. 32–3.

Garbarino, J. (1986), 'Where does social support fit into optimizing human development and preventing dysfunction?', *British Journal of Social Work*, **16**(suppl't), pp. 23–37.

Giddens, A. (1998), *The Third Way: The Renewal of Social Democracy*, Polity Press, Cambridge.

Gilchrist, A. (1997), 'A more excellent way: developing coalition and consensus through informal networking', *Community Development Journal*, **33**(2), pp. 100–108.

Gottlieb, B.H. (ed.) (1981), *Social Networks and Social Support*, Sage, London.

Greig, R. and Poxton, R. (2001), 'From joint commissioning to partnership working – will the new policy framework make a difference?', *Managing Community Care*, **9**(4), pp. 32–8.

Higham, P.E. (2001), 'Changing practice and an emerging social pedagogue paradigm in England: the role of the personal adviser', *Social Work in Europe*, **8**(1), pp. 21–9.

Hutton, W. (1997), *The State to Come*, Vintage, London.

Jones, R.V.H. (1992), 'Teamwork in primary care: how much do we know about it?', *Journal of Interprofessional Care*, **6**(1), pp. 25–9.

Jordan, B. (1970), *Client–Worker Transactions*, Routledge and Kegan Paul, London.

Jordan, B., with Jordan, C. (2000), *Social Work and the Third Way: Tough Love as Social Policy*, Sage, London.

Mackintosh, M. (2000), 'Flexible contracting? Economic cultures and implicit contracts in social care', *Journal of Social Policy*, **29**(1), pp. 1–19.

Maguire, L. (1983), *Understanding Social Networks*, Sage, London.

Mayo, M. and Taylor, M. (2001), 'Partnerships and power in community regeneration', in Balloch, S. and Taylor, M. (eds), *Partnership Working: Policy and Practice*, Policy Press, Bristol, pp. 39–56.

Mitchell, J.C. (1969), 'The concept and use of social networks', in Mitchell, J.C. (ed.), *Social Networks in Urban Situations: Analyses of Personal Relationships in Central African Towns*, Manchester University Press, Manchester, pp. 1–50.

Parton, N. (2000), 'Some thoughts on the relationship between theory and practice in and for social work', *British Journal of Social Work*, **30**(4), pp. 449–63. (An earlier version, presented in the *Theorising Social Work Research* seminar series, no. 1, 26 May 1999, Brunel University, is now available at
<http://www.elsc.org.uk/socialcareresource/tswr/seminar1/parton.htm>.)

Payne, M. (1993), *Linkages: Effective Networking in Social Care*, Whiting and Birch, London.

Pedison, J. and Sorenson, J.S. (1989), *Organisational Cultures in Theory and Practice*, Avebury, Aldershot.

Pratt, J., Gordon, P. and Plamping, D. (1998), *Working Whole Systems: Putting Theory into Practice in Organisations*, King's Fund, London.

Rao, N. (1991), *From Providing to Enabling: Local Authorities and Community Care Planning*, Joseph Rowntree Foundation, York.

Seebohm Committee (1968), *Report of the Committee on Local Authority and Allied Personal Social Services*, Cmnd 3703, HMSO, London.

Seed, P. (1990), *Introducing Network Analysis in Social Work*, Jessica Kingsley, London.

Seed, P. and Kaye, G. (1994), *Handbook for Assessing and Managing Care in the Community*, Jessica Kingsley, London.

Senge, P. (1990), *The Fifth Discipline: The Art and Practice of the Learning Organisation*, Doubleday, New York.

Smale, G., Tuson, G., Cooper, M., Wardle, M. and Crosbie, D. (1988), *Community Social Work: A Paradigm for Change*, National Institute for Social Work, London.

Speck, R.V. and Attneave, C.L. (1973), *Family Networks*, Pantheon, New York.

Statham, D. (2000), 'Partnership between health and social care', *Health and Social Care in the Community*, **8**(2), pp. 87–9.

Treanor, J., Wintour, P. and Harper, K. (2002), 'Fury at Byers bail-out for air traffic', *Guardian*, 20 February.

Trevillion, S. (1988), 'Conferencing the crisis: the application of network models to social work practice', *British Journal of Social Work*, **18**(3), pp. 289–307.

Trevillion, S. (1999), *Networking and Community Partnership*, Arena, Aldershot.

Trevillion, S. (2000), 'Social work, social networks and network knowledge', *British Journal of Social Work*, **30**(4), pp. 505–17. (An earlier version was presented in the *Theorising Social Work Research* seminar series, no. 1, 26 May 1999, Brunel University.)

Wasserman, S. and Faust, K. (1994), *Social Network Analysis: Methods and Applications*, Cambridge University Press, Cambridge.

Chapter 6

Taking Sides: Social Work Research as a Moral and Political Activity

Beth Humphries

Introduction

Years ago in the 1960s, Howard Becker argued that all research, and particularly social research, is always conducted, reported, interpreted from someone's point of view, and is therefore partisan. He thought the most important question was 'whose side are we on?' (Becker, 1967). Impartiality is neither possible nor desirable; to claim impartiality is pretence. Researchers should declare their partiality openly, putting research to work in the interests of 'the underdog'. In other words, research is both a moral and a political activity, and taking sides is inevitable. The issue is particularly important at a time when social work is pushing to be accepted as a distinctive research-based discipline, competing for recognition and resources from government and the wider research community.

This chapter will attempt to locate social work research in the current political and policy context of welfare in the UK, focusing particularly on the status of its claim to operate in anti-oppressive ways. Using the example of immigration and asylum controls, the area of my ongoing research, I comment on the separation that has taken place between social work and social policy. I ask whether policy is indeed informed by evidence from research, and what research tells us about social work practice in this field. I examine the implications of this for social work's claim to be on the side of 'the oppressed'.

Research, objectivity and partisanship

The 'taking sides' debate that arose 30 years ago is no less relevant now. Social work research, in particular the evidence-based practice movement which is currently influential in the UK and elsewhere, with its urge to separate practice from politics and to identify and measure only 'what works', implicitly embraces the myth of value-free research. This requires examination.

The claim that impartiality is neither possible nor desirable is based on a concept of power and the ways its distribution in society regulates both material and ideological relations. The definition, interpretation, and solution of social problems and social need lie largely with relatively powerful groups and in professional and bureaucratic contexts. These institutional arrangements exclude the participation and perception of less powerful and less advantaged groups. The invisibility and enforced silence of such groups in setting the terms of the debate are what make it impossible and undesirable for researchers not to take sides. Whether acknowledged or not, the questions that affect research can never be only with 'what works'. Ethical research is concerned also with the conditions that lead to or hinder the self-realisation of individuals and groups, including the impact of social policy interventions.

The main accusation made against the call to 'take sides' consciously and explicitly in research is that in the process objectivity is sacrificed, reliability and validity are compromised, and the result is research that is biased and invalid. Truth must be sought for its own sake, and the methods used to pursue it must be technically sound. This doctrine, prevalent at least since Weber, demands the separation of facts and values, requiring a moral effort on the part of the researcher to prevent her/his personal views from intruding into purely technical decisions. But the emphasis on technique can be overstressed. Are we to believe that researchers' (and funders') personal values and the manner in which they are held, or their sanity or maturity, are irrelevant if the impersonal machinery of research is irreproachable?

Gouldner (1973, see especially chapters 1–5), like Becker, saw no incompatibility between partisanship and objectivity, and gave a number of reasons why social researchers need to take sides. I have referred above to the issue of the power to define need; the presence of suffering is another of these reasons. Gouldner gave the example of the physician whose objectivity is not affected because he has made a partisan commitment to his patient and against the disease and its causes. Objectivity is secured because of a commitment to a specific value: health. 'Insofar as [we] are capable of distinguishing the side to which [we] are attached, from the *grounds* on which [we] are attached to it, [we] are, to that extent, capable of a significant objectivity' (1973, p. 58, emphasis in original). The physician's objectivity can of course be compromised if he loses sight of the value and focuses on the character of the patient (resulting, for example, in refusal of treatment because the lung cancer sufferer continues to be a smoker). Our most basic commitment as researchers is to particular values, not to particular factions. In social work those values include an opposition to injustice and a commitment to alleviating and even preventing suffering. Research that is concerned to expose and challenge inequalities is entirely compatible with these values. Research that attempts solely to measure the impact of interventions, regardless of their relationship to the social context, is not value-free. Rather, it has taken the side of whatever values have inspired the interventions it uncritically 'evaluates'.

Researchers are in a position to bring to public notice realities unknown to the powerful and respectable, and new perspectives on worlds that have been taken for granted. The fact that disempowered people suffer should make a compelling demand on us. Gouldner makes the point that one possible meaning of objectivity in social science is the contribution the latter might make to what he calls a 'human unity of mankind' (1973, p. 67). However, to make such a contribution social scientists cannot and should not be impartial towards human suffering; they must not make their peace with any form of human unity that complacently accommodates itself to or imposes suffering. It is here that partisanship and objectivity can be brought together without conflict, and it is also here where social work research has the potential to make a unique contribution because of the values it espouses and because of what it *knows* about inequality. Taking sides should imply neither an absence of rigour and care in the conduct of research, nor the use of a sloppy methodology. It should not result in ignoring ways in which oppressed groups can also be oppressors (for example, see Wise (1990) on the dangers of social workers ignoring child abuse by mothers because of a commitment to women as an oppressed group). And in any event, research need not focus exclusively on 'the oppressed'; rather, in constructing an holistic understanding of social processes, it should also investigate the workings of institutions and 'power élites'. In other words, research holds no particular virtue in those who are oppressed, and no particular mendacity in those with power over them. It is when research attaches itself to *factions* (regardless of whether right or wrong) and not to *values* that 'taking sides' becomes a problem.

The politics of research in social work

The recent flurry of events in the UK to highlight the importance of research in social work – such as the ESRC-sponsored seminar series conducted during 1999–2000 and the development of a code of research ethics for social work (Butler, 2002) which was one of its aims and outputs – signals more than simply a renewed emphasis on the importance of research. Research in social work has taken on *political* significance as a result of changes in recent governments' policies related to the governance of research, and the possibilities of financial reward to institutions that are research-active – along with financial penalties for those that are not. Thus leading members of the UK social work academy have trained their sights on enhancing the profile of social work research, and through it the status of social work itself.

So whilst we may glibly – or even genuinely – declare that we are on the side of the oppressed, the urge for status and resources requires us to seek favour with the powerful; commitment to the oppressed is often compromised by attachment to self-interest. As Gouldner (1973, p. 32) put it: 'We are, in short, also on our own side.' The price to be paid for wider approval may be control of the topics to be pursued, the questions to be asked, the critical demeanour of research, and the directions to be recommended for policy and practice. The codes of ethics so enthusiastically pursued may turn out to be routine and banal, substitutes for a concern with the morality of policy, involving a loss of objectivity and independence in interrogating it. In Britain we have seen increasing restrictions on research financed by government departments, designed, for example, to ensure that published findings will support current policy (Hammersley and Gomm, 1997). The government-sponsored research that people in the social work academy aspire to is, more often than not, narrowly defined and based on a pseudo-scientific positivism focused on 'what works', isolating individual behaviour from the wider social and political context (examples include Macdonald, 1994; 1998; Macdonald and Sheldon, 1992). In fact it is the real objectivity of social work research that is at risk in a climate where motives and ideology lie unquestioned and where 'outcomes' hold the only value. Critics of the model of evidence-based practice which is increasingly hegemonic have highlighted its blinkered and limited focus: its obsession with individualism and prescription, particularly the emphasis on accomplishing measurable changes in behaviour, and the selection and application of outcomes of quantitative studies as the most appropriate to inform practice [eds: see also James, this volume]. As Jordan points out:

> Despite the grandiose claims of scientific probity and methodological soundness, most of the studies undertaken are context-specific: they examine the effects of interventions undertaken in a very specific set of cultural, environmental and administrative circumstances, such as a particular residential or day care regime, or battery of investigative procedures. (Jordan, 2000, p. 208)

The evidence-based practice movement does not ask questions about the ideological basis that informs practice. It assumes that the *origins* and *aims* of intervention are unproblematic; it is only the *methods* about which questions are asked, as to whether they are appropriate and effective. If there is a quest for 'truth' here, one suspects that 'allegiance [is] to the *flag* of truth, while saying nothing about the *country* for which it stands' (Gouldner, 1973, p. 65, emphases added).

Moreover, the approach carries with it a confidence in the possibility of certainty. It is reluctant to acknowledge that most research is ambiguous and does not give definitive answers. Research findings are open to a range of interpretation and seldom offer 'proof' of the efficacy or otherwise of particular interventions [eds: see also Butler and Pugh, this volume]. In both the physical and the social sciences caution is a fundamental principle in assessing and interpreting research findings, yet the push for evidence-based practice not only rejects other possible research approaches, but also puts its faith in clear and unambiguous results, capable of providing prescriptions for practice. A range of methods has a place in social research, and the need for rigour is no less important whatever the approach employed (Humphries, 1999; Humphries and Martin, 2000) [eds: see also Gould, this volume]. The point is that an insistence on the so-called 'scientific' model, and on adopting a narrow, individualistic, practice focus as the only legitimate way to conceptualise research for social work, ignores the decades of epistemological and methodological debates within social research communities. This also results in a barren, mechanistic and distorted construction of practice and its possibilities, and in a denial of the contribution of research to a moral and a just society.

Social policy and social work – evidence-based, or not?

Here I want to move from a focus on the relationship between research and social work practice and attend to another aspect of the drive for an 'evidence base': that of the relationship of research to social policy initiatives. My argument here is that not only are assertions about the appropriateness and/or adequacy of the 'scientific' model misleading, but despite rhetoric about the importance of the results of impartial research in informing policy there are examples to suggest that policy and legislation commonly *ignore* evidence from research where this does not support the direction already set or taken, which tends rather to be based primarily on ideological commitments, supported with selective evidence. For example, New Labour youth justice policies have resulted in an increase in the numbers of 18–20-year-old young men in prison in the belief that 'prison works', ignoring research that suggests that locking up young offenders increases the risk of youth crime (National Association for the Care and Resettlement of Offenders, 2001; Ramsbotham, 2001). Modood's (1997) study examining the position of Asian communities in Pennine towns warned that segregated failing schools, poverty, discrimination, and neglect were building into resentment and racial tension. Yet this Government's policy has reinforced the idea that poverty is an issue of individual character, and has encouraged the proliferation of segregated education. Its condemnation of the race riots of 2001 as 'wanton criminality' (Home Secretary David Blunkett, reported in the *Observer*, 15 July 2001) and subsequent call for 'proof' of loyal citizenship, ignores the evidence, confirms stereotypes, aggravates grievances, and nurtures the ground for the activities of groups on the extreme Right. Much of Government policy is based on populism rather than evidence.

Beresford and Evans have pointed out that social research in the latter half of the twentieth century shifted from a role in initiating policy developments to one of evaluating, monitoring and legitimating them. In other words, it now primarily occupies a reactive position in relation to social policy, with an emphasis on exploring the 'effectiveness, efficiency and economy of policy … reflected in its increasing preoccupation with managerially and professionally defined outcomes and outcome measurement' (1999, p. 672). Any role involving an examination of policies themselves has been removed. Research about social work is no exception to this; the trend has been towards an uncritical treatment of the policy context in which social work is practised. This separation of social work and social work research from a critique of social policy, and the enthusiasm for this in some quarters within social work, suggests a moral and political conservatism in the profession. This is evidenced in a willingness to collaborate with what Butler and Drakeford (2001, p. 7) call 'a particular form of social authoritarianism', which has robbed social work of its radical and transformatory potential [eds: see also Butler and Pugh, this volume].

The danger in the direction being taken by social work research is obvious. To go down the road of separating the 'effectiveness' of social work from the ideological basis on which policy affecting service provision depends is to ignore the potentially oppressive origins of such policy, and to construct social work as 'part, not of an inclusive but of an incorporative agenda, in which awkward, troublesome and risky individuals who do not play by the rules of their own volition, must be made to do so' (Butler and Drakeford, 2001, p. 15). The purpose of social work research in this scenario is to evaluate just how effective strategies for control are. It is important for a critical social work research to resist the separation of social work from social policy, to commit itself to asking questions about the implications for practice of such a separation, and particularly to ask whose best interests are served by these moves.

The example of immigration controls

Immigration control provides an example of the need for research to be drawn into the service of preventing human suffering and exposing the myths that legitimate unequal treatment. In this regard it exemplifies the need to resist a separation of policy, research and practice in social affairs. Immigration control has relevance for social work in ways that, sadly, social workers are only beginning to appreciate. Immigration legislation operates in respect of a country not only externally (as it were), at the level of pre-entry and on-entry controls, but also after entry, in the shape of internal controls. Such after-entry controls are applied not by immigration officials alone. Other public officials administering housing benefits, income support, child benefit, attendance allowance, aspects of social care, and so on, all have a part to play in internal controls.

Since the inception of immigration controls in this country in 1905, a relationship has existed with welfare entitlement. An 'undesirable' immigrant is someone who cannot support themselves and their dependents, or who because of disease or infirmity is likely to become a burden on the tax-/rate-payer. Eligibility for benefits has been inextricably linked to immigration status; entitlement was further eroded with each piece of legislation introduced during the twentieth century and this has continued into the twenty-first. The 1999 Immigration and Asylum Act removed the right to claim welfare benefits from all who are subject to immigration legislation; for destitute asylum seekers it set up a segregated and inferior system of welfare in the shape of the National Asylum Support Service (NASS), located within the Immigration and Nationality Directorate of the Home Office (Cohen, 2001). Support to asylum seekers shifted to being 'in kind', mainly through food vouchers (which specific approach was later abandoned as a failure). A forced dispersal scheme, which remains in operation, involves one offer of housing with no choice as to location; anyone leaving the accommodation loses any right to support. Yet another Act was approved by Parliament on 7 November 2002. Among other changes it provides for locating asylum seekers in large centres in rural areas, which will surely worsen their housing situation. There are some ambiguous aspects of the 2002 Act, and local authorities retain responsibility for certain categories of asylum seeker and immigrant under the National Assistance Act, 1948, and the Children Act, 1989. These include, for example, unaccompanied asylum seekers under the age of 18, families with children who are not asylum seekers but subject to immigration control and not entitled to benefits, and certain groups who as well as being destitute are old, sick, or disabled.

The Nationality, Immigration and Asylum Act which came into force in January 2003 will set up virtual prisons for asylum seekers. Moreover, Section 55 of the Act denies welfare support to anyone not claiming asylum 'as soon as reasonably practicable' [*sic*] after they arrive in the UK – which in practice, it seems, means 'immediately'. The operation and the legality of this latter provision, not least its compatibility with human rights legislation, have already been challenged via a number of 'test cases' in the High Court under the judicial review process, with the Home Office subsequently going to the Court of Appeal on several judgements which have gone against them. [Eds: as this book goes to press, the picture emerging from the string of cases which have been through the courts seems to be that, despite the Home Office's claim (following an adverse judgement on the first test cases) to have 'made changes to our procedures to ensure that individual cases get full and fair consideration' (Home Secretary David Blunkett, Press Release, 18 March 2003), it is quite possible, though not inevitable, for the application of Section 55 of the 2002 Act (see above) to breach any of several Articles of the European Convention on Human Rights.]

The questions I now address here are: first, what research, if any, informed the policy and legislation initiatives reported above; and second, what does the available research say about how social work interprets and implements its role in relation to people subject, in one way or another, to immigration controls?

Social policy and the available evidence on immigration

UK immigration controls are justified – both officially and in the general understanding – in a number of ways: to control the numbers of people on what is already an overcrowded little island; to preserve the jobs, wealth and welfare of the country against the perceived threat of 'economic migrants', who would take jobs away from natives and exploit the country's wealth and welfare; to allay fears that immigration leads to an increase in racial tension; and to ensure good race relations within Britain. Let us look at the available research.

With regard to numbers, the 1991 Population Census records that the 'ethnic minority' population of Britain (i.e. non-Europeans) was 5.5 per cent of the total population (Layton-Henry, 1992). The Organisation for Economic Co-operation and Development (OECD) published figures in 1998 showing the 'foreign' population (i.e. those without citizenship of the country concerned) as a proportion of total resident population in various European countries in 1997. The highest proportion was in Austria (9.1 per cent), and the lowest in the UK (3.6 per cent). These statistics are, of course, partial and may be misleading. They tend to exclude, for example, both 'illegal' immigrants and people who have citizenship of the country concerned but were born abroad. However, a factor often omitted relates to people *leaving* Britain and other European countries. The official British figure for net migration to/from this country between 1971 and 1991 – the difference between the known number of those arriving and those leaving – is minus 705,000 (Layton-Henry, 1992). Sutcliffe (1998, cited in Hayter, 2000, p. 11) comments that as the overall demographic effect of immigration and emigration appears to be almost insignificant, its apparent political significance is all the more striking. He suggests that part of the explanation for this is due to the opportunistic use of the topic of immigration by the extreme Right and others.

In current discourses, 'immigrants' and 'asylum seekers' have been conflated and criminalised. But the numbers of people seeking asylum in European countries are directly related to persecution, war and civil disturbances. In 1998–

99 for instance, applications from the Federal Republic of Yugoslavia made up over half of all asylum applications to the countries of the European Union, with 90 per cent of those involved being Kosovo Albanians. In 2001 the level of asylum applications to the UK was 1.5 per thousand of the population, seventh highest among the countries of the European Union on this measure, whilst the equivalent ratio for Sweden was 2.6 and that for Austria was the highest at 3.7 per thousand (Information Centre about Asylum and Refugees in the UK (ICAR), 2003). Although authoritative figures show a numerical increase in applications to Britain from around 32,000 in 1987 to nearly 90,000 in the late 1990s, this is misleading, as the Office of the United Nations High Commissioner for Refugees (UNHCR), which produces these and related statistics, changed its method of calculation during this period to include dependents.

These problems of interpretation are common in the use of any official statistics. The latter are subject to whatever definition of an issue is dominant; such definitions are liable to change, as are methods of calculation. The figures often do not take account of balancing factors, and usually are not placed in a wider context for comparison. They also need to be read in the light of fluctuations in the pattern of the events being measured, rather than being seen as representing a steady upward or downward movement. Yet these complexities do not figure in the image of overwhelming numbers of asylum seekers/immigrants which pervades public debate. Some newspapers claim thousands of 'bogus' refugees are being admitted (e.g. the *Mail on Sunday*, 15 March 1998; the *Daily Mail*, 28 July 1998). The White Paper *Fairer, Faster and Firmer* (Home Office, 1998a) was, according to the Home Secretary, 'intended to curb the rapid increases in asylum applications from migrants simply seeking a better life in Britain' (reported in *The Sunday Times*, 31 October 1999). None of these public utterances paid the slightest attention to the available research, in the frenzy to be 'tougher than thou' and to make political hay out of the suffering and despair of other human beings.

A myth that fuels immigration discourses is that immigrants and refugees take work that should go to people already living here, so that without immigration controls the jobs and living standards of existing residents would be threatened. The UK Government states that its concern is with 'economic refugees', and most rejected applications are turned down for that reason, with much being made of rooting out those who are 'bogus' asylum seekers. Interestingly, in this context the desire to find work is interpreted negatively, whereas New Labour policies such as the various 'New Deal' arrangements encourage work as a virtue. Moreover, the Government is actively recruiting workers from abroad to fill vacancies resulting from a shortage of native labour. Unskilled work which the natives concerned are unwilling to do, such as casual employment in hotels, restaurants, supermarkets and hospitals, features in this context; but so too does work in areas needing highly skilled practitioners, such as medicine, nursing, teaching, social work, and information technology (Hayter, 2000; Sassen, 1999). Economic migration is taking place in response to labour demand in rich countries, and is likely to increase with declining birth rates there.

The picture is in fact even more bizarre. The present Government's rhetoric condemns 'economic migrants', while at the same time there is a thriving exploitation of illegal labour, which rich countries have come to depend upon. Sassen (1999) reports that in the USA the practice of employing foreigners illegally as cheap exploitable labour is virtually institutionalised, with these workers a recognised part of the labour force, much valued by employers. The UK research is still tentative, but Hayter (2000) reports Rwandan women working in the clothing industry in London for £1.50 an hour; Chinese businesses employing Chinese 'illegals' seven days a week, giving them no money and little food; British farmers employing illegal immigrants for a pittance. The *Observer* of 14 March 1999 reported that Filipinos and Mauritians were working on oilrigs in 'slave' conditions for 81 pence an hour. As for the impact on local wages and conditions, an OECD publication declared that the methodological arsenal of modern econometrics could find no evidence that immigrants have a major adverse effect on earnings and job opportunities (Borjas, 1993). The indications are that immigrants do not cause unemployment, and have little effect on wage levels and conditions; their effect on employment levels is if anything positive, because they take jobs shunned by natives.

The studies, as always, are not conclusive. However, as Hayter (2000, p. 159) says, 'supposing there was, after all, any negative effect on wages and conditions ... the obvious response is to make more effort to incorporate them as fully as possible into union structures'. A secure and legal resident status would benefit immigrant workers and their families. The question is whether the economic benefits of an illegal workforce are such that it is expedient for governments to criminalise rather than protect them.

A myth that gained credence from 1962 onwards involved the belief that immigration controls are necessary to maintain good race relations, and with it the assumption that not all those wishing to enter the UK as immigrants should be excluded, but rather only those who are clearly different from the majority population in appearance and culture. This argument exposes the relationship between immigration controls and 'race', and with it the belief held by its proponents that both numbers and 'difference' are offending factors. Margaret Thatcher's rhetoric of 'swamping' and her misuse of statistics exemplify the argument: 'If you want good race relations, you have got to allay people's fears about numbers' (*World in Action*, ITV, 30 January 1978); and she quoted figures predicting that by the year 2000 there would be 'four million people of the New Commonwealth or Pakistan'. The group she predicted as becoming a 'frightening minority' was at the time less than 4 per cent of the population.

The evidence that exists in any substance is of systematic discrimination against immigrants and black British people in jobs, education, health and public life, and of officially sanctioned violence against them. The statistics show that of over a million people stopped and searched, the proportions were 37 per 1000 for whites, 66 per 1000 for Asians, and 180 per 1000 for Caribbeans and Africans (Home Office, 1998b). Research for 2001–02 suggests that African Caribbeans are eight times more likely than whites to be stopped and searched, and Asians three times more likely (Home Office, 2002). The list of black people who have died in police cells, or during attempts to deport them, far exceeds (in proportional terms) that of whites who have died in similar circumstances (see Hayter, 2000, p. 36 for a catalogue of the deaths).

If improving race relations is a concern, successive governments have done nothing to pursue this goal. Modood's (1997) research in the former mill towns of northern England revealed years of neglect, low quality housing and schooling, and unemployment. Oldham Metropolitan Borough is in the top one per cent of deprived boroughs in the country. Twenty per cent of its school children are from ethnic minorities. An OFSTED[1] report on the area's schools in January 2001 identified tensions related to schooling (*Observer*, 15 July 2001). Have the problems arisen because a large minority of Asians live in the area, and thus threaten race relations, or because of a more general alienation, deprivation and division? Various far-Right neo-fascist groups are active in fuelling fear and promoting a distorted image of racist violence – it is the white pensioner with the bloodied face who has suffered anti-white racism. Decades of neglect of working class communities (black and white) fades into the background of burning cars and circling machetes.

It is too simplistic – irresponsible – for a government to claim that improving race relations depends on controlling numbers of black people entering Britain. The argument disguises a motive of controlling immigration to exclude poor people, and especially black people. The justification of controls is not based on the available research, which is either inconclusive or suggests that immigrants and asylum seekers are an asset rather than a problem, and that violence is more likely to be perpetrated against them than by them.

The present Government emphasises practice and policy that is based on systematic evidence. Indeed, when the Labour Party – then still the Opposition – produced the ideas for immigration controls which later appeared in *Fairer, Faster and Firmer* (Home Office, 1998a), it announced that research would be carried out. Instead of research we have seen the 1999 Immigration and Asylum Act, and its successor the Nationality, Immigration and Asylum Act, 2002, deal further brutal blows in the fields of asylum and immigration.

Moreover, in the Government's 'what works' parlance there are data available to suggest that controls do *not* work. During the 1990s there were increasingly repressive measures in the form of fines on carriers and airlines, spot checks, sniffer dogs, carbon dioxide detectors, all of them employed to ensure 'illegal' immigrants and 'bogus' asylum seekers were not allowed to enter Britain. Yet the numbers of asylum seekers remained roughly constant during the 1990s. Now, within the UK, asylum seekers carry 'smart' cards and have their fingerprints taken. People fleeing persecution and war are desperate, and they employ desperate and innovative methods to flee their oppressors, sometimes losing their lives in the process. Further, in a period of growing power on the part of international private capital, the contradiction of maintaining freedom of movement for the latter whilst at the same time preventing the free movement of labour will not indefinitely withstand the pressures of globalisation (Hayter, 2000).

---

[1]   The Office for Standards in Education (OFSTED) is the Office of Her Majesty's Inspector of Schools in England.

There are also problems around deporting people. The costs of detention and of assessing claims are prohibitive, and deportation may not be practicable following the rejection of an application. Countries of origin may not readmit people, they may have developed family links in Britain, or they may have disappeared. The poor publicity surrounding attempts to deport forcibly, and the campaigns to prevent deportations, lead officials to despair at their inability to carry them through efficiently.

Immigration policy and anti-oppressive social work practice

All of this raises a fundamental question. If there is no clear evidence that immigrants and asylum seekers take jobs and will 'swamp' the majority population numerically; if the demographic effect is insignificant; if the main issue affecting race relations is not numbers; and if the whole paraphernalia of immigration control is both costly and ineffectual; what then *does* inform Government policy?

The key objection to immigration control is not any of those addressed thus far. Immigration controls affect some people more than others, and are not applied uniformly to all of those people wanting to enter the UK who are not British citizens. The rules treat people differently according to ethnicity, country of origin, parentage, sexuality, gender, physical ability, age and economic means (Humphries, 2002a). In other words, *they discriminate against people on all the grounds that social work claims to oppose.* Those who are rich and white are the most likely to have least problems in gaining entry and citizenship. Exclusion of people from this country depends on a nationalist construction of certain groups as 'other', as 'not of us', as 'alien'. The law reinforces these notions by classifying those who 'belong', and nationality legislation grants full British citizenship to people whose ancestry is likely to be white and European (Cohen, 2001; Cohen *et al.*, 2002; Hayter, 2000). Immigration policy also treats women as dependents of men. Even where they have an entitlement to come to Britain in their own right this is lost on marriage, and they have no independent right to stay here unless their husbands are settled and they too are granted settlement. They are literally appendages (Bhabha and Shutter, 1994). Where a couple is granted leave to marry, and the wife does not have settlement status, she may be deported if she leaves her husband after less than a year of marriage, potentially forcing women to stay in violent and dangerous circumstances. Gay and lesbian couples are also treated differently from heterosexual couples, both as regards the length of time they have to have lived together before making application for settlement, and the probationary period afterwards (Stonewall, 2000).

However, even if changes were made to treat women in the same ways as men in the relevant respects, and likewise gays and lesbians in the same ways as heterosexuals, the fundamental problem remains; white people would be treated differently from black people. Immigration law is intrinsically racist, because it depends on ideas about 'kith and kin', and about 'the Other' as 'abusing ("our") services', 'bogus', and unwelcome (Hayes, 2002; Humphries, 2002a).

Social work and internal controls

There has been very little by way of debate in social work about the fundamental question raised by the above discussion. If immigration controls are intrinsically discriminatory, and therefore contradict the values of social work, should the profession co-operate with their implementation at even the most basic level? Because of the individualistic orientation of dominant discourses in social work, and the separation of social work from social policy (in the sense argued earlier), questions about policies that perpetuate inequalities can be ducked. What then is expected of social work in relation to immigration controls, and what do studies of practice tell us about how social work interprets its role?

Local authorities, and social services departments in particular, have a responsibility to offer help to certain people subject to immigration control. Alongside this, since 1993 social work and other health, education and welfare services have been drawn in to play their part in the internal control of access to services. (This is not inconsistent with the changing rhetoric of welfare and the redefinition of social work in terms of a more explicit authoritarian and controlling function (Humphries, 2002b; Jones and Novak, 1999; Parton, 1996).) The Home Office's 'efficiency scrutiny' signalled an intention that each state worker would in effect become an arm of that government department to ensure that no one should benefit from state provision who is not entitled to it (Hudson, 1997). A 'help line' was set up for workers unsure of a person's immigration status to check with the Home Office before offering a service. The 1999 Immigration and Asylum Act enshrined this 'partnership' in the legislation. Section 20 provides for information to be supplied to the Home Secretary for 'immigration purposes' by a range of policing agencies. It also allows the Home Secretary to make an order obliging a 'specified person' to pass on information for 'immigration purposes' (Cohen, 2001). I am not aware of any debate in social work circles about the ethics of this, or about the anti-discrimination implications of the relationship between an expectation to report a person's immigration status and the professional obligation to offer help where it is needed. Is the absence of a public discussion of the contradictions an indication that these are not experienced or identified in practice? What does the evidence tell us about what *is* happening in social work practice?

Social work practice and immigration control: the evidence

The research carried out in this field to date has been sparse, but those studies that do exist paint a worrying picture. Düvell and Jordan carried out interviews with members of 'asylum teams'[2] in London, and reported that asylum seekers were receiving a second class service, well below the standard seen as acceptable for UK citizens (Düvell and Jordan, 2000; Jordan, 2000). They found that staff lacked preparation and training for work with refugees, with little support given by way of

---

[2]   The 1996 Asylum and Immigration Appeals Act excluded asylum seekers from welfare benefits. Some local authorities set up 'asylum teams' to provide help to these people under the National Assistance Act, 1948.

interpretation of policy from central or local government, and that practice was inconsistent and guided by 'bureaucratic rules of thumb' (Jordan, 2000, p. 141).

Although the researchers were sympathetic to the teams in terms of the restricted resources available to them, their findings 'illustrated the fact that social workers will volunteer to do the "dirty work" of social policy, even when this involves intentional and systematic deprivation by official agencies of the means of dignified existence' (*ibid.*, p. 140). These social workers were, by some criteria, violating human rights. Jordan quotes a social worker attempting to give a morally adequate account of her/his work:

> [I]n the afternoons when we do reviews, social work with clients ... to talk about other problems they have ... that is the moment I am really doing social work ... This is the first time I am seeing the client as a person, as a human being. (*ibid.*)

No doubt this social worker saw this as 'anti-oppressive', in view of her/his recognition of clients' humanity. There is nothing more unacceptable than the administration of cruelty in a kindly way, except perhaps when those doing the administering pride themselves on their kindness. The social workers acknowledged that they were assessors and rationers rather than counsellors, and they

> echoed the unease, guilt and resentment felt by the whole profession, simply taking to the extreme the tendency ... to become trapped in a downward spiral of compromise between client need and resource scarcity – always pressed, rushed and conscious of their shortcomings, but never able to draw a firm line where falling standards have sunk to unacceptably low levels. (*ibid.*, p. 143)

Jones (1998) studied the child welfare implications of UK immigration and asylum policy. She found lawyers and social workers ill-prepared, resulting in vulnerability and risk for many of the children in the study, some of whom were detained in adult prisons and subjected to conditions of hardship, deprivation, and sometimes physical and sexual assault. Where there were concerns about 'significant harm', Jones observed that since the primary legislation applicable is immigration law, the lesser requirement of 'reasonable cause to suspect' (Children Act, 1989) is subsumed within the greater requirement of proof required by immigration authorities that the issues raised are not merely a ploy designed to prevent the child's deportation. Jones describes material deprivation, separation from family, and inconsistent responses on the part of local authorities to children regarded as 'in need'. Social workers seemed to have little knowledge, interest, or regard for the immigration problems of their clients, even if the latter were children in public care, for whom they thus had specific responsibilities. Although there were examples of careful and imaginative practice, Jones identified failings in the protection of children in public care that raised questions about whether young people who are asylum seekers are regarded as having the same rights to protection from harm as other children.

Uncertainty and lack of knowledge were also evident amongst the social workers in research conducted in Greater Manchester examining the needs of young separated asylum seekers (Humphries and Mynott, 2001). The latter experienced vulnerability in terms of decisions about their asylum status, separation from family, accommodation, education, health and well-being, and facing racism. There was no explicit inclusion of targets for young separated asylum seekers in *Quality Protects* strategies. In one authority the children and families team had no specialist training, nor were there any pre-planned procedures for dealing with this group of young people. Team members were aware of and concerned about the trauma experienced by the young refugees, but had little knowledge of their immigration status or of the legislation. Although the young people should have been assessed as 'children in need' under Section 17 of the 1989 Children Act, assessment was likely to take place under the 'children at risk' provision. This reclassifying of the problem was explained as the most likely way to obtain a positive response. It is clearly not an appropriate procedure through which to help separated asylum-seeking children, yet it appears to be the only way to secure help in rigid, bureaucratic settings [eds: see Kearney, this volume, for some related discussion]. Decisions about an offer of help also entailed social workers checking immigration status with the Home Office, the implications of which those interviewed did not appear to appreciate. They were operating internal controls as envisaged by the Home Office's 'efficiency scrutiny', without any real reflection on the ethical implications for their role or the possible consequences for the children. The practice seemed to be regarded as no more than an irritating bureaucratic hurdle.

These studies – which predate and therefore do not reflect any impact of the Nationality, Immigration and Asylum Act, 2002 – illustrate the consequences of separating social work from social policy analysis, in the sense and manner discussed earlier in this chapter. They raise worrying questions about the policies of local authorities and about social work practice in the field of immigration controls. There is evidence that people subject to immigration control receive an inferior service, in that workers do not have the training, legal knowledge or expertise to equip them to offer a fit service. Their employers have not supported them with advice, briefing and interpretation of policy; they have not confronted the implications of co-operation with the Home Office, nor have they made attempts to place young asylum seekers' needs on a par with those of other children. Where good practice exists it does so despite these circumstances; the more common picture is one of workers who feel guilty, resentful and frustrated, and service users who are neglected, vulnerable and exploited.

The research reported here *does* have messages for practice. These concern resources, recognition, policy development, training, and, crucially, moral, ethical and political direction. They expressly do *not* take the form of or include suggestions for 'what works' in terms of behaviourist targeting and further controlling of the movements of people subject to immigration controls.

Conclusion: whose side are we on?

In this chapter I have described the negative consequences of the split between social work research and social policy research, and the divorce of both from a critique of social policy itself. I have also argued that current policy and practice in the UK are not necessarily based upon the available evidence, and that such evidence as exists is seldom conclusive and is always influenced by partisan interests. Much of the available evidence in fact tends to contradict recent and current government policy. I have asserted that immigration controls are intrinsically racist, and I have offered examples of research that consciously takes sides – in the sense in which I have used this phrase – against such racism. That is, such studies are rigorous, methodologically sound, and attempt to construct knowledge in a clear and informed way, but do not claim to be impartial in the sense of maintaining a pretence that researchers and their political masters do not have their own interests, which inform the topics they pursue and the questions they ask. These studies involve approaches that have concerns about inequality and injustice at their heart. Crucially, they do not ignore the ideological perspectives that inform the social policies directing the efforts of social workers. They endorse, rather, what Haraway (1988) describes as the partial 'view from somewhere', as having more credibility than the relativist view from everywhere, or the transcendent, objectifying, view from nowhere. The 'somewhere' is a commitment to truths emerging out of experiences of oppression (including oppression from social policies and their consequences), a desire to uncover hidden articulations of need, an urge to expose conditions of poverty and misery, and an effort to understand frameworks that lead to survival and resistance. The view from somewhere does not involve blind allegiance to either a flag or a faction, nor the distortion of inconvenient and hostile truths.

The view from somewhere does, however, also need to be wary of complacency. Gouldner warns against thinking 'that we have solved the problem of objectivity by good-naturedly confessing that, yes, we do have a standpoint, and by openly specifying what it is' (1973, p. 54). Such a bland confession of partisanship, he says, betrays smugness and naïveté – smug because it assumes the values that we have are good enough; naïve because it assumes we know what values we have. Describing complacency as 'the mind's embalming fluid' (*ibid.*), Gouldner recommends an examination of the *consequences* of the commitment(s) confessed: 'without considering these, confession becomes a meaningless ritual of frankness' (*ibid.*, p. 55). An interrogation of our mixed motives and allegiances as researchers, our relationship to the people and the topics studied – to know our values and to see that such knowledge is problematic – is crucial to authenticity in research.

The concerns discussed above suggest different kinds of focus from those that target individual behaviour and outcomes. They imply that an examination of policy and policy makers is a fundamental activity for social work research and should not be abandoned. They assert the compatibility of a commitment to objectivity and a commitment to making visible the suffering of oppressed groups. They raise again the need for social work research to grasp the moral and political realities of its positioning in contemporary Britain. They question the 'what works' agenda and its implications for human rights and welfare principles. They point to a continuing awareness of connections between policy and practice, the nature of anti-oppressive practice, the role of ethics, politics, and strategies of resistance. The evidence examined here raises alarming questions about the alignment of social work with forces that contradict its expressed values. The profession cannot avoid the moral and political aspects of its operation. It is time either to learn the lessons of the research, or to cease the pretence that current practice genuinely pursues 'empowerment'.

References

Becker, H.S. (1967), 'Whose side are we on?', *Social Problems*, **14**(3), pp. 239–47.

Beresford, P. and Evans, C. (1999), 'Research Note: Research and empowerment', *British Journal of Social Work*, **29**(5), pp. 671–7.

Bhabha, J. and Shutter, S. (1994), *Women's Movement: Women Under Immigration, Nationality and Refugee Law*, Trentham Books, Stoke-on-Trent.

Borjas, G.J. (1993), *The Impact of Immigrants on the Employment Opportunities of Natives*, OECD, Paris.

Butler, I. (2002), 'Critical Commentary: A code of ethics for social work and social care research', *British Journal of Social Work*, **32**(2), pp. 239–48. (An earlier version, presented in the *Theorising Social Work Research* seminar series, no. 6, 11 July 2000, University of Luton, is now available at
<http://www.elsc.org.uk/socialcareresource/tswr/seminar6/butler.htm>.
The Code itself is also available on the web page of the Joint Universities Council Social Work Education Committee (JUC/SWEC), which is in turn accessible via
<http://www.york.ac.uk/depts/poli/juc/jucwelc.htm>.)

Butler, I. and Drakeford, M. (2001), 'Which Blair project? Communitarianism, social authoritarianism and social work', *Journal of Social Work*, **1**(1), pp. 7–19.

Cohen, S. (2001), *Immigration Controls, the Family and the Welfare State*, Routledge, London.

Cohen, S., Humphries, B. and Mynott, E. (eds) (2002), *From Immigration Controls to Welfare Controls*, Routledge, London.

Düvell, F. and Jordan, B. (2000), *'How Low Can You Go?' Dilemmas of Social Work with Asylum Seekers in London*, Department of Social Work and Probation Studies, University of Exeter, Exeter.

Gouldner, A.W. (1973), *For Sociology: Renewal and Critique in Sociology Today*, Allen Lane, London.

Hammersley, M. and Gomm, R. (1997), 'Bias in social research', *Sociological Research Online*, **2**(1), <http://www.socresonline.org.uk/socresonline/2/1/2.html>.

Haraway, D. (1988), 'Situated knowledges: the science question in feminism and the privilege of partial perspective', *Feminist Studies*, **14**(3), pp. 575–99.

Hayes, D. (2002), 'From aliens to asylum seekers: a history of immigration controls and welfare in Britain', in Cohen, Humphries and Mynott, *op. cit.*, pp. 30–46.

Hayter, T. (2000), *Open Borders: The Case Against Immigration Controls*, Pluto, London.

Home Office (1998a), *Fairer, Faster and Firmer: A Modern Approach to Immigration and Asylum*, Cm 4018, Home Office, London.

Home Office (1998b), *Statistical Bulletin, 1998*, Home Office, London.

Home Office (2002), *Statistical Bulletin, 2002*, Home Office, London.

Hudson, D. (1997), 'Excluded at home, excluded in the UK', *Adults Learning*, **8**(5), pp. 121–3.

Humphries, B. (1999), 'Feminist evaluation', in Shaw, I. and Lishman, J. (eds), *Evaluation and Social Work Practice*, Sage, London, pp. 118–32.

Humphries, B. (2002a), 'Fair immigration controls – or none at all?', in Cohen, Humphries and Mynott, *op. cit.*, pp. 203–19.

Humphries, B. (2002b), 'From welfare to authoritarianism: the role of social work in immigration controls', in Cohen, Humphries and Mynott, *op. cit.*, pp. 126–40.

Humphries, B. and Martin, M. (2000), 'Disrupting ethics in social research', in Humphries, B. (ed.), *Research in Social Care and Social Welfare: Issues and Debates for Practice*, Jessica Kingsley, London, pp. 69–85.

Humphries, B. and Mynott, E. (2001), *Living Your Life Across Boundaries: Young Separated Refugees in Greater Manchester*, Save the Children Fund, London.

Information Centre about Asylum and Refugees in the UK (2003), *ICAR Statistics Paper 1: Statistics About Asylum Seekers in the UK*, ICAR, London.

Jones, A. (1998), *The Child Welfare Implications of UK Immigration and Asylum Policy*, Department of Applied Community Studies, Manchester Metropolitan University, Manchester.

Jones, C. and Novak, T. (1999), *Poverty, Welfare and the Disciplinary State*, Routledge, London.

Jordan, B., with Jordan, C. (2000), *Social Work and the Third Way: Tough Love as Social Policy*, Sage, London.

Layton-Henry, Z. (1992), *The Politics of Immigration*, Blackwell, Oxford.

Macdonald, G. (1994), 'Developing empirically-based practice in probation', *British Journal of Social Work*, **24**(4), pp. 405–27.

Macdonald, G. (1998), 'Promoting evidence-based practice in child protection', *Clinical Child Psychology and Psychiatry*, **3**(1), pp. 71–85.

Macdonald, G. and Sheldon, B., with Gillespie, J. (1992), 'Contemporary studies of the effectiveness of social work', *British Journal of Social Work*, **22**(6), pp. 615–43.

Modood, T. (1997), *British Asian Self-Employment: The Interaction of Culture and Economics*, Policy Studies Institute, London.

National Association for the Care and Resettlement of Offenders (2001), *Grow Up and Be Responsible*, NACRO, London.

Parton, N. (ed.) (1996), *Social Theory, Social Change and Social Work*, Routledge, London.

Ramsbotham, Sir D. (2001), *Report of the Fourth Inspection of HMYOI & RC, Feltham*, Her Majesty's Inspector of Prisons, Home Office, London.

Sassen, S. (1999), *Guests and Aliens*, The New Press, New York.

Stonewall Immigration Group (2000), *Briefing Document on Immigration Rules*, <http://www.stonewall-immigration.org.uk/Briefing%20Doc.htm>.

Sutcliffe, B. (1998), *Naçido in Otra Parte: Un Ensayo sobre la Migratión Internaçional, el Desarollo y la Equidad*, Hegoa, Bilbao, cited in Hayter, *op. cit.*

Wise, S. (1990), 'Becoming a feminist social worker', in Stanley, L. (ed.), *Feminist Praxis: Research, Theory and Epistemology in Feminist Sociology*, Routledge, London, pp. 236–49.

Chapter 7

Qualitative Research and Social Work: The Methodological Repertoire in a Practice-Oriented Discipline

Nick Gould

Introduction

In a recent book, Williams and Popay describe the dichotomised nature of welfare research and draw out the implications that these dichotomies have for the future direction of welfare policy and professional practice (Williams and Popay, 1999). A primary dichotomy has been between those forms of research study which foreground structural and policy contexts which constrain the subject, and those which prioritise the individual and focus on the construction of meaning and agency. To a large extent this polarity maps onto the duality of quantitative research (dealing with the structural and measurable) and qualitative research (dealing with meaning and discursive practices). As in so many aspects of Western culture (Haste, 1996) these oppositions are aligned with other deep-level polarities. For example, there is a gendered aspect of the quantitative/qualitative research divide [eds: see also Lyons and Taylor, this volume], with the implication that, 'real men don't do soft data' (although Ann Oakley's book *Experiments in Knowing* (2000) is an important step in reclaiming the relevance of quantitative methods for feminist research). Reductionism has predominated on both sides, with one camp asserting that 'there is no such thing as qualitative data, everything is 1 or 0', the other that 'all forms of statistical analysis involve the insertion of qualitative judgement'.

Inevitably, social work research does not stand outside these oppositions. In a discussion of the characteristics of academic debate over social work theory, Rojek and Collins (1987) coined the phrase, 'the gladiatorial paradigm'. The recent re-emergence of epistemological and theoretical debates within social work sometimes engenders a similar feeling that a fight to the death is ensuing and that there can be only one victor. This has focused around the enthusiastic importation of the concept of evidence-based practice from medicine, and the reaction of researchers who feel that this is inimical to the development of non-oppressive forms of research and practice in social work. Both perspectives involve – indeed to some extent they share – caricatures: of a hierarchical valuation of research designs that always places randomised controlled trials and systematic reviews at the top of a food chain that descends to qualitative case studies (a rigid ranking that has in reality become more nuanced in evidence-based medicine), opposed to qualitative researchers characterised as uninterested in technical issues such as validity and generalisation (about which they have in fact written libraries of books).

The most recent evidence-based practice debate in social work was captured almost before it had emerged by 'gladiatorial' position-taking. In the UK this was institutionally represented by the Department of Health/Association of Directors of Social Services funding of a centre for evidence-based social services, which has primarily been identified with individuals whose research provenance lies in behavioural and clinical social work, and with the research paradigms associated with experimental and variable-based research studies. This action has had its reaction, for instance in an informal grouping of researchers known as the 'Toronto Group' and predominantly identified with qualitative methods. This chapter itself grew out of the *Theorising Social Work Research* seminar series,[1] which seemed to define itself in fairly oppositional terms to the evidence-based persuasion. This author argued over ten years ago that social work suffers from a tendency to latch on to intellectual trends once they have passed in other disciplines; instances were given then of social work's late discovery of systems theory, behaviourism and poststructuralism (Gould, 1990). We need to be careful that we do not again expend energy fighting causes that have already moved on.

First, let us consider evidence-based medicine, where for a few years now there has been a growing pluralism:

> There are clear signs that the status of qualitative research within evidence-based medicine is changing. Criteria for the appraisal of qualitative research have been developed, and continue to be developed ... and there appears to be an increasing acknowledgement that the principle which determines what kind of research is of value is dictated by the specific clinical question. (Reynolds, 2000, p. 33)

There is also an evidence base to show that different professional groups will have differing views about what constitutes usable evidence. Doctors are more likely to give a narrower view based on generalisable quantitative evidence (represented primarily by randomised controlled trials), as compared with nurses, who include qualitative evidence, local information, and practice knowledge (Greenhalgh and Douglas, 1998, cited in Lipman, 2000, p. 55). One suspects that social work is rather like nursing in this respect, and my own research into practitioner constructions of learning suggests a similar mix of the formal and the informal (Gould, 2000).

---

[1]   An earlier version of the present chapter, entitled 'Qualitative research and the development of best attainable knowledge in social work', was presented at the fifth seminar in the *TSWR* series, 27 April 2000, University of Wales, Cardiff, and is now available at <http://www.elsc.org.uk/socialcareresource/tswr/seminar5/gould.htm>. It was in turn part of work then in progress towards Ian Shaw and Nick Gould (2001), *Qualitative Research in Social Work: Context and Method*, Sage, London.

This chapter considers the contribution of qualitative research to social work from a non-hierarchical perspective which accepts that social work practice can be informed by knowledge which is derived from a trinity of qualitative, quantitative and experiential sources. Forms of inquiry emphasising each of these have their own respective epistemologies and logics, but all constitute resources for the development of more effective practice. Underpinning the discussion which follows are two related observations which are not themselves considered in any detail: one is that social work markedly lacks an adequate sense of the historical development of its own knowledge base; the other is that because of social work's tendency to assimilate both theoretical perspectives and empirical findings from other social sciences and professions rather than generate its own indigenous understandings, there is (as already noted) often a time delay or 'catching up' quality to its internal debates (Gould, 1990). With these thoughts in mind, the chapter attempts four tasks: to situate qualitative social work research within a historical overview of its own and wider methodological developments; to identify some of the substantive themes and associated practice and policy issues which have proved amenable to inquiry through qualitative research methods; to explore the relationship between qualitative research and social work practice, including the idea of practice-based and/or experiential knowledge; to suggest evaluative criteria by which findings from qualitative social work research can be judged as evidence or knowledge.

Qualitative research in social work – a historical overview

The characterisation of the history of qualitative research in general has come to be dominated by Denzin and Lincoln's (1994) overview, which presents it in five broad 'moments'. First the *traditional period*, running from the beginning of the twentieth century until the Second World War, largely but not exclusively characterised by the dominance of the 'lone ethnographer', but also incorporating the Chicago School of sociology. The central object of interest was 'the Other', be it in the anthropological field study of foreign cultures or the sociological observation of marginal or outsider individuals and communities within the researcher's own society. Second the *modernist phase*, existing until the 1970s and typified by various projects to systematise and formalise the procedures of qualitative research. This would thus include Glaser and Strauss's development of grounded theory (1967). Although Denzin and Lincoln would see the high point of qualitative modernity as having passed by the 1970s, this moment continues in the work of writers like Miles and Huberman (1994), who advocate highly procedural-ised and systematic approaches to data collection, analysis and display. Denzin and Lincoln's third moment, *blurred genres*, describes developments until the mid 1980s and is evidenced by the coexistence of a plurality of approaches and a *laissez-faire* attitude to their combination (from amongst, for example, symbolic interactionism, ethnomethodology, phenomenology, semiotics, etc.). From the mid 1980s this phase gave way to the *crisis of representation*, with various critiques within the sociology of science and ethnography beginning to challenge the presumption that the researcher's account of events had a privileged relationship to an external reality, and/or that the author could escape the subjectivity of their own biography and cultural assumptions. Finally, Denzin and Lincoln's *fifth moment* indicates the influence of postmodernist deconstruction of grand theory, and the recasting of research as a series of narratives producing provisional, local accounts.

Denzin and Lincoln's periodisation is not without its problems (Shaw and Gould, 2001). It is a US-centric view of the research literature and in particular under-represents developments in European and non-English-language contexts (Flick, 1998). It also suffers the usual problems of such taxonomies in being over-schematic, not to mention short-sighted – the further back the period covered (for instance before the Second World War) the more the perspective offered becomes over-generalising and too homogeneous. Such historical frameworks tend also to focus on the doctrinal differences between certain researchers and, as we shall see, play down the persistence of pragmatic research approaches which in practice deploy qualitative methodologies as part of a mixed repertoire in addressing practice- or policy-based research questions. Finally, as Atkinson has argued, the paradigm argument sometimes seems to confuse three (or more) distinct levels of discussion: theoretical traditions (symbolic interactionism, ethnomethodology, phenomenology), research methods (grounded theory), and meta-theories (deconstructionism, feminism, critical theory) which have no necessary – and certainly no linear – connection to particular methodological approaches (Atkinson, 1995, p. 121).

Consideration of qualitative research in social work shows that such 'moments' as may be identified are not like geological seams which are mined to extinction; rather they overlap and are often worked simultaneously (Shaw and Gould, 2001). Nevertheless, despite the caveats entered above, an approach akin to Denzin and Lincoln's offers a sensitising framework for thinking about the evolution of qualitative research in social work.

The first moment is broadly indicated by the predominance in the social work literature of the clinical case study [eds: see also Lorenz, this volume]. Sherman and Reid briefly chart the place of the case study in social work journals from Richmond to Hollis:

> Indeed we could justifiably say that the case study method developed by Mary Richmond in *Social Diagnosis* is a legitimate form of qualitative research. The case study has been defined as an in-depth form of research that may focus on a person, a cultural incident or a community. Certainly, the in-depth study involved in 'social diagnosis' could be construed as applied qualitative research in which research findings guide intervention. (Sherman and Reid, 1994, p. 2)

For Sherman and Reid, from the 1950s until around 1970 social work experienced a period when qualitative research went underground and the dominant paradigm became variable-based evaluative studies with a psychological orientation. Outside social work this was a 'golden age' of qualitative research, particularly with the consolidation of social constructionism. Until the 1970s the influence of qualitative research on social work was (with a few notable exceptions) one of importation, primarily via sociologists who studied topics or issues which were of interest to social workers, such as institutions or the cultural life of marginalised groups of outsiders, notably classics from the Chicago School (e.g. Becker, 1963; Liebow, 1967; Whyte, 1955). Studies of institutional life, such as Goffman's *Asylums* (1961) or Polsky's *Cottage Six* (1962), became influential resources in emergent critiques of residential care. The landmark qualitative study indigenous to social work during this period or moment was Mayer and Timms's *The Client Speaks* (1970), based on in-depth interviews with clients of social workers to gain their views on being the recipients of casework. This became the first in a series of so-called 'client studies', giving voice to service users (Fisher, 1983).

By the late 1970s a series of studies was emerging in social work which reflected the methodological pluralism of 'blurred genres' (Shaw and Gould, 2001), although it is interesting to note how within this there was a particular flourish of ethnographic research. Ethnography was being used particularly as an approach for studying the dynamics of social work practice within changing organisational contexts – either social work as a totality or some sub-unit or particular substantive aspect. A number of these studies took as their point of departure certain organisational preoccupations of the time, such as intake or assessment processes and the functional organisation of teams. For example, both Maluccio (1979) and Rees (1978) used ethnographic methods to explore intake: the processes by which agencies receive, prioritise and allocate work relating to new referrals, and how the definition of problems is negotiated. Carole Satyamurti (1981) showed how social workers cope with working within irreconcilable frames of reference; her study remains highly relevant to contemporary conditions of continuous change. This form of inquiry, ethnography, has continued to be used to describe and understand the contradictions and tensions in social work, both personal and organisational – for instance Pithouse's study (1987) of a UK social services department.

Meanwhile, Denzin and Lincoln's 'modernist moment', and in particular grounded theory which has been taken to typify it, did not disappear and has continued to be an influential and active tradition. Grounded theory has been described by Sherman and Reid as 'particularly promising for the development of indigenous social work theory and knowledge ...' (1994, p. 6) and, as we shall see below, has been drawn upon as a source for arguing for the recognition of synergies between qualitative research and social work practice. It has continued to be an ongoing stimulus within the social work research field, with many examples in the literature. Mizrahi and Abramson (1985) used grounded theory to study interaction between social workers and physicians, developing a typology of professionals, who could be placed on a continuum of collaboration – traditional, transitional and transformational. Belcher (1994) reports on a grounded theory study of how people become homeless. Using material from open-ended interviews, Belcher and colleagues sought to develop a more complex model of multiple factors involved in the drift into homelessness. Similarly, grounded theory approaches to data collection and analysis have been used in studying the contribution made to change by community activists (Lazzari *et al.*, 1996). Ward *et al.* (1996) used continuous comparative techniques from grounded theory to compare how qualified and student social workers attributed motivation to sexual abusers of children.

The fourth moment reflects the wider crisis of representation associated with postmodernism and feminism, rendering problematic the processes of doing fieldwork and analysis, and foregrounding the subjectivity of the researcher. These themes are instanced in narrative research, which is prominent among the methodologies favoured by feminists as sharing their concern to give voice to those who may not be heard. Narrative research in social work draws on models of therapeutic intervention, such as narrative family therapy, as both research and practical engagement (Besa, 1994; Fish and Condon, 1994), and also on the methods of oral historians. Thus, the construction of narratives about an individual life is not only a communication of the subjective experience(s) of events, but also a process of reintegration for people whose lives may have been fractured by violence or oppression (Riessman, 1990). For Flick, 'Narrative analyses start from a specific form of sequentiality' (1998, p. 204). Narrative research is both methodological and epistemological in character: a life is regarded as a biographical narrative which can be elicited and thereby 'reconstructed'. Narrative inquiry restores the voice of the service user and contests the hierarchies between researcher and researched manifest within positivistic research. Riessman, in particular, sees narrative research as a counter to some of the perceived reductionist tendencies of positivism. As an example, she contrasts narrative accounts by people experiencing divorce with more quantitative studies of the divorce process, which produce, for instance, gender bias within standardised symptom scores, and with survey research, which neglects personal meaning (Riessman, 1991). Borden has also used narrative methods to show their capacity to identify the strengths and personal resources that individuals who have experienced adverse life events are able to mobilise, in contrast to the 'deficit models' which problem-centred approaches tend to produce (Borden, 1992).

The movements into narrative and postmodernism shade into Denzin and Lincoln's fifth moment, characterised in terms of reflection, co-operative inquiry, empowerment, and the positioned investigator. Here the concept of narrative moves from the more literal meaning of telling life stories towards the argument that research theories or methods are forms of rhetoric, persuasion or story-telling, and that 'truth' is a series of metaphors. This is where, as Flick has argued, 'narratives have replaced theories, or theories are read as narratives' (Flick, 1998, p. 10). Feminists' use of narrative methods has already been noted; the interest in subjectivities allies some strands of feminist research with postmodernist ideas.

These general intellectual developments are indicative of three emergent, interlocking themes in wider qualitative methodology, which are reflected in turn in social work research. First there is what is generally called 'the crisis of representation', involving, crucially, a questioning of the tendency to write up fieldwork in positivistic language so that the author is hidden as an agent who interprets, prioritises and owns the research. Though this was prefigured in Geertz's seminal book *The Interpretation of Cultures*, first published in the 1970s, postmodern deconstruction more radically and fundamentally places the author at the centre of methodological argumentation. In turn, the reflexive positioning of the author within research accounts tends to declare the political stance of the researcher and reveals research as an intentional political project, typically one intended to contribute to the emancipation of the subjects of the research. This builds on Marxist conceptions of *praxis* – the dialectical interaction of theory and practice – and in particular (in social work) on the field of action research. But there are also suggestions for reframing less overtly or directly political research traditions such as ethnography, identifying what are seen as the moral and political implications of adopting these approaches. For example, Altheide and Johnson argue that 'Ethnography is ... a way to study justice as well as to "do justice"', suggesting, moreover, 'that ethnographers are "justice workers" in so far as they clarify the nature, process and consequences of human expectation which are manifested in everyday life as social definitions' (1997, pp. 173–4). Third, we have the promotion of those usually described as the subjects or respondents of research as equal collaborators: the service user or practitioner as co-researcher. This further collapses traditional dualities between the researcher and the researched.

From these perspectives, conventional, modernist, qualitative research is a morally compromised endeavour, in which respondents consent to participate without having opportunity to influence or control the research process. Some social work researchers have looked to the contribution to epistemology and methodology of writers such as John Heron (1996) and Peter Reason (1994) to provide a co-operative approach in which the formally-designated researcher enables a process which is democratically steered by people who traditionally might be 'respondents' or service users. Examples would be Bess Whitmore's (1990) work on user participation in programme evaluation or Baldwin's account of working with people with learning disabilities as co-inquirers into day centre services (Baldwin, 1997). However, it is arguable that what we often see here is a continuation of modernist research methodologies, but located within a research sensibility which has become cautious of claims to universality or generalisibility beyond the local.

Qualitative research in social work – a thematic overview

Another way to 'cut the cake' of qualitative social work research, in contrast to the rather deductive approach of aligning it with an essentially predetermined historical framework which emphasises epistemology and methodology, is to sort it inductively to identify substantive themes or preoccupations of qualitative social work researchers. In the language of variable-based research, this is to take a cross-sectional rather than a longitudinal approach. Such a project has been undertaken in the field of qualitative health research by Popay and Williams (1998), and the author acknowledges that the following attempt to sketch what this looks like from a social work or social care perspective is aligned with their work. This approach has the additional advantage of showing where social work's qualitative evidence base can pick up continuities with qualitative health care evidence.

Some of the categories which emerge are in fact prefigured by the foregoing historical overview of qualitative social work research; there are identifiable clusters of studies which over time have addressed such topics as understanding organisational culture, investigating 'invisible' processes in social work, eliciting service user perceptions of practice, and evaluating complex policy initiatives. Some of these studies are instances of what Popay and Williams call a 'difference' model, i.e. they are stand-alone qualitative studies; others involve combination with quantitative methods as part of an 'enhancement' model, that is they compensate for some of the deficits of pure quantitative studies.

What this begins to look like is sketched below; the studies cited in the five inductive groupings are illustrative examples only.

- *'Taken for granted' practices in social work* – studies which reveal the 'invisible trade' of social work and make tacit dimensions of practice available for analysis:
  Maluccio (1979): intake practice in social work;
  Dingwall, Eekelaar and Murray (1983): decision making in child protection practice;
  Stenson (1993): deconstructing social work interviews;
  Parton, Thorpe and Wattam (1997): risk management in child protection.
- *Understanding service user and/or social worker behaviour*:
  Mizrahi and Abramson (1985): collaboration between social workers and doctors;
  Gilgun and Connor (1989): how perpetrators view child sexual abuse;
  Belcher (1994): social drift among homeless people;
  Martin (1994): oral history narratives of African-American people.
- *Representing service users' voices*:
  Mayer and Timms (1970): the language of social casework;
  Rees (1978): social work face to face;
  Fisher (1983): speaking of clients;
  Whitmore (1990): participatory approaches to programme evaluation.
- *Organisational culture and change management*:
  Satyamurti (1981): strategies of professional adaptation to stressful environments;
  Pithouse (1987): the occupational invisibility of social work;
  Baldwin (2000): managing the transition from social work to care management;
  White (2001): 'insider' (auto-)ethnography of child care practice.
- *Understanding complex policy implementation*:
  McGrath (1991): multi-disciplinary teamwork;
  Lewis and Glennerster (1996): implementation of community care in social services departments;
  Gould (1999a): multi-disciplinary child protection practice.

Apart from being a heuristic device to cluster research themes, this analysis reveals continuities and complementarities between the qualitative evidence base in social work and that in health care – an increasingly important professional frontier. In addition, it illustrates that qualitative research is not limited to the exploration of subjectivity, identity and social position; it also contributes to knowledge about the institutional context of policy making and implementation, and about the structural context of practice – i.e. social and economic change. This can be related to the more recent argument of Williams and Popay (1999) that a framework for research which links analytical levels – specifically those of the individual, social topography, institutions, and social structure – transcends the conventional wisdom which constrains methodological approaches to discrete levels of analysis.

Qualitative research and practice

So far we have considered at some length the development of qualitative social work research in the wider context of the social sciences. In recent years there have been vigorous debates within the discipline about whether qualitative research has a special relationship to social work as regards influencing practice. Often this view is associated with the writing of Jane Gilgun (1989; 1994), who has proposed and explored the metaphor that social work practice fits qualitative research 'like a hand fits a glove', but it is also an assumption of writers like Goldstein (1991) who describe qualitative research and practice as 'partners in discovery'. Gilgun's argument is specifically located in grounded theory, though there has been a tendency on the part of commentators to extrapolate from this to other areas of qualitative research, particularly ethnography. Fundamental to Gilgun's position is the contention that practice and qualitative research are delineated by a number of common processes: they both start where the client is; the qualitative attention to the contextualisation of data-fit is congruent with the social work emphasis on locating the person within their environment; 'thick' description of individual cases by researchers is comparable to social work's individualisation of the service user; and so on.

Several years after Gilgun first proposed the hand-in-glove analogy it was strongly challenged by Deborah Padgett, herself a protagonist of qualitative research in social work; she suggested that under closer scrutiny the glove really did not fit (1998; 1999). While confirming the value of the contribution of qualitative research to the knowledge base of social work, Padgett identifies several ways in which practice and research are dissimilar undertakings, concluding that there are both methodological and ethical reasons for ensuring that the two are not confused. Essentially, Padgett's argument is that social work research and social work practice are located in different assumptive frameworks; for her, practice is fundamentally theory- and model-based, and located within normative views of social or individual functioning, whereas (qualitative) research is concerned with theory generation, and is non-normative. She goes on to assert that the goals of the two activities are divergent. Practice is embedded within a nexus of contracts established amongst the practitioner, legal duties, the agency, and the service user; these may be contested or in conflict, but are presumed to be contributing to a notion of 'helping'. In contrast, the goals of research are the development of knowledge and scholarship. Underlying these differing aims, Padgett argues, are contrasting forms of relationship. Practice is often time-limited and terminated by the judgement of at least one party that further progress cannot be made. Research is characterised by prolonged immersion in 'the field', which is concluded when the researcher judges that no more understanding can be extracted; moreover, with research the 'real work' begins when the fieldwork is ended, and consists in transcribing, analysing and writing up the data.

Various rejoinders to Padgett's argument have been made, for instance that it caricatures social work, primarily in that it views practice as a privatised, clinical activity, imprisoned in anachronistic, psychological paradigms (Bein and Allen, 1999). It is also not clear, if Padgett nonetheless accepts that qualitative research makes an important contribution to social work as a professional activity, just how she considers that contribution to be made. This is where we need to explore appropriate criteria in terms of which qualitatively-derived knowledge might be judged as providing usable evidence for social work.

Qualitative research as evidence

If qualitative research makes – or claims to make – a contribution to policy and practice it is reasonable to expect that some criteria can be established to set standards of quality and utility for that research. As the debate about evidence-based practice stands in relation to social work, its protagonists argue that the value of evidence for practice is determined by a methodological hierarchy, with randomised controlled trials (RCTs) at the apex. Ironically, within evidence-based medicine, from which the social work variant initially draws its model, there is a more elaborated debate. Thus, although the effectiveness of some clinical interventions is best established by an RCT, the range of additional factors involved in deciding upon a course of action – appropriateness, cost, professional decision-making behaviour, geographical location, to name but a few – demands a more differentiated and pluralistic approach to determining what counts as evidence, including the contribution of qualitative research (Popay and Williams, 1998). Within the literature there are extensive and arcane discussions concerning markers of validity and reliability for qualitative research equivalent to those for quantitative work. Elsewhere this author has discussed some of the technical aspects of this matter (Gould, 1999b), suggesting that some of the contributions seem to be motivated by a defensive impulse to show that qualitative research, whilst lacking the scientistic techniques of quantitative research, can also make itself difficult and obscure. As Reid has argued, the issues need to be settled in language which has meaning for both practitioners and researchers; we need evaluative criteria for research, whether quantitative or qualitative, which are meaningful to the larger professional community rather than solely to elites within it such as academics or policy makers (Reid, 1994).

It may perhaps be conceded that quantitative researchers ask reasonable questions about methodology; but these – to continue the gladiatorial metaphor –

are not the *coup de grâce* for qualitative research. For instance, it is a reasonable expectation that both quantitative and qualitative research publications should contain enough description of the research question, design and methods for the reader to judge the adequacy of the study being reported. Within these descriptions it again seems reasonable to expect of all research that details of sampling and analysis are provided, even accepting that the substantive expectations concerning these matters will vary as between qualitative and quantitative work. However, beyond these points of convergence it may be entirely reasonable for issues of validity and reliability to take a different form in qualitative research from that which is conventional in quantitative studies. Following Popay and Williams (1998), the judgement of the adequacy of qualitative research follows from what they call the 'primary marker', that is: does the research illuminate the subjective meaning, actions and contexts of those being researched? From this primary and distinguishing concern flow various standards which can be employed to assess the evidential adequacy of qualitative research findings:

- *Responsiveness to social context*: Is the research design sensitive and adapted to the real-life setting in which it is conducted?
- *Evidence of theoretical or purposeful sampling*: Is the sample constructed in such a way that the structures and processes within which the individuals or situations being researched are located are adequately represented?
- *Adequate description*: Is the description of the individuals or events being researched sufficiently detailed to allow meaning to be inferred?
- *Data quality*: Are subjective perceptions and experiences treated as knowledge in their own right without 'expert' translation? How are different sources of information prioritised and reconciled?
- *Theoretical and conceptual adequacy*: If the research is 'grounded', how does it move from description of data, including quotations and examples, to analysis, interpretation and theorisation? If not grounded, how adequately is the study theorised, and the findings related to the cited body of theory?
- *Typicality*: What claims are made and how persuasive are they for transfer-ability of findings to other populations?
- *Policy relevance*: Has sufficiently extensive consideration been given to the full range of stakeholders implicated by the research?

Qualitative research in social work – a new tradition

It has been argued in this chapter that qualitative research in social work continues to develop within a range of theoretical and methodological traditions. Social work researchers draw eclectically from methods reflecting and representing the diversity of qualitative 'moments' outlined in an earlier section, including ethnography, grounded theory, case studies, narrative, discourse analysis, conversation analysis, and co-operative inquiry. They have also generally been conscripted only loosely to the 'paradigm wars' which have beset methodological debates in other fields of research, such as, notably, education. (This is deliberately to pass over the 'gladiatorial' aspect of recent UK discussions around evidence-based practice in social work and social care, noted at the beginning of this chapter.) Social work researchers bring this variety of methods to bear on the kinds of questions which preoccupy qualitative researchers in other domains of social research, including health. These include: exploratory research to describe and map out new fields of inquiry; researching issues of sensitivity where surveys are too blunt an approach; research to capture the frames of reference and meaning constructed by professionals and service users; evaluations of programmes and interventions where there is a desire to capture process rather than or as well as to identify quantified outcomes; case studies where holism is more important than measurement of specified variables; and politically committed research which rejects the claimed neutrality of positivism. Although it would be difficult to show that social work has made an identifiably distinct contribution to qualitative methodology, qualitative social work research has made and continues to make a substantial contribution to social work's knowledge base.

At the same time the chapter has sought to avoid any insinuation that qualitative research has a privileged position in relation to social work. Earlier the argument was cited that there is a growing view that the principle determining what kind of research is of value is – or should be – guided by the specific clinical question or practice scenario. This echoes an earlier argument developed by William Reid (1994), that we need to 'reframe the epistemological debate' in social work so that, rather than argue for a hierarchy of forms of knowledge, we identify the particular contribution that qualitative research makes to practice, alongside quantitative research and practice-based knowledge. This acknowledges that social work as a form of practice is a complicated and unpredictable activity, involving the reflective synthesis of both inductive and deductive reasoning. It is within this synthesis that qualitative research contributes to 'best attainable knowledge', in Reid's words 'a network of propositions with origins in practice experience and research' (Reid, 1994, p. 464). Thus, quantitative methods can identify the linkage between variables, evaluate alternative explanations through experimental and quasi-experimental designs which control variables, make precise measurements, and deal with sufficiently large samples for the purposes of generalisation (though how to apply population-based generalisations to the individual case remains problematic). On the other hand, qualitative research describes the holistic functioning of social systems, explores processes which link variables, identifies the influence of contextual factors on change processes, makes explicit dimensions of practice which are tacit or elusive, and through thorough description provides a basis for transferability of knowledge. Finally, knowledge developed experientially from practice represents *de facto* social work's most pervasive form of knowledge; it is grounded in the realities of the practitioner's world, is task-focused, and can be developed into indigenous theories and methods of practice. Practice knowledge is tested and validated through iterative cycles of action, evaluation, hypothesising, and action.

The challenge is to examine the architectures and logics of research methods in order to relate them to the kinds of questions which are salient for social work practitioners and service users. The diversity of social work militates against a neat functional analysis that can match tasks to specific research designs, be they qualitative or quantitative. At the same time, and certainly in the current UK context, the profession needs to challenge a Governmental policy framework which, despite the rhetoric, seeks improvement not, in fact, through an evidence-based approach of any persuasion [eds: see also Butler and Pugh, this volume; Humphries, this volume], but rather through standard-setting, regulation, and inspection. As Trinder has argued, managerial rather than scientific or professional discourse characterises the Government's agenda (Trinder, 2000a, p. 157; 2000b, pp. 8–13). In turn, social workers make decisions in contexts where the preferences of service users, wider public anxieties about risk, professional ethics, legislation, and resource scarcities all interact with research evidence to influence decisions about intervention. What this ultimately requires is practitioners with, in Hugh England's words, 'uncommonly good common sense' (England, 1986); the educated critical and reflective skills to make judgements about the relative significance of these forms of knowledge in unique circumstances.

References

Altheide, D. and Johnson, J. (1997), 'Ethnography and justice', in Miller, G. and Dingwall, R. (eds), *Context and Method in Qualitative Research*, Sage, London, pp. 172–84.

Atkinson, P. (1995), 'Some perils of paradigms', *Qualitative Health Research*, **5**(1), pp. 117–24.

Baldwin, M. (1997), 'Day care on the move: learning from a participative action research project at a day centre for people with learning difficulties', *British Journal of Social Work*, **27**(6), pp. 951–8.

Baldwin, M. (2000), *Care Management and Community Care: Social Work Discretion and the Construction of Policy*, Ashgate, Aldershot.

Becker, H.S. (1963), *Outsiders: Studies in the Sociology of Deviance*, Sage, London.

Bein, A. and Allen, K. (1999), 'Hand in glove? It fits better than you think', *Social Work*, **44**(3), pp. 274–7.

Belcher, J.R. (1994), 'Understanding the process of drift among the homeless: a qualitative analysis', in Sherman, E. and Reid, W.J. (eds), *Qualitative Research in Social Work*, Columbia University Press, New York, pp. 126–34.

Besa, D. (1994), 'Evaluating narrative family therapy using single-system research designs', *Research on Social Work Practice*, **4**(3), pp. 309–25.

Borden, W. (1992), 'Narrative perspectives in psychosocial intervention following adverse life events', *Social Work*, **37**(2), pp. 135–41.

Denzin, N. and Lincoln, Y. (1994), 'Entering the field of qualitative research', in Denzin, N. and Lincoln, Y. (eds), *Handbook of Qualitative Research*, Sage, London, pp. 1–18.

Dingwall, R., Eekelaar, J. and Murray, T. (1983), *The Protection of Children: State Intervention and Family Life*, Blackwell, Oxford.

England, H. (1986), *Social Work as Art: Making Sense for Good Practice*, Allen and Unwin, London.

Fish, B. and Condon, S. (1994), 'A discussion of current attachment research and its clinical applications', *Child and Adolescent Social Work Journal*, **11**(2), pp. 93–105.

Fisher, M. (ed.) (1983), *Speaking of Clients*, Joint Unit for Social Services Research, University of Sheffield/*Community Care*, Sheffield.

Flick, U. (1998), *An Introduction to Qualitative Research*, Sage, London.

Geertz, C. (1973), *The Interpretation of Cultures: Selected Essays*, Basic Books, New York.

Gilgun, J. (1994), 'Hand in glove: the grounded theory approach and social work practice research', in Sherman, E. and Reid, W.J. (eds), *Qualitative Research in Social Work*, Columbia University Press, New York, pp. 115–25.

Gilgun, J. and Connor, T. (1989), 'How perpetrators view child sexual abuse', *Social Work*, **34**(3), pp. 249–51.

Glaser, B. and Strauss, A. (1967), *The Discovery of Grounded Theory: Strategies for Qualitative Research*, Aldine, Chicago.

Goffman, E. (1961), *Asylums*, Anchor, New York.

Goldstein, H. (1991), 'Qualitative research and social work practice: partners in discovery', *Journal of Sociology and Social Welfare*, **18**(4), pp. 101–19.

Gould, N. (1990), 'Political critique of Kantian ethics: a contribution to the debate between Webb and McBeath, and Downie', *British Journal of Social Work*, **20**(5), pp. 495–9.

Gould, N. (1999a), 'Developing a qualitative approach to the audit of inter-disciplinary child protection practice', *Child Abuse Review*, **8**(3), pp. 193–9.

Gould, N. (1999b), 'Qualitative practice evaluation', in Shaw, I. and Lishman, J. (eds), *Evaluation and Social Work Practice*, Sage, London, pp. 63–80.

Gould, N. (2000), 'Becoming a learning organisation: a social work example', *Social Work Education*, **19**(6), pp. 585–96.

Greenhalgh, P. and Douglas, H.R. (1998), *'Life's Too Short and the Evidence Too Hard to Find': A Training Needs Analysis of GPs and Practice Nurses in Evidence-Based Practice in North Thames Region*, Unit for Evidence-Based Practice and Policy, Department of Primary Care and Population Sciences, University College London, London, cited in Lipman, *op. cit.*

Haste, H. (1996), *The Sexual Metaphor*, Jossey-Bass, San Francisco.

Heron, J. (1996), *Co-operative Inquiry: Research into the Human Condition*, Sage, London.

Lazzari, M., Ford, H. and Haughey, K. (1996), 'Making a difference: women of action in the community', *Social Work*, **41**(2), pp. 197–205.

Lewis, J. and Glennerster, H. (1996), *Implementing the New Community Care*, Open University Press, Buckingham.

Liebow, E. (1967), *Tally's Corner: A Study of Negro Streetcorner Men*, Little, Brown and Co., Boston.

Lipman, T. (2000), 'Evidence-based practice in general practice and primary care', in Trinder, L. (ed.), with Reynolds, S., *Evidence-Based Practice: A Critical Appraisal*, Blackwell Science, Oxford, pp. 35–65.

McGrath, M. (1991), *Multi-Disciplinary Teamwork*, Avebury, Aldershot.

Maluccio, A.N. (1979), 'The influence of the agency environment on clinical practice', *Journal of Sociology and Social Welfare*, **6**(6), pp. 734–55.

Martin, R. (1994), 'Life forces of African-American elderly illustrated through oral history narratives', in Sherman, E. and Reid, W.J. (eds), *Qualitative Research in Social Work*, Columbia University Press, New York, pp. 190–99.

Mayer, J.E. and Timms, N. (1970), *The Client Speaks: Working Class Impressions of Casework*, Routledge and Kegan Paul, London.

Miles, M. and Huberman, A. (1994), *Qualitative Data Analysis: A Sourcebook of New Methods*, Sage, Thousand Oaks, CA.

Mizrahi, T. and Abramson, J. (1985), 'Sources of strain between physicians and social workers', *Social Work in Health Care*, **10**(3), pp. 33–51.

Oakley, A. (2000), *Experiments in Knowing: Gender and Method in the Social Sciences*, Polity, Cambridge.

Padgett, D.K. (1998), 'Does the glove really fit? Qualitative research and clinical social work practice', *Social Work*, **43**(4), pp. 373–80.

Padgett, D.K. (1999), 'The research–practice debate in a qualitative research context', *Social Work*, **44**(3), pp. 280–82.

Parton, N., Thorpe, D. and Wattam, C. (1997), *Child Protection: Risk and the Moral Order*, Macmillan, Basingstoke.

Pithouse, A. (1987), *Social Work: The Social Organisation of an Invisible Trade*, Avebury, Aldershot.

Polsky, H.W. (1962), *Cottage Six: The Social System of Delinquent Boys in Residential Treatment*, Wiley, New York.

Popay, J. and Williams, G. (1998), 'Qualitative research and evidence-based healthcare', *Journal of the Royal Society of Medicine*, **91**(suppl't 35), pp. 32–7.

Reason, P. (1994), *Participation in Human Inquiry*, Sage, London.

Rees, S. (1978), *Social Work Face to Face*, Edward Arnold, London.

Reid, W.J. (1994), 'Reframing the epistemological debate', in Sherman, E. and Reid, W.J. (eds), *Qualitative Research in Social Work*, Columbia University Press, New York, pp. 464–81.

Reynolds, S. (2000), 'The anatomy of evidence-based practice: principles and methods', in Trinder, L. (ed.), with Reynolds, S., *Evidence-Based Practice: A Critical Appraisal*, Blackwell Science, Oxford, pp. 17–34.

Riessman, C.K. (1990), 'Strategic uses of narrative in the presentation of self and illness: a research note', *Social Science and Medicine*, **30**(11), pp. 1195–1200.

Riessman, C.K. (1991), 'Beyond reductionism: narrative genres in divorce accounts', *Journal of Narrative and Life History*, **1**(1), pp. 41–68.

Rojek, C. and Collins, S. (1987), 'Contract or con trick', *British Journal of Social Work*, **17**(2), pp. 199–211.

Satyamurti, C. (1981), *Occupational Survival: The Case of the Local Authority Social Worker*, Blackwell, Oxford.

Shaw, I. and Gould, N. (2001), *Qualitative Research in Social Work: Context and Method*, Sage, London.

Sherman, E. and Reid, W.J. (1994), 'Coming of age in social work: the emergence of qualitative research', in Sherman, E. and Reid, W.J. (eds), *Qualitative Research in Social Work*, Columbia University Press, New York, pp. 1–20.

Stenson, K. (1993), 'Social work discourse and the social work interview', *Economy and Society*, **22**(1), pp. 42–76.

Trinder, L. (2000a), 'Evidence-based practice in social work and probation', in Trinder, L. (ed.), with Reynolds, S., *Evidence-Based Practice: A Critical Appraisal*, Blackwell Science, Oxford, pp. 138–62.

Trinder, L. (2000b), 'Introduction: the context of evidence-based practice', in Trinder, L. (ed.), with Reynolds, S., *Evidence-Based Practice: A Critical Appraisal*, Blackwell Science, Oxford, pp. 1–16.

Ward, T., Connolly, M., McCormack, J. and Hudson, S. (1996), 'Social workers' attributions for sexual offending against children', *Journal of Child Sexual Abuse*, **5**(3), pp. 39–56.

White, S. (2001), '(Auto-)ethnography as reflexive inquiry: the research act as self-surveillance', in Shaw and Gould, *op. cit.*, pp. 100–115.

Whitmore, E. (1990), 'Empowerment in program evaluation: a case example', *Canadian Social Work Review*, **7**(2), pp. 215–29.

Whyte, W. (1955), *Street Corner Society: The Social Structure of an Italian Slum*, University of Chicago Press, Chicago.

Williams, F. and Popay, J. (1999), 'Balancing polarities: developing a new framework for welfare research', in Williams, F., Popay, J. and Oakley, A. (eds), *Welfare Research: A Critical Review*, UCL Press, London, pp. 156–83.

Chapter 8

Research as an Element in Social Work's Ongoing Search for Identity

Walter Lorenz

Social work has always had an uneasy relationship with research. It is therefore to
be welcomed that the various important issues involved have recently received so
much attention, particularly in the UK, where during 1999–2000 the ESRC for the
first time sponsored a series of seminars on *Theorising Social Work Research*.
Undoubtedly, taking research findings and above all taking the debate about
research methodology seriously contributes to the social status of the profession –
an area of considerable uncertainty for British social work. Reviewing these
developments in their wider social and political context reveals that the options
being debated with regard to the research methodology most appropriate to social
work do not just represent technical or instrumental possibilities for the
achievement of given goals; rather, these controversies are closely linked to the
issue of the identity of social work. Moreover, it is suggested here that these
debates do not coincide accidentally but that there is in fact an intricate and
historical connection between them. Thus an adequately comprehensive answer to
the question of how to engage in social work research requires a clearer account
and understanding of the formation of social work identities than has generally
been evident.

The most striking feature of social work's current identity is the fragmentation
of the profession and discipline, not just in an international context, where it
presents a bewildering variety of professional titles and intellectual discourses, but
also at national level, where in every country several professional profiles exist in
parallel, sometimes contesting each other's territories. In the UK this relates not
just to the still relatively recent split between social work and probation and to the
older tensions in the relationship between social work and youth and community
work, but above all to the dichotomy between social work and social care. The
growing emphasis on care management in recent years has now begun to fragment
the professional field further, and while the introduction of national Social Care
Councils may formalise the relationship between the distinctive traditions
concerned, it will do little to create a common sense of identity or to invigorate the
intellectual dialogue amongst them. In fact, while creating a unified identity might
be a justifiable interest for any profession in general terms, in the case of social
work and social care this might run counter to the actual social mandate that this
professional group has acquired and has striven to develop, which involves setting

the interests of service users above professional self-interests. Person-centred needs never correspond neatly to professional boundaries and the plurality of perspectives in the social professions can serve as a reminder of the creative, critical potential of inter-professional boundary disputes, as long as they are regarded as more than merely matters of power and group interests. It is precisely in order to unlock this potential that it is necessary to understand social work's inherent diversity and to identify common features across its different forms, which requires in turn a clear and careful historical and conceptual analysis.

For theoretical, but also for practical purposes it is important to understand this diversity as neither the product merely of the vagaries of historical and administrative forces impinging on the development of the social professions, nor as the differentiated, self-generated unfolding of principled intellectual positions. The diversity arises, fundamentally, from the tension between the necessity for the profession to engage with a given historical, social and political reality and its desire, also necessary for its survival as a recognisable profession, to distance itself from these structural contexts and to establish fields and methods of relatively autonomous thought and action to underline its mediating capacity. This tension, and the ensuing contradictions, closely reflects the profession's ambivalent position between 'the lifeworld' (the realm of society in which people take care of their own affairs, individually and collectively) and 'the system' (where organised control and steering mechanisms operate), to use the key terms of Habermas's analytical grid (Blindenbacher, 1999; Habermas, 1987), which will be discussed further below. The social professions came into existence, in their various forms and in different countries, during a very distinct historical period in the development of modern societies in which these domains – system and lifeworld – moved apart, and they still reflect that split in their actions and appearance. Therefore the tension, like the diversity presented within and amongst these professions, is not something that should or indeed could be resolved. Rather, the very possibility of a distinct kind of social action, and thereby the possibility of realising social work's social mandate, lies precisely in the ability to maintain, and to operate accountably within, this tension. Thus an answer to the vexing question about social work's contemporary identity depends not on the definitive resolution of the current controversy over research methods – which, as will be shown, is not a new phenomenon at all – but very much on establishing a connection between the epistemological questions of concern in social work and a wider theory of society. Social work research methodology must therefore never focus on epistemology in isolation, but always in the context of a theory of society.

Social work between system and lifeworld

This chapter will approach these matters via Habermas's particular way of analysing the development of modern societies, which as already mentioned uses the distinction between lifeworld and system. These concepts refer together to a given state of society; 'lifeworld' captures those aspects and processes in which people experience themselves as communicating actors capable of expressing intentions and giving meaning to their world, whereas 'system' denotes what are in fact the structural consequences of those actions and which ensure the material reproduction of society via the media of power and money [eds: see also Lovelock and Powell, this volume]. Modern societies, according to Habermas, are characterised by increasing differentiations within and between those two domains which results in their 'uncoupling' and, on account of the sheer 'success' of rationality in the system, the gradual 'colonisation' of the lifeworld by the system. In more concrete terms, arguments embodying instrumental rationality and conducted with reference to money and power have come to dominate the welfare state project, at the expense of communicative processes.

It is important to recognise that the origins of social work lie in both 'domains' – system and lifeworld – (Rauschenbach, 1999). The emergence of social work received significant impetus from initiatives at the level of the lifeworld in as much as voluntary activities, of both the charitable middle-class as well as the self-help and solidarity-creating working-class type, reflected the prevalent diversity of values and aspirations for a 'better society'. At the same time the integrative requirements of industrialising societies outlined the contours of welfare systems not as philanthropy but as calculated and organised attempts at social control. Social work was allocated its place and function in relation to the system's need for setting firm boundaries and limits to destabilising forces. This increased the pressure on the emergent profession to become incorporated into public systems of social policy and national agendas of social and cultural integration.

Thus, and crucially, social work became an intermediary between lifeworld and system, sharing in the differentiation and specialisation of both but also developing its mediating functions in both directions. Contemporary tensions in social work represent 'professionally alienated, displaced social contradictions' and manifest themselves in various perceived dichotomies:

> social work as social commitment v. social work as a paid occupation, as resulting from the mandate given by clients v. the result of an organisational and societal mandate, as self-help v. help from the outside, as care v. control – all still echoing the old basic controversy: does social change reflect the actual lived interests of people or is it social reform in the interest of the stability of the system? (Marzahn, 1982, p. 20, trans. this author)

These contradictions also show up in some of the fundamental ambiguities which are evident in the area of research. For instance, when studies have recourse to notions of 'community building' or to 'female qualities of caring', and latterly also to the concept of 'empowerment', and when research methodologies favour 'emancipatory research', we sense at once the 'promise' of these reference points resonating from their lifeworld qualities and roots. However, closer inspection of their use in particular contexts reveals that each of these same ideas can also have implications with regard to social control and can be used instrumentally for such purposes (Humphries, 1997). Conversely, adhering to principles and criteria of objectivity and rationality, key instruments enabling the system to hold and legitimise power in modernity, has been at times a means by which social work research, on behalf of the profession, can resist that colonisation and provide a critical counter-reference to a system that seeks to use the social professions merely for purposes of social control.

Given the intermediary function of social work already outlined, the wider significance of discourses on research methodology cannot be elaborated adequately without reference to the intersection of these two sets of dynamics. They play a role on the one hand in the epistemological ambiguity between what has been described classically as the alternatives of social work as art and as science, and on the other hand in the ambivalence between striving for the status of a full, autonomous profession and retaining the empowering elements of 'voluntarism' and the solidarity with service users which they can convey.

Some elements of these complex interconnections have become visible in recent and current debates on social work research methods in the UK. While the pragmatism which prevails in the approach both to research and to practice methods in Britain (Powell, 2002) has hindered full recognition of the issues that are at stake, the political implications of the polarisation affecting professional practice as well as approaches to research nevertheless become apparent. Broadly speaking the debate divides into two camps, although in characterising it in this way we should not overlook the interlinking complexity of interests referred to above, which is present within each of the positions and which therefore gives rise to further differentiations in terms both of the pragmatics of organisational policies and of the impact of poststructuralist critiques (Kazi, 2000; Shaw, 1999) [eds: see also Gould, this volume].

On the one hand there is renewed interest in and advocacy for the relevance to social work of research methods which take up the traditions of positivism and empiricism, with the promise of providing accuracy of measurements, reliability of results, and transparency of actions, and hence of enhancing the public accountability of the profession (Dillenburger, 1998; Macdonald, 1994; Reid, 1994). Social work has always been suspected of lacking an empirical base for its methods of intervention, particularly an empirical base that was not borrowed from studies conducted by other disciplines, and there is certainly good reason to suggest that the profession has a need to confront data about the outcomes of its interventions (Shaw, 1999).

On the other hand this positivist stance is being contested from a perspective on research in social work which emphasises the elaboration and evaluation of subjective meanings as the key to understanding social phenomena. These meanings remain hidden to quantitative enquiry on account of the 'detachment' required by that method; they can be captured best by qualitative approaches which aim at giving expression to the authentic voice of the 'research subject' (Ruckdeschel, 1985; Sherman and Reid, 1994; White, 1998). Among other things this approach inverts, or at least relativises, the relationship between 'experts' and 'people with mere experience', and thereby exposes and criticises the differentials in power involved (Beresford and Evans, 1999).

Categorising the parties to the ongoing debate about social work research in terms of such opposing methodological or philosophical positions is problematic, since the differences between the 'two sides' are far from simple and clear-cut.

Crucially, the discussion is overlaid with a host of agendas which have a direct bearing on the gravitational pull of the various options and which can prompt curious 'border crossings' between theoretical perspectives. Chief among those is the renewed focus on assuring the quality of services, which itself has both a professional and a political side. The political agenda, noticeable particularly in the UK but spreading also to other parts of Europe (Rauschenbach, 1999), is about a restructuring of social work in terms of management criteria which emphasise cost-effectiveness and thereby outcome orientation. In research terms this is reflected in a shift from a focus on issues of principle and problem causation towards studies of policy implementation and effectiveness (Fisher, 1999; Gibbs, 2001). The professional agenda amounts to an attempt to reconstitute the status and to that extent the autonomy of the social work profession under these changed policy conditions by seeking to develop 'evidence-based practice', which of course feeds directly back into the same political agenda (see Webb (2001) for an incisive analysis consistent with the argument of the present chapter) [eds: see also Butler and Pugh, this volume; James, this volume; Jordan and Parton, this volume]. This concern emphasises reliance on research findings rather than on established intervention methods as the constitutive part of professional social work (Taylor and White, 2001). It implies that once a secure knowledge base has been established with regard to a given situation, intervention becomes a matter of following given procedures (and thereby avoiding 'mistakes'). Achieving and maintaining service quality, in this version, seeks to combine a basically empiricist research framework with the underlying concern of 'quality assurance' for consumer views and participation. This approach purports to subvert the dichotomies of positivism and phenomenology, quantitative and qualitative methods, and adjustment (control) and emancipation which had beset the agenda, thereby seducing an insecure profession with the promise of bringing it intellectually into the fold of postmodernism while providing certain assurances against the angst of total relativism. In this line of development, not only is British pragmatism showing itself at its acrobatic best (Trinder, 1996), it also, by claiming to have resolved the various tensions referred to, marks a surrender to the logic (and the power) of the system, with action reduced to procedures.

It is not surprising, therefore, that intellectual discontent over such an alluring but flawed settlement is manifesting itself. The question is how to mobilise resistance and counter-arguments effectively against a development that takes colonisation to new heights. In the UK the concept of 'realism' (Kazi, 1998; Pawson and Tilley, 1997; Taylor and White, 2001) is being suggested as a reference point for a possible settlement of the at times strongly conflicting interests, and as a means of giving the social work profession a unifying profile and more secure social status while retaining the lifeworld link in the form of an action perspective. In 'realistic evaluation', 'Practitioners construct models of their practice, which include their theoretical orientation, practice wisdom, accepted knowledge amongst peers, tacit knowledge and previous experience of what works, for whom and in what contexts' (Kazi, 2000, p. 764). The process continues through the participative testing of the hypotheses thus derived to lead to a context-specific intervention programme that 'harnesses enabling mechanisms and steers clear of disabling mechanisms' (*ibid.*, pp. 764–5). The resultant models of 'scientific realism' (Kazi, 2000), 'sturdy relativism'/'realistic realism' (Taylor and White, 2001), or 'practice-focused reflexivity' (Sheppard, 1998), appear to satisfy the societal demands for greater accountability, the political interests in efficiency and effectiveness, and the professional concerns for autonomy based on scientific stringency.

However, there is a sense of premature settlement about these 'solutions', foreclosing on discussion, with a new emphasis on inclusiveness (empirical practice, interpretivist, and pragmatic approaches all under the roof of this type of 'realism') before the depth of the conflicts and the implications of social work's inherent diversity and plurality have been fully explored. Their concern with integration (of science and art, of rationality and emotions, of knowledge and values, of quantitative and qualitative models of research, of objectivity and subjectivity, of professional and consumer interests, of political agendas of control and of empowerment) paradoxically confirms their rootedness in and continued adherence to a dualistic epistemology disconnected from a theory of society. 'Realism' as the reliance on an objectivity which, though hidden and unreachable, serves as a given yardstick, surrenders the understanding of social processes to a scientific project which, by its very success in the area of science and technology, blocks the elaboration of values and meanings constitutive of societies and thereby the communicative potential constitutive of social work.

An alternative approach is explicitly to explore social work's intermediary role between lifeworld and system as this impacts in the area of research. This leads first of all to a sharper realisation of the conflicts and contradictions involved. But staying with this aspect of diversity, and acknowledging the apparent impossibility of uniting models of research and models of social work under one common approach, prompts the recognition that social work has its place in both lifeworld and system, and thereby releases its communicative potential. For Habermas the heuristic distinction between lifeworld and system marks two related realms of action in society, communicative and instrumental action, reflecting the sharp philosophical distinction he makes between communicative and instrumental reason (Habermas, 1987). The system is guided by principles and criteria of efficiency, necessary for the structural integration and material reproduction of society, by impersonal mechanisms best exemplified by the workings of the market. Communicative action, however, cannot come about on the basis of such 'given' reference points of meaning and understanding, but strives instead to constitute, out of the infinite diversity of subjective and conflicting meanings, the conditions for consensus. The openness of this process, its precarious ability to invoke reflection and critique, are for Habermas the very conditions – the only conditions – under which communication in its full sense can come about (Habermas, 1990).

Habermas emphasises the importance of the distinction between instrumental and communicative reason and action not only for the epistemological process of establishing different forms and regimes of knowing as such, but also for the creation of identities (Habermas, 1972). He elaborates on C.S. Peirce's observations that the (individual) human self which derives its identity solely from the success or failure of instrumental action can only develop in a negative way. It learns to become aware of itself only in moments where the discrepancy between its own position and the given, generalised consensus of 'common sense wisdom' becomes apparent. This observation could also be extended to the constitution of social work's professional identity, albeit that due care must be taken not to exaggerate the homogeneity of the latter. Once social work surrenders to the rationalistic requirements of the system and therefore adopts the dogma of positivism, it becomes set on an instrumental perspective on action and its identity becomes negatively constituted in terms of the 'remaining' discrepancy between claims (to efficiency and effectiveness) and resultant achievements. Since this discrepancy will always remain considerable, such negative constitution of the identity of social work is also likely to result in a negative public image.

These consequences cannot be avoided by means of the recourse to 'client participation' in research, at least not as long as such participation is conceived or employed purely as an instrumental device to give the results greater validity. Used in this way it simply preserves and transfers the basic underlying conception of research as instrumental action to an expanded 'community of researchers and practitioners'. Even though the results of such research can render themselves less vulnerable to criticism, seeming to satisfy both methodological and ideological criteria of 'representation' and 'representativeness' to a greater extent than does research conducted 'on them', the views of users, however representative they might be in statistical terms, are always going to be partial and in many ways 'parochial'. From an instrumental perspective on research the greater 'fit' of needs and outcomes achieved through client participation might represent a quantitative gain, but already in the application of such results the negative effects become tangible in as much as the approach renders those users who do not 'fit' into the framework totally defenceless and without representation, their right to subjectivity and to having a public voice having been further eroded.

This strongly suggests an ongoing need for social work research to be conceptualised and realised as communicative action, and hence the need to develop fully a hermeneutic approach in a research context. This is not to juxtapose a superior research *method* to the ones touched on so far, but rather to establish some *meta-theoretical criteria* which could guide the search for appropriate methods that might have to differ from situation to situation but which can be evaluated against criteria established by means of consensus-oriented communication. The existence of a diversity of possible methods necessitates communication; the imposition of one dogma – which essentially *is* positivism (Habermas, 1972) – but equally the 'anything goes' indifference to relativity which poses as postmodern (Fook, 2002) forecloses communication and thus understanding. It might therefore be less important to see social work as either a science or an art and to endorse the choice with the promotion of the corresponding research methods, than to recognise more fully the historical nature of social work in relation to the differentiation of modern societies.

Historical reflections

Reflection on key moments in the development of the social professions might illustrate the usefulness of the perspective just intimated. A defining moment for the emergence of a distinct social work identity in the UK was the divergence between the 'case-by-case' approach, pioneered by the Charity Organisation Society (COS) at the end of the nineteenth century, and the 'sociological' (structural) approach promoted during the same period by the Fabian Society. This controversy was not just about practice methodology, nor was it a clear-cut ideological conflict; rather it can also be regarded as paradigmatic as regards the different epistemologies of either side and as such it is an important indication of the early differentiation of research methods in this discipline in relation to lifeworld and system.

The individualism of the COS approach reflected a moral commitment to the transmission of values through direct interaction with the poor and destitute; the moral principles were applied not purely in a dogmatic, 'top-down' way, but through the 'study' of individual life circumstances. 'Investigation' became a characteristic key method of the Society, with which it sought to justify the shift from 'spontaneous' and indiscriminate (and thereby in its view socially and morally deleterious) almsgiving, to rational, evidence-based intervention, which it sought to promote as its contribution to the improvement of social conditions. Social enquiry at the individual level became at once both a research and an intervention method for the COS worker; in Octavia Hill's famous definition, given in an address to the Social Science Association in 1869: 'By knowledge of character more is meant than whether a man is a drunkard or a woman dishonest, it means knowledge of the passions, hopes and history of the people ... how to move, touch, teach them' (Hill, 1869, quoted in Woodroofe, 1962, p. 52). The gathering of copious case notes by the charity workers (Bosanquet, 1914) reflected a mode of research that sought to engage and to understand from 'within' the life context of the clients and hence 'the lifeworld', no matter how much the actual evaluation and the resulting decisions were overlaid with the requirements of 'the system' in the form of given economic and political norms. The Society's own struggle to resolve the ensuing contradictions with reference to philanthropy as 'scientific charity' show the mediating function which social work, even in this early pre-professional form, had taken on. It placed itself between the requirements of a lifeworld, in which countless interests and value positions sought to articulate themselves and to maintain the viability of family and community life in the face of urbanisation and industrialisation, and the impersonal integrative requirements of national political and economic systems.

The agenda of the Fabian Society started from the system end of the spectrum, with the aim of achieving stability and integration through structural reforms. Scientific enquiry, inspired by positivism and a firm belief in the impact of social data obtained through painstaking social research, as undertaken by Booth and Rowntree, formed its natural basis, although actual reforms by no means followed 'automatically' on the back of convincing data but rather had to be campaigned for. The agents of Fabianism therefore had to engage with the lifeworld very directly if they were to bring about changes, and this, despite their opposing positions on the 1905 Royal Commission on the Reform of the Poor Law (Woodroofe, 1962), provided an eventual meeting ground between COS and Fabians in the form of joint training courses for social workers at the London School of Economics.

Another instance of these unfolding dynamics is the wide acclaim and positive reception attracted by the earliest 'social work textbook', Mary Richmond's *Social Diagnosis* (1917). This can be attributed to the resonance the book had for early social workers finding themselves in the mediating role suggested above but without recourse to a systematic method. It is significant that this text elevates 'research' to a central position in *intervention*, thereby revealing both the pioneering potential and the limitations of the work. With this textbook casework became a defining method of social work rather than being simply a description of its way of operating. Casework could lay claim to being a scientific method on account of the positivism in which it is ultimately rooted and which it seeks to share with the great model profession of medicine, where diagnosis based on scientific principles formed the proof of a decisive turn away from quackery. The limitations of Mary Richmond's approach lay in the epistemological emptiness of her concept of diagnosis, which purported to be a gathering of 'facts' but which failed to problematise the relationship between fact and evaluation. As Annette Garrett wrote, recalling her own mistaken beliefs derived from training at that time: 'If we could just have enough facts we would know what to do' (Garrett, 1949, p. 222). By trying to resolve the tension between demands on the part of both the lifeworld and the system, of which practitioners like Richmond were so acutely aware, the casework approach deprived itself of its actual communicative potential; but it did render the profession socially acceptable.

Alice Salomon, the pioneer of German social work and social work education, articulated the same dilemmas and under the very title borrowed from Mary Richmond's work. Her book *Soziale Diagnose* (Salomon, 1926), for which she also considered the title *Soziale Recherche*, reflects on the epistemological problems facing social work(ers) and suggests a combination of inductive and deductive approaches to the acquisition of knowledge, both in individual cases and as the research basis for specific intervention methods in general. In her account she clearly struggles between holding on to the respectability which a scientific approach can convey and doing justice to the hermeneutic processes which practice experience suggests: 'The data collected have different meanings. The essential aspect is the correct evaluation of these details, their comparison, their interpretation' (Salomon, 1926, p. 7). Elsewhere Alice Salomon resorts to appeals to 'motherliness' as a key ingredient of social work epistemology, and for her this is not a biological reference point but rather indicates the level at which the experience of caring can be universalised, such that her overall conception contains a very distinctive vision of a classless society (Salomon, 1919). Here the need for an integration of research and practice, of methodological and political concerns, for an objectivity that does not silence the voice of subjectivity, especially of women, finds an appealing though 'old-fashioned' expression. What is lacking is not only, as Salomon herself acknowledges, the contribution of an appropriate psychology that elaborates on the helping process as a process of (self-)discovery (for both client and helper), but also an explicit epistemology which does not devalue as 'unscientific' the intermediary stance such approaches try to maintain.

The eventually almost universal acceptance which Freudian psychology achieved in social work served exactly the purpose of gaining respectability through the adoption of a seemingly positivist method, almost obliterating thereby the element of hermeneutic reflexivity contained in Freud's original approach. Freud's achievement, as Habermas emphasises in his historical review of social epistemology, was to elevate the process of self-reflection to the level of a properly scientific undertaking and thereby to expand the scope and method of hermeneutics significantly (Habermas, 1972). The logic of the seemingly illogical sphere of the unconscious reveals itself not through a standardised, objectivised code of symbols applied by an all-knowing expert who penetrates those barriers (even though this misrepresentation has often been attributed to Freud); on the contrary the 'truth' of the unconscious reveals itself only through acts of self-reflection which the therapist is merely instrumental in bringing about. This defines the mediating role of the therapist in very stringent terms. It gives each therapeutic encounter the character of a discovery, of research; not, however, research conducted *on* a patient, but the self-searching work *of* the patient herself.

Applied to casework the psychoanalytic method has the potential both to satisfy the requirements of the system within which social service work takes place and which aims ultimately at producing adjustment to the 'inevitable' in the form of social norms, and at the same time to engage with and support the communicative abilities of individuals in their lifeworld which aim at being better understood – by others and by themselves. The original sense of the much maligned term 'working through' expresses this dual aspect of the encounter between client and social worker; a complex process in which social workers are, on account of their societal position and mandate, always already engaged by necessity, but for which they had so far lacked a comprehensive heuristic tool that could capture this complexity without reducing it to a mechanistic, instrumental activity.

The Freudian mode of enquiry was by no means immune against reductionist interpretations and uses, and had a similar impact on parts of the intellectual tradition of 'applied social science', prevalent mostly in Anglo-Saxon countries, as it had on that of social pedagogy, which prevailed in most continental European countries (Lorenz, 2000; 2001). When the interests of the respective social professions in status and public recognition link with the societal process of rationalisation and bureaucratisation they tend to promote practice and research models geared towards objectivity, value neutrality and effectiveness. From the 'applied social science' perspective Freudian concepts supplemented the tools available for 'manipulating the environment' with tools that remedied individual pathology rationally and effectively (Garrett, 1949). Paradoxically, this concern with making comprehensive objective assessments generated very little in the way of primary research, a requirement which greater public acceptance of the approach had to some extent obviated. Commenting on the expansion of casework services in the US in the 1920s and 1930s, Leiby observes: 'It is curious that the demand for these services expanded steadily, despite the fact that their practitioners were never able to offer either a very cogent argument or impressive efficacy for their practice' (Leiby, 1969, p. 314). The answer to this puzzle doubtless lay in the social acceptance of the methods themselves and of their proponents who had found a place in society.

Social pedagogy; the hermeneutic tradition and its betrayal

While the effect of the incorporation of social pedagogy into the growing welfare bureaucracy of the Weimar Republic was very similar in terms of the instrumental use of new psychological insights such as those presented by psychoanalysis, there were differences in the way this academic tradition raised issues concerning the relationship between lifeworld and system. Pedagogy, in contrast to social science grounded in positivism, was initially not so much an academic discipline as representative of a social and intellectual movement – to which, to some extent, the unified German nation of the late nineteenth century owed its existence, or at least its identity. Both Romantic and Liberal movements went beyond simply exposing the deficits and dangers of modern society, proposing and articulating cultural alternatives to the growing fragmentation and alienation of the population and calling for cultural renewal and opportunities for self-improvement. Particularly in the form of social pedagogy, an alternative approach to education as such was set out, rather than just a supplementary structure of education outside the school system. Rather than beginning with the requirements of the political system for having a well-adjusted population, the starting point was the potential of each individual, which required fostering towards a sense of community. The defining form of enquiry of this 'reform movement' became hermeneutics, elaborated above all in the work of Dilthey, who by contrasting the epistemologies of the physical or natural sciences and the 'human sciences' (*Geisteswissenschaften* – usually, and unsatisfactorily, rendered as 'arts' or 'humanities' in the British context) addressed very specifically the needs of pedagogy for a reliable basis of knowing. The question was whether the practice of social pedagogy, in seeking to find a place within the overall (largely authoritarian) educational and social policies of the state, would be able to apply this methodology for the purposes of both primary research and the search for hermeneutic forms of intervention.

This project was realised to some extent in the Weimar Republic when social pedagogues developed their own research approaches to the study of youth in direct contrast to the prevailing methods in the positivistically orientated social sciences. Qualitative methods, such as diaries and accounts of their daily lives given by young people themselves, came to play an important role (Böhnisch *et al.*, 1997), not just in understanding the pressures and dilemmas these youngsters were facing but also in constructing methods of engaging them that started from those very experiences. The influence of Freudian concepts on this type of research was considerable, particularly in the area of residential child care, where child-oriented approaches were being promoted and old regimes changed drastically. It is noteworthy that psychoanalytic concepts in the version promoted by Alfred Adler inspired numerous pedagogical grassroots movements in German-speaking countries and also in the USA, and these often combined with socialist political movements which criticised and opposed the authoritarianism that prevailed in public child and youth services (Schille, 1997).

Overall, the 1920s in Austria and Germany were marked by sharply contrasting 'social experiments', on the Right as well as on the Left of the political spectrum. The progressive reform projects foundered, however, partly on the ideological controversies in which they became embroiled, and partly due simply to their lack of financial resources. Conceptually, the pedagogical reform movement hypothesised that starting with the subjective notions and wishes of young people would not heighten their alienation from society nor increase the latter's fragmentation, but rather that this type of socialisation would eventually realise a more solid sense of community and social integration. The evidence in terms of the outcomes of these practice methods did not tend to support this claim, as many youngsters were simply too disruptive in groups and communities to endorse the ideal of such integration. The (perverse) realisation of the project of establishing a correspondence between the spontaneous unfolding of the enthusiastic social commitment of youth and a wider, national community providing a 'home' for youthful ideals was engineered by the welfare politics of Hitler's fascism, whose youth policies incorporated those very ideas. It institutionalised an ideology-based populist sense of belonging, declaring this to be the realisation of the wishes of the youth movement, albeit – and this was regarded as the price to be paid – through the exclusion and, sometimes quite literal elimination of those individuals who did not fit the concept. The imposition of a totalitarian system along these lines disarmed or silenced many formerly critical pedagogues and 'validated' the role of those who were willing to provide fitting epistemologies, of whatever intellectual kind – and/or quality.

Nazi welfare concepts replaced the emergent welfare consensus pertaining to the integrative responsibilities of the state, based on political negotiations and professional as well as intellectual controversies, with a 'given' criterion of belonging: the racist concept of an organic body of the 'folk'. This ideology changed the epistemology of social service staff (in both public and non-governmental agencies) decisively. There was no longer any ground for the understanding of subjectivity and the negotiation of shared goals; their task became solely the application of objectivised criteria of social pathology, which were to be used for the purposes of the 'selection' of those whose attitude and physique qualified them as belonging to the national community, and the exclusion, incarceration, 'treatment' (including sterilisation) and eventual murder of those who did not belong (Sünker and Otto, 1997). Nazi welfare represents the triumph of instrumental rationality, a system that purports to represent the lifeworld whilst actually swallowing it up, thus leaving social work no scope for mediation, only for detached, mechanical diagnosis.

The link between social work's attraction to positivist epistemologies and its receptiveness to fascist ideology, or indeed the more general link between epistemology, methodology and the functional requirements of political systems, was not recognised – or at least not reflected upon – in the period of reconstruction and anti-fascist re-education following the Second World War. UN- and US-led training programmes emphasised the objectivity which casework methods introduced into the assessment and intervention process as an antidote to the apparent receptiveness of pedagogy to ideological interference (Lorenz, 1994). The approach was infused with an ethos which C. Wright Mills identified as prevailing in sociological research and which he called 'the professional ideology of social pathologists' (Mills, 1943): 'The ideal of practicality, of not being "utopian", operated in conjunction with other factors as a polemic against the "philosophy of history", brought into American sociology by men trained in Germany' (*ibid.*, p. 168). The 'thinking in situations unrelated to structures' fitted, for Mills (*ibid.*, p. 170), into a social work epistemology that was still shaped by Richmond's *Social Diagnosis*; the goals of adjustment to a given normative reality were presupposed uncritically.

In terms of social work's identity, the first two decades after the Second World War were a time when a unified, universal model of social work seemed achievable, based on the assumption, expressed in terms of ethical principles, that people had basically the same needs everywhere, regardless of culture and social and political context. Parsonian functionalist sociology, which prevailed not only in the US but also in large parts of Europe, provided the backdrop (and an explanation) for the way in which the social professions effected their task and status arrangements with the welfare states in whose rapid rise they played an increasingly central role. Universality and identity seemed to be secured even before the claims made to them had been empirically endorsed. This provided renewed evidence that once the link between social work's interest in being fully recognised as a profession and society's need for social work as a factor contributing to social stability and integration has been established, pragmatic/functionalist interests in research and methodology will tend to outweigh those aimed at communicative differentiation of and engagement with lifeworld processes.

Where unease about the nature and function of research in social work emerged at all, it was explored from the perspective of whether social work needed its own approach to research or whether it should 'borrow' prevailing models from the social sciences. The 'traditional' instrument of research in social work had been the evaluation of case records, undertaken with a view to understanding the complexity of practice situations and thence improving intervention accordingly (Lyons, 2000; Walton, 1975). But increasingly this was seen as less respectable than the large-scale quantitative research approach which represented the contemporary social science standard but which could not at that time be replicated with the resources available to social work. Heineman observed of the establishment of this hierarchical ranking order between models of research, based on experimental designs and geared towards prediction and *ex post facto* evaluative studies:

> The problem is not that these assumptions about what constitutes good science and hence good social work research never lead to useful knowledge, but, rather, that they are used normatively, rather than descriptively, to prescribe some research method-ologies and proscribe others. (Heineman, 1981, p. 374)

Research and the question of identity

One much-noted exception to conventional preferences, an example of qualitative research that received wide acclaim, was the study by Mayer and Timms (1970), *The Client Speaks*, although the self-critical implications of this research were seen immediately as handing arguments to a political lobby in Britain critical of social work's growing professional autonomy. The trend towards the dominance of positivist research standards was only halted, and that only temporarily perhaps, with the advent of new social movements in the 1970s and 1980s; these posed a profound challenge to the unifying and consolidating trend in the formation of social work's identity – a challenge encompassing but reaching beyond research methodology. Once the possibility of a plurality of fundamentally contrasting approaches to social work has been conceived, as demonstrated for instance by the emergence of feminist social work, and in its wake by the renewed interest in and valuing of personal experience over formal qualifications and expertise, the profession's position in society becomes insecure and contested. But precisely in this uncertainty, new stances on research can also form, leading in turn to a further differentiation of models of practice and a widening of the boundaries of social work overall.

In this situation a starker polarisation has set in between universalism and positivism-inspired empiricism on the one hand and a newly self-confident subjectivism and constructivism on the other. 'Experience' has come to be taken seriously again as a subject of and as a vehicle for welfare research, particularly in studies inspired by feminist ideas, which simultaneously challenge the alleged neutrality of conventional approaches. Hanmer and Hearn argue that 'Because gender-absence and gender-neutrality in social science is impossible to obtain, presentations in these traditions do not eliminate power relations between women and men, but rather only serve to obscure them' (1999, p. 107). Other social movements, notably those of black people, people with disability, psychiatric illness, social care users and trauma survivors, have added their voice to the critique of 'top-down research' and struggle to reclaim the right to authentic representation in research (Beresford and Evans, 1999).

With these challenges questions of identity have moved centre stage once more, not just in terms of the identities of service users, but also those of service providers, both individually and collectively. For the movements promoting emancipatory, user-led research have had a very distinct agenda of challenging the power of established professions, seeing this as maintained not least by means of 'authoritative' research. Here the interplay between intellectual, professional and political factors has come into play once again, for the shift in emphasis and orientation has really only become effective on the back of social policy changes aimed at altering fundamentally the role and structure of public social services (Gibbs, 2001).

It appears at first a curious and dangerous coincidence for social work that the issues of 'de-constructing' its power and structure are forced onto the agenda as it were from both directions, from neo-liberal policies and from user movements, and this makes it very difficult for social work to respond. The discipline and profession may well have considerable sympathy with the 'emancipatory' approach to research as it concurs with some of its own central values, but such sympathy is going to be short-lived if it results in the gradual abolition of social work's recognised place in society. However, once this conflict is seen in the light of social work's position straddling system and lifeworld, new, less defensive responses become possible, not least in terms of research strategies.

Similar problems and possibilities may pertain with regard to social work facing the dilemmas attendant upon the fundamental philosophical challenges posed to all 'truth claims' by poststructuralist and postmodern positions, which compound the uncertainty already long experienced by social work over its approach to research. Their programme has been to lay bare the power structures contained in all regimes of truth and has resulted in the destabilisation and decentring of all positions previously held to be authoritative. Identities can therefore no longer be taken as simply given, but only as constructed and transient. It must be stressed that this sobering realisation not only suspends the authority of empirical studies but also relativises the seeming authenticity of subjective accounts.

Seen from the historical perspective sketched above, the sharp divisions over the function of research and the choice of research methods apparent in social work today are not new phenomena [eds: see also Gould, this volume]. However, they present themselves currently with unprecedented force, and this indicates not simply that social work *per se* is in a confused state but that the rupture between system and lifeworld and the processes of differentiation within each of those domains have become more acute. Social work is unavoidably caught up in these tensions and finds its role and identity threatened by the bewildering plurality of demands and of reference points in the associated debates. What seems to be more important than making decisions on whether to pursue this or that research methodology is to relate the discourse on research back to more fundamental reflections on the place and role of social work in society. Noting the plurality of forms of social work can serve as a heuristic device to provide a better understanding of the dilemmas it faces. On the one hand there are many parallel ways of interpreting social work's role on account of the nature of the discipline and profession in its historical context, and this means its dual mandate between system and lifeworld. On the other hand this perspective also provides a basic understanding for the shared themes connecting those different manifestations.

In its link to lifeworld processes, their often contradictory effects on both epistemology and practice notwithstanding, social work keeps open its potential for communicative action, action that engages with conflicting norms, wishes and aspirations in such a way that it creates the conditions for reaching a consensus (Lorenz, 2001). Social work research can ultimately only make sense as research that is congruent with the profession's social mandate, and this means that it needs to develop as communicative action, in Habermas's sense. The many attempts at framing social work research as a reflexive process which are currently under debate are hopeful signs in this direction. However, this discussion needs to be linked to a critical theory of society in order to prevent its function and its results from becoming absorbed into the system, with its pursuit of instrumental action, and thereby risking the unintended consequence of contributing to tighter and more powerful social control. As Habermas put it some years ago:

... an exclusively technical civilization, which is devoid of the interconnection between theory and praxis ... is threatened by the splitting of its consciousness, and by the splitting of human beings into two classes – the social engineers and the inmates of closed institutions. (Habermas, 1974, p. 282)

References

Beresford, P. and Evans, C. (1999), 'Research Note: Research and empowerment', *British Journal of Social Work*, **29**(5), pp. 671–7.

Blindenbacher, R. (1999), 'The task dilemma in human service organizations and its impact on efficacy – a possible solution developed out of the theory of society of Jürgen Habermas', *European Journal of Social Work*, **2**(2), pp. 131–8.

Böhnisch, L., Niemeyer, C. and Schröer, W. (1997), 'Die Geschichte der Sozialpädagogik öffnen – ein Zugangstext', in Niemeyer, C., Schröer, W. and Böhnisch, L. (eds), *Grundlinien Historischer Sozialpädagogik – Traditionsbezüge, Reflexionen und übergangene Sozialdiskurse*, Juventa, Weinheim/Munich, pp. 7–32.

Bosanquet, H. (1914), *Social Work in London, 1869–1912: A History of the Charity Organisation Society*, John Murray, London.

Dillenburger, K. (1998), 'Evidencing effectiveness: the use of single-case designs in child care work', in Iwaniec, D. and Pinkerton, J. (eds), *Making Research Work*, Wiley, Chichester, pp. 71–91.

Fisher, M. (1999), 'Social work research, social work knowledge and the research assessment exercise', in Broad, B. (ed.), *The Politics of Social Work Research and Evaluation*, Birmingham, Venture Press, pp. 91–108.

Fook, J. (2002), 'Theorizing from practice: towards an inclusive approach for social work research', *Qualitative Social Work*, **1**(1), pp. 79–95. (A version entitled 'Theorising from frontline practice: towards an inclusive approach for social work research' was presented in the *Theorising Social Work Research* seminar series, no. 6, 11 July 2000, University of Luton, and is now available at <http://www.elsc.org.uk/socialcareresource/tswr/seminar6/fook.htm>.)

Garrett, A. (1949), 'Historical survey of the evolution of casework', *Journal of Social Casework*, **30**(6), pp. 219–29.

Gibbs, A. (2001), 'The changing nature and context of social work research', *British Journal of Social Work*, **31**(5), pp. 687–704.

Habermas, J. (1972), *Knowledge and Human Interests*, trans. J.J. Shapiro, Heinemann, London.

Habermas, J. (1974), *Theory and Practice*, trans. J. Viertel, Heinemann, London.

Habermas, J. (1987), *The Theory of Communicative Action*, Vol. II: *Lifeworld and System – A Critique of Functionalist Reason*, trans. T. McCarthy, Polity, Cambridge.

Habermas, J. (1990), *Moral Consciousness and Communicative Action*, trans. C. Lenhardt and S.W. Nicholsen, Polity, Cambridge.

Hanmer, J. and Hearn, J. (1999), 'Gender and welfare research', in Williams, F., Popay, J. and Oakley, A. (eds), *Welfare Research: A Critical Review*, UCL Press, London, pp. 106–30.

Heineman, M.B. (1981), 'The obsolete scientific imperative in social work research', *Social Service Review*, **55**(3), pp. 371–97.

Hill, O. (1869), 'The importance of aiding the poor without almsgiving', address to the Social Science Association, quoted in Woodroofe, *op. cit.*, who cites as her source Maurice, C.E. (ed.) (1913), *Life of Octavia Hill as Told in Her Letters*, Macmillan, London, pp. 257–8.

Humphries, B. (1997), 'From critical thought to emancipatory action: contradictory research goals?', *Sociological Research Online*, **2**(1), <http://www.socresonline.org.uk/socresonline/2/1/3.html>.

Kazi, M.A.F. (1998), *Single-Case Evaluation by Social Workers*, Ashgate, Aldershot.

Kazi, M.A.F. (2000), 'Contemporary perspectives in the evaluation of practice', *British Journal of Social Work*, **30**(6), pp. 755–68.

Leiby, J. (1969), 'Social work and social history: some interpretations', *Social Service Review*, **43**(3), pp. 310–18.

Lorenz, W. (1994), *Social Work in a Changing Europe*, Routledge, London.

Lorenz, W. (2000), 'Contentious identities – social work research and the search for professional and personal identities', paper presented in the *Theorising Social Work Research* seminar series, no. 4, 6 March, University of Edinburgh, and now available at <http://www.elsc.org.uk/socialcareresource/tswr/seminar4/lorenz.htm>.

Lorenz, W. (2001), *Understanding the 'Other': European Perspectives on the Ethics of Social Work Research and Practice*, 12th Annual CEDR Lecture, Centre for Evaluative and Developmental Research, Department of Social Work Studies, University of Southampton, Southampton.

Lyons, K. (2000), 'The place of research in social work education', *British Journal of Social Work*, vol. **30**(4), pp. 433–47. (An earlier version, presented in the *Theorising Social Work Research* seminar series, no. 1, 26 May 1999, Brunel University, is now available at <http://www.elsc.org.uk/socialcareresource/tswr/seminar1/lyons.htm>.)

Macdonald, G. (1994), 'Developing empirically-based practice in probation', *British Journal of Social Work*, **24**(4), pp. 405–27.

Marzahn, C. (1982), 'Zur Entwicklung des historischen Selbstverständnisses der Sozialpädagogik als wissenschaftlicher Disziplin', *Literatur Rundschau*, **5**(7), pp. 6–22.

Mayer, J.E. and Timms, N. (1970), *The Client Speaks: Working Class Impressions of Casework*, Routledge and Kegan Paul, London.

Mills, C.W. (1943), 'The professional ideology of social pathologists', *American Journal of Sociology*, **49**(2), pp. 165–80.

Pawson, R. and Tilley, N. (1997), *Realistic Evaluation*, Sage, Thousand Oaks, CA.

Powell, J. (2002), 'The changing conditions of social work research', *British Journal of Social Work*, **32**(1), pp. 17–33.

Rauschenbach, T. (1999), *Das sozialpädagogische Jahrhundert – Analysen zur Entwicklung Sozialer Arbeit in der Moderne*, Juventa, Weinheim/Munich.

Reid, W.J. (1994), 'The empirical practice movement', *Social Service Review*, **68**(2), pp. 165–84.

Richmond, M. (1917), *Social Diagnosis*, Russell Sage Foundation, New York.

Ruckdeschel, R.A. (1985), 'Qualitative research as a perspective', *Social Work Research and Abstracts*, **21**(2), pp. 17–21.

Salomon, A. (1919), *Die deutsche Frau und ihre Aufgaben im neuen Volksstaat*, Teubner, Leipzig/Berlin.

Salomon, A. (1926), *Soziale Diagnose*, Heymanns, Berlin.

Schille, H.-J. (1997), 'Zu Einflüssen der Individualpsychologie auf die Sozialpädagogik zwischen 1914 und 1933', in Niemeyer, C., Schröer, W. and Böhnisch, L. (eds), *Grundlinien Historischer Sozialpädagogik – Traditionsbezüge, Reflexionen und übergangene Sozialdiskurse*, Juventa, Weinheim/Munich, pp. 217–25.

Shaw, I. (1999), 'Evidence for practice', in Shaw, I. and Lishman, I. (eds), *Evaluation and Social Work Practice*, Sage, London, pp. 14–40.

Sheppard, M. (1998), 'Practice validity, reflexivity and knowledge for social work', *British Journal of Social Work*, **28**(5), pp. 763–81.

Sherman, E., and Reid, W.J. (eds) (1994), *Qualitative Research in Social Work*, Columbia University Press, New York.

Sünker, H. and Otto, H.-U. (eds) (1997), *Education and Fascism*, Falmer, London.

Taylor, C. and White, S. (2001), 'Knowledge, truth and reflexivity: the problem of judgement in social work', *Journal of Social Work*, **1**(1), pp. 37–59.

Trinder, L. (1996), 'Social work research: the state of the art (or science)', *Child and Family Social Work*, **1**(4), pp. 233–42.

Walton, R. (1975), *Women in Social Work*, Routledge, London.

Webb, S.A. (2001), 'Some considerations on the validity of evidence-based practice in social work', *British Journal of Social Work*, **31**(1), pp. 57–79.

White, S. (1998), 'Analysing the content of social work: applying the lessons from qualitative research', in Cheetham, J. and Kazi, M.A.F. (eds), *The Working of Social Work*, Jessica Kingsley, London, pp. 153–69.

Woodroofe, K. (1962), *From Charity to Social Work in England and the United States*, Routledge and Kegan Paul, London.

Chapter 9

'Knowing How to Go On': Towards Situated Practice and Emergent Theory in Social Work

Jeremy Kearney

Can one learn this knowledge? Yes; some can. Not, however, by taking a course in it, but through '*experience*'.—Can someone else be a man's teacher in this? Certainly. From time to time he gives him the right *tip*.—This is what 'learning' and 'teaching' are like here.—What one acquires here is not a technique; one learns correct judgements. There are also rules, but they do not form a system, and only experienced people can apply them right. Unlike calculating-rules.

What is most difficult here is to put this indefiniteness, correctly and unfalsified, into words.

(Wittgenstein, 1953, p. 227, emphases in original)

One of the key themes in this book is the complex relationship between research, theory and practice in social work, and in this chapter I want to consider this issue from a perspective which draws on the later work of the philosopher Ludwig Wittgenstein, particularly his notion of 'language-games', and also on social constructionist thinking. In the approach which I propose, research and theory are regarded as being neither in opposition to practice nor foundational to it, but rather as weaving into and emerging out of forms of situated practice experience. In such particular situations the issue is not only – or not so much – the application of the right rule or procedure, as being able to answer the question 'how should I act in this specific context?'

Wittgenstein described our everyday ability to understand the meanings of words and to use them correctly in context as 'knowing how to go on' (1953, para. 154), seeing this as involving a relational–responsive approach in which we act not only out of our own experiences and ideas but also respond in a moral way to the actions of others. In similar vein, John Shotter describes such practices as a 'social poetics', succeeding not in the sense applicable to theories worked out beforehand, but in terms of 'certain practical uses of language, at crucial points within the ongoing conduct of practice, by those involved in it' (Shotter and Katz, 1996, p.

213). I shall attempt to explore the implications of these ideas in relation to social work.

The debate on the relationship between knowledge and practice in social work has been described – with very good reason – as 'interminable' (Sheppard *et al.*, 2000, p. 466). It has also been, for the most part, rather repetitive, in that the same 'oppositions' emerge at different times and in various contexts in different guises – theory versus practice, the 'thinkers' versus the 'doers', or the 'academy' versus the 'agency'. However, this creation of oppositions is neither a specific characteristic of social work, nor a recent phenomenon.

Vernon Cronen (2001) puts the notion of theory/practice dualism in a historical context, noting John Dewey's view that such dualism is neither original nor primitive. Dewey saw its roots in the ancient European and Middle Eastern disparagement of labour, where work was 'associated with a curse and done under the pressure of necessity, while intellectual activity [was] associated with leisure' (Dewey, 1960 [1926][1], pp. 4–5, cited in Cronen, 2001, p. 15). In our own day this is reflected in the common idea of a split between those reclining in 'ivory towers' and those getting their hands dirty 'at the coal face'. Greek philosophers from Parmenides onwards looked for the certainty behind appearances and regarded direct participation in everyday life as a poor source of reliable knowledge. What was needed to secure this was a method that put the inquirer in an independent, external, or objective position, so that he or she could look behind appearances to unchanging laws of nature. Some influences of this tradition can be seen in the positivist approaches of our own era, with their search for objective truth (although there are of course important differences between ancient and modern understandings of science). However, Cronen also identifies an equally long-standing but less influential alternative tradition, with philosophers like Heraclitus arguing that the world was constantly changing and that human actions had an impact upon it.

Cronen notes that Aristotle regarded the behaviour of human beings as intrinsically contingent and not fully determined by the laws of nature (Cronen, 2001). The distinctions that Aristotle made in the *Nichomachean Ethics* between the physical world and the world of human activities have been described as involving the difference between a world where things 'have to be as they are' and a world where things 'can be other than what they are' (Pearce, 1994, p. 12). As regards the domain of what was universal and invariable, the appropriate mode of cognition was, for Aristotle, *theoria*, detached (though not passive) contemplation, through which pure and certain (including 'scientific') knowledge (*epistēmē*), was possible. In the world of human affairs, things were contingent upon each other and changeable through *praxis*, to which the appropriate form of knowing was practical wisdom or good judgement (*phronēsis*). *Praxis* and *phronēsis* involve mediation between the universal and the particular, and therefore deliberation and choice; thus they have a moral quality. Aristotle used politics and public speaking as key examples of these contingent and uncertain aspects of human experience; in

---

[1]   Dates given in the text for Dewey's works are those of the editions cited, followed (in square brackets) by dates of original publication.

the process of being involved in these activities people's views might change, so affecting the outcome. For Aristotle a third domain of human experience could also be distinguished, that of *poiēsis*, in which things (i.e. artefacts) are made and knowledge takes the form of *technē*, skill.

In some sense the debates on knowledge in social work can be seen as reflecting these three ways of knowing, or types of knowledge, outlined by Aristotle. Evidence-based approaches and procedural and regulated models of practice see the social world in rationalistic terms, as open to understanding, explanation, prediction and control by using the logic and methods of science (*epistēmē*). Approaches based on competencies assume that change can be brought about by the use of the right skills and techniques and that people can be trained to apply these correctly (*technē*). Those who see social work as uncertain and ambiguous feel that social workers need the wisdom to make good judgements in particular case situations (*phronēsis*).

It is this notion of 'things being contingent' that I wish to explore here; such thinking is very much part of a social constructionist approach to knowledge, which sees a fundamental, interactional relationship between meaning and action, knowledge and practice. It is an approach that emphasises the 'activities of makings and doings' and that 'the reality of the social world is continually made and remade in conjoint activities ...' (Pearce, 1992b, p. 137). In this approach language and meaning are 'matters of use and doing in conjoint action' (Cronen and Lang, 1994, p. 6), rather than conveying 'representations' of 'the real world' (so to speak). This is of course different from the Cartesian account of knowledge still dominant in the modern West, which separates the individual from what is observed, with knowledge seen as the recording of objective reality and language as a means of representing that reality. From a social constructionist perspective 'reality' or 'truth' is not *represented by* language but is *constructed in* language. Therefore we need to look at the situated contexts in which particular forms of language are used. And consequently, rather than attempting to separate them radically, one would see theory, research and practice in social work as intertwined, and as historically situated and emerging forms of acting/living rather than timeless, fixed entities.

Language-games

The later work of Ludwig Wittgenstein provides one way of thinking about these ideas that can also suggest ways to move forward in action. For Wittgenstein, to know the meaning of a word, a phrase or a sentence is to know how to use it and how to respond to it appropriately (Wittgenstein, 1953, para. 43). Take the word 'mean' for example; it can be used to describe someone as miserly or ungenerous, or the middle point between two extremes, or the sense or significance of something. The word can only be fully understood when one knows the context in which it is being used, and a person shows they know the meaning of a word by the way in which they use it coherently to continue – or 'go on' – in conversations.

Wittgenstein uses the term 'rule' to describe how people develop coherent patterns of behaviour in their interactions with others. People do not get up each morning and start from scratch thinking about how they should behave throughout the day; they have certain rules to guide them. The rules that a particular conversant is able to bring to bear on an episode constitute what are described as that person's 'grammatical abilities' (Cronen and Lang, 1994). For Cronen and Lang, 'both the terms – "rules" and "grammar" – refer to words, sentences, paragraphs, gestures, emotions and patterns of behaviour. These are inter-related in the process of co-ordination' (*ibid.*, p. 18).

For example, the various professionals attending a case conference have certain ways of acting which make sense in relation to their own general work contexts and the more specific contexts of case conferences. The case conference itself has a form, a grammar, which people usually act into appropriately, which in turn allows the meeting to continue. However, there can be times when the grammar(s) of the individual professions/professionals can clash with the grammar of the wider shared context. For example, at one case conference the parents of the child involved were invited in to discuss the situation, and in response to a question one of them acknowledged injuring the child. Immediately, the representative of the police who was present arrested the person concerned and the normal process of the conference was temporarily thrown into confusion. At that point the (specific) grammar of the police in dealing with criminal offences had overridden the (shared) grammar of the meeting in discussing the child in question.

Wittgenstein calls 'the whole, consisting of language and the actions into which it is woven, the "language-game"' (1953, para. 7). He uses this term, 'language-game', analogically, and not to suggest that language is always or necessarily playful but rather to bring out the way in which language is characterised by a diversity which may be grasped especially well by reflecting on our notion of a 'game' (1953, paras 65–6). He points out that there is a great range of different activities, all of which we call 'games', for example board-games, card-games, ball-games, Olympic games, etc. However, we mislead ourselves if we think that because these are all called 'games' they *must* all share certain characteristics in common. Rather, they are related to each other in many different ways, each sharing some characteristics with some others and others with yet others:

> Look for example at board-games, with their multifarious relationships. Now pass to card-games; here you find many correspondences with the first group, but many common features drop out, and others appear. When we pass next to ball games, much that is common is retained, but much is lost. ...
>
> And the result of this examination is: we see a complicated network of similarities overlapping and criss-crossing: sometimes overall similarities, sometimes similarities of detail. (1953, para. 66)

Wittgenstein crystallises his point by reminding us of the idea of 'family resemblances' – the ways in which 'the various resemblances between members of a family: build, features, colour of eyes, gait, temperament, etc. etc. [*sic*] overlap and criss-cross ... "games" form a family' (*ibid.*, para. 67). To counter any idea that this makes language appear weak in some sense, he also draws attention to the way in which the strength of a thread woven of many fibres consists not in the fact that one fibre extends throughout its length but in the overlapping of a changing plurality of different fibres at each point (*ibid.*).

The wide variety of language-games in human social life exhibits this characteristic diversity and people have to work out how to act appropriately in each different context. In the example I gave earlier the action of the police representative was coherent within the language-game of law enforcement but was incoherent within the language-game of case conferences. Along similar lines we can understand the variety of discussions and activities in social work indicated by 'theory', 'research', and 'practice' in terms of language-games. For example, evidence-based practice and user involvement could be described as current language-games within social work research. Each has its own grammar and rules, which different researchers act into in different ways. Some aspects of the grammar of evidence-based practice, for example the emphasis on the importance of randomised controlled trials, may make it difficult to co-ordinate coherently with the grammar of user-based approaches. So while it is possible to reflect that a group of users may decide to enter the grammar of evidence-based practice in order to carry out some particular research project, it is probably less easy to imagine advocates of evidence-based approaches adopting a user-focused philosophy. At this point it becomes a question of the different moral orders within which the two approaches exist, and whether adopting another grammar would change that moral order.

Wittgenstein makes clear that his use of the idea of language-games expressly seeks to highlight that speaking language is part of an activity; language is embedded in broader patterns of actions and objects, which he calls 'forms of life' (1953, para. 23). Gergen comments that '[l]anguage, in this sense, is not a mirror of life, it is the doing of life itself' (Gergen, 1999, p. 35).

In developing his 'analogy between language and games' (1953, paras 83–8) to illuminate his ideas about meaning as use, and to elucidate the particular sense in which understanding and speaking a language involve following rules, Wittgenstein observes that some games, such as chess, involve following definite rules, and these rules are unchanged by the playing of the game. As social constructionist writers such as those discussed in this chapter (notably Shotter, Gergen, Pearce, Cronen and Lang) have suggested, these may be called fixed rule language-games. In the example of the game of chess there are rules about who can play, how many can play together and how each piece can be moved. By playing, people reconstitute the game and reconstitute the rules that give it its coherence (Wittgenstein, 1953, para. 197). The chess pieces and the board would just be pieces of wood outside the game. As Gergen says, 'each piece in the chess set acquires its meaning from the game as a whole' (1999, p. 34).

In interactions with long-term users of services who have considerable experience of talking about their problems and who exhibit repetitive patterns of 'problem' behaviour over time, to ask them to retell the story of what their problem is can risk reconstituting a fixed rule language-game of 'problem talk', which can quickly become frustrating for the social worker (and often for the service user) involved.

Wittgenstein draws attention to the fact that there are contexts in which rules are not fully fixed or definite, using informal ball games as an example: 'And is there not also the case where we play and—make up the rules as we go along? And there is even one where we alter them—as we go along' (1953, para. 83). He emphasises that the rules of conversation and social interaction differ in important ways from the rules of chess or algebra. In everyday conversations rules have much more of an emergent quality, arising from the process of conversation; they are not pre-given as in chess. As Stevenson and Beech say, 'emergent rule language games are those in which the person's ideas about how to create meanings, put words, sentences, gestures, emotions and patterns of behaviour together, arise from the playing of the game' (1998, p. 791). Wittgenstein gives the example of telling someone to 'Stand roughly here' (1953, para. 88), which although it may be regarded as inexact in fixed rule language-game terms may yet be quite usable. The statement may work perfectly as an instruction or explanation in the context of the specific conversation that is taking place. The meaning of 'Stand roughly here' emerges from the context in which it is spoken. In emergent rule language-games, the rules emerge from within the language-game itself; they are not pre-given or fixed.

Some of these ideas can be useful for thinking about our ways of acting. For example, procedures for dealing with cases of child abuse are formalised in organisations and intended to be applied consistently to appropriate cases, and so can be seen as a kind of fixed rule language-game. Workers are expected to act in set ways within fixed parameters. As a result, whenever there is an inquiry or investigation into a failure of the child protection system, it is often argued that the procedures were not followed properly and the action is then to tighten up the procedures. However, as Wittgenstein says, knowing a rule is very different from following a rule, and in an important sense use is primary. Moreover, 'to *think* one is obeying a rule is not to obey a rule' (1953, para. 202, emphasis in original). For Wittgenstein, grasping a rule is not an individual psychological task or problem, but rather a question of co-ordination with others. On this understanding, it is doubtful that there is much more to be learned at this stage from further child abuse inquiries of the conventional kind, as the basis for these in the first place is that the formal 'rules' (i.e. the regulations and procedures) have not been followed. The issue at stake in these cases is rarely lack of knowledge of the 'rules'. The regulations and procedures exist and are almost certainly well-known to the professionals involved, so that revising them or adding extra ones will not in itself improve practitioners' or managers' 'ability' to use them in specific circumstances. This is because, as Wittgenstein points out, '"obeying a rule" is a practice. ... Hence it is not possible to obey a rule "privately": otherwise thinking one was obeying a rule would be the same thing as obeying it' (1953, para. 202). The ability to use the rule is shown in the doing of it.

It is more likely that in those cases where there has been a 'failure' of the system, meanings emerged from the interactions between the adults, children and workers within the actual circumstances of the situation which were not covered by the rules and procedures. The process became an emergent rule language-game, in which rules of behaviour developed unique to that particular situation. Of course, in the cases that become subject to public scrutiny, the result of the emergent process has generally had a negative outcome. It might in fact be more useful to have an 'inquiry' examining some successful cases of work in child protection, in order to see what 'emergent' practices made a difference.

Similarly, from the perspective of language-games it might be said that the debate about theory and practice in social work has mostly been conducted as a fixed rule language-game. It is often suggested that there is a particular grammar of theory, involving academic contexts, research, writing, conferences, and complexity, and a particular grammar of practice, involving lived experience, working in the field, and listening to the voice of users and clients. These grammars are very widely seen as incommensurate, and people often feel that they need to be either on one 'side' or the other. However, if we consider social work as more of an emergent rule language-game, where theory is embedded in and emerges from social work practice, then the emphasis shifts away from fixed outcomes to possible and potential 'ends in view' (Dewey, 1958 [1921]). Such outcomes are – or would be – constructed jointly in the process of negotiating how to go forward.

Recently, some writers have been attempting to outline possible under-standings of the production and use of knowledge in social work which have some affinity with the notion of emergent rule language-games. Parton (1998; 2000) has discussed the need to address issues of uncertainty and ambiguity in social work practice. Fook (2000) talks about the 'theory of knowledge which is implicit in action, the hidden assumptions enacted in practice', and the type of theory which 'practitioners use ... which is built up in their own private store, devised, developed and adapted from a variety of sources' (p. 10). Sheppard (1995) focuses on the difference between 'knowledge as product' and 'knowledge as process'.

The importance of process

The contemporary ideas about the form(s) of knowledge appropriate to social work mentioned at the end of the previous section fit very well with certain developments within social constructionist thinking which are themselves particularly useful to those who are engaged in various forms of practice.

Pearce (1992a) sees the key distinction among different social constructionist thinkers as being between those who foreground the products of the formative process, focusing on the events and objects of the social world, and those who foreground the process of formation itself. The focus on socially constructed products involves concentrating on the creations of language such as age, the self, gender, child abuse, the family, as units of observation (i.e. as data) rather than as units of analysis. This 'product-orientated' constructionism can be useful in that it allows entry to the standard academic discourse in terms of what is understood to constitute a 'theory' or 'research project', while at the same time maintaining a social constructionist perspective. However, it also involves certain difficulties, as there is something of a disjunction between the focus on the 'product' and the centrality of the idea of process characteristic of social constructionism. For although the process is felt to be open to change by experience, the end product is regarded as sufficiently robust not to change too much during the process of, or as a function of, being observed. For example, it is now commonplace to talk about social work being socially constructed. Howe (1987) and Payne (1997) have used an overall constructionist frame to look at theories in social work and the words 'social construction' are appearing in titles of social-work-related texts (Harding and Palfrey, 1997; Symonds and Kelly, 1998). In publications over a number of years Parton and his colleagues (Parton, 1985; 1996; Parton *et al.*, 1997), among others, have discussed the question of the social construction of child abuse and the implications for practice in the field of child protection. However, in general these writers have utilised the approach as a framework for their thinking rather than as a 'form of practice'.

An explicit focus on the *process* of social construction involves examining 'specific, local, situated *activities* in the social construction of reality, not as data points or illustrations of more general matters, but as themselves appropriate objects of enquiry' (Pearce, 1992a, p. 151, emphasis in original). This approach is consciously self-reflexive in that it focuses both on the process of (our) enquiry and the end result of that enquiry. On this view social work is not something that *has been* constructed and so can be examined objectively, but rather is *constantly being* constructed and reconstructed both by the way it is talked about and in the sites where this talk takes place. So the fact that people often talk about 'social work and social care' as a pair nowadays, or that two new Government bodies are called the Social Care Institute for Excellence (SCIE) and the General Social Care Council (GSCC), illustrates that the 'talk' about social work is in the process of changing; it is being reconstructed. Recently it has been suggested that whereas many of the practices engaged in by people involved in Government-funded initiatives such as Health and Education Action Zones and economic and social regeneration schemes would in the past have been called social work, current political discourses surrounding social work – which are mostly negative – mean that these practices are now not so described (Jordan, 2000).

Pearce (1992a, p. 152) notes Wittgenstein's view that language, the way we talk, ensnares us: 'a *picture* held us captive. And we could not get outside it, for it lay in our language and language seemed to repeat it to us inexorably.' (Wittgenstein, 1953, para. 115, emphasis in original). In this sense it is our way of talking 'as if' theory was foundational, and/or 'as if' research produced eternal truths, that hinders our ability to grasp what is taking place before our eyes and to acknowledge the part we play in it. For this reason, Wittgenstein says we should abandon the effort to see behind appearances to the truth, i.e. 'theory' (in the dominant/traditional sense): 'We must do away with all *explanation*, and description alone must take its place' (1953, para. 109, emphasis in original). We should, therefore, describe the 'actual use of language', which in an important sense 'leaves everything as it is' (*ibid.*, para. 124). To take this approach with respect to social work focuses our attention on the sites where the latter is being constructed and reconstructed, which is in the 'talk' and practices of governments, academics, practitioners and service users. To understand what social work 'is' is to examine the diverse contexts where this talk and action takes place: institutions, offices, conferences, meetings, books, user groups, and so on.

Constructing forms of practice

To concentrate on situated practices as practices, for their own sake, is to be willing to live with uncertainty, in situations where meaning is always emerging. As Branham and Pearce (1985) write, the relation between 'texts' (actions performed in a given moment) and 'contexts' (the circumstances in which those actions take place) is inherently unstable. Each derives meaning from and constructs the other in a reflexive co-evolutionary process. To treat either individually as a product leads to problems. On the one hand, in family therapy for example, the foregrounding of 'texts' (specific actions) as if they existed independently, floating in space, has led to notions of neutrality in relation to such political issues within the family as abuses of power, violence and exploitation, which are thereby left unchallenged and so are perpetuated, to the disadvantage of women, children, minority groups and older people (Dale *et al.*, 1986). On the other hand, always to foreground 'context' (the wider picture) as the arbiter of possibilities may serve to disempower individuals and fail to recognise the importance of personal interactions.

Such a focus changes our view of what constitutes research, theory and practice, and presents each of these as always emerging and unfinished. Indeed, Vernon Cronen (1994) has suggested that we have to shift our idea of what a theory is, recommending that we think of theory as a means by which we explore the creation, evolution and change of ideas in social action. He describes his own approach as a form of 'practical theory', which he says 'offers principles informed by engagement in the details of lived experience that facilitate joining with others to produce change' (Cronen, 2001, p. 14). For Cronen the importance of a theory is to be judged in terms of its consequences; theories are developed in order to make life better. From this perspective practical theories are morally committed theories.

John Shotter (1993) has described the kind of knowledge that emerges from such a self-consciously situated approach as 'knowing of the third kind', which is a *knowing from within* in contrast to *knowing how* (a technical skill or craft) and *knowing that* (facts or theoretical principles). But Shotter does not mean that this knowledge rests wholly within oneself; it is, rather, 'the kind of knowledge one has *only from within a situation* ... and ... thus takes into account (and is accountable to) the *others* in the social situation within which it is known' (Shotter, 1993, p. 7, emphases in original). In this way it is knowledge of a practical and a moral kind. This form of knowing has less to do with discovering or understanding than with making, but importantly, as with Aristotle (see above), not the making of artefacts but making in a social sense and context.

As we construct together our realities in language we are involved in what Shotter calls 'joint action', where we jointly create the ongoing processes in which we are mutually involved. This therefore places us in a moral position, where we are both responsible for and responsive to the joint actions that are constructed with others. As Pearce (1994) suggests, the form of knowledge involved here is very different from the positivist idea of unchanging factual knowledge. It is about practical wisdom, intelligence, local knowledge, and *praxis*. That is to say, what Wittgenstein has described as 'knowing how to go on' (1953, para. 154).

Knowing how to go on

As we have already seen, to use a word meaningfully is, for Wittgenstein, the same as being able to use it to 'go on' coherently in conversation. To act coherently in a particular situation is to know how to go on in an interaction with another person or persons. So when we ask for the meaning of an utterance we are in effect asking for an explanation of how to use it an ongoing situation, which in turn involves not only the use of the word itself, but also how to relate to others now and in the future, and in what contexts it is appropriate to act in this way (Cronen and Lang, 1994). It is this ability to act coherently that Wittgenstein wishes to emphasise when he says 'understanding is like knowing how to go on, and so is an ability: but "I understand", like "I can go on", is an utterance, a signal' (1980, I, no. 875). Shotter has described this responsiveness in 'going on' in the following terms:

> In this kind of activity – what elsewhere I have called joint action (Shotter, 1980, 1984, 1993) – what we do is 'shaped', not so much by us acting out of our own inner plans or desires, as by acting 'into' the social circumstances in which we must fit our actions. So, although participants respond to each other in a 'fitting' manner, to the extent that they influence each other's actions in a moment-by-moment fashion, its nature is intrinsically unpredictable and indeterminate: none of the participants will contain within themselves a complete grasp of its nature. (Shotter, 1994, p. 4)

These understandings of language and meaning offer a useful perspective on social work, which may be seen in Wittgenstein's terminology as a 'form of life', made up of many different language-games which both constrain and allow different possibilities for acting coherently. Practitioners, team members, managers, service users, supervisors and supervisees are all 'persons-in-conversation' (Harré, 1984), jointly making and remaking, through language, the social worlds in which they live. While we all bring our beliefs and theoretical perspectives, our knowledge and experience, into new situations, the actual process of engagement with the other person, if we are open to it, can lead to something new and unexpected taking place.

Meaning and action go together and by acting into situations we create meaning. When people have problems, or organisations are in difficulties, they often say they 'don't know what to do next' or 'don't know how to go forward'. Such situations are described as 'crazy' or 'stuck' or 'not making sense'. Social work, by its nature, has to deal with many such circumstances. Therefore, I want to consider the processes that can be used in social work to help practitioners and users find better ways of 'knowing how to go on', and thence how to create more meaningful interactions (and outcomes) for themselves. If we recognise that social workers, as part of a process of 'joint action', have some power in a situation, either to maintain it or to change it, they therefore also have some responsibility for their behaviour. And if we can see how something has been put together and, more importantly, what part we have played, or do play, in keeping it the way it is, there is then the opportunity to do something different and so *make* something different.

Take as an example the use of the term 'a Section', which is common in social work duty rooms when dealing with mental health situations. Social workers say things like 'a Section has just come in' or 'I am going on a Section'. On the surface this language of course refers to the fact that approved social workers' powers to make an application for a compulsory admission to hospital in mental health cases are governed by certain Sections of the 1983 Mental Health Act. But to use such shorthand language to refer to a potentially complex situation, on the basis of the limited information provided by an initial referral and before the person is actually seen, is already to create certain meanings and to begin to construct some potential outcomes. In other words, this language limits the potential ways of 'going on' in such cases.

It is interesting to note that a similar process is now taking place in child protection work. As a result of the 1989 Children Act the linguistic shorthand currently employed in this field is based similarly on legal procedures, with child care referrals being described as 'a Section 17' or 'a Section 47'. Some social services departments divide up their duty system between a 'general intake team' and a 'Section 47 team', so that the likely way of 'going on' is already enshrined in these very names. These phrases, 'Section 17' and 'Section 47', are part of a process of classification and it is widely agreed that the system as it currently operates is classifying many more families than it needs to as potential child protection cases at the referral stage (Dartington Social Research Unit, 1995; Parton *et al.*, 1997). A number of studies have concluded that only about 15–20 per cent of initial referrals eventually arrive at a point where they can be categorised clearly as child protection cases (Gibbons *et al.*, 1995; Thorpe, 1994). In an attempt to address this difficulty, Thorpe and Bilson (1998) have suggested some ways that cases can be identified at the initial referral stage so as not to 'create' child protection cases. They report that their approach has been implemented in Australia with very positive effects. This change should not be seen as some kind of 'disappearing act', whereby potential children at risk are 'wished away', but rather as recognising and responding to the fact that one of the ways in which the child protection system is maintained and reproduced is through systems of classification, and that it is people who do the classifying. In other words, classification is intervention and has real effects, intended or otherwise.

Research shows that social workers and their agencies 'know how to go on' in implementing the child protection system, but that they are much less clear how to work with families in need (Dartington Social Research Unit, 1995). A recent study (Kearney, 1998) into how and in what terms front-line social workers made the initial decision to classify new child care referrals, revealed that although the administrative system decreed that each new referral should be categorised immediately, some social workers responded pragmatically to the fact that many referrals were initially ambiguous and uncertain. They constructed and maintained an 'undefined zone' for a period of time, where referrals were categorised within the administrative system yet remained uncategorised within the worker's head while more information was gathered. The construction of this 'undefined zone' was a means of creating a space separate from the options offered by the administrative system. It was a response to the circumstances that workers experienced in particular case situations, where it was 'not possible' to categorise a case within the administrative timescale and framework. By adopting this approach the social workers were open to the possibility of new information and thence to the emergence of new ways to go on that might have been closed off by a definitive categorisation of the family and its situation.

To take an example from another context, during a Masters programme workshop one of the students (who was also a senior manager in a large voluntary organisation working with young people) described her concerns about how policy on dealing with staff safety and the risk of violence was being implemented differently in various parts of her organisation. As this was explored it emerged that groups in different areas of the organisation were responding in different ways to similar violent actions towards staff by users. The issue for the manager was how to rewrite the policy document covering this issue in a way that would ensure that it was applied uniformly across all parts of the organisation. It was noticeable that the manager frequently used such words as 'staff safety' and 'consistency'. The workshop discussion focused on asking questions about the meaning of these words for the manager and the organisation, but no final position was reached. When the students met again about three weeks later the manager reported that she had decided not to rewrite the policy document herself, but to engage in dialogue with colleagues from all parts of the organisation itself and with service users on how to go forward with this issue. About three months later, at another workshop, the manager described what had taken place and with what outcome. As a result of the process of dialogue all the organisation's directly interested parties had participated in thinking about the meaning of 'safety' in the context of the organisation's work; what had emerged was a sense that the issue needed to be seen in relation to the needs of the user group. This had the effect of reconstructing the meaning of the word to include both staff and users' safety, and also so as to acknowledge the organisation's responsibility to meet the needs of those users who were being difficult and aggressive. So the (unexpected) outcome of the review process was an agreement, within the overall policy framework, that parts of the organisation could apply sanctions differently for what might seem to be the same offence, depending on the particular circumstances in each case. As 'persons -in-conversation' the staff of the organisation and its users had established what might be called a policy of 'inconsistent' consistency. As a consequence of the dialogic process it had proved possible for the organisation as a whole still to 'know how to go on' in a coherent way. The new policy was comprehensible – and worked – because everyone understood how it had been 'made'.

Social poetics as a form of practice

Having elaborated above a particular tradition of thought which focuses on language and the relationship between meaning and action, I want now to consider what forms of practice might be most consistent with such a perspective and how they might be described. One possible approach is that which John Shotter calls 'social poetics' (Shotter, 1995). He proposes this as a means of developing forms of practice that at once both emerge from and influence the immediate and ongoing interactions between people. In place of professional monologue from the expert to the client/user he suggests a dialogical approach to these human inter-relations, a relational–responsive approach, which notices the responses that others' words, actions, emotions and behaviours call out from us (see, for example, Shotter and Katz, 1996). It pays attention to the possibilities of what can be constructed in the moment, rather than viewing the other's words and actions as data to be interpreted.

Shotter is arguing that we do not need a specific theory to 'get at' something behind appearances, but instead, as Wittgenstein says, we need to change our 'way of looking at things' (1953, para. 144) and '[give] prominence to distinctions which our ordinary forms of language easily make us overlook' (*ibid.*, para. 132). Shotter sees practices orientated by these ideas as having a 'poetic' quality; picking up Wittgenstein's notion of a (more) 'perspicuous representation' (*ibid.*, para. 122), this is about creating an 'understanding which consists in "seeing connections"' (*ibid.*). Shotter's approach entails a

> new, relational attitude to the patient's use of words, an attitude that invites a creative, poetic sensibility, as well as a 'boundary crossing' stance that creates comparisons useful in relating what (people) say to the rest of their lives. (Katz and Shotter, 1996a, p. 919)

Therefore it is about working with what arises in the moment and finding ways to connect it to the wider aspects of people's lives.

Such an approach to professional practice has been described in a number of different contexts, including doctor/patient interactions (Katz and Shotter, 1996a), a mentoring programme for medical students (Katz and Shotter, 1996b), and, most strikingly, in an analysis of the famous study by Oliver Sachs (1985) in which Sachs recounts the case of Dr P. – 'the man who mistook his wife for a hat' (Shotter, 1998). Shotter calls the practices that Sachs describes himself engaging in with Dr P. as 'poetic', 'as they are to do with novelty, with processes of creation ... with "first time" makings and "first time" understandings – with ... only "once-occurrent" events' (Shotter, 1998, p. 34). In Shotter's view it is through such events that Sachs is both able to relate to Dr P. and also to illustrate his ways of relating to him to the reader. In his analysis Shotter notes that in order to respond to Dr P., Sachs had to find a way, a means, to 'go on with him' in a practical manner:

[T]his was Sacks's [*sic*] task ... to 'go on' with him to a sufficient degree, as to be able to build up a grasp of what Dr P.'s strange 'inner world' was like, from a whole set of responses in relation both to Sacks's probes and other events. (1998, p. 41)

And what Sachs discovers through his efforts to respond to the strange behaviour of Dr P. is that 'music, for him, had taken the place of [the visual] image. He had no body-image, he had body music ...' (Sachs, 1985, p. 17, quoted by Shotter, 1998, p. 42). In fact that was the way he recognised people – by their 'body-music', when they moved. How Sachs came to understand this man was by being open to and responding to some unique moments in their interactions which gave him crucial information, which his standard neurological tests had not provided. He responded in a 'living, embodied ... [way to] Dr P.'s strange style of interacting' (Shotter, 1998, p. 44). As Shotter says:

It is this emphasis on the living, embodied, gestural aspect of people's social practices, and the direct and immediate, sensuous responses that they call out of us, that gives us a clue as to how non-informational, 'poetic' events can give us access to worlds utterly unfamiliar to us. Their function is not so much to help us see, in contemplation, the supposedly true nature of what a certain thing or event actually is, as with drawing our attention, practically, to the possible relations and connections such things or events might have with other aspects of our lives. And it was to the 'musical' dimension in Dr P.'s life that Sacks's attention was drawn. (Shotter, 1998, p. 44)

Another practitioner whose way of working might be described as having fitted the concept of social poetics is the hypnotherapist Milton Erickson. There are many examples in his work of how he found unusual and creative ways to 'go on' with people towards positive outcomes (Haley, 1973). He was willing to accept working within metaphors, not only of a verbal kind but also working with people who live 'a metaphoric life', for example those diagnosed as schizophrenic. In one hospital where he worked there was a young man who said he was Jesus. He paraded about as the Messiah, wore a sheet, and attempted to impose Christianity on people. So one day Erickson approached him and said, 'I understand you have had some experience as a carpenter?' The man could only reply that he had, and then Erickson involved him in building a bookcase.

In another example, there was a patient in hospital who would only speak in 'word salad' – meaningless phrases – for hours on end. Erickson decided to have some of this man's speech transcribed, then analysed it for repetitive patterns in the actual, meaningless, language. Having done this he went up to the man and said 'Hello', to which the man replied in word salad for 15 minutes. Erickson then responded with similar meaningless language for 15 minutes. The man then replied for half-an-hour, whereupon Erickson in turn spoke for half-an-hour. This process continued over a number of days in the same way. Eventually the man spoke in word salad to Erickson for three hours and Erickson replied for the same length of time; at which point the man said, 'I'm tired of this, let's have a normal conversation'. From then on he and Erickson engaged in ordinary conversations, except that each of these would end with the man saying one sentence in word salad. The man's condition improved and he left the hospital, and Erickson told of getting a friendly postcard a few years later which ended with one meaningless phrase.

In each of these cases Erickson focused on the specific detail of the patient's behaviours and used what initially seemed like senseless actions as a means of connecting with the patient's inner world. From this focus on detail he then managed to connect the patients to wider and more positive forms of living.

Stevenson (2000) suggests that the approach of Romme and Escher (1989) to people 'hearing voices' also has a poetic quality, as they find new ways to make sense of this experience without using traditional diagnostic frameworks.

All these examples are in my view highly congenial to social work practice, for as Parton and O'Byrne argue, direct face-to-face work with users is 'still the core of social work' (2000, p. 3). The ideas discussed above attempt to get us to focus on what is actually emerging in the specific, interactional moment between the social worker and the service user; to be able to respond on all levels (emotional, intellectual, physical) to what is taking place and to notice, in Gregory Bateson's phrase, 'the difference that makes a difference' (1972). As Wittgenstein says, it is

> Not ... [that] we had to hunt out new facts; it is, rather, of the essence of our investigation that we do not seek to learn anything *new* by it. We want to *understand* something that is already in plain view. For *this* is what we seem in some sense not to understand. (1953, para. 89, emphases in original)

Conclusion

The approach outlined above offers a different way of thinking about the relationship between theory and practice, along similar lines to Lang's[2] elegant notion of making theory 'lived practice' and practice 'lived theory'. Such phrasing aims to make an intimate connection between theory and practice and to illustrate that our ways of talking have practical consequences and our ongoing activities help construct our ways of talking (and thinking).

From a philosophical perspective, Wittgenstein helps us to see the effects of traditional/explanatory theorising and urges us to abandon attempts to produce such forms of theory, claiming that philosophical problems occur when '[w]e predicate of the thing what lies in the method of representing it' (1953, para. 104). However, he was very aware that the effort not to theorise in this way involves equal difficulties and does not in itself avoid these dangers, for we cannot thereby escape from language. For Wittgenstein, 'Philosophy is a battle against the bewitchment of our intelligence by means of language' (*ibid.*, para. 109). Perhaps more immediately useful in the social work context are the ways in which Cronen draws on these ideas in developing his notion of 'practical theory'. Agreeing with Dewey (1948 [1920]), Cronen claims that 'beginning with Plato, the formalisation of inquiry took an unhelpful turn ... [which] ... moved theory itself rather than the

---

[2] Personal communication, cited in Burnham, 1992, p. 12.

use of theory into the foreground' (Cronen, 2001, p. 26). Cronen wishes to emphasise the practical use of theory, and with 'practical theory' he is proposing an approach that holds on to a framework which helps the *inquirer* know where to go next, while also being committed to *joining with others* in situated action. Thereby, practical theory is 'importantly informed by data created in the process of engagement with others' (*ibid.*). In this way the understanding of what to do next is open to change as a result of engagement with others' lived experience. It is this willingness to put our ways of thinking 'on the line' that can help us engage with the uncertainties and ambiguities that constitute social work.

This chapter has drawn on social constructionist ideas and the later work of Wittgenstein in an attempt to present a view of language and meaning in which social worlds are made by persons-in-conversation. In considering social work as a series of 'language-games' which can facilitate or inhibit different possible outcomes, we are always faced with the questions 'how should we act?' in particular circumstances, and 'what am I making if I act this way?' In exploring social work as a 'form of life' that is primarily concerned with relationships and face-to-face interactions, my aim has been to focus on ways in which we can pay close attention to what takes place in specific interactional moments and how we can use them as creative opportunities to help produce outcomes that those involved regard as useful, helpful or good. I have tried to present some examples of practice which illustrate some such 'moments'. I see these perspectives as being relevant to social work practice in that they acknowledge the complexity of human interaction and do not attempt to reduce it to set formulae or final definitions. As has been argued, the 'notions of ambiguity, indeterminacy and uncertainty are at the core of social work' (Parton and O'Byrne, 2000, p. 44). It should be clear that the ideas, approaches and methods sketched here constitute neither a theoretical model nor a specific guide to practice; rather the chapter is a call to acknowledge the importance of focusing our awareness on specific situated moments of interaction with others and an invitation to pay attention to what emerges or might emerge from such moments.

References

Note: dates given below for Dewey's works are those of the editions cited in the text, where dates of original publication are also shown (in 'square brackets').

Bateson, G. (1972), *Steps to an Ecology of Mind*, Ballantine Books, New York.
Branham, R.J. and Pearce, W.B. (1985), 'Between text and context: toward a rhetoric of contextual reconstruction', *Quarterly Journal of Speech*, **71**(1), pp. 19–36.
Burnham, J. (1992), 'Approach–method–technique: making distinctions and creating connections', *Human Systems*, **3**(1), pp. 3–26.
Cronen, V. (1994), 'Coordinated management of meaning: practical theory for the complexities and contradictions of everyday life', in Siegfried, J. (ed.), *The Status of Common Sense in Psychology*, Ablex, Norwood, NJ, pp. 183–207.
Cronen, V. (2001), 'Pragmatic theory, practical art, and the pragmatic–systemic account of inquiry', *Communication Theory*, **11**(1), pp. 14–35.

Cronen, V. and Lang, P. (1994), 'Language and action: Wittgenstein and Dewey in the practice of therapy and consultation', *Human Systems*, **5**(1–2), pp. 5–44.

Dale, P., Davies, M., Morrison, T. and Waters, J. (1986), *Dangerous Families: Assessment and Treatment of Child Abuse*, Tavistock, London.

Dartington Social Research Unit (1995), *Child Protection: Messages from Research*, HMSO, London.

Dewey, J. (1948), *Reconstruction in Philosophy*, Beacon, New York.

Dewey, J. (1958), *Experience and Nature*, Dover, New York.

Dewey, J. (1960), *The Quest for Certainty*, Capricorn Books, New York.

Fook, J. (2000), 'Theorising from frontline practice: towards an inclusive approach for social work research', paper presented in the *Theorising Social Work Research* seminar series, no. 6, 11 July, University of Luton, and now available at <http://www.elsc.org.uk/socialcareresource/tswr/seminar6/fook.htm>.
(A version appears as Fook, J. (2002), 'Theorizing from practice: towards an inclusive approach for social work research', *Qualitative Social Work*, **1**(1), pp. 79–95.)

Gergen, K.J. (1999), *An Invitation to Social Construction*, Sage, London.

Gibbons, J., Conroy, S. and Bell, C. (1995), *Operating the Child Protection System*, HMSO, London.

Haley, J. (1973), *Uncommon Therapy: The Psychiatric Techniques of Milton H. Erickson, M.D.*, W.W. Norton, New York.

Harding, N. and Palfrey, C. (1997), *The Social Construction of Dementia: Confused Professionals?*, Jessica Kingsley, London.

Harré, R. (1984), *Personal Being: A Theory for Individual Psychology*, Harvard University Press, Cambridge, MA.

Howe, D. (1987), *An Introduction to Social Work Theory*, Wildwood House, Aldershot.

Jordan, B., with Jordan, C. (2000), *Social Work and the Third Way: Tough Love as Social Policy*, Sage, London.

Katz, A. and Shotter, J. (1996a), 'Hearing the patient's "voice": toward a social poetics in diagnostic interviews', *Social Science and Medicine*, **43**(6), pp. 919–31.

Katz, A. and Shotter, J. (1996b), 'Resonances from within the practice: social poetics in a mentorship programme', *Concepts and Transformations*, **1**(2–3), pp. 239–47.

Kearney, J. (1998), *Exploring Everyday Social Work Practices in Child Protection*, unpublished research report, Centre for Social Research and Practice, University of Sunderland, Sunderland.

Lang, P., personal communication, cited in Burnham, *op. cit.*

Parton, N. (1985), *The Politics of Child Abuse*, Macmillan, London.

Parton, N. (1996), 'Child protection, family support and social work', *Child and Family Social Work*, **1**(1), pp. 3–11.

Parton, N. (1998), 'Risk, advanced liberalism and child welfare: the need to rediscover uncertainty and ambiguity', *British Journal of Social Work*, **28**(1), pp. 5–27.

Parton, N. and O'Byrne, P. (2000), *Constructive Social Work: Towards a New Practice*, Macmillan, Basingstoke.

Parton, N., Thorpe, D. and Wattam, C. (1997), *Child Protection: Risk and the Moral Order*, Macmillan, Basingstoke.

Payne, M. (1997), *Modern Social Work Theory* (2nd edn), Macmillan, Basingstoke.

Pearce, W.B. (1992a), 'A "camper's guide" to constructionisms', *Human Systems*, **3**(3–4), Special Issue: 'Concepts and Applications of Social Constructionism', ed. W.B. Pearce, pp. 139–61.

Pearce, W.B. (1992b), 'Editorial', *Human Systems*, **3**(3–4), Special Issue: 'Concepts and Applications of Social Constructionism', ed. W.B. Pearce, pp. 137–8.

Pearce, W.B. (1994), *Interpersonal Communication: Making Social Worlds*, Harper Collins, New York.

Romme, M. and Escher, S. (1989), 'Hearing voices', *Schizophrenia Bulletin*, **15**(2), pp. 209–16.

Sachs, O. (1985), *The Man Who Mistook His Wife for a Hat*, Duckworth, London.

Sheppard, M. (1995), 'Social work, social science and practice wisdom', *British Journal of Social Work*, **25**(3), pp. 265–93.

Sheppard, M., Newstead, S., Di Caccavo, A. and Ryan, K. (2000), 'Reflexivity and the development of process knowledge in social work: a classification and empirical study', *British Journal of Social Work*, **30**(4), pp. 465–88. (Some of the material discussed in this article was presented (by Sheppard), in the *Theorising Social Work Research* seminar series, no. 1, 26 May 1999, Brunel University, under the title 'Reflection, reflexivity and knowledge for social work practice'.)

Shotter, J. (1980), 'Action, joint action, and intentionality', in Brenner, M. (ed.), *The Structure of Action*, Blackwell, Oxford, pp. 28–65.

Shotter, J. (1984), *Social Accountability and Selfhood*, Blackwell, Oxford.

Shotter, J. (1993), *Cultural Politics of Everyday Life: Social Constructionism, Rhetoric and Knowing of the Third Kind*, Open University Press, Buckingham.

Shotter, J. (1994), 'Now I can go on: Wittgenstein and communication', paper presented at the University of Calgary, 30 September.

Shotter, J. (1995), 'Wittgenstein's world: beyond "the way of theory" toward a "social poetics"', paper presented at a conference on *Social Construction, Culture and the Politics of Social Identity*, New School for Social Research, New York, 7 April.

Shotter, J. (1998), 'Social construction as social poetics: Oliver Sacks [*sic*] and the case of Dr P', in Bayer, B.M. and Shotter, J. (eds), *Reconstructing the Psychological Subject: Bodies, Practices and Technologies*, London, Sage, pp. 33–51.

Shotter, J. and Katz, A. (1996), 'Articulating a practice from within the practice itself: establishing formative dialogues by the use of a "social poetics"', *Concepts and Transformations*, **1**(2–3), pp. 213–37.

Stevenson, C. (2000), 'Living within and without psychiatric language games', in Barker, P. and Stevenson, C. (eds), *The Construction of Power and Authority in Psychiatry*, Butterworth Heinemann, Oxford, pp. 17–34.

Stevenson, C. and Beech, I. (1998), 'Playing the power game for qualitative researchers: the possibility of a post-modern approach', *Journal of Advanced Nursing*, **27**(4), pp. 790–97.

Symonds, A. and Kelly, A. (eds) (1998), *The Social Construction of Community Care*, Macmillan, Basingstoke.

Thorpe, D. (1994), *Evaluating Child Protection*, Open University, Milton Keynes.

Thorpe, D. and Bilson, A. (1998), 'From protection to concern: child protection careers without apologies', *Children and Society*, **12**(5), pp. 373–86.

Wittgenstein, L. (1953), *Philosophical Investigations*, trans. G.E.M. Anscombe, Blackwell, Oxford.

Wittgenstein, L. (1980), *Culture and Value*, ed. G.H. von Wright, with H. Nyman, trans. P. Winch, Blackwell, Oxford.

Chapter 10

Habermas/Foucault for Social Work: Practices of Critical Reflection

Robin Lovelock and Jackie Powell

Taken together, the works of Jürgen Habermas and Michel Foucault highlight an essential tension in modernity. This is the tension between the normative and the real, between what should be done and what is actually done ... the tension between consensus and conflict. (Flyvbjerg, 1998, pp. 210–11)

... cultural practices are more basic than any theory and ... the seriousness of theory can only be understood as part of a society's on-going history. (Dreyfus and Rabinow, 1986, p. 115)

... the characterisations of the modern welfare state and of civil society provided by Habermas and by Foucault ... provide different ways of thinking politically about the challenges which confront us. (Ashenden, 1999b, p. 143)

... the regimes of law and power are constantly at loggerheads. To be able to address [this] adequately, we need both Foucault and Habermas ... (Kelly, 1994b, p. 378)

It is through rational dialogue, and especially through political dialogue, that we clarify, even to ourselves, who we are and what we want. ... Here politics functions as a normative concept describing what collective agency should be like. (Beiner, 1983, p. 152, quoted in Timms, 1989, p. 22)

... our unexamined assumptions block our view and our situation ... [S]ocial work cannot simply roll along in the present storm ... We need to act—contemplating, in doing so, alternative possibilities. (Chambon, Irving and Epstein, 1999, p. 266)

This chapter is about 'thinking about thinking'. More specifically, it is about thinking about thinking about social work. How are we to reflect critically and self-consciously about the discipline and profession? How are we to discuss the issues this raises, both as academic colleagues and in wider public arenas? We thus address the question 'What is critical reflection?', and (in a less detailed and a less direct way) the question 'What can critical reflection *do*?' – i.e. in respect of acting in/on 'the world'.

Several contributors to this book have argued, here and elsewhere, that social work's origins and ambiguities lie in changes which were taking place at a crucial point in the history of modern liberal states and, relatedly, that social work is both a political and a moral activity (see, for example, Jordan, 1978; 1989; 1990; Jordan and Parton, 1983; Parton, 1991; 1994a; b; 1996a; 1999; 2000). We too proceed from these understandings. Moreover, we are *in the midst* of another major (and arguably global) transition; one whose outcome is as yet – and necessarily – unclear, as signalled in Richard Bernstein's perceptive characterisation (1991) of the leading themes and issues in contemporary thought in terms of a pervasive *mood* of 'modernity/postmodernity'. Consequently, there is a pressing need to think broadly and deeply about social work in its historical and intellectual context. The social work community as a whole – whether practitioners or managers, or primarily educators, researchers and/or theorists – may be said to have not only a need but also a responsibility to think about, and indeed to discuss, the nature of their work and how they do it. With this in mind, the focus in this chapter is primarily on alternative ways of being critically reflective, as a contribution to re-examining the nature and purpose of social work in a context of uncertainty and rapid change.

To describe social work as 'inherently political' is to point to something more than the fact that social work in both its statutory/mandatory and its non-statutory/permissive aspects is either directly implementing government policy enshrined in law or otherwise acting within a framework of legislation and 'guidance', significant though these aspects are in themselves. Moreover, since the very words 'politics' and 'political' currently have negative connotations in many contexts, both academic and more general, it perhaps also needs underlining that our intention is quite specifically *not* that of attaching guilt to social work by association.

Bill Jordan's writing over several decades has consistently brought out the moral and political nature of social work in a particularly cogent way (see especially Jordan, 1989; 1990), showing how social work is necessarily concerned with justice and that in their day-to-day practice social workers are faced with dilemmas

> not just about *how* to help the client, but also about what the *right* thing is to do. The choices ... are ones of morals as well as methods. ... The issues at stake are ones in which the community, through the state and in the profession of social work ... [has decided] to use power and resources to promote certain outcomes which are valued, and avoid certain others which are disapproved. (Jordan, 1990, p. 25, emphases in original)

These matters are not fundamentally altered by the 'reform' or 'modernisation' of the UK welfare state which has been undertaken by successive governments since those words were written, nor by the social work/social care 'conundrum' embedded in current discussions.

Walter Lorenz, like Jordan, argues that social workers intervene in situations where issues of personal autonomy, conflicts of interest, and different ways of living somehow have to be reconciled, more often than not in a situation of limited resources. Emphasising the broader context within which social work is located, Lorenz notes that social workers' actions are legitimated through legal authority, professional knowledge and expertise, and the cultural and societal norms of the context in which they practice:

> Social work has a 'dual mandate' for [the] negotiations [it involves], from individuals and from society at large, either through state agencies or through non-governmental organisations. It was originally not just a private, charitable movement but an organised, systematic activity which took account of the overall societal context in which it operated and developed. (Lorenz, 1994, p. 4)

Thus to put it at its most general, social work, like politics – indeed as part of politics – is essentially about the 'relationship' 'between' 'the individual' and 'society'.[1] Politics and social work, both generally and more specifically, in effect give and represent constantly changing answers to a perennial and unavoidable question: 'How shall we live together?' This necessarily has an ethical dimension: 'How *should* we live together?' And these questions in turn subtend – among others – the more detailed, yet no less large questions indicated in the introduction to this book (p. 12, quoting Plant, 1991, pp. 1–2) as characteristic and recurrent themes in political theory/philosophy;[2] for example: 'Are there human rights and if so what are they?'; 'Do individuals have definable needs and if so who has an obligation to satisfy them?' The implicit orientation of such questions towards a future means neither that the fleeting present embodies no 'answers' to them nor that the slate ever was or can be a blank one. 'Answering' them involves, at least implicitly, the articulation and justification *both* of claims to knowledge *and* of judgements of value and of prudence [eds: see also Butler and Pugh, this volume]. In this, in the associated and unavoidable concern with 'the question of theory and practice' (both in theory and in practice), and in the very similar challenges to their academic credibility attendant upon acknowledging explicitly normative concerns, the disciplines of social work and political theory/philosophy have much in common. Because of the importance we attach to this perception we give it some attention – albeit unavoidably superficial – in the overall introduction to this collection (especially pp. 11–17). The present chapter may serve to further demonstrate, exemplify and develop the points made there.

The contemporary context is one of powerful managerialist tendencies in many governments' general approaches and associated pressures to adopt particular forms of 'evidence-based' practice, and of 'positions' (*sic*) opposing these orientations which are not always notably more reflective or self-critically open. The perspective sketched immediately above suggests perhaps above all a

---

[1] We use 'scare quotes' here in an attempt to forestall any unreflective reading or use of the key terms they 'enclose'.

[2] See p. 12, note 4.

need in this situation to preserve the intelligibility of an idea of critical reason and so to keep alive the possibility of reasoned discussion of normative issues. For this a 'space' is needed, as it were 'between' the positivistic would-be avoidance of normative discussion and the mere assertion of value-commitment; the latter being in many respects a mirror-image of the former.

This chapter explores what has been constructed as 'the Foucault/Habermas debate'. This encounter concerns 'the relation between society, critical reason and modernity' (Dreyfus and Rabinow, 1986, p. 109); a detailed overview provides an opportunity to examine two different approaches to critical reflection and what is at stake between them. Following a general account of the Foucault/Habermas debate in which we seek to bring out the two distinct modes of thinking which lie at its heart, we focus on the differing understandings of state/society relations offered by Habermas and Foucault respectively, and the contrasting ways in which the concept of 'civil society' has been and may be understood and employed to delineate a potential site for resistance against the increasing bureaucratisation and managerialism of the welfare state. In the final part of the chapter we consider more directly the relevance of the Foucault/Habermas debate to reflecting critically on social work. Contemporary social work literatures suggest, and increasingly acknowledge, a need to develop our ideas and our practice through open discussion and debate. We explore the problematic notion of 'dialogue', frequently encountered in recent social work discourses, with a view to finding possible ways 'to think and act differently' (Tully, 1999). Our suggestion is that we need to draw upon the ideas of both Habermas and Foucault in this regard.

Michel Foucault (1926–84) and Jürgen Habermas (b. 1929) are incontestably two of the most important social and political theorists of the past fifty years; this latter designation – i.e. *political* theorists (see previous page and the introduction to this book) – notwithstanding that Foucault's conception of power and its operation led him away from traditional accounts of politics in terms of sovereignty and of the activities of governments as essentially legislative, and that he himself wrote little political theory as such in conventional academic terms. For example, he did not reflect directly and systematically on topics such as democracy and the rule of law (Dean, 1999, pp. 166–8). Moreover, like Wittgenstein (among others) he resisted the very notion of theory as generally understood in these and other, social scientific, contexts [eds: see Kearney, this volume].

Both Habermas and Foucault have given sustained attention to such large themes as truth, subjectivity and progress; indeed they have often been held, both inside and outside academe, to represent opposing views on these and related matters, with their names commonly invoked as 'standard-bearers' in respect of modernity and postmodernity, modernism and postmodernism. Whilst not wishing to give credence to this rather unhelpful way of framing what is at stake between them, it is certainly the case that Habermas has repeatedly identified himself with 'the unfinished project of modernity'; however, it is imperative to understand precisely what he means by this (d'Entrèves and Benhabib, 1996). Foucault's affiliations in these respects are in some ways rather less clear, or rather perhaps less overtly stated, but there is evidence that they differ from what is widely thought or implied. For example, reflecting on his own intellectual reference points in a 1983 interview in which, not insignificantly, Habermas's ideas were being referred to, Foucault both indicates considerable unease about the usefulness of the terms 'modernity' and 'postmodernity' and firmly distances himself from any association with the idea of 'a collapse of reason' (Foucault, 1988a, pp. 33–5). Despite what are certainly deep philosophical differences, both thinkers reject the idea of 'a transcendental, self-constituting (theoretical and practical) subject'; a rejection which is 'distinctive of philosophers in the late twentieth century' (Kelly, 1994c, pp. 3–4).

The writings of both Habermas and Foucault are centrally concerned with knowledge, especially knowledge produced by the social and human sciences, and with the use and abuse of power. Simons notes the different ways in which each was 'haunted by the Third Reich' (1995, p. 110) and the influence on their work of their respective childhood experiences during the rise of Nazism and fascism should not be ignored. The fundamental issues surrounding the role, including the public role, of the critical intellectual are of deep concern to both, representing a common central dimension of their work.

Habermas and Foucault in the social work literature

In reflecting on the nature of social work in a changing Europe, Walter Lorenz (1994) acknowledges the tradition of critical theory associated with 'the Frankfurt School', and in particular the work of Jürgen Habermas. Lorenz argues that Habermas's theory of communicative action has the potential to 'provide practice paradigms for social work in a broader sense on the strength of its analysis of communicative processes' (Lorenz, 1994, p. 85). Habermas's ideas connect and resonate with the German tradition of 'social pedagogy' (Lorenz, 1999), the roots of which lie in wider attempts to find and develop – in hermeneutics – a philosophical and methodological alternative to positivism. In his recent work, Lorenz (2000; 2001; this volume) further explores these themes both with regard to social work research and its actual and potential relation to practice, and, inter-relatedly, with regard to the identity of social work as a discipline and profession, drawing on Habermas's work to offer a theoretical basis for the increasingly frequently asserted 'need for dialogue'. However, Lorenz's writings and certain other specific contributions excepted, the social work literature of the English-speaking world contains relatively few references to the work of Habermas and very little by way of systematic attention to his ideas (Powell, 2001, p. 84). Henkel's reflections (1995; 1996) on the forms of education and evaluation appropriate to social work make use primarily of Habermas's early attempts (1972)[3] to counter the dominance of positivism in the human sciences and,

---

[3]   Where single dates are given in this chapter for the works of Habermas and Foucault they refer to English translations. Original publication dates in German (Habermas) or French (Foucault) are not only invariably earlier, but the order in which translations of key texts have appeared in English differs somewhat from that of initial publication in their authors' respective first languages. Where it is important to the argument – mainly in those

correspondingly, of scientism and decisionism in the wider culture, by setting it alongside alternative philosophical accounts of knowledge. So too does Webb's recent welcome and penetrating critique (2001) of the version of evidence-based practice currently dominant – or at least apparently officially endorsed (i.e. by the Government) – in the UK. Like Henkel, Blaug (1995) finds in Habermas's work theoretical grounds on which to base a critique of the increasing managerialism and associated instrumentalism and bureaucracy which he too perceives in UK social work. But he draws primarily on Habermas's later theory of communicative action (1979; 1984; 1987b) and his discourse ethics (1990; 1993) to argue the importance of face-to-face discussion aimed at mutual understanding in a variety of practice, organisational, policy, and research contexts across social work and social care. It should be noted, however, that Blaug has also written on a wider canvas about the abiding gap between the theoretical promise and the practical impact of Habermas's/Frankfurt critical theory in terms of progressive change (1997).

By comparison, references to Foucault, both direct and indirect, abound in the social work literature in English, where his work has influenced both theoretical ideas and more immediately practical or institutional discussions. In these latter contexts this is doubtless partly because many of his historical studies focused upon substantive areas of interest to social work, for example institutions such as hospitals and prisons and the practices associated with them. The recent collection of mainly Canadian/North American contributions edited by Chambon, Irving and Epstein (1999) demonstrates the range and diversity of Foucault's influence in and on social work. Noting the link 'between (professional) practices, self, and power', Chambon herself (1999a, p. 53) sees Foucault's importance in uncovering 'the microdynamics of power by examining the particular mechanisms that shape individuals and groups'. Parton's writing on child welfare policy and practice (e.g. 1985; 1991; 1998; 1999) adopts Foucault's 'history of the present' approach and, especially latterly, also makes explicit use of his concept of 'governmentality'; likewise Ashenden (1996; forthcoming). Chambon (1999a, p. 52) emphasises the 'critical and transformative ... purpose of Foucault's investigations', and with Irving argues that in our contemporary world of rapid change and uncertainty his various writings collectively offer 'a particularly relevant means for examining such indeterminacies and cultural transformations and for revisiting social work's mission, activities, and objectives' (Chambon and Irving, 1999, p. *xiii*). Chambon highlights the 'formidable challenge' involved in 'step[ping] back from those practices and forms of knowledge that we experience as most natural, that we have been socialized into, and to which we actively contribute as scholars, educators, practitioners, policy makers' (1999a, p. 54), but insists that '[t]his unsettling work can become surprisingly useful during historical periods of change, such as now, when established ways of knowing are no longer helpful guides' (*ibid.*, p. 53).

Habermas himself has written very little about social work as such – and in any case we need of course to be mindful of the different traditions and organisational arrangements regarding welfare provision as between Germany,

parts of the next section where the development of Habermas's and Foucault's ideas is discussed – dates of original publication are also given (in square brackets) for major texts.

France, the UK, US, etc., when making reference to any statements on these topics either by Habermas or by Foucault. Foucault, however, offered some pertinent observations on the role of social workers in the French context of the time during a round-table discussion in the early 1970s on the role and status of social work, especially in relation to social control and normalisation:

> *Foucault:* … What is important is that social work is inscribed within a larger social function that has been taking on new dimensions for centuries, the functions of surveillance-and-correction: to surveil individuals and to redress them, in the two meanings of the word, alternatively as punishment and as pedagogy. (Chambon (trans.), 1999b, p. 92)

These tensions, emanating from its ambiguous and uncertain role in relation to the state, form part of social work's historical origins, as Parton in particular has argued in several publications (e.g. 1994a; b; 1996a; b; 1999; 2000); and such tensions are clearly being further underlined in the contemporary context of uncertainty and rapid change. As Ife observes:

> [M]any of the older certainties of social work practice no longer seem relevant. The apparently unproblematic commitment to ideals such as human rights and social justice, the idea that empirically verified social science could guide practice, and the assumption of a universalist and prescriptive code of ethics no longer seem to meet the needs of many practitioners. (Ife, 1999, p. 211)

Ife's vision for social work (1997; 1999), which he acknowledges as being strongly influenced by the ideas of Habermas and earlier Frankfurt School critical theorists – as well as by the work of Freire (1970) – is rooted in a philosophy of user participation and of 'a dialogical … form of practice' (Ife, 1999, p. 221). Noting the contemporary appeal of postmodernism, Ife is nonetheless wary of the relativism and the scepticism towards meta-narratives and any form of universalist ideals which go with its stronger versions. He identifies the linking of theory and practice and the consciously normative orientation of critical theory as among the latter's attractions and strengths, and presents his own view as consistent with Habermas's 'concern to retain some of the modernist notions of morality and justice, while freeing up individuals to define their own realities and to act in order to improve their circumstances' (*ibid.*, p. 222). Ife argues that 'postmodernism is a necessary, but not a sufficient, basis for conceptualising [social work] theory and practice' (p. 212), and claims that 'critical theory provides a paradigm within which the postmodernist critique can be largely incorporated, while at the same time fully legitimising social work's traditional commitments to universalist ideals of human rights and social justice' (p. 222).

Responding directly to Ife's contribution to their edited collection *Transforming Social Work Practice* (Pease and Fook, 1999b), Fook and Pease note Ife's 'doubts about the dangerously relativist tendencies of postmodern thinking' and acknowledge – indeed they say they 'share' – his 'serious concerns about the relevance and applicability of postmodern theorising to critical social work' (Fook and Pease, 1999, p. 227). However, they suggest that 'there are many forms of postmodernism', exhibiting different degrees of distance from 'notions of modernity' and 'retreat from an emancipatory politics' (Pease and Fook, 1999a, p. 12). What they find and endorse in 'a [*sic*] postmodern perspective' is 'a *new way of thinking about thinking*, rather than trying to *replace the content of ... old ways of thinking*' (Fook and Pease, 1999, p. 228, emphases in original). They identify with 'a "weak" form of postmodernism informed by critical theory', which they suggest 'can contribute effectively to the construction of an emancipatory politics concerned with political action and social justice' (Pease and Fook, 1999a, p. 12). They call their perspective a 'postmodern critical approach', and present this as linking yet in the process transforming 'both postmodern theory and critical theory' (Fook and Pease, 1999, p. 227), and see welcoming this mutual transformation as their main point of difference from Ife.

Other social work academics (for example, Fawcett *et al.*, 2000), many of them directly or indirectly and variously influenced by the work of Foucault in their engagement with postmodernist ideas and orientations, choose and order their terms very carefully and self-consciously in styling themselves 'postmodern feminists', to signal – like Ife, Fook and Pease (who align with them), and others – a recognition that strongly relativist variants of postmodernist thought pose severe problems for the reasoned justification of a feminist – and for that matter any – political project (see Benhabib *et al.*, 1995; Nicholson, 1990). These ongoing debates are making a valuable contribution to the discipline and profession, not least by promoting an appreciation of broader contemporary theoretical ideas and currents of thought; *inter alia* they are assisting a more widespread and thorough-going critical appropriation of Habermas's ideas in social work discourses (see, for example, Rossiter, 2000; Rossiter *et al.*, 2000).

It would be unfair to suggest that some of what is going on in, for example, the relatively brief exchange between Fook and Pease, and Ife, to which we have just rather summarily referred, is rather of the order of a dispute about whether a glass is half full or half empty, since deep and serious issues are certainly at stake. But it is striking that the protagonists do not actually seem very far apart – or, perhaps more precisely, one cannot see very clearly what is at stake between them. For example, both 'sides' in the end strongly emphasise 'process', 'dialogue', and 'partnership'. One of the factors reflected in the exchange, and in many similar contexts, is doubtless the concern amongst social work academics to keep – and to be seen to be keeping – an eye on the practical, on social work 'itself', so to speak, with a consequent and perhaps inevitable degree of superficiality in the theoretical discussion, as indicated by a widespread use of 'labels' – 'critical theory', 'postmodernism', 'poststructuralism' etc. – thereby gesturing towards generalised perspectives rather than exploring the detailed arguments of particular leading theorists, thus at best glossing complex and differentiated ideas and intellectual commitments. For this very reason we indicated earlier our wish to steer clear of any simplistic identification of Habermas with 'modernism' and Foucault with 'postmodernism'. In the next section we attempt to distinguish at some length and with some care between the respective approaches to critical reflection of these two major thinkers. In doing so we have tried to take up Chambon and Irving's challenge to 'move away from the kind of academic carpentry that is all too prevalent in academic social work and toward a much more penetrating and thorough analysis of significant philosophical issues' (1999, p. *xiv*).

Habermas and Foucault; critique and genealogy

'Reflection' is a widely used term in current social work circles, denoting something generally perceived as a worthwhile activity, one that not only promotes self-understanding but also effective practice (Fook, 1999). The scepticism expressed by Ixer (1999) as regards just what – if anything – is meant by 'reflection' in social work discourses, how it can be recognised, taught, assessed, especially in the context of or in relation to 'reflective practice', should be taken seriously. Our concerns here, however, lead us in different directions.

'Reflection' suggests a questioning of the taken-for-grantedness of a situation or an idea, perhaps a certain degree of puzzlement. The addition of 'critical' to 'reflection' – 'critical reflection' – underlines this sense of 'standing back' or distancing. For Bernstein, 'There is always a moment of negativity or distancing in critique, but a critique demands that one seeks to understand what is being criticized' (1986, p. x). In insisting on these two dimensions, taking a degree of reflective distance and seeking to understand, Bernstein introduces key issues relevant to our concerns in the present chapter and those of this book as a whole. As he further observes:

> The expression 'critical' and its cognates 'critic' and 'critique' have been sadly abused in recent times. There is a vulgar sense of 'critical' where it means little more than 'scoring negative points'. But this abuse of the term should not blind us to the tradition of critique which was initiated by Kant ... (*ibid.*)

As we hope to clarify in what follows, 'critical reflection' may be a preferable term to 'theory' in many social work contexts, certainly for the ideas this chapter draws attention to and the ways of thinking it seeks to encourage. As we hinted in introducing our subject matter, the overall orientation we have in mind is captured by the title of a recent essay by James Tully, 'To think and act differently' (1999), which appears in the recent edited collection *Foucault Contra Habermas* (Ashenden and Owen, 1999a).

The introduction to Ashenden and Owen's book begins as follows:

> The encounter between the practices of critical reflection elaborated by Michel Foucault and by Jürgen Habermas is a source of continuing debate in social and political philosophy. The concern of both of these thinkers with topics of enlightenment, modernity and critique indicates the possibility of a productive philosophical dialogue ... [y]et, with some honourable exceptions ..., the history of this encounter is characterised by the marked absence of open dialogue. (Ashenden and Owen, 1999b, p. 1)

As a reviewer has commented, the essays in Ashenden and Owen's collection 'presume a considerable familiarity on the part of the reader with the texts of the principals' (Hunt, 2000, p. 1). In the present context it seems necessary to offer a brief overview of their respective ideas and orientations before identifying the 'debate' alluded to in the foregoing quotation and exploring the issues at stake. It may be helpful to note even at this early stage that Kant provides a key common reference point for Habermas and Foucault. Moreover, it is also their distinctively different interpretations of Kant's project of a critical philosophy – his attempt to secure our knowledge of the world in the face of Humean scepticism by specifying the limits of reason and thereby at once preserving its power – which crucially separates them (Dreyfus and Rabinow, 1986; Hutchings, 1996; Owen, 1996).

Kant's continuing importance lies in his philosophical articulation of fundamental changes taking place in Western understanding and in Western life during his time:

> For both Foucault and Habermas, Kant's specification of the task of critical reflection, of enlightenment, in terms of the achievement of maturity (i.e. the autonomous deployment of one's capacity for critical reflection) marks the emergence of our modernity. (Owen, 1996, p. 121)

Dreyfus and Rabinow similarly note that both Foucault and Habermas hold that 'our modernity begins with Kant's attempt to make reason critical; i.e. to establish the limits and legitimate use of reason' (1986, p. 111). Moreover,

> Foucault and Habermas agree with Kant [both] that critical reason begins with the rejection of the Western project of developing a theory which mirrors substantive universal truths about human nature ... [and] that the problem of moral action and social bonds must be faced anew once revealed religion and metaphysics have lost their authority. (*ibid.*, p. 110)

Beyond this lie the crucial differences between Habermas and Foucault, which, as suggested a little earlier, again may be summarised with reference to Kant:

> ... Habermas locates the central feature of Kant's project in its recognition of the limits of reason and its simultaneous preservation of the critical-transcendental power of reason to ground claims to truth and to normative rightness. ... Foucault focuses on Kant's reflections on enlightenment as exemplifying a certain form of reflection on the present. (Owen, 1996, p. 121)

The significance of these different understandings of Kant – of 'what he was about', so to speak – is as follows: '[W]hereas Habermas seeks to rearticulate Kant's project in terms of a weak transcendental argument grounded in a reconstruction of our communicative competences ...' (Owen, *ibid.*), which Dreyfus and Rabinow (1986, p. 111) refer to in terms of maturity seen as 'the discovery of the quasi-transcendental basis of community as all we have and all we need, for philosophy and human dignity', 'Foucault offers a reworking of what it is to think "today" as difference in history' (Owen, 1996, p. 121). For Foucault, unlike Habermas, what is most significant is not Kant's acknowledged attempt to show that the critical use of reason is in fact its universal nature, thus preserving the normative role of reason whilst rejecting any dogmatic metaphysical claim to provide truths about a transcendent reality (Dreyfus and Rabinow, 1986, pp. 110–11). Rather, 'What Foucault finds distinctive and insightful in Kant's essay ['An answer to the question: "What is enlightenment?"'] is a philosopher *qua* philosopher realizing for the first time that his thinking arises out of and is an attempt to respond to his historical situation' (*ibid.*, p. 111). As Owen puts this: 'For Foucault, Kant's differential relation to the present lies "at the crossroads of critical reflection and reflection on history"' (1999b, p. 601, quoting Foucault, 1984d, p. 38).

Thus Habermas and Foucault may be understood as 'debating' what we mean by 'enlightenment', 'maturity', 'modernity', and 'critical reason'/'reflection'; and because they have acted publicly as well as professionally (i.e. academically) on the basis of their deepest understandings of these matters and their interconnections, they 'embody two opposed but equally serious and persuasive ways of interpreting the philosophic life' (Dreyfus and Rabinow, 1986, p. 109). Moreover, as Dreyfus and Rabinow further comment, this seriousness sets *both* Foucault and Habermas in opposition to 'the anti-thinkers who, in the name of post-enlightenment and postmodern discourse, question seriousness in general' (*ibid.*).

Habermas – the universal presuppositions of communication

Since the mid 1960s the 'guiding thread' of Habermas's critical project has been the idea that

> a rational basis for collective life would be achieved only when social relations were organized 'according to the principle that the validity of every norm of political consequence be made dependent on a consensus arrived at in communication free from domination'. (White, 1995, p. 6, quoting Habermas, 1972, p. 284)

This encapsulates Habermas's reformulation of Frankfurt School critical theory whilst reaffirming its original, pre-Second-World-War spirit. He has pursued a conception of reason or rationality that is 'more comprehensive' than the culturally dominant one in which it is reduced to 'the instrumental-technical or strategic calculations of an ... individual subject' (White, *ibid.*). At the same time he has developed the idea that an 'emancipated', just – and in that sense 'rational' – society can now only make sense in terms of corresponding to such a broader conception of rationality.

In his programmatic Inaugural Lecture given in 1965 (Habermas, 1966), and in *Knowledge and Human Interests* (Habermas, 1972 [1968])[4] the book developed from it, Habermas postulated three anthropologically deep-seated cognitive – 'knowledge-guiding' or 'knowledge-constitutive' – interests, to which three forms of human knowledge and rationality – 'technical', 'practical' and 'emancipatory' – were said to correspond [eds: see also Lyons and Taylor, this volume]. However,

---

[4]   See note 3 above.

in light of his own and critics' reflections on the serious philosophical difficulties attending this epistemological thesis (see, for example, McCarthy, 1978; Thompson and Held, 1982), Habermas made his 'linguistic turn', developing the conceptual framework which has since remained at the heart of his wide-ranging work, namely the theory of communicative action and communicative reason/ rationality.

Habermas claims that as speakers of natural languages we can and do distinguish sharply between trying to reach understanding and agreement with others, which he calls the 'communicative' use of language, and trying to bring about compliance by whatever means possible, including deceit, manipulation, or outright coercion, which he terms the 'strategic' use of language (1979 [1976]; 1984 [1981], especially pp. 8–42; 1990 [1983]). He further claims that the communicative form is primary, being presupposed by the strategic form, which depends upon it for its force.

He then observes that

> In contexts of communicative action we call someone rational not only if he [*sic*] is able to put forward an assertion and, when criticized, to provide grounds for it by pointing to appropriate evidence, but also if he is following an established norm and is able, when criticized, to justify his action by explicating the given situation in the light of legitimate expectations. We even call someone rational if he makes known a desire or an intention, expresses a feeling or a mood, shares a secret, confesses a deed etc., and is then able to reassure critics in regard to the revealed experience by drawing practical consequences from it and behaving consistently thereafter. (Habermas, 1984, p. 15)

Thus Habermas contends that natural language speakers demonstrate an implicit, pre-theoretical, mastery of rules for raising and redeeming 'validity claims' in ordinary language; claims regarding the (propositional) truth of what is said, its normative rightness or appropriateness, and the truthfulness or sincerity of the speaker – in addition to sharing the meanings of the words used. Clearly, whereas claims to truth and/or rightness are in principle redeemable discursively if explicitly challenged, truthfulness, or sincerity, can only be tested in further interaction. It is important to keep in mind that Habermas uses the term 'discourse' in a quite specific sense; speakers engage in 'theoretical discourse' and 'practical discourse' respectively when claims to truth or rightness are challenged and redeemed. (See Warnke, 1995a, for a particularly useful discussion of the several important aspects of Habermas's theory outlined in this and the immediately preceding paragraphs.)

The idea of a 'universal pragmatics', a rational reconstruction of what he sees as the unavoidable – and in that sense 'transcendental' – presuppositions of rational argumentation, aiming at mutual understanding and agreement, is central to Habermas's conception and practice of critical reflection. The universality and necessity that Habermas claims for these implicit but necessary rules of rational argumentation – in summary, equal and reciprocal access for all to participation – stem from their entailing that understanding and agreement are generated solely by the force of the better argument. His central and most controversial claim is that the validity – in the sense just indicated – of these pragmatic presuppositions, and reason as such seen as expressed in and through them, is not context-bound. However, the presuppositions themselves are context-dependent, i.e. they arose in a substantive historical context, that of modernity; any rational reconstruction of them (including his own) is fallible (Owen, 1996, p. 123).

Habermas has never claimed that the ideal conditions embodied in his theory are usually or could ever be fully realised in practice. It is significant that in his later work he refers to an 'unlimited communication community', mindful of misunderstandings of his earlier term 'ideal speech situation' on the part of both critics and followers. Moreover, not only is he not constructing an ideal discourse, he is 'concerned with actual discourses between affected parties and is simply trying to delineate the conditions of argumentation which participants must assume to be approximately realized if they are concerned to validate a norm ...' (Owen, 1996, p. 124, citing Habermas, 1990, pp. 91–2). Through being logically pre-supposed by entering discourse at all (in Habermas's sense of the term – see above), the 'rules of argumentation' provide a counterfactual against which actual discourses can be critically assessed.

But Habermas *does* claim that questions of morality, and thus of justice, are, in some strong sense, capable of being settled by reason. This is expressed in his 'discourse principle' (Habermas, 1990, p. 93): 'Only those norms can claim to be valid that meet (or could meet) with the approval of all affected in their capacity as participants in a practical discourse.' And correlatively, 'The question that has *priority* in legislative politics is how a matter can be regulated in the equal interest of all' (Habermas, 1996, p. 282, emphasis in original). An overtly racist proposal is a good example of suggested legislation which could and would not gain such approval under the conditions of universal participation stipulated by Habermas.

Moreover, Habermas distinguishes sharply between 'moral discourses ... [which] aim at the impartial evaluation of action conflicts' (Habermas, 1996, p. 97) and 'ethical deliberations [which] rely on substantive, contextual understandings of the good and are rooted in particular ways of life' (Ashenden, 1999a, p. 232). Both arise and intermingle in real-life political discussion – along with pragmatic reflections on questions of means (Habermas, 1993, pp. 1–17). Habermas insists that the moral dimension (in his conceptualisation) alone requires detachment from an individual's perspective and from the concrete ethical life of a society and culture, and that such detachment is possible.

Clearly Habermas's approach is procedural rather than substantive – the actual issues for discussion are matters for participants. It is also crucially *inter*-subjective; the discourse principle is essentially a restatement of Kant's categorical imperative in a dialogical, as against a monological form – valid norms are to be established by discussion, not by individual thought. Indeed Habermas (1987a [1985]; 1992 [1988]) presents his intersubjective theory as an alternative 'escape' from modernity's 'philosophy of consciousness' to that with which he credits – or rather charges – postmodernists. Habermas's attempt to ground universals in argumentative procedures is clearly different from traditional attempts to ground them in self-consciousness, as in the 'philosophy of the subject', whose rejection, as stated earlier, Habermas and Foucault share.

In *The Theory of Communicative Action* (1984 and 1987b [both 1981]), Habermas attempts to show how his communicative approach to reason and action provides the basis for a critique of certain features of Western modernity, whilst at the same time clarifying the positive value of other aspects. In a controversial evolutionary account of modern societies he makes an analytic distinction between two 'levels': 'the system' (the economy and state administration) and 'the lifeworld' (essentially the private nuclear family and the public political sphere). A critical standpoint is provided by the idea of 'the rational potential implicit in cultural modernity' and the unbalanced development of its potential.

Habermas argues that modern culture has made available what he calls a 'rationalised lifeworld', with an increasing number of spheres of social interaction having ceased to be guided by unquestioned tradition and become subject to co-ordination by consciously achieved agreement; i.e. (in the terms of his theory) through communicative action, oriented towards mutual understanding and agreement. That is to say, there is a shared expectation that the various validity claims raised in speech have to be cognitively distinguished and redeemed in the different ways outlined above. Alongside this advance in communicative rationalisation there has been an advance in the rationality of society as seen from a functionalist or systems perspective, with an expansion of social subsystems in which action is co-ordinated through the 'delinguistified' media of money (the capitalist economy) and administrative power (modern, centralised states). In Habermas's view, whereas the expansion of these media was beneficial at first, it has progressed to a pathological level, involving what he calls the 'colonisation of the lifeworld', so that areas of social life that have been, could, and in some sense should, be co-ordinated communicatively, through understanding and agreement, 'solidarity', have increasingly been invaded.

Of particular interest to a social work audience is the way in which the development of welfare states features prominently in Habermas's analysis in *The Theory of Communicative Action* [eds: see also Lorenz, this volume]. He presents certain pathological effects of the modern, Western, welfare state as resulting from one-sided societal rationalisation in which law as a medium of state administration introduces money and power into lifeworld contexts. For Habermas 'the ambivalence of guaranteeing freedom and taking it away has attached to the policies of the welfare state ... from the start' (1987b, p. 361).

However, notwithstanding the apparent pessimism of this account of welfare states, Habermas sought to theorise a necessary shift in the system/lifeworld balance. The purposive rationality and the media of money and power characteristic of the system are not in Habermas's view inherently harmful, but they must be brought under the control of the communicative rationality of the lifeworld. Habermas indicated at the time – harking back to his earlier historical study *The Structural Transformation of the Public Sphere* (published in German in 1962 but not available in English until 1989) – that possible advances lay in developing enhanced forms of democratic dialogue in the public political spheres of civil society. Moreover, in emerging 'new social movements' he saw signs of resistance to functionalist/instrumental reason and further colonisation. Yet while he saw environmentalists' critiques and feminists' and gay and lesbian groups' rejection of traditionally prescribed identities as offering some grounds for hope and as potential catalysts in this regard, his 1980s discussion is marked by a sense of their activities being essentially limited to opposition and struggle at the margins of organised politics (White, 1995, pp. 10–11). We return to these themes later.

Foucault – a critical ontology of ourselves

Unlike Habermas, Foucault does not seek to provide us with a universal or transcendental argument, even one in qualified or weakened form. Instead, he presents us with a series of historical studies, which he calls 'philosophical exercises', as exemplars of his practice of critical reflection (Owen, 1996, p. 125). For as Rabinow points out, 'Foucault is highly suspicious of claims to universal truths. He doesn't refute them [however]; instead, his consistent response is to historicize grand abstractions' (1984, p. 4). Foucault's work is characterised by David Owen (1999b) in terms of its '*ethos* of ... self-critical reflection, continually transforming the limits of its thinking and developing its self-understanding', (p. 593, emphasis added). Words like 'unsettling', 'disturbing', 'destabilising' are commonly used with reference to Foucault's way of 'showing the historical construction of the underlying conventions of our perception' and 'disturbing our complacent presumption of progress' (*ibid.*, p. 594). We noted earlier Chambon's comments along these lines in a social work context (Chambon, 1999a, pp. 53–4).

Owen 'trace[s] Foucault's thought to his final self-understanding' by examining his work in three broad 'stages': (i) his early 'archaeological' studies concerning madness, medicine, and the human sciences; (ii) his genealogical explorations of power/knowledge relations in respect of punishment practices, constructions of sexuality, and rationalities of government; (iii) his final studies of ethical subjectivity in Ancient Greece and Rome and his reflections on Kant's 1784 essay 'An answer to the question: "What is enlightenment?"' (Owen, 1999b, p. 593). These 'stages' – or 'phases' – become evident in the light of several key reflections by Foucault himself on both his subject matter and his methods.

In his major archaeological works, *Madness and Civilisation* (1965 [1961]),[5] *The Birth of the Clinic* (1973 [1963]), and *The Order of Things* (1970 [1966]), and his subsequent methodological reflections in *The Archaeology of Knowledge* (1972 [1969]), Foucault's focus was on discontinuities between what were presented as distinct Renaissance, Classical and Modern *epistemes* (configurations of knowledge) and the characteristic social practices and institutions associated with them. One of his main concerns was to unsettle 'the seeming naturalness and necessity of our [modern] epistemic perceptions – ... [e.g.] madness as mental illness – by showing [their] historical construction ...' (Owen, 1999b, p. 594). Moreover, the discomfort associated with having our customary ways of thinking disturbed is intensified by Foucault's demonstration that the changes in our

---

[5] See note 3 above.

patterns of thought cannot be regarded with any degree of philosophical coherence as products of increases in moral compassion and/or scientific objectivity.

It has been argued that in beginning to develop his genealogical approach in *Discipline and Punish* (1977 [1975]) and *The History of Sexuality* (1979b [1976]), Foucault was seeking to overcome two important theoretical limitations to his archaeological method of which he had become aware: failure to address the inter-relationship of discursive and non-discursive practices (Dreyfus and Rabinow, 1982), and failure to clarify the critical relevance to our contemporary concerns of an account stressing historical contingency (Dean, 1994). Owen summarises this 'transformation of [Foucault's] project' in terms of his 'now locat[ing] the critical import of genealogy in its questioning of the necessity of certain power/knowledge relations and thus opening a reflective space within which resistance to those relations can be mobilised' (1999b, p. 597).

In this context, Foucault developed his concepts of 'biopower' and 'bio-politics'. The former is for Foucault the specifically *modern* form of power/ knowledge, the emergence of which 'brought life and its mechanisms into the realm of explicit calculations and made knowledge-power an agent of transform-ation of human life' (Foucault, 1979b, p. 143, quoted in Ashenden, 1999b, p. 151). It is a form of power over life which developed through the eighteenth century, replacing 'the ancient right to *take* life or *let* live ... by a power to *foster* life or *disallow* it to the point of death' (Owen, 1999b, p. 597, quoting Foucault, 1979b, p. 138, emphases in Foucault's original). Biopower and biopolitics have two dimensions and a dual focus: the individual human body as an object to be made useful through discipline; and the supervision, health and regulation of the wider population or species body. Thus, for example, we find the coterminous emergence of the idea of documenting the details of an individual's life – the case history – and the development of statistics. For Foucault these individualising and totalising forms of knowledge and power are at once linked and made possible by the development of the human sciences and by panoptic and confessional technologies as the institutional sites for their emergence and concerns. In addition, they constitute new ways in which the welfare of individuals is linked with the nation state and forms of political rule (Ashenden, 1999b, p. 152).

It should be clear even from this necessarily brief account that Foucault 'is not asserting the identity of power and knowledge, but [rather] their mutual constitution' (Owen, 1999b, p. 596), notwithstanding that the works of his 'middle period' provide grounds in some places for such 'misreadings'. Neither did he 'abandon himself to the free play of self-referential signifiers' (Dreyfus and Rabinow, 1986, p. 113). Chambon (1999a, p. 53), writing for a social work audience, implicitly draws attention to the dangers of seizing on particular studies or interpretations reflecting only the early or middle phases of Foucault's thought. More specifically, Chambon notes (*ibid.*) that 'commentators have tended to stress power relations in Foucault's work, detached from his focus of interest: the person', quoting in support 'The subject and power' (Foucault, 1982), one of the most important of the 'reframings' of his own work which, as stated earlier, are characteristic of Foucault's approach:

[T]he goal of my work during the last twenty years ... has not been to analyze the phenomena of power, nor to elaborate the foundations of such an analysis. ... My objective, instead, has been to create a history of the different modes by which, in our culture, human beings are made subjects. (Foucault, 1982, p. 208)

Foucault reflected that his work to that point had 'dealt with three modes of objectification which transform human beings into subjects' (*ibid.*); Rabinow (1984, p. 11) presents these as 'dividing practices', 'scientific classification' and 'subjectification'. 'Thus', Foucault argued, 'it is not power, but the subject, which is the general theme of my research' (1982, p. 209).

While retaining his fundamental and to many readers no doubt familiar understanding of power as 'productive, relational and everywhere' (Cooper, 1994), in his later work Foucault (1982) clearly distinguishes between power and domination and addresses several related points concerning human agency which had been – and continue to be – the source of much misunderstanding. Power in Foucault's sense '[can be exercised] only over free subjects and only insofar as they are free' (Foucault, 1982, p. 221); 'exercises of power can act to modify the actions of human subjects only insofar as they have the capacity to act in various ways, including that of resisting the modification of their actions' (Owen, 1996, p. 128). Thus Foucault came to use the term 'domination' to refer to 'stable and asymmetrical systems of power relations' in which 'the possibility of effective resistance has been removed' (Patton, 1994, p. 64).

Foucault's posthumously published final studies of forms of ethical subjectivity evident in Ancient Greece and Rome (1985 [1984]; 1986 [1984]) had led him to see that he had previously used 'power' to refer only to how we act on others, so that his genealogies had thus far provided 'only a partial account of the transformation of our ways of thinking' (Owen, 1999b, p. 599). Alongside power and knowledge he now introduced ethics, conceptualised as the power one exercises over oneself in, as it were, conducting one's own conduct. It is important to keep this 'definition' in mind in what follows, since most common contemporary usages of 'ethics' do not embody the Ancient ideas of virtue and character formation which inform Foucault's thinking here. Patton argues that these clarifications – developments – on Foucault's part of his concepts of power and ethics indicate that, and importantly, his approach does presuppose 'a ... conception of the subject of thought and action', albeit a 'thin' one (Patton, 1994, p. 61). Certainly the capacities for thought and action available at any juncture are historically located, but human beings endowed with such capacities are involved in their exercise.

Foucault's essay 'What is enlightenment?' (Foucault, 1984d) has come to be seen by many contemporary scholars as 'the clearest [and most succinct] statement of his own philosophical work and of his understanding of the tasks of modern philosophy' (Owen, 1999b, p. 601). Here Foucault reconceptualised his investigations as 'problematisations' and redescribed his project as 'a critical ontology of ourselves', 'genealogical in its design and archaeological in its method' (Owen, *ibid.*, p. 599, quoting Foucault, 1984d, p. 46). It is a 'practical critique ... which opens up the possibility of being otherwise [than we are] by calling what we are into question through reflecting on how we have become what we are' (Owen, 1999b, p. 602). Foucault (1984d, p. 45) argues for '[turning] the critical question today ... back into a positive one ... to transform the critique conducted in the form of necessary limitation into a practical critique that takes the form of a possible transgression'. He saw such a form of critique as incapable of final delimitation, as always beginning again, and as leading not to apathy but to a 'hyper- and pessimistic activism' (Owen, 1996, p. 126, quoting Foucault, 1984b, p. 343), orientated to the main dangers of modern society, identified by reflecting on 'the "contemporary limits of the necessary"' (Owen, *ibid.*, quoting Foucault, 1984d, p. 43). This clearly and necessarily 'entails abandoning the project of *total* critique ... and thus any radically utopian aspirations or longings for total revolution' (Owen, *ibid.*, p. 603, emphasis in original).

The Foucault/Habermas debate

We have shown above how Habermas attempts to set out a *theory* of reason in the form of a regulative ideal, and how this contrasts with Foucault's interest in the *historicity* of reason (Hoy, 1998, p. 23), in 'forms of rationality', especially 'the forms of rationality applied by the human subject to itself' (Foucault, 1988a, pp. 28–9), and his insistence that 'no given form of rationality is actually reason' (Foucault, *ibid.*, p. 35).

Michael Kelly encapsulates the key issues at stake between them as follows:

> Foucault introduces power ... into the contemporary philosophical landscape ... [and] claims that power is, in fact, productive of both knowledge and practice. While acknowledging power, Habermas insists that it be tempered by a critical theory able to make normative distinctions between legitimate and illegitimate uses of power. To make such distinctions, he introduces ... the idealizing presuppositions of discourse ... Foucault challenges not so much the presence of such presuppositions as Habermas's attempts to establish them as unavoidable universals. Arguing instead for a form of local rather than global critique, Foucault defiantly practices [it] ... without universal norms and within a discourse demarcated by the axes of knowledge and self as well as power. (Kelly, 1994c, pp. 1–2)

For Kelly (*ibid.*, p. 2), the question is 'Which paradigm of critique – Foucault's or Habermas's – is most defensible philosophically and most effective practically ...?'. To answer it is to take a position on whether: (i) philosophical discourse is what links critique and power (Foucault), 'where power itself is discursive and critique is just one of many discursive practices tied to power'; or whether (ii) 'power undermines the rational basis and practical efficacy of critique' (Habermas), so that 'philosophical discourse ideally separate[s] critique and power', with the role of critique being 'to hold power in abeyance and then to justify the universal norms pragmatically presupposed in ethical, political, and social theory'. Foucault denies that discourse – including these last-mentioned forms of philosophical discourse – and power can be radically separated from each other in the way Habermas wants them to be; for Foucault there can be no 'power-free discourse with which to conduct critique'.

Although Foucault and Habermas did meet at least once, in 1983, when Habermas lectured in Paris, they never debated formally (Kelly, 1994c, pp. 2–3). Hence what has come to be referred to as 'the Foucault/Habermas debate' is, as far as the two leading figures are directly concerned, largely a construction. However, through the writings of theorists mainly influenced by one or the other which appeared during the decade following Foucault's death, something approaching a debate began to develop. Kelly's collection (1994a) brings together the main publications in which either Habermas or Foucault directly takes issue with or comments upon the other's work, along with several examples of the secondary contributions just referred to. The two chapters devoted to Foucault in *The Philosophical Discourse of Modernity* (Habermas, 1987a) – the most extended and directly focused examples – are included, along with Foucault's well-known 'Two lectures' from *Power/Knowledge* (1980) and a number of significant shorter pieces by each. Foucault's essay 'What is enlightenment?' (1984d) is a notable omission.

Kelly notes that 'the debate' as exhibited in the two key figures' own writings is rather 'lopsided', and that subsequent 'exchanges' have continued both to be skewed and indeed to be conducted largely on Habermas's terms. Among the reasons is that *The Philosophical Discourse of Modernity* appeared only after Foucault's death, so that the discussion of his work there received no direct response. Moreover, whereas Habermas's analysis was clearly directed at Foucault's writings of the 1970s, responses 'on Foucault's behalf' have generally drawn on his more mature work (Kelly, 1994c, pp. 4–5).

Kelly argues that in this unbalanced 'debate' Foucault has been expected to satisfy Habermas's demand for a normative justification of critique without sufficient attention being given to whether such a justification – at least as understood by Habermas – is necessary or possible (Kelly, 1994c, p. 4). He (Kelly) sees Habermas and Foucault as sharing 'the predicament of critique in modernity' (Kelly, 1994b, p. 366). No longer able to rely on religion or metaphysics, claims to truth and justice look to critique for justification; but 'how can critique justify any truth or justice claims without being able ... to justify its own norms?' (*ibid.*). For Kelly, critique is therefore unavoidably self-referential (and thus, possibly, a 'hopelessly paradoxical' enterprise (see also Hutchings, 1996)). He views the rival ontological claims made by Habermas and Foucault concerning the status of universals – 'the possible transhistorical significance of historical validity claims' (Kelly, 1994b, p. 390) – as their respective responses to this situation, in which the ultimate superiority of either one over the other cannot be determined, at least for the time being.

Owen (1996, p. 120) acknowledges that Kelly not only reasonably describes and to some extent accounts for the nature of the debate thus far, but also that in his own concluding chapter (Kelly, 1994b) he both defends Foucault's approach and goes some way towards offering a critical rejoinder to Habermas. However, Owen and Ashenden want to go further in a number of inter-related ways: first, in analysing the nature and quality of the Foucault/Habermas debate, which as noted earlier they see as 'characterised by the marked absence of open dialogue' – Hoy and McCarthy's (1994) book-length exchange being acknowledged as a note-worthy exception (Ashenden and Owen, 1999b, p. 1); second, with regard to what is fundamentally at stake in terms of practising critical reflection; and third, in pointing a way forward and encouraging a more even-handed discussion of the key issues involved. As they see it, Habermas and those sympathetic to him have shown a marked tendency to 'directly take up the challenge posed by Foucault's work in order to exhibit its shortcomings' (Owen, 1996, p. 120), 'attempt[ing] to demonstrate the incoherence of Foucault's practice of critical reflection while also incorporating its admitted insights' (Ashenden and Owen, 1999b, p. 1). This is seen as most famously expressed in Nancy Fraser's characterisation of Foucault's studies and analyses as offering a mixture of 'empirical insights and normative confusions' (Fraser, 1989a), and in Habermas's own inter-related claim (1987a, p. 284) that Foucault's work cannot answer the question 'Why fight?', i.e. 'Why oppose domination?'. Consequently, 'advocates of Foucault's practice ...' have been put, and by and large have remained, on the defensive (Owen, 1996, pp. 119–20; Ashenden and Owen, 1999b, pp. 1–2).[6]

Ashenden and Owen draw attention to how, in order to support the strong claims which he makes for his theory of communicative rationality (see above), Habermas is committed to showing that the latter 'can generate more powerful conceptual, moral and empirical insights than its competitors' (1999b, p. 1). Indeed his major contributions across four inter-related fields – the philosophy and methodology of the social sciences, the development and characterisation of modernity, contemporary moral philosophy, and the theory of democratic legitimacy – constitute his attempt to do just that (White, 1995, p. 7). However, Ashenden and Owen claim that Habermas's actual practice may be seen as seeking to 'show that alternative projects' – crucially here Foucault's – 'are either capable of being subsumed under the theory of communicative action or involve a performative contradiction' (Ashenden and Owen, 1999b, p. 7). Their aim is to outline 'a Foucauldian response which is, simultaneously, a criticism of Habermas' own understanding of critique' (*ibid.*, p. 13).

They suggest that 'Foucault's practice of critical reflection is radically distinct from that of Habermas' (*ibid.*, p. 11), and bring into sharp relief what they see ultimately as the key differences in both *content* and *form* between the mature work of each by echoing a remark of Wittgenstein's[7] (1953, para. 115):

> Foucault is, as it were, concerned to loosen the grip of a picture which currently holds us captive and, simultaneously, [both] to open up the possibility of being otherwise than we are by loosening this picture and to exhibit a mode of being otherwise than we are through [this] practice. (Ashenden and Owen, 1999b, p. 11)

---

[6]   A slightly modified and updated version of the 1996 paper by David Owen to which we have been referring so far now forms the introduction to Ashenden and Owen's 1999 collection *Foucault Contra Habermas: Recasting the Dialogue Between Genealogy and Critical Theory*.

[7]   We noted in our introduction to this book (pp. 10–11) that there are resonances between in each case the later work of Wittgenstein and Foucault (see Tully, 1995, especially pp. 34–43), while Ashenden and Owen (1999b, p. 19, note 5) also refer positively to Tully's (1989) 'Wittgensteinian critique' of Habermas's conception and practice of critical reflection.

The three main criticisms of Foucault's historical approach associated with Habermas are that it is tied hermeneutically to present concerns ('presentistic'), that it is thereby 'relativistic', and that it cannot account for its own normative foundations ('cryptonormative') (Habermas, 1987a, p. 276). Ashenden and Owen argue persuasively that, over and above what can be shown to be misunderstandings, confusions and misrecognitions regarding Foucault's work, the force of each of these three challenges actually depends on Habermas's strong claim to have articulated a form of critique in which reason – conceived as embodied in rules for reaching understanding and agreement – is expressed as a context-*transcending* power. Here they go further than Kelly (see above) in not only seeing Habermas's claims as so far not having been sustained, but proposing that they are incapable of ever being sustained (for the detailed argument see Ashenden and Owen, 1999b, pp. 12–15; see also Schmidt (1996) for a similar analysis and conclusion).

An aspect of this which is relevant to our discussion of dialogue in the next section is that Ashenden and Owen regard as unsatisfactory (1999b, p. 14) the successive refinements Habermas has made to his theory (see especially Habermas, 1993 [1990 and 1991]), in response to criticisms of its claim to radical separation from concrete ethical life and accusations of emptiness and practical impotence levelled at its highly abstract and formal conceptualisation of morality – along similar lines to Hegel's critique of Kant (see Habermas, 1990, pp. 195–215). Whereas Ashenden and Owen clearly 'side' with Foucault, a number of Habermas's 'most sympathetic interpreters ... criticize ... his formalism, idealism and insensitivity to context' (Flyvbjerg, 1998, p. 218). Perhaps most notably, Seyla Benhabib (1986; 1992; 1996b), whilst endorsing Habermas's universalist hopes, wishes to acknowledge their historicity more fully than he does, and above all to insist that the 'rules of discourse' involve concrete ethical commitments (see also Warnke, 1995a). This perspective potentially enables the 'use' of Habermas's 'rules' to guide institutional arrangements for democratic decision making without being committed to his transcendental perspective. We take up this line of development in relation to social work in the third section of this chapter.

It is, notwithstanding, necessary to address directly and from a theoretical perspective the entirely legitimate question of Foucault's alleged lack of normative criteria, which as Ashenden and Owen note 'is often admitted in part by Foucault's sympathetic readers' (1999b, p. 14). We hope to have said enough in this section to indicate why Foucault cannot answer the criticism in the terms in which it is put by Habermas. Habermas's charges are articulated precisely in terms of his view that it is necessary to provide a general answer to the question 'Why fight?', and to do this by grounding universal norms, which in turn – in a post-metaphysical age (Habermas, 1992) – requires, in Habermas's view, (his) specification of the transcendental structure of rational argumentation.

Many readers may very well take the view that the proper – perhaps the only possible – answer to 'Why resist domination?' is 'Who needs theoretical justification for valuing autonomy?!'. Be that as it may, Ashenden and Owen (1999b, pp. 14–15) find important elements of a useful and more philosophical response in the paper by Paul Patton (1994) to which we referred a little earlier. While Patton notes that the 'thin' or minimalist conception of the human subject (as a 'subject of power'), which, as we saw, he shows to be present in Foucault's later work, 'will not provide any basis for a single universal answer to the question, "Why ought domination to be resisted?"', he (Patton) immediately adds that 'given certain minimal assumptions about the nature of human being, and about the particular capacities which human beings have acquired, Foucault's conception of the subject does provide a basis on which to understand the inevitability of resistance to domination' (Patton, 1994, p. 61, quoted in Ashenden and Owen, 1999b, p. 15).

The crux of Patton's argument here is that 'to account for the experience of ... systems of power as forms of domination', Foucault must and demonstrably does have a 'conception of human subjectivity which takes into account both the interpretative and the self-reflective dimensions of human agency' (Patton, 1994, p. 71):

> So long as human capacities do in fact include the power of individuals to act upon their own actions ... Foucault's conception of human being in terms of power enables us to distinguish between those ... exercise[s] of power which inhibit and those which allow the self-directed use and development of human capacities. [Moreover, t]o the extent that individuals and groups acquire the meta-capacity for the autonomous exercise of certain of their own powers and capacities, they will inevitably be led to oppose forms of domination which prevent such activity. (*ibid.*, p. 68)

Ashenden and Owen endorse and significantly develop Patton's perceptive reading of Foucault, which for them

> clarifies [Foucault's] *rejection* of the *legislative* project of providing 'universal moral norms or criteria of evaluation' and his *recommendation* of an 'ethics of existence' ... [b]ut ... is limited to the extent that it does not further recognise the way in which Foucault's *practice* of critical reflection *grounds* its recommendation of an ethics of existence ... in its *exemplification* of such an ethics ...   [Making good this interpretative deficit] provide[s] both a rejoinder to the criticism offered by critical theorists and a problematisation of the form in which that criticism is posed. (Ashenden and Owen, 1999b, p. 15, quoting Patton, 1994, p. 71, emphases ours)

Owen has elaborated on this elsewhere (1995a) and further develops it in his individual contribution (Owen, 1999a) to *Foucault Contra Habermas*.   Now reserving the term 'critique' for Habermas's mode of critical reflection, and 'genealogy' for Foucault's contrasting practice, Owen argues that

> critique is characterised by a specific way of orienting thinking ... [which] constructs a conception of enlightenment as the project of striving to reconcile the real and the ideal through the lawful use of reason which acts as the standard for the normative evaluation of other practices of critical reflection. (Owen, 1999a, pp. 29–30)

> ... genealogy exemplifies an orientation in thinking in which thinking is oriented to an immanent ideal and this orientation ... is articulated in terms of the process of

becoming otherwise than we are through the agonic use of reason.[8] (*ibid.*, p. 30, emphases in original omitted, footnote ours)

Thus Ashenden and Owen can justifiably present their recent collection (1999a) as a significant intervention in the Foucault/Habermas debate, recasting it in terms of two different *practices* of critical reflection and clarifying what is at stake between them. They make no claim to settle matters; rather, 'by providing a Foucauldian riposte to Habermas' criticisms of genealogy', as we have seen, they seek to redress the imbalance of the debate thus far and to promote further, more genuine, and productive 'dialogue between these two ways of reflecting critically on our historical being in the present' (Ashenden and Owen, 1999b, p. 19). The various contributions to their collection reflect this orientation, broadly share the understandings and interpretations set out in the editors' introduction, and develop the debate in a number of directions. Intriguingly, some contributors find common cause and/or complementary elements in the respective ideas and approaches of Foucault and Habermas, thereby perhaps suggesting grounds and scope for somehow 'combining' them. Three chapters address key and inter-related themes in contemporary political theory which are of particular interest to a social work audience; these focus upon civil society (Ashenden, 1999b), democracy (Dean, 1999), and the recognition of difference (Thompson, 1999).

Earlier we introduced the different accounts of state/society relations offered by Habermas and Foucault, in particular their critical perspectives on the modern welfare state, the context of social work's historical emergence and contemporary existence throughout much of the world. By further exploring both approaches to these topics in the following section we hope to encourage the adoption of a broader and more theoretically informed framework for the discussion of the nature, role and future of social work, and thence to enhance the possibility for transformation. The idea of 'dialogue', which seems to appear with increasing frequency in contemporary social work discourses, emerges as a key area for further reflection.

---

[8]   The concepts of 'the agonic', 'agonism', and 'agonistic (or agonal) politics', have achieved a certain currency in political theory in recent years, largely through the work of writers such as William Connolly (e.g. Connolly, 1991) and Bonnie Honig (e.g. Honig, 1993). There is in these ideas both a reference back to Ancient notions of contest and a strongly Nietzschean flavour and influence. A perspectivist account of reason is reflected in a primary concern to locate difference and a positive view of conflict as at the heart of 'the political', and as somehow both essential and inevitable – as against emphases on consensus and/or concerns with rights. O'Sullivan (1997) and Mouffe (1999) offer useful overviews of some of the main themes, on which David Owen's book on Nietzsche (Owen, 1995b), especially chapters 1, 2 and 6, also repays close reading. We touch on some of these ideas and issues in the final section of this present chapter, although we do not directly make use of the concept of 'agonism'.

State, society and social work

State/society relations

In this section we turn our attention to how the very different approaches to critical reflection adopted by Habermas and Foucault, and more specifically how grasping what is at stake between them, can inform our understandings of state/society relations and our thinking about welfare legislation and provision. We consider how together these alternative ways of making sense of our contemporary world, of reflecting critically upon it, might help us promote and shape wider discussion and debate about the place of social work in our changing welfare context and thence act collectively to change it.

Despite their different orientations to the justification of normative criteria, and the associated differences in their analyses of the history of Western societies, there are, as Simons (1995, pp. 110–16, especially p. 111) indicates, close similarities between Foucault's and Habermas's substantive views on contemporary welfare states. For both,

> [T]he legal-bureaucratic form of welfare organization ... undermine[s] subjective capacities of agency at the same time as ... provid[ing] the space or material resources for it. Habermas (1987[a]: 291) ... argues that in welfare-state democracies 'it is the legal means for securing freedom that themselves endanger freedom'. ... Moreover, both thinkers look favourably on similar social movements that resist what Habermas refers to as the colonization of the life world (its invasion by instrumental rationality) and Foucault as normalization (White, 1986: 422–3). (Simons, 1995, p. 111, references to both Habermas and White in original)

Continuing to work within the framework of his theory of communicative action and reason, and retaining his discourse principle as a key critical element, in *Between Facts and Norms* (1996 [1992]) Habermas returns to the topic of welfare states, offering a less pessimistic account than before (see previous section), especially in terms of the possibilities and means available for change. He now seeks to articulate interdependent procedural approaches to law and to democracy, the former involving a more subtle understanding of the role of modern law than that of his previous analysis, the latter a return to and development of some of his earlier suggestive ideas for a radicalised form of participative democracy.

Habermas now identifies two competing paradigmatic understandings of law in modern society, involving different conceptions of basic rights and constitutional principles: first, liberal-bourgeois formal law, concerned essentially with securing formal equality, individual liberty, etc; second, social welfare 'materialised' law, developed on the basis of acknowledging a need for positive social supports to citizenship and participation. As Habermas argued earlier, this welfare paradigm has generated new problems in the form of unfreedom in terms of 'clientelism'. He suggests that the two paradigms of law share a common error in misunderstanding the legal constitution of freedom by assimilating it to the model of the equal distribution of goods. He exemplifies this via the equality/

difference debate in feminism and associated campaigns for equal treatment (Habermas, 1996, pp. 418–27), suggesting that whereas early demands for strict gender equality in access to education, occupations, political institutions, etc., failed to recognise the impact of substantially different life experiences and positions in the social structure, later recognition of this resulted in various forms of welfare state paternalism, with women given special rights and privileges, which have had the opposite effect to that sought, for example bringing greater risks of job loss for women and/or confining them to secondary labour markets. He locates the reasons for this in the combined effect of over-generalisations in respect of disadvantaged persons and disadvantaging situations, and the continued use of traditional stereotypical gender roles in legislative and adjudicative contexts.

Habermas suggests that a perpetual tension exists in modern constitutional states between the functional role of law in respect of stability and social control, and the positive focus and vehicle for individual and collective identity and solidarity which modern legal institutions such as constitutions and charters of basic rights *also* provide – and in ways which traditional institutions no longer can. Citizens can identify with legal institutions 'understood as representations of the idea of a self-determining community of free and equal subjects who wish to guide their collective life through binding rules' (White, 1995, pp. 11–12). Thus modern law can provide 'solidarity' as well as stability and social control. Habermas claims that his theory of communicative rationality makes it possible to reconfigure the long-standing problem in Western political theory concerning the conflict between private and public autonomy, between individual rights and popular sovereignty. In his view, liberal accounts of democratic politics give priority to individual rights over collective autonomy, neglecting the need for social solidarity; communitarian or republican approaches either assume or seek too 'thick' a form of community and give collective autonomy priority over the individual. Habermas suggests that both of these accounts are rooted in notions of subjectivity, whether individual or collective, and that they also share a state-centred view of social and political life. He claims that the intersubjective orientation of his overall theory and his new, procedural paradigm of law capture what he posits as the reciprocal relationship between private and public autonomy, between the traditional individual liberal freedoms and political participation. He expresses and proposes the institutionalisation of this in a system of five sets of rights: rights to equal individual liberties; membership rights; rights of legal protection and due process; rights of political autonomy or participation; and social welfare rights, necessary for citizens to exercise the other four groups of rights.

Law gains its legitimacy from the possibility of consensus achieved through open democratic participation. In contemporary pluralistic societies, without shared comprehensive or metaphysical world views, such democratic procedures represent, for Habermas, the only possible source for societal rules. The institutional framework he now proposes as a means to entrench the required form of public discussion and so provide for the discursive legitimation of law – his solution to the pathologies of the welfare state in terms of undermining human freedom – involves both reaffirming the importance of the established legislative institutions of constitutional representative democracy *and* linking these more closely with the independent associations of civil society, with the latter enabled to provide communicative inputs and thereby reinvigorated. Thus what he envisages is 'a differentiated "network" of communicative arrangements for the discursive formation of public opinion and will' (White, 1995, p. 12). We might note in passing that this approach to participative democracy does go some way towards acknowledging the significant difficulties generally seen as facing it as regards the time and numbers involved and the complexity of the issues facing us in the contemporary world.

In three linked papers Samantha Ashenden (1998; 1999a; b) critically dissects this, i.e. Habermas's more recent (1996) analysis of and projected 'solution' to our contemporary social and political ills, in ways which reflect her reading of Foucault and the Foucault/Habermas debate as presented elsewhere (Ashenden and Owen, 1999a; b). She implicitly acknowledges the continuing force of Habermas's earlier analysis of the 'peculiarly ambivalent effects of the welfare state' (Habermas, 1996, p. 42), and welcomes his attempt to make good its democratic deficits. She also notes approvingly how his recent work both makes use of feminist analyses of welfare (as indicated above and discussed further below) and 'provides powerful theoretical support for … [those] who have criticized … welfare states' normalising assumptions and called for the recognition of different ways of life in the framing of legislation' (1999a, p. 231). However, she draws out a number of problems, at once theoretical and with practical import in terms of the potential fruitfulness of Habermas's ideas in assisting social and political change, each turning on Habermas's deep-seated drive for 'an outside of power disclosed by the immanent features of communication' (1999b, p. 159).

Although he expressed similar views about the increasing bureaucratisation of the modern welfare state, and the need to oppose this, Foucault's analysis takes a very different form from that of Habermas. It has at its heart his general concern with biopower and biopolitics, concepts through which, as we saw in the previous section, he identifies the specifically modern form of power over life. He links this with the issue of 'rationalities of rule', or political rationality via the concept of 'governmentality' (Foucault, 1979a; Burchell *et al.*, 1991). Foucault understands the idea of 'government' in a very general way – which has a long history – as 'the conduct of conduct', both individual and collective, and as an 'art'. In this sense (modern) government involves a wide range of practices and refers not only to states and to narrowly political structures. Foucault's historical thesis is that the 'governmentalisation' of the state results from 'a confluence of new knowledges and techniques of rule which emerge in the sixteenth century and develop as practices of government from the eighteenth century' (Ashenden, 1999b, p. 152). He suggests that 'a new art of government is formed' when population and the possibility of managing it come to be recognised as issues (see previous section). This involves 'the emergence of a domain of the social and the development of a range of new techniques of government … [in the form of] institutions, apparatuses and knowledges which constitute, regulate and survey … this domain' (Ashenden, *ibid.*). 'Governmentality' signifies this concern with a broadened field of politics, and readers of Nigel Parton's work (see multiple references listed) will of course find familiar resonances here, not least concerning the origins and context of social work.

As we hope this brief summary at least indicates, Foucault distinguishes clearly between juridical or sovereign forms of power (law, rights), and disciplinary or normalising forms of power (capacities to organise, sustain, enhance life), whilst seeing them as crucially linked. 'The welfare state problem' is absolutely central here: 'the tricky adjustment between political power wielded over legal subjects and pastoral power wielded over live individuals' (Ashenden, 1999b, p. 152, quoting Foucault, 1988b, p. 67). The modern individual is at once both a citizen with rights produced through law as a member of a juridical *polity*, and a subject of discipline and normalisation as a member of a welfare *society* (Ashenden, *ibid.*, pp. 152–3). Moreover, while modern conceptions of citizenship entail practices involving the management of populations they employ discourses of sovereignty as justification. 'The "welfare state problem" is [for Foucault] that of reconciling "law" with "order", producing "the social" as a governed domain' (Ashenden, *ibid.*, p. 153). This involves continual negotiation of the public and the private, achieved through normalising (not least professional) knowledge and expertise. Clearly Foucault's analysis problematises the notion of civil society and its relation to the state; the former becomes an object and an end of government. Indeed Foucault remarks: 'I haven't spoken about civil society. And on purpose, because I hold that the theoretical opposition between the state and civil society which traditional political theory belabors is not very fruitful' (Foucault, 1991, pp. 163–4, quoted in Ashenden, 1999b, p. 154).

Key aspects of Ashenden's critique are particularly relevant to the concerns of this chapter and the present book as a whole. The respective accounts of state/society relations which Foucault and Habermas offer illustrate very clearly the different forms of critical reflection advocated and practised by each of them. Ashenden shows how Habermas essentially presupposes civil society in an ideal or counterfactual form as the very ground of critique, and so in effect merely 'refines and reiterates the terms of contemporary political reason' (Ashenden, 1999b, p. 158). Indeed as Dean argues in his contribution to Ashenden and Owen's collection, 'the construction of the diverse deliberative public spheres that will both legitimise the exercise of power and be capable of correcting pathological forms of political thought and practice' necessarily presupposes normalising powers for which Habermas's theory cannot account. (See also next subsection, where this is in effect taken up in more concrete terms.) Habermas cannot adequately 'address the question of how to make subjects act discursively', whereas Foucault's 'account of the normalising practices of biopower' makes this possible (Dean, 1999, p. 192). Thus Foucault addresses what are arguably prior questions about the emergence and use of the term 'civil society', thereby challenging and enabling us 'to think again about our conceptual and practical limits' (Ashenden, 1999b, p. 158), 'question[ing] what we are and ... open[ing] space in which to reflect critically on what we might become' (*ibid.*, p. 159).

None of this is to say that the concept of 'civil society' may not be useful in contemporary circumstances [eds: see, for example, Jordan and Parton, this volume], to express commitments and to explore avenues of change, just as at various times in various contexts and places in the past it has marked 'an ethical arena, a space of interaction and not simply of market exchange', and 'a private sphere of trade and social interaction counterpoised to the public realm of law and government, the state' (see Ashenden, 1999b, pp. 144–5). Whilst the dominant current conceptualisation – usually employed favourably and in criticism of the status quo in a variety of 'state-centred' contexts – refers to a non-market and non-state sphere, the association of civil society with 'individualism, the rule of law and markets' also persists (*ibid.*, p. 146). What Ashenden's reading certainly suggests is that to employ the term 'civil society' unreflectively, not least in the context of a critique of contemporary arrangements, may actually limit our possibilities for thinking and acting politically.

As we have seen, both Habermas and Foucault regard resisting the rationalisation and misuse of power as the key problem of our time, and each seeks a critical influence, in effect both theoretical and practical, on actual relations of dominance. Habermas approaches this via a universalistic theory; Foucault seeks a genealogical understanding of actual power relations in specific contexts. Habermas emphasises procedural macro-politics, Foucault substantive micro-politics:

> Habermas's approach is oriented toward universals, context-independence and control via constitution-writing and institutional development. Foucault focuses his efforts on the local and context-dependent and toward the analysis of strategies and tactics as basis [*sic*] for power struggle. (Flyvbjerg, 1998, p. 227)

As Flyvbjerg further observes, both are 'bottom-up' thinkers as regards the content of political action, definition of which they *both* leave to participants. However, Habermas is a 'top-down' moralist as regards procedural rationality, whereas Foucault would not prescribe any particular process either, 'only recommend[ing] a focus on conflict and power relations as the most effective point of departure for the fight against domination' (*ibid.*, p. 224). And this fight is central both to the relationships between groups within civil society, such as groups of different gender or ethnicity, and in the relationship of civil society to the state (*ibid.*).

Foucault clearly has normative commitments, but (as we saw in the previous section), rather than claiming or seeking universal grounding for them, he insists that they are based on historical and personal context – although widely shared (Flyvbjerg, *ibid.*, p. 221).

> For Foucault, our history endows us with the possibility to become aware of those social arrangements which create problems, for instance a weak civil society, and those which create satisfaction, for instance empowering civil society. It follows that we have the possibility to either oppose or promote these arrangements. This is Foucault's point of departure for social and political change, not global moral norms. (*ibid.*, p. 222)

But there is more to be said. As Flyvbjerg argues, 'The value of Habermas's approach is ... [its] clear picture of what [he] understands by "democratic process", and what preconditions must be fulfilled for a decision to be termed "democratic"' (*ibid.*, p. 228). Foucault, on the other hand, did not give sustained or systematic attention to these matters, as we noted earlier. Habermas may perhaps be seen as idealistic and his account as 'contain[ing] little understanding of how power functions or of those strategies and tactics which can ensure more of the sought after democracy' (*ibid.*). Foucault's strength 'is his emphasis on the dynamics of power', how power works in particular contexts; power which is inescapable and in terms of which action needs to be understood and undertaken (*ibid.*). Any practical attempt to engender free and open public discussion, for example about the way in which we organise the welfare functions of the state, including setting a framework for related non-state activities, must certainly be rooted in such an understanding. Yet we surely also need a framework of institutions and a 'set of rules' as to how we might conduct ourselves in discussing matters of public concern, and it is these which Habermas offers us. Following Foucault in starting from the particular and the local may lead us 'to overlook more generalized conditions concerning, for example, institutions, constitutions and structural issues' (Flyvbjerg, *ibid.*).

The following quotation from a discussion with Foucault a few months before he died – and which therefore reflects his final studies of ethical practices in the Ancient World – hints at what we have in mind here, whilst encapsulating much of what has been said thus far in this chapter:

> The thought that there could be a state of communication which would be such that the games of truth could circulate freely, without obstacles, without constraint and without coercive effects, seems to me to be Utopia. It is being blind to the fact that relations of power are not something bad in themselves, from which one must free one's self. I don't believe there can be a society without relations of power, if you understand them as means by which individuals try to conduct, to determine the behaviour of others. The problem is not of trying to dissolve them in the utopia of a perfectly transparent communication, but to give one's self the rules of law, the techniques of management, and also the ethics, the *ethos*, the practice of self, which would allow these games of power to be played with a minimum of domination. (Foucault, 1987, p. 129, emphasis in original)

Foucault is here quite explicitly speaking about Habermas; although clearly expressing deep reservations he seems not to be dismissive of Habermas's preoccupations. These remarks may therefore help point a way forward, perhaps through somehow 'adding a Foucauldian (self-)interpretation' to Habermas's work (see Conway, 1999; Dean, 1999), or seeking to 'bring together' Habermas's and Foucault's 'distinctive – and ... sometimes complementary – contributions' (Thompson, 1999). This is certainly the direction in which we seek to influence the discussion, since notwithstanding the positive interpretation of 'the later Foucault' offered by Ashenden and Owen, among others (e.g. Moss, 1998; Simons, 1995), which we have implicitly endorsed in this chapter, it seems to us essential – as the foregoing paragraphs indicate – to attend also to Habermas's ideas, and especially to draw upon his most recent proposals, but with, so to speak, a specifically Foucauldian sensitivity to what is problematic about them.

Although rarely discussed amongst members of the social work community in such an abstract manner, many of the concerns explored in this section currently preoccupy them, including and not least in ongoing debates about the role and purpose of the profession and the discipline in the changing context of welfare provision – as other contributions to this collection variously demonstrate. In the remainder of this chapter we turn our attention to the relevance of an understanding of the key issues at stake between Habermas and Foucault for thinking about and debating the nature, role and place of social work in the twenty-first century. Indeed it seems to us that social work is a particularly significant site for further exploring the ideas and approaches of Habermas and Foucault, both in practice and in theory. The theory and practice of social work requires not only continuous critical reflection in both academic and professional contexts; it demands wider public debate, and thus a strengthening of both democracy and civil society.

Dialogue – academic, public, democratic

Our primary focus for most of this chapter has been on providing a detailed understanding of the Foucault/Habermas debate and seeking to indicate how it bears upon some current themes and issues in social and political theory which in turn have relevance for social work. As we put it at the outset, our concern is with 'thinking about thinking', more particularly with how to reflect critically and self-consciously on social work in a changing context of state/society relations.

The importance to the social work community of what is at stake between Habermas and Foucault is surely indicated quite clearly by the juxtaposition of two current concerns, both touching upon the nature of social work as a moral and political activity. One is the commitment of governments such as that in the UK to the active pursuit of what they tellingly label 'modernisation', including as part of this agenda the application (*sic*) of a particular conception of 'evidence-based policy and practice' which leans heavily on a rationalistic model of decision making and a scientistic world-view (see Webb, 2001), as variously discussed in many of the contributions to this book. This seems either to deny that social work is an expression of a collective commitment to certain values, or to conceive the pursuit of its aims in purely technical, means-to-ends terms. Those putting up oppositionary arguments variously seek (like Webb, *op. cit.*) to mount a primarily philosophical attack on the assumptions behind these dominant positions and/or to take refuge in particularly unreflective forms of 'value-talk' (Timms, 1983; 1989), asserting their/social work's commitment to normative ideals such as 'empower-ment' and 'anti-oppressive practice' as if these were somehow 'above' critical examination. The second current concern – intersecting with the first on just this terrain – is the currency of postmodernist and poststructuralist ideas in social work literatures, and in particular (for present purposes) the possibility of preserving the intelligibility of normative 'commitment' in the face of the perceived relativism of at least some postmodernist approaches. The issues around this were exemplified early in this chapter with reference to recent exchanges in the literature (Ife, 1997; 1999; Fook and Pease, 1999; Pease and Fook, 1999a); the matter of reasoned justification of such commitment(s) has been a theme throughout.

Broadly speaking, we ourselves have taken a position, following Ashenden and Owen and others, that precisely does not see Foucault as a relativist; indeed one which interprets him as going as far as seems possible, though not as far as Habermas attempts to go, in terms of justifying a commitment to human freedom, or better, a commitment to opposing domination.

With the characteristic flavour of many of the discussions in both of the areas referred to in the previous paragraph in mind, the following observation by David Owen is of interest:

> Foucault and Habermas manifestly failed to engage with each other at the level of a *mutual* process of dialogic contestation, let alone one in which a concern with understanding the other's position is tied to an openness with respect to the status of one's own claims. (Owen, 1996, p. 119)

As we noted at the end of section two, Owen (1995a; 1999a) has developed his interpretation of what is at stake between Habermas and Foucault, between critique and genealogy as distinct practices of critical reflection, in terms of contrasting 'ways of orienting thinking': '*legislat[ing]* … the *project* of striving to reconcile the real and the ideal through the *lawful* use of reason … [and] *exemplif[ying]* … the *process* of becoming otherwise than we are through the *agonic* use of reason' (Owen, 1999a, p. 21, emphases in original). '[T]his encounter poses important questions concerning the ethics of dialogue' (*ibid.*), which Owen elaborates in terms of both Foucault and Habermas 'conceptualis[ing] dialogue as a practice of mutual respect', but articulating – and practising – this in very different ways, such that

> what is at stake in the encounter is the character of our ethical understanding of ourselves and of our relations to each other as self-governing beings, which is simply to say that what is at stake is the very concept of enlightenment. (*ibid.*, p. 42)

With these ideas in mind, of particular interest to the concerns of this chapter is the argument of Rossiter and her colleagues (Rossiter *et al.*, 2000) that the possibility of genuine dialogue in 'relations of mutual respect' (*ibid.*, p. 98) is a condition of ethics – which latter they understand as being socially produced in relations of power (*ibid.*, p. 97) – actually being central in professional practice rather than, as at present, being thought of largely as codes to be applied by individual actors as cognitive solutions to dilemmas which they encounter, and thereby being essentially marginalised, at best discussed occasionally and then in a very constrained way. This perspective clearly reflects the way in which Foucault's later writings seek 'to broaden how we understand morality and ethics … bring[ing] out … the role individuals themselves play in implementing or refusing a particular type of subjectivity', including how they reflect upon and change aspects of themselves (Moss, 1998, p. 4). Rossiter *et al.* (p. 99) acknowledge the problematic nature of 'unconstrained dialogue', but insist on the importance of attending 'less to regulating methods of individual reflection and more to intersubjective communication' in conceiving ethics. They explore the potential of this not least through specifically addressing the tension between Habermas's theory of discourse ethics and postmodern feminism. In our view, the process of reflection and communication which Rossiter *et al.*'s work exemplifies is 'academic' in the best sense, and with a practical intent. It embodies a bringing together of perspectives associated with and developed from the work of both Foucault and Habermas, and suggests how these approaches, often presented in oppositional terms, can when brought together offer a productive way forward in engaging in critical reflection as a shared enterprise.

An emphasis on dialogue as a form of active participation is evident in much of the writing on 'empowerment' in social work literatures. However, given an apparent commitment to empowerment as such as the primary goal, there is (as, for example, Healy (2000), and Parton and O'Byrne (2000), point out) a danger that the current emphasis on dialogue in these and related contexts will – if it has not indeed already done so – have a reifying and/or an ossifying effect, so that 'dialogue' will acquire an equivalent status to that given to 'core values' in social work – a list to be adhered to – essentially without critical reflection on what is at once a problematic concept and a challenging form of practice.

'Dialogue' is generally understood as being necessarily reciprocal, requiring preparedness on the part of each of those involved to be influenced by the other – indeed others – as well as seeking to influence her/him – them. It is also often seen – for example, and not least, by Habermas – as involving a search for common understanding and agreement. Foucault himself remarked in an interview shortly before his death: 'The farthest I would go is to say that perhaps one must not be for consensuality, but one must be against nonconsensuality' (1984c, p. 379). His point seems to be that the former is a stronger claim which might connote intolerance of difference, whereas the latter is weaker, and means that when we encounter others with seemingly very different views we should try to find out why this is so and whether there is mutual ground for discussion, which does not presuppose that understanding will lead to agreement (Hoy, 1998, p. 28). The notion of dialogue as a mode of interaction that aims at and facilitates shared understanding, possibly leading to agreement, and the conditions that make this possible, are explored further in what follows.

If it is understood as both discipline and profession, it is surely central to the development of social work that thinking about and discussing its nature and purpose is regarded as a valid form of 'doing' social work, and one where the social work academy has a key contribution to make. In addition, there is a need to promote and engage in such dialogue in much broader public arenas, not least at a time when far-reaching changes in social work and in social and health care services are taking place nationally (in the UK) and around the world. In thinking about how to address this dual challenge, the necessarily abstract ideas and arguments on which we have concentrated in this chapter seem to us particularly important. Struggling to connect the particular theoretical issues explored here with the messiness of everyday social encounters, and attending consciously to the structures of power and authority within which we all live and work, may help us develop a more critical understanding of the complexity of the idea of dialogue and the difficulty of engaging in it, and thus how we might pursue just such dialogue with the nature and role of social work as a topic.

We noted earlier that in *Between Facts and Norms* (1996) Habermas pays close attention to feminist discussions and campaigns concerning equality and difference in articulating his main theses on democracy, law and the welfare state. He argues that a prerequisite to being able to create the conditions for genuinely equal opportunities for women and men is 'public discussion ... in order to establish *which* differences between men and women are *relevant*' in the given context (Ashenden, 1999a, p. 225, citing Habermas, 1996, p. 425, emphases ours). That is to say, there is a need for what Nancy Fraser (1989b) has called a 'politics of need interpretation'. For Habermas this requires 'a transformation in our understanding of the legitimacy of law and a more thorough grounding of this in discursively achieved consensus in public debate' (Ashenden, 1999a, p. 226). Habermas's proposal for a politics of need interpretation involves precisely

> not a blanket treatment of men and women as the same, nor legislation which *assumes* different roles for women and men, but rather ... instituting the conditions for ongoing public political discussion in which the respective roles of women and men are thoroughly debated and society's assumptions concerning the welfare of children and the independence and security of its members are subject to critical scrutiny. (Ashenden, 1999a, p. 230)

Ashenden (as we have also already noted) welcomes Habermas's recent contribution to rethinking – indeed 'relegitimating' – the welfare state 'in a manner capable of recognizing and drawing upon the plurality of modern societies' (Ashenden, 1999a, pp. 216–17). She sees the procedural framework for public discussion which Habermas proposes as 'offer[ing] a potential way of recognizing difference whilst maintaining a focus on the importance of the inclusive character of political debate' (*ibid.*, p. 237). However, she argues that the very aspects of Habermas's recent work which promise most in this regard also closely reflect those elements of his overall theoretical position which have been the objects of major and in her view justified criticism.

Ashenden argues (1998; 1999a) that Habermas's theoretical appeal to rational consensus achieved under ideal conditions of argumentation, and his privileging of consensus as the goal of political dialogue, limit the form and extent of cultural diversity which his model can actually recognise – rather than 'transcend', bracket or marginalise. In the context of a politics of need interpretation, the privileging of consensus arises both with respect to 'the definition of problems and issues to be addressed ... [and] ... the need to reach agreements concerning what to do about such issues once identified' (Ashenden, 1999a, p. 231). For Ashenden and others (see below), separating propositional and normative validity claims from ethical deliberations and from expressive and world-disclosing and world-creating forms of language (as Habermas does), and denying the latter modes of language-use similar weight, is to take too narrow a view of discourse. As Ashenden points out,

> Habermas assumes that differences can be subsumed within an overarching account of justice and on this basis forwards a procedural account for the generation of just norms. ... [He] could be said to be trying to produce an account of argumentation without culture or with culture 'bracketed'. This offers a voice to diverse groups in the framing of legislation ... but severely delimits the terms in which such groups can argue for anything. (*ibid.*, p. 237)

This sits ill with Habermas's insistence that some form of direct participation is required for decision making to be deemed democratic, and effectively rules out a good deal of diversity *a priori*.

In our discussion of Habermas in the previous section of this chapter we noted Seyla Benhabib (1986; 1992; 1996b) and others' wish to acknowledge concrete ethical commitments in endorsing Habermas's 'rules of discourse' as guides for institutionalising democratic decision making. Simone Chambers, similarly concerned to explore and make use of Habermas's ideas in relation to actual political discussion and social change, reflects on the 'feminist discursive experiment' (Chambers, 1995b, p. 164) of the Seneca Peace Camp – which was in turn inspired by the Greenham Common women in the UK – in her contribution to an edited collection entitled *Feminists Read Habermas* (Meehan, 1995). Chambers argues that 'implementing practical discourse' is an arduous process, which is 'not so much a matter of setting up a constitutionally empowered "body" ... as ... of engendering a practice' (*ibid.*, p. 177). She underlines the need for

> ... fostering a political culture in which citizens actively participate in public debate and consciously adopt the discursive attitudes of responsibility, self-discipline, respect, cooperation, and productive struggle necessary to produce consensual agreements. (*ibid.*)

To avoid misunderstanding, given the wide recent currency of the word itself, we need to recall here from our earlier discussion Habermas's special use of the term 'discourse' – which Chambers herself adopts – for the kind of reflective moment of discussion where normative claims, especially questions of justice, are, so to speak, 'up for grabs'. We must also remember that while Habermas is concerned with actual not ideal discourses, his analysis does not bear directly on their content but rather with the logical and procedural conditions necessary for the only force involved in them to be the force of the better argument. As we saw earlier, with his concept of communicative action Habermas seeks to delineate a mode of intersubjective action 'in language' which aims at understanding and agreement, rather than at compliance, as with strategic action. Moreover, he sees his theory as providing the basis for consensual will-formation in practice. Chambers seeks to develop this by reflecting on the conditions that would make the latter a possibility (see also Chambers, 1995a). Again with close reference to Habermas's terminology she emphasises the 'necessity of *learning* how to be discursive actors as opposed to strategic actors' (Chambers, 1995b, p. 163, our emphasis). She suggests that Habermas possibly overstresses the purely proced-ural requirements of discursive democracy in the context of public debate. She also draws attention to features of our contemporary world that can actively undermine such a project, arguing that

> In a world where negotiation, instrumental trade-offs, and strategic bargaining are the most common routes to achieving collective 'agreement' and resolving disputes, it is plausible that the most serious barrier to discourse can be found in the conversational habits that citizens have become used to. (*ibid.*, p. 176)

Moreover, Chambers argues that while certain institutional rules may be necessary conditions for taking decisions discursively, they are not sufficient conditions; for her, 'the defining characteristics of discourse' do not lie in a set of institutional rules (*ibid.*). Practical discourse involves reciprocal requirements which by their very nature cannot be enforced:

> ... to *listen* to what others have to say; ... to attempt to *understand* the other's point of view; ... to *refrain* from manipulating or deceiving others; ... to be *swayed* only by the force of the better argument. Only we can require these things of ourselves; institutions cannot force us to do them. (*ibid.*, emphases in original)

Focusing on issues of difference and diversity in relation to facilitating participation in deliberative democratic processes, Iris Marion Young also proposes a broader conception of such means of decision making than that associated with Habermas; one that she terms 'communicative democracy'. She regards difference as a resource, proposing that '[e]xpressing, questioning, and challenging differently situated knowledge ... adds to the social knowledge of all the participants' (Young, 1996, p. 128).

In developing her ideas, Young explicitly draws support from Plato's accounts of the dialogues of Socrates to challenge the tenability of a sharp distinction between critical reasoning and argument in pursuit of truth and the skills of persuasion; for 'argument also persuades' (Young, *ibid.*). Thus Young's conception of communicative democracy acknowledges and encompasses 'greeting, rhetoric and storytelling' as well as critical argument. These additional modes of communication specifically recognise that participants are embodied and particular [eds: see also Gould, this volume; Kearney, this volume]; thereby they help to establish and maintain a plurality of perspectives and 'supplement argument by providing ways of speaking across difference in the absence of significant shared understandings' (*ibid.*, p. 129). With this in mind, Young states that

> A theory of democratic discussion useful to the contemporary world must explain the possibility of communication across wide differences of culture and social position. Such a theory of democracy needs a broad and plural conception of communication that includes both the expression and the extension of shared understandings, where they exist, and the offering and acknowledgement of unshared meanings. (*ibid.*, pp. 132–3)

The observations of Young, Chambers (1995a; b), and others (for example Braaten, 1995; Warnke, 1995b), also draw attention to a number of issues of practical relevance to pursuing a form of dialogue which is inclusive, although not necessarily conflict-free or with the potential to result in total agreement. Acknowledging the possibility of conflict as *part of* dialogue opens up a way to exploring difference and promoting participation for those previously ignored, marginalised or excluded. Although they work with a notion of dialogue which neither fundamentally presupposes nor aims at consensus in the ways in which Habermas's account does, such writers do not seek to undermine or dismiss Habermas's concept of communicative action, which they acknowledge as providing a theoretical backing for the widespread contemporary assertion of the need for democratic legitimation and thence, given diversity and difference, the need for genuine dialogue [eds., see also Lorenz, this volume]. Rather, they explore the usefulness of Habermas's formulation as a means of thinking about and pursuing dialogue in the context of building more discursive or deliberative forms of democracy (Benhabib, 1996a; b; Blaug, 1996; Dryzek, 1990; Habermas, 1994) in ways which both recognise and consciously engage with power, which, like Foucault, they regard as inescapable in human inter-relationships.

Seeking a more adequate conceptualisation of what we might understand and mean when using the term 'dialogue' than is often apparent – including in social work discourses – seems an appropriate academic contribution, one which might in and of itself contribute to developing 'a communicative community'. We might envisage a 'space' where differences can be explored in ways which are mutually respected, opening up to the possibility of new, shared understandings, albeit temporary and negotiated ones, as a basis for – indeed as part of already – 'thinking and acting differently'.

That, of course, is to make a very general – and doubtless somewhat idealistic – point about 'developing democracy'. More specifically, but with such a larger perspective in view, social work academics and educators could be said to have a key role and responsibility in fostering a communicative community, especially in and around their own discipline and profession, but also, given our broad understanding of social work, in a wider context. By thinking and talking, including about how to talk with each other, with students, with practitioners, with managers, with policy makers, and ultimately in wider public arenas, among other things about what social work is and what it could be, the space for dialogue might be extended precisely by engaging in dialogue, thereby widening and deepening the space for thinking and learning together. More substantively – in each of the contexts just listed, albeit in appropriately different ways – the subject matter for such dialogic exploration should include and be informed by, *inter alia*, what hopefully will be a growing number and variety of genealogical accounts of social work in its many aspects and local instantiations, as exemplified by Samantha Ashenden's contributions (1996; forthcoming), Nigel Parton's continuing studies (e.g. 1996b; 1998; 1999), Walter Lorenz's comparative analyses (2000; 2001; this volume), and Laura Epstein's sadly uncompleted 'Origins' project (see Chambon and Irving, 1999; Epstein, 1999). Though of a somewhat different kind, Bill

Jordan's varied contributions (e.g. 1989; 1990; 1998; 2000) are equally relevant in these contexts, informed as they are by a similar spirit.

As well as suggesting a *means* of 'rethinking' social work, these reflections seem to point towards and connect with a *substantive conception* of and role for the discipline and equally the wider profession itself, very much in the pedagogic tradition as discussed, for example, by Walter Lorenz in this collection and elsewhere (1994; 1999; 2000; 2001) and by Pat Higham (2001).

Concluding thoughts

In his last lectures (see Flynn, 1987), Foucault discussed *parrhesia*, distinguishing this direct mode of truth-telling that endangers the speaker – 'the practice of truth-telling [seen] as a moral virtue in the ancient world' (Bernauer and Rasmussen, 1987, p. 111) – from the modes of truth-telling exemplified by the prophet (truth as destiny), the sage (truth as being), and the teacher/technician (truth as learned skill) (Owen, 1999a, p. 603; Rabinow, 1994, pp. 204–7). In various contexts philosophers – including Foucault himself – unavoidably adopt each of these roles and modes of truth-telling, sometimes in combination. However, *parrhesia* represents for Foucault the form of ethical self-relation engaged in when calling conventions into question, 'rendering [them] up for judgement' (Ashenden, 1999b, p. 158) through a critical ontology of ourselves. In this way Foucault's own work 'exemplifies the *ethos* it recommends' (Owen, 1999a, p. 603, our emphasis) – in colloquial language he 'practised what he preached', or in terms familiar to social work educators made an attempt to model or mirror the kinds of behaviour and relationships he advocated.

Thus:

> Foucault as *parrhesiast* – the engaged truth-teller speaking within a field of power – is not simply a philosopher talking away. Rather, he is negotiating the relation of philosophy and politics, of the contemplative life (*bios theoretikos*) and the active life (*bios politicos*) ... As simultaneously critical-historical contemplation and ethical/political activity ... Foucault's work negotiates the paradox of political philosophy ... (Owen, 1999b, p. 603)

This seems to offer us a way of fully grasping the situation – in its own ways both 'timeless' and contemporary – of social workers in the academy.

References

Note: dates given below for the works of Foucault and Habermas are those of English translations; dates of original publication in French or German respectively are included in the main text (at certain points) in 'square brackets'.

Ashenden, S. (1996), 'Reflexive governance and child sexual abuse: liberal welfare rationality and the Cleveland enquiry', *Economy and Society*, **25**(1), pp. 64–88.

Ashenden, S. (1998), 'Pluralism within the limits of reason alone? Habermas and the discursive negotiation of consensus', *Critical Review of International Social and Political Philosophy*, **1**(3), pp. 117–36.

Ashenden, S. (1999a), 'Habermas on discursive consensus: rethinking the welfare state in the face of cultural pluralism', in Chamberlayne, P., Cooper, A., Freeman, R. and Rustin, M. (eds), *Welfare and Culture in Europe: Towards a New Paradigm in Social Policy*, Jessica Kingsley, London, pp. 216–39.

Ashenden, S. (1999b), 'Questions of criticism: Habermas and Foucault on civil society and resistance', in Ashenden and Owen, 1999a, pp. 143–65.

Ashenden, S. (forthcoming), *Governing Child Sexual Abuse*, London, Routledge.

Ashenden, S. and Owen, D. (eds) (1999a), *Foucault Contra Habermas: Recasting the Dialogue Between Genealogy and Critical Theory*, Sage, London.

Ashenden, S. and Owen, D. (1999b), 'Introduction: Foucault, Habermas and the politics of critique', in Ashenden and Owen, 1999a, pp. 1–20.

Beiner, R. (1983), *Political Judgement*, Methuen, London, quoted in Timms, 1989.

Benhabib, S. (1986), *Critique, Norm, and Utopia: A Study of the Foundations of Critical Theory*, Columbia University Press, New York.

Benhabib, S. (1992), *Situating the Self: Gender, Community and Postmodernism in Contemporary Ethics*, Polity, Cambridge.

Benhabib, S. (ed.) (1996a), *Democracy and Difference: Contesting the Boundaries of the Political*, Princeton University Press, Princeton, NJ.

Benhabib, S. (1996b), 'Toward a deliberative model of democratic legitimacy', in Benhabib, 1996a, pp. 67–94.

Benhabib, S., Butler, J., Cornell, D. and Fraser, N. (1995), *Feminist Contentions: A Philosophical Exchange*, Routledge, London.

Bernauer, J. and Rasmussen, D. (1987), 'An introductory note', *Philosophy and Social Criticism*, **12**(2–3), Special Issue: 'The Final Foucault: Studies on Michel Foucault's Last Works', eds J. Bernauer and D. Rasmussen, pp. 109–11.

Bernstein, R.J. (1986), *Philosophical Profiles: Essays in a Pragmatic Mode*, Polity, Cambridge.

Bernstein, R.J. (1991), *The New Constellation: The Ethical/Political Horizons of Modernity/ Postmodernity*, Polity, Cambridge.

Blaug, R. (1995), 'Distortion of the face to face: communicative reason and social work practice', *British Journal of Social Work*, **25**(4), pp. 423–39.

Blaug, R. (1996), 'New theories of discursive democracy: a user's guide', *Philosophy and Social Criticism*, **22**(1), pp. 49–80.

Blaug, R. (1997), 'Between fear and disappointment: critical, empirical and political uses of Habermas', *Political Studies*, **45**(1), pp. 110–17.

Braaten, J. (1995), 'From communicative rationality to communicative thinking: a basis for feminist theory and practice', in Meehan, *op. cit.*, pp. 139–61.

Burchell, G., Gordon, C. and Miller, P. (1991), *The Foucault Effect: Studies in Governmentality*, Harvester Wheatsheaf, Hemel Hempstead.

Chambers, S. (1995a), 'Discourse and democratic practices', in White, S.K. (ed.), *The Cambridge Companion to Habermas*, Cambridge University Press, Cambridge, pp. 233–59.

Chambers, S. (1995b), 'Feminist discourse/practical discourse', in Meehan, *op. cit.*, pp. 163–79.

Chambon, A.S. (1999a), 'Foucault's approach: making the familiar visible', in Chambon *et al.*, *op. cit.*, pp. 51–81.

Chambon, A.S. (trans.) (1999b), 'Social work, social control, and normalisation: roundtable [*sic*] discussion with Michel Foucault', in Chambon *et al.*, *op. cit.*, pp. 83–97. (This round-table discussion was arranged by the editors of *Esprit* and published (in French) as 'Pourquoi le travail social?' in a special edition of that journal, no. 413, avril–mai

1972, pp. 678–703. An earlier and differently edited English translation (by J. Herman) appears as 'Confining societies' in Foucault, 1996, pp. 83–94.)

Chambon, A.S. and Irving, A. (1999), 'Introduction', in Chambon *et al., op. cit.*, pp. *xiii–xxx.*

Chambon, A.S., Irving, A. and Epstein, L. (eds) (1999), *Reading Foucault for Social Work*, Columbia University Press, New York.

Connolly, W.E. (1991), *Identity\Difference: Democratic Negotiations of Political Paradox*, Cornell University Press, New York.

Conway, D.W. (1999), '*Pas de deux*: Habermas and Foucault in genealogical communication', in Ashenden and Owen, 1999a, pp. 60–89.

Cooper, D. (1994), 'Productive, relational and everywhere? Conceptualising power and resistance within Foucauldian feminism', *Sociology*, **28**(2), pp. 435–54.

Dean, M. (1994), *Critical and Effective Histories: Foucault's Methods and Historical Sociology*, Routledge, London.

Dean, M. (1999), 'Normalising democracy: Foucault and Habermas on democracy, liberalism and law', in Ashenden and Owen, 1999a, pp. 166–94.

Dreyfus, H.L. and Rabinow, P. (1982), *Beyond Structuralism and Hermeneutics*, Harvester, Brighton.

Dreyfus, H.L. and Rabinow, P. (1986), 'What is maturity? Habermas and Foucault on "What is enlightenment?"', in Hoy, D.C. (ed.), *Foucault: A Critical Reader*, Blackwell, Oxford, pp. 109–21.

Dryzek, J.S. (1990), *Discursive Democracy: Politics, Policy, and Political Science*, Cambridge University Press, Cambridge.

d'Entrèves, M.P. and Benhabib, S. (eds) (1996), *Habermas and the Unfinished Project of Modernity*, Polity, Cambridge.

Epstein, L. (1999), 'The culture of social work', ed. A. Chambon, in Chambon *et al., op. cit.*, pp. 3–26.

Fawcett, B., Featherstone, B., Fook, J. and Rossiter, A. (eds) (2000), *Practice and Research in Social Work: Postmodern Feminist Perspectives*, Routledge, London.

Flynn, T. (1987), 'Foucault as parrhesiast: his last course at the Collège de France (1984)', *Philosophy and Social Criticism*, **12**(2–3), Special Issue: 'The Final Foucault: Studies on Michel Foucault's Last Works', eds J. Bernauer and D. Rasmussen, pp. 213–29.

Flyvbjerg, B. (1998), 'Habermas and Foucault: thinkers for civil society?', *British Journal of Sociology*, **49**(2), pp. 210–33.

Fook, J. (1999), 'Critical reflectivity in education and practice', in Pease and Fook, 1999b, pp. 195–208.

Fook, J. and Pease, B. (1999), 'Emancipatory social work for a postmodern age', in Pease and Fook, 1999b, pp. 224–9.

Foucault, M. (1965), *Madness and Civilisation*, trans. R. Howard, Tavistock, London.

Foucault, M. (1970), *The Order of Things: An Archaeology of the Human Sciences*, trans. unidentified, Tavistock, London.

Foucault, M. (1972), *The Archaeology of Knowledge*, trans. A.M. Sheridan Smith, Tavistock, London.

Foucault, M, (1973), *The Birth of the Clinic: An Archaeology of Medical Perception*, trans. A.M. Sheridan Smith, Tavistock, London.

Foucault, M. (1977), *Discipline and Punish: The Birth of the Prison*, trans. A. Sheridan, Allen Lane, London.

Foucault, M. (1979a), 'Governmentality', trans. R. Braidotti, *Ideology and Consciousness*, **6**, pp. 5–21.

Foucault, M. (1979b), *The History of Sexuality*, Vol. I: *An Introduction*, trans. R. Hurley, Penguin, Harmondsworth.

Foucault, M. (1980), 'Two lectures', trans. K. Soper, in *Power/Knowledge: Selected Interviews and Other Writings 1972–1977*, ed. C. Gordon, Harvester, Brighton, pp. 78–108.

Foucault, M. (1982), 'Afterword: The subject and power', trans. (part) L. Sawyer, in Dreyfus and Rabinow, 1982, pp. 208–26.

Foucault, M. (1984a), *The Foucault Reader*, ed. P. Rabinow, Penguin, Harmondsworth.

Foucault, M. (1984b), 'On the genealogy of ethics: an overview of work in progress', in Foucault, 1984a, pp. 340–72.

Foucault, M. (1984c), 'Politics and ethics: an interview', trans. C. Porter, in Foucault, 1984a, pp. 373–80.

Foucault, M. (1984d), 'What is enlightenment?', trans. C. Porter, in Foucault, 1984a, pp. 32–50.

Foucault, M. (1985), *The Use of Pleasure: The History of Sexuality*, Vol. II, trans. R. Hurley, Penguin, Harmondsworth.

Foucault, M. (1986), *The Care of the Self: The History of Sexuality*, Vol. III, trans. R. Hurley, Penguin, Harmondsworth.

Foucault, M. (1987), 'The ethic of care for the self as a practice of freedom', trans. J.G. Gautier, *Philosophy and Social Criticism*, **12**(2–3), Special Issue: 'The Final Foucault: Studies on Michel Foucault's Last Works', eds J. Bernauer and D. Rasmussen, pp. 112–31.

Foucault, M. (1988a), 'Critical theory/intellectual history', trans. J. Harding, in *Politics, Philosophy, Culture: Interviews and Other Writings 1977–84*, ed. L.D. Kritzman, Routledge, London, pp. 17–46.

Foucault, M. (1988b), 'Politics and reason', in *Politics, Philosophy, Culture: Interviews and Other Writings 1977–84*, ed. L.D. Kritzman, Routledge, London, pp. 57–85.

Foucault, M. (1991), 'Remarks on Marx: Conversations with Duccio Trombadori', trans. R.J. Goldstein and J. Cascaito, Semiotext(e), New York, quoted in Ashenden, 1999b.

Foucault, M. (1996), *Foucault Live: Interviews 1961–84* (expanded edn), ed. S. Lotringer, trans. L. Hochroth and J. Johnson, Semiotext(e), New York.

Fraser, N. (1989a), 'Foucault on modern power: empirical insights and normative confusions', in *Unruly Practices: Power, Discourse and Gender in Contemporary Social Theory*, Polity, Cambridge, pp. 17–34.

Fraser, N. (1989b), 'Women, welfare, and the politics of need interpretation', in *Unruly Practices: Power, Discourse and Gender in Contemporary Social Theory*, Polity, Cambridge, pp. 144–60.

Freire, P. (1970), *Pedagogy of the Oppressed*, Penguin, Harmondsworth.

Habermas, J. (1966), 'Knowledge and interest', trans. G. Flöistad, *Inquiry*, **9**(4), pp. 285–300. (Habermas's Inaugural Lecture as Professor of Philosophy and Sociology at the University of Frankfurt, 28 June 1965. Also appears (in a different translation) as an appendix to Habermas, 1972, pp. 301–17.)

Habermas, J. (1972), *Knowledge and Human Interests*, trans. J.J. Shapiro, Heinemann, London.

Habermas, J. (1979), *Communication and the Evolution of Society*, trans. T. McCarthy, Heinemann, London.

Habermas, J. (1984), *The Theory of Communicative Action*, Vol. I: *Reason and the Rationalization of Society*, trans. T. McCarthy, Polity, Cambridge.

Habermas, J. (1987a), *The Philosophical Discourse of Modernity: Twelve Lectures*, trans. F. Lawrence, Polity, Cambridge.

Habermas, J. (1987b), *The Theory of Communicative Action*, Vol. II: *Lifeworld and System – A Critique of Functionalist Reason*, trans. T. McCarthy, Polity, Cambridge.

Habermas, J. (1989), *The Structural Transformation of the Public Sphere: An Inquiry into a Category of Bourgeois Society*, trans. T. Burger, with F. Lawrence, MIT Press, Cambridge, MA.

Habermas, J. (1990), *Moral Consciousness and Communicative Action*, trans. C. Lenhardt and S.W. Nicholsen, Polity, Cambridge.

Habermas, J. (1992), *Postmetaphysical Thinking: Philosophical Essays*, trans. W.M. Hohengarten, Polity, Cambridge.

Habermas, J. (1993), *Justification and Application: Remarks on Discourse Ethics*, trans. C. Cronin, Polity, Cambridge.

Habermas, J. (1994), 'Three normative models of democracy', *Constellations*, **1**(1), pp. 1–10.

Habermas, J. (1996), *Between Facts and Norms: Contributions to a Discourse Theory of Law and Democracy*, trans. W. Rehg, Polity, Cambridge.

Healy, K. (2000), *Social Work Practices: Contemporary Perspectives on Change*, Sage, London.

Henkel, M. (1995), 'Conceptions of knowledge and social work education', in Yelloly, M. and Henkel, M. (eds), *Learning and Teaching in Social Work: Towards Reflective Practice*, Jessica Kingsley, London, pp. 67–82.

Henkel, M. (1996), *Professional Practice: Alternative Conceptions of Education and Evaluation*, 7th Annual CEDR Lecture, Centre for Evaluative and Developmental Research, Department of Social Work Studies, University of Southampton, Southampton.

Higham, P.E. (2001), 'Changing practice and an emerging social pedagogue paradigm in England: the role of the personal adviser', *Social Work in Europe*, **8**(1), pp. 21–9.

Honig, B. (1993), *Political Theory and the Displacement of Politics*, Cornell University Press, New York.

Hoy, D.C. (1998), 'Foucault and critical theory', in Moss, J. (ed.), *The Later Foucault: Politics and Philosophy*, Sage, London, pp. 18–32.

Hoy, D.C. and McCarthy, T. (1994), *Critical Theory*, Blackwell, Oxford.

Hunt, A. (2000), Review of Ashenden and Owen (1999a), *Canadian Journal of Sociology Online*, May/July, <http://www.arts.ualberta.ca/cjscopy/reviews/foucaulthabermas.html>.

Hutchings, K. (1996), *Kant, Critique, and Politics*, Routledge, London.

Ife, J. (1997), *Rethinking Social Work: Towards Critical Practice*, Longman, Melbourne.

Ife, J. (1999), 'Postmodernism, critical theory and social work', in Pease and Fook, 1999b, pp. 211–23.

Ixer, G. (1999), 'There's no such thing as reflection', *British Journal of Social Work*, **29**(4), pp. 513–27.

Jordan, B. (1978), 'A comment on "Theory and practice in social work"', *British Journal of Social Work*, **8**(1), pp. 23–5.

Jordan, B. (1989), *The Common Good: Citizenship, Morality and Self-Interest*, Blackwell, Oxford.

Jordan, B. (1990), *Social Work in an Unjust Society*, Harvester Wheatsheaf, Hemel Hempstead.

Jordan, B. (1998), *The New Politics of Welfare: Social Justice in a Global Context*, Sage, London.

Jordan, B., with Jordan, C. (2000), *Social Work and the Third Way: Tough Love as Social Policy*, Sage, London.

Jordan, B. and Parton, N. (eds) (1983), *The Political Dimensions of Social Work*, Blackwell, Oxford.

Kelly, M. (ed.) (1994a), *Critique and Power: Recasting the Foucault/Habermas Debate*, MIT Press, Cambridge, MA.

Kelly, M. (1994b), 'Foucault, Habermas, and the self-referentiality of critique', in Kelly, 1994a, pp. 365–400.

Kelly, M. (1994c), 'Introduction', in Kelly, 1994a, pp. 1–13.

Lorenz, W. (1994), *Social Work in a Changing Europe*, Routledge, London.

Lorenz, W. (1999), 'Social work and cultural politics: the paradox of German social pedagogy', in Chamberlayne, P., Cooper, A., Freeman, R. and Rustin, M. (eds), *Welfare and Culture in Europe: Towards a New Paradigm in Social Policy*, Jessica Kingsley, London, pp. 26–42.

Lorenz, W. (2000), 'Contentious identities – social work research and the search for professional and personal identities', paper presented in the *Theorising Social Work Research* seminar series, no. 4, 6 March, University of Edinburgh, and now available at <http://www.elsc.org.uk/socialcareresource/tswr/seminar4/lorenz.htm>.

Lorenz, W. (2001), *Understanding the 'Other': European Perspectives on the Ethics of Social Work Research and Practice*, 12th Annual CEDR Lecture, Centre for Evaluative and Developmental Research, Department of Social Work Studies, University of Southampton, Southampton.

McCarthy, T. (1978), *The Critical Theory of Jürgen Habermas*, Hutchinson, London.

Meehan, J. (ed.) (1995), *Feminists Read Habermas: Gendering the Subject of Discourse*, Routledge, London.

Moss, J. (1998), 'Introduction: the later Foucault', in Moss, J. (ed.), *The Later Foucault: Politics and Philosophy*, Sage, London, pp. 1–17.

Mouffe, C. (1999), 'Deliberative democracy or agonistic pluralism?', *Social Research*, **66**(3), pp. 745–58.

Nicholson, L.J. (ed.) (1990), *Feminism/Postmodernism*, Routledge, London.

O'Sullivan, N. (1997), 'Difference and the concept of the political in contemporary political philosophy', *Political Studies*, **45**(4), pp. 739–54.

Owen, D. (1995a), 'Genealogy as exemplary critique: reflections on Foucault and the imagination of the political', *Economy and Society*, **24**(4), pp. 489–506.

Owen, D. (1995b), *Nietzsche, Politics and Modernity: A Critique of Liberal Reason*, Sage, London.

Owen, D. (1996), 'Foucault, Habermas and the claims of reason', *History of the Human Sciences*, **9**(2), pp. 119–38.

Owen, D. (1999a), 'Orientation and enlightenment: an essay on critique and genealogy', in Ashenden and Owen, 1999a, pp. 21–44.

Owen, D. (1999b), 'Power, knowledge and ethics: Foucault', in Glendinning, S. (ed.), *The Edinburgh Encyclopedia of Continental Philosophy*, Edinburgh University Press, Edinburgh, pp. 593–604.

Parton, N. (1985), *The Politics of Child Abuse*, Macmillan, London.

Parton, N. (1991), *Governing the Family: Child Care, Child Protection and the State*, Macmillan, London.

Parton, N. (1994a), 'The nature of social work under conditions of (post)modernity', *Social Work and Social Sciences Review*, **5**(2), pp. 93–112.

Parton, N. (1994b), '"Problematics of government", (post)modernity and social work', *British Journal of Social Work*, **24**(1), pp. 9–32.

Parton, N. (1996a), 'Social theory, social change and social work: an introduction', in Parton, N. (ed.), *Social Theory, Social Change and Social Work*, Routledge, London, pp. 4–18.

Parton, N. (1996b), 'Social work, risk and "the blaming system"', in Parton, N. (ed.), *Social Theory, Social Change and Social Work*, Routledge, London, pp. 98–114.

Parton, N. (1998), 'Risk, advanced liberalism and child welfare: the need to rediscover uncertainty and ambiguity', *British Journal of Social Work*, **28**(1), pp. 5–27.

Parton, N. (1999), 'Reconfiguring child welfare practices: risk, advanced liberalism, and the government of freedom', in Chambon *et al.*, *op. cit.*, pp. 101–30.

Parton, N. (2000), 'Some thoughts on the relationship between theory and practice in and for social work', *British Journal of Social Work*, **30**(4), pp. 447–63. (An earlier version, presented in the *Theorising Social Work Research* seminar series, no. 1, 26 May 1999, Brunel University, is now available at <http://www.elsc.org.uk/socialcareresource/tswr/seminar1/parton.htm>.)

Parton, N. and O'Byrne, P. (2000), *Constructive Social Work: Towards a New Practice*, Macmillan, Basingstoke.

Patton, P. (1994), 'Foucault's subject of power', *Political Theory Newsletter*, **6**(1), pp. 60–71.

Pease, B. and Fook, J. (1999a), 'Postmodern critical theory and emancipatory social work practice', in Pease and Fook, 1999b, pp. 1–22.

Pease, B. and Fook, J. (eds) (1999b), *Transforming Social Work Practice: Postmodern Critical Perspectives*, Routledge, London.

Plant, R. (1991), *Modern Political Thought*, Blackwell, Oxford.

Powell, F. (2001), *The Politics of Social Work*, Sage, London.

Rabinow, P. (1984), 'Introduction', in Foucault, 1984a, pp. 3–29.

Rabinow, P. (1994), 'Modern and counter-modern: ethos and epoch in Heidegger and Foucault', in Gutting, G. (ed.), *The Cambridge Companion to Foucault*, Cambridge University Press, Cambridge, pp. 197–214.

Rossiter, A. (2000), 'The postmodern feminist condition: new conditions for social work', in Fawcett *et al.*, *op. cit.*, pp. 22–38.

Rossiter, A., Prilleltensky, I. and Walsh-Bowers, R. (2000), 'A postmodern perspective on professional ethics', in Fawcett *et al.*, *op. cit.*, pp. 83–103.

Schmidt, J. (1996), 'Habermas and Foucault', in d'Entrèves and Benhabib, *op. cit.*, pp. 147–71.

Simons, J. (1995), *Foucault and the Political*, Routledge, London.

Thompson, J.B. and Held, D. (1982), *Habermas: Critical Debates*, Macmillan, London.

Thompson, S. (1999), 'The agony and the ecstasy: Foucault, Habermas and the problem of recognition', in Ashenden and Owen, 1999a, pp. 195–211.

Timms, N. (1983), *Social Work Values: An Enquiry*, Routledge and Kegan Paul, London.

Timms, N. (1989), 'Social work values: context and contribution', in Shardlow, S. (ed.), *The Values of Change in Social Work*, Tavistock/Routledge, London, pp. 11–23.

Tully, J. (1989), 'Wittgenstein and political philosophy: understanding practices of critical reflection', *Political Theory*, **17**(2), pp. 172–204.

Tully, J. (1995), *Strange Multiplicity: Constitutionalism in an Age of Diversity*, Cambridge University Press, Cambridge.

Tully, J. (1999), 'To think and act differently: Foucault's four reciprocal objections to Habermas' theory', in Ashenden and Owen, 1999a, pp. 90–142.

Warnke, G. (1995a), 'Communicative rationality and cultural values', in White, S.K. (ed.), *The Cambridge Companion to Habermas*, Cambridge University Press, Cambridge, pp. 120–42.

Warnke, G. (1995b), 'Discourse ethics and feminist dilemmas of difference', in Meehan, *op. cit.*, pp. 247–61.

Webb, S.A. (2001), 'Some considerations on the validity of evidence-based practice in social work', *British Journal of Social Work*, **31**(1), pp. 57–79.

White, S.K. (1986), 'Foucault's challenge to critical theory', *American Political Science Review*, **80**(2), pp. 419–32.

White, S.K. (1995), 'Reason, modernity, and democracy', in White, S.K. (ed.), *The Cambridge Companion to Habermas*, Cambridge University Press, Cambridge, pp. 3–16.

Wittgenstein, L. (1953), *Philosophical Investigations*, trans. G.E.M. Anscombe, Blackwell, Oxford.

Young, I.M. (1996), 'Communication and the other: beyond deliberative democracy', in Benhabib, 1996a, pp. 120–35.

Index